P9-DGV-246

Fodor's
BAHAMAS

Welcome to the Bahamas

Little did we realize that the emergence of a novel coronavirus in early 2020 would abruptly bring almost all travel to a halt. Although our Fodor's writers around the world have continued working to bring you the best of the destinations they cover, we still anticipate that more than the usual number of businesses will close permanently in the coming months, perhaps with little advance notice. We don't expect things to return to "normal" for some time. As you plan your upcoming travels to the Bahamas, please confirm that places are still open and let us know when we need to make updates by writing to us at this address: editors@fodors.com.

TOP REASONS TO GO

★ **Beaches.** The powdery, soft sand creates some of the world's best strands.

★ **Boating.** Ideal conditions draw small dinghies, serious sailboats, and luxury yachts.

★ **Family Fun.** From sprawling water parks to horseback rides along the beach.

★ **Out Islands.** Quiet and uncrowded, these islands are hard to reach but worth the trip.

★ **Fishing.** From fly-casting for tarpon and bonefish to fighting with a giant marlin.

Contents

MAPS

Fodor's Features

Chapter 1

EXPERIENCE THE BAHAMAS

19 ULTIMATE EXPERIENCES

Bahamas offers terrific experiences that should be on every traveler's list. Here are Fodor's top picks for a memorable trip.

1 Scuba Diving

Discover aquatic wonders when you explore the region's ultra-clear waters, from the shallows of the world's third-largest barrier reef to the ocean depths. Coral, blue holes, drop-offs, and sea gardens abound here. *(Ch. 4)*

2 Lucayan National Park

Kayak through wild tamarind and gumbo-limbo trees, a mangrove swamp, and one of the world's largest underwater cave systems on Grand Bahama Island. *(Ch. 4)*

3 The Out Islands

Seek refuge at these sparsely populated islands. Ascend the cut stone staircase to Mount Alvernia, the country's highest natural point, 206 feet above sea level. *(Ch. 8)*

4 Rum Drinks

Revisit the bootlegging days of the Prohibition Era. Treat yourself to a Goombay Smash. *(Ch. 1)*

5 Horseback Riding

Even without prior experience, visitors can take guided tours of several of the islands on horseback; gallop across the sand and even into the sea. *(Ch. 6)*

6 Sailing

In July, Grand Bahama hosts a Regatta and Heritage Festival with sailing races and more. *(Ch. 4)*

7 Nurse Sharks

Interact with harmless nurse sharks in their natural habitat at Compass Cay in the Exumas, where a handful of them swim and sunbathe at the private island marina. *(Ch. 7)*

8 Swimming with Pigs

World-famous pigs live on Big Major Cay in the Exumas. The animals swim out to greet tourists, but be respectful on their home turf, and don't pick any up for selfies. *(Ch. 7)*

9 Aquaventure at the Atlantis Resort

This 141-acre aquatic wonderland on Paradise Island has river rides, a 200-foot body slide, and pools. It's the ultimate playground for kids and adventurous adults. *(Ch. 3)*

10 Bonefishing

Shallow waters and mangroves filled with "gray ghosts," or silvery white fish, make bonefishing the fly-fishing sport of choice in the Bahamas. *(Ch. 1)*

11 Private Resorts

Complete your island getaway with a stay at a secluded, all-inclusive luxury resort like Fowl Cay, just a 7-minute boat transfer from Staniel Cay Airstrip. *(Ch. 7)*

12 Dolphin Spotting

Take a boat into Freeport, and a pod of dolphins may splash and dive along beside you. Jump into the water to swim with them in their natural environment. *(Ch. 4)*

13 Fish Fry

At Arawak Cay, brightly colored restaurants serve local fish specialties like fried fish and cracked conch. Wash it down with "sky juice" (gin, coconut water, and milk). *(Ch. 3)*

14 Junkanoo Festival

This celebration with dancing, brass bands, and vibrant costumes is the Bahamas' answer to Mardi Gras. Junkanoo happens on Boxing Day and New Year's Day. *(Ch. 3)*

15 Snorkeling

Explore Thunderball Grotto in the Exumas and its limestone cave, or Paradise Point in Bimini where dolphins and black coral await you just offshore. *(Ch. 1)*

16 Spas

Retreat to top-rated spas in idyllic settings throughout the region, where you can indulge in massages, body treatments, aromatherapy, and much more. *(Ch. 3)*

17 The Exumas

Across the Tropic of Cancer lies this chain of hundreds of islands with white sand and calm blue water. Look for exquisite wildlife: giant starfish, iguanas, and pigs. *(Ch. 7)*

18 Beaches

With powdery white and pink sand and kaleidoscopic blue water, beaches extend for a total of 800 miles in the Bahamas and offer parties on the sand or complete solitude. *(Ch. 1)*

19 Harbour Island

Modern but with an old-world feel, Harbour Island is home to pastel-colored clapboard houses, a 3½-mile pink sand beach, and the mysterious lone tree. *(Ch. 6)*

WHAT'S WHERE

1 New Providence and Paradise Islands. Nassau and nearby Paradise Island are the most action-packed places in the Bahamas. From flashy megaresorts like Atlantis and Baha Mar to fine dining and high-end shopping, development here is unrivaled on any of the other islands.

2 Grand Bahama Island. Urban and deserted vibes mix to create a quieter alternative to fast-paced Nassau. Lucaya has shopping, golfing, scuba diving, and beach parties, but old-island fishing settlements and vast expanses of untouched nature appeal to adventurous travelers.

3 Andros, Bimini, and the Berry Islands. In the northwest corner of the Bahamas, these islands share many characteristics, most notably their reputation for excellent fishing and diving. Each exudes a casual, old-island atmosphere and abundant natural beauty.

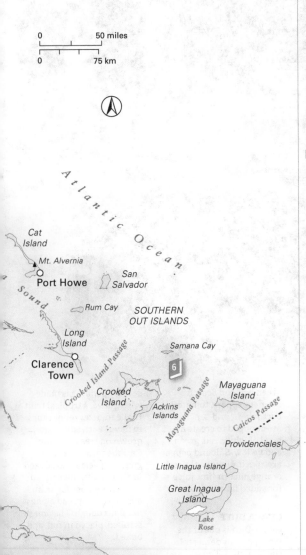

0   50 miles

0   75 km

Atlantic Ocean

Cat
Island

Mt. Alvernia

Port Howe

San
Salvador

Sound

Rum Cay

SOUTHERN
OUT ISLANDS

Long
Island

Samana Cay

Clarence
Town

Crooked Island Passage

6

Crooked
Island

Acklins
Islands

Mayaguana
Island

Mayaguana Passage

Caicos Passage

Providenciales

Little Inagua Island

Great Inagua
Island

Lake
Rose

4 Eleuthera and Harbour Island. The Nantucket of the Bahamas, Harbour Island—rimmed by its legendary pink-sand beach—is the chicest Out Island. Eleuthera is the opposite, with historic churches and pretty fishing villages, unpretentious inns, and a few upscale, intimate beach resorts.

5 The Exumas. Hundreds of islands skip like stones across the Tropic of Cancer, all with gorgeous white beaches and the most beautiful water in the Bahamas. Mainland Great Exuma has friendly locals, great beach parties, and the popular Pig Beach where tourists can go swimming with the friendly pigs.

6 The Southern Out Islands. The Bahamas' southernmost islands have so few visitors and so many natural wonders. Cat Island boasts the highest natural point in the country and Inagua is home to one of the largest flamingo colonies in the world.

What to Eat and Drink in the Bahamas

Rum Cake

CRACKED CONCH

Cracked conch is made from the meat of the shelled marine mollusk found in the Bahamian waters, and it is guaranteed to be on every Bahamian restaurant's menu.

CONCH SALAD

You haven't had a taste of authentic Bahamian cuisine until you've had a conch salad. Bits of onions, green bell and Scotch bonnet peppers, tomato, cucumbers, and conch meat are chopped to create a bowl of white, red, green, and yellow. Salt and pepper are added, along with fresh orange juice or lime juice for added flavor.

GUAVA DUFF

Guava Duff is one of the most popular desserts in the Bahamas. The soft and spongy pudding is made with guava, a tropical fruit that can be sweet or tangy in flavor with edible seeds grown on trees in many Caribbean islands. The guava is peeled and cooked until it is soft, then mixed with cinnamon, sugar, and allspice, and spread along a flat flour dough. The dough is rolled, placed in foil, and boiled.

Conch Fritters

JOHNNY CAKE
The Bahamian Johnny Cake falls somewhere between a dense bread and a slightly sweet cake and is made with flour, milk, butter, sugar, and baking powder, and baked in a round baking tin.

PEAS 'N' RICE
The dish is the country's most popular staple, traditionally served with heavy lunches or dinners, alongside fish, meat, or chicken (you won't find Bahamians having peas and rice for breakfast). The ingredients of the dish are in its name: white rice and brown pigeon peas. Bahamians will typically add thyme, diced vegetables, tomato paste, salt pork, or pieces of bacon for added flavor.

BAHAMIAN MAC 'N' CHEESE
Bahamians bake their mac and cheese, and include ingredients such as chopped onions, bell peppers, and spices to make it their own. The finished product is cut in small squares that resemble lasagna.

RUM PUNCH
Rum Punch in the Bahamas is made with Wray & Nephew rum, Malibu Coconut Rum, a splash of Campari, orange juice, and pineapple juice.

CONCH FRITTERS
Locals use conch to make fritters. The flour batter is mixed with chopped vegetables, seasoning, and conch meat, and deep-fried until it is golden brown.

GOOMBAY SMASH
The Goombay Smash is the unofficial cocktail of the Bahamas and was created in the 1960s by Emily Cooper, aka "Miss Emily," the owner of Miss Emily's Blue Bee Bar in Green Turtle Cay, Abaco. The official recipe of the drink contains coconut rum, dirty rum, apricot brandy, and pineapple juice.

RUM CAKE
Bahamian rum cake is moist and buttery, like a sponge cake. The popular dessert is made with dark or light rum (not spiced) and is baked in a bundt baking pan. The coating is made using white rum, sugar, butter, and/or pineapple juice. The island has its own factory just for the production of Bahamian rum cakes in Nassau.

10 Animals to Meet in the Bahamas

SEA STARS
One of the most recognizable underwater creatures is the large, spiny, orange Bahama Sea Star. Tour guides are often outfitted with at least one sea star to show to visitors. Snorkeling is the best way to view the sea star in its natural habitat, thriving among the coral reefs and in seagrasses.

SPIDER CRABS
Crabs roam all over the Bahamas, especially on Andros Island, known as the "The Land of the Crabs." This island hosts the Bahamas' largest population of land crabs, many of which are threatened due to overdevelopment. All crabs are influenced by the ocean's cycles.

IGUANAS
On the small shore of Allen's Cay, the familiar rumble of approaching boats summons a reptilian army of rock iguanas to the water where the tourists wait, armed with bananas and grapes. Rock iguanas are indigenous to only three islands in the world, all in the Bahamas.

DOLPHINS
Bimini is where the wild dolphins are. When sailing around these islands, a pod of wild Atlantic Spotted dolphins might decide to swim alongside the boat and play in the wake, making the trip a memorable one.

SHARKS
At the marina in Compass Cay, nurse sharks congregate in the shallow waters where free meals are sprinkled from above, their only inconvenience being the tourists who stand among them while they feed.

FLAMINGOS
Preferring an isolated existence, the West Indian Flamingo can be found balancing in the salt flats of Lake Rosa on the Inagua Islands. Roughly 70,000 flamingos flock to these marshes to feast on the fly larvae and brine shrimp that are packed to the gills with beta carotene, imparting their deep pink hue into the flamingos' plumage.

PIGS
Visitors to the beach at Big Major Cay in Exuma witness a sight that is highly unusual in any part of the world. A litter of pigs in varying colors and sizes splashes and waddles along an idyllic white sand beach on their own private pig island, surrounded by the electric blue waters of the Caribbean, living high on the hog. The pigs look very out of place against this backdrop, and most visitors become downright gleeful at the strange existence and enviable lifestyle of these tropical pigs.

Pigs

FISH

Strap on a snorkel for an immersive experience in the caves and coral reefs of Thunderball Grotto. What appears to be a not very interesting rock is actually a system of small caves that is home to lively, colorful coral reefs and many brightly colored tropical fish.

Made famous by a cameo in two James Bond films, Thunderball Grotto is a popular stop for many visitors to Exuma. Visitors arrive to the Grotto via boat and then snorkel or dive their way inside the cavernous rock. Low tide is easier to navigate, as there are five entrances that can only be accessed by diving underwater and two entrances that are accessible above water. Streams of light find their way into the cave, illuminating the calm blue water and the array of wildlife that darts in and out of reefs on the shallow sea floor. Spot some of the Bahamas' finest such as triggerfish, rock beauty, angelfish, yellowtail snappers, and sergeant majors.

CONCH

The most celebrated ocean floor resident and a staple of Bahamian cuisine, the Queen Conch (pronounced "konk") is a sea snail that thrives in these warm blue waters.

TURTLES

The sea turtles in the Bahamas can be found in their largest concentration on Eleuthera Island. Four of the world's seven turtle species live here, and each species has its own preferred habitat—mangrove forests, shallow coastal areas, coral reefs, and the open ocean.

Ways to Explore the Myths and Mysticism of the Bahamas

PRETTY MOLLY BAY

Pretty Molly Bay is a tiny, unoccupied beach located on Little Exuma, whose namesake was allegedly a slave who drowned at the beach in the 1800s. Locals say that she still visits the beach at night, haunting the island. Some say she was a young woman who was turned into a mermaid.

MYSTERIOUS BLUE HOLES

Created over thousands of years, the limestone bedrock of the island eroded to form intricate cave systems, and Andros is known to have the largest collection in the world. Thus far, 178 blue holes on land and at least 50 in the sea have been discovered, and they provide habitat for unusual cave fish and invertebrates found nowhere else on earth. Fossils, shipwrecks, and the remains of a crocodile not native to the Bahamas have also been found within the blue holes. Noted oceanographer and conservationist, Jacques Cousteau, visited the island in 1970 to explore and film these wonders, and divers from around the world continue to be drawn to them.

LOST ISLAND OF ATLANTIS

For centuries, the fictional city of Atlantis has been the subject of focus by marine researchers. Many have speculated that the legendary underwater city would be located somewhere in Europe, while others have found evidence that suggests Atlantis could have been in North Bimini.

BUSH MEDICINE AND USE OF LOVE POTIONS

The use of plants for medicinal purposes is a tradition brought by African slaves and Native Americans to the Bahamas in the 18th and 19th centuries and passed on to younger generations by practitioners called "grannies." Cures for ailments can be found all over the Bahamas.

LUSCA MYTHICAL UNDERWATER CREATURE

Androsians believe that a gigantic half-octopus, half-shark dwells in the depths of the blue holes. They have named it Lusca, and folklore suggests it's 75 feet long and uses its strong tentacles to drag humans and boats into its underwater lair.

Pirates of Nassau Museum

THE CHICKCHARNEY

Sightings of the mysterious Chickcharney, a feathered three-foot-tall creature with one red eye, three-toed claws, a prehensile tail, and a 360-degree rotating head are still being reported. This flightless bird may have a basis in the large, 3.3-foot-tall barn owl, Tyto pollens, whose remains were found on Andros. That species, however, disappeared in the 16th century due to hunting and habitat destruction.

PIRATES OF NASSAU

During the Golden Age of Piracy (1650 to 1730), Nassau was notorious for being a pirate haven. The city once served as the capital of the "Pirate Republic," a pirate-run colony that existed in the Bahamas between 1706 and 1718. Edward Teach, better known as Black-beard, was the leader of the pirates that lived and "worked" in New Providence. They ran the colony until the British invaded the island in 1718. Black-beard was killed in battle.

HAUNTED HOUSE IN HARBOUR ISLAND

In 1945, a young, newlywed couple moved into this mansion. According to locals, they had a terrible argument shortly after, and left everything just as it was and never returned. Children playing on the grounds talked of seeing two figures in white floating about the house.

The Bahamas Today

Development is no longer on the back burner in the Bahamas. One of the island's five-star resorts, the Baha Mar, took more than 10 years to open, but once it officially opened its doors in 2017, the resort attracted scores of visitors from around the world, which led to a boost in the country's tourism industry. Many other new hotels, restaurants, and other tourist attractions are underway across all the islands, and Bahamians are using the increase in tourism as an opportunity to spruce up existing properties and improve an infrastructure that was starting to show signs of age and neglect.

THE BRITISH FEEL REMAINS

From driving on the left side of the road, to tea parties, to the wig-wearing lawyers who stroll into court, British influence is still apparent in the Bahamas. Though the country gained independence from England in 1973, Bahamians learn British spelling in school, and the country still uses the Westminster style of government. At the same time, a constant diet of American media has had an impact on the country. Bahamians measure temperature in Fahrenheit instead of Celsius, and although the English gentleman's cricket is the national sport, you'll be hard-pressed to find a local who plays the game.

A PLAYGROUND FOR THE RICH AND FAMOUS

With its near-perfect year-round weather, modern infrastructure and amenities, and proximity to the United States, it's no wonder that the Bahamas is a home away from Hollywood for many celebrities. Sean Connery lives behind the gates of the exclusive Lyford Cay community on New Providence Island. Tim McGraw and Faith Hill, David Copperfield, and Nicolas Cage own private islands in the Exumas. Mariah Carey owns a private Eleuthera estate, and the island is also home to Lenny Kravitz, whose mother, actress Roxie Roker, grew up there.

MANY DIFFERENT DESTINATIONS

The majority of the 6 million tourists who visit the Bahamas each year experience only Nassau, Paradise Island, or perhaps Grand Bahama. But with more than 700 islands, there's so much more to see and do. Each island has a different way of life; none of them have the liveliness of big-city life experienced in the capital. The farther south you venture, the slower the pace.

STILL DEVELOPING

Bay Street, once Nassau's Madison Avenue, is on the road to recovery after years of neglect. The esplanade just west of downtown has seen the addition of new renovated hotels and restaurants, the renovation of existing establishments, and new shopping areas, with other major additions currently underway. The Lynden Pindling International Airport is now a modern gateway that truly welcomes visitors. And following a number of false starts, the multibillion-dollar Baha Mar transformation of the Cable Beach strip is now a reality. As Nassau continues to develop, many parts of the Out Islands remain untouched, preserving the quaint nature that attracts adventure travelers each year.

SUSTAINABLE DEVELOPMENT

The government works closely with the Bahamas National Trust to identify and develop protected green spaces, adding more and more land each year to the National Park System, and any developer interested in putting up a sizable or potentially environmentally sensitive project anywhere in the country is required to pay for and submit an Environmental Impact Assessment before consideration is granted.

Kids and Families

It might not be an exaggeration to say that the Bahamas is a playground for children—or anyone else who likes building castles in the sand, searching for the perfect seashell, and playing tag with ocean waves.

Although water-related activities are the most obvious enticements, these relaxed and friendly islands also offer a variety of land-based options, particularly in Nassau and on adjacent Paradise Island. For tales of the high seas, **Pirates of Nassau** has artifacts and interactive exhibits of the original pirates of the Caribbean.

The **Ardastra Gardens, Zoo and Conservation Center** is home to a variety of animals, like pink flamingos, a pair of guenons, and Madagascar lemurs.

Let the kids pick out their favorite pony at the **Surrey Horse Pavilion** on Prince George Wharf and take a leisurely clip-clopping ride through the old city of Nassau. For a few extra dollars, most guides will extend your tour beyond the typical route to include other sites.

Megaresort **Atlantis** has lots of appeal, with everything from pottery painting to remote-control car-making and racing, to an 8,000-square-foot, state-of-the-art kids' camp, and the Bahamas' and Caribbean's largest casino and water park.

In Freeport, older children and adults can spend a day learning how dolphins are trained from **UNEXSO** (one of whose founders was Jacques Cousteau) at Sanctuary Bay, a refuge for dolphins.

For water-sports enthusiasts, snorkeling, parasailing, and boating opportunities abound. In the Exumas, rent a powerboat and take the kids to Big Major Cay to see the famous **swimming pigs.** If you are staying in Nassau, book a day trip to see the pigs with **Harbour Safaris.** Don't forget some scraps! Kids will also get a kick

out of the hundreds of **iguanas** on nearby Allan's Cay and the **giant starfish** near mainland Great Exuma.

Much of the Bahamas' most incredible scenery is underwater, but kids of all ages can enjoy the scenes beneath the sea without even getting wet. At **Stuart Cove's Dive Bahamas** in Nassau, kids 12 and up can go 15 feet under with a SUB (Scenic Underwater Bubble) and zoom around the reefs. **Seaworld Tours'** semisubmarine explores Nassau Harbour and Paradise Island for 1½ hours with sightseeing above and below water.

What to Watch and Read

ISLAND IN THE STREAM

First published in 1970, nine years after Ernest Hemingway's death, *Islands in the Stream* follows the adventures of Thomas Hudson, a wandering artist, from his experiences as a painter on the Gulf Stream island of Bimini where he is paid a visit by his three young sons, to the coast of Cuba during World War II. This book is the first of the posthumously published works of Ernest Hemingway.

THUNDERBALL: JAMES BOND SERIES

Published in 1961, *Thunderball* is the ninth book in Ian Fleming's James Bond series, and the eighth full-length Bond novel. The book is where we first meet Bond's number one enemy, SPECTRE leader Ernst Stavro Blofeld, who steals two atomic bombs and attempts to blackmail Western powers for their return. James Bond, Secret Service operative 007, travels to the Bahamas to work with his friend Felix Leiter, for the CIA's investigation.

THE NOBLE PIRATES

Rima Jean's time travel romance novel *The Nobel Pirates* (2014) tells the story of a workaholic attorney named Sabrina who, on vacation in the Bahamas in 2009, gets transported back in time to 1718 amidst the pirates of Nassau. Surrounded by the notorious bad boys of the Golden Age of Piracy, Edward England, Howel Davis, and "Black Bart" Roberts, Sabrina now has to learn how to survive in the present-past and figure out how to get back to her time.

CASINO ROYALE

In *Casino Royale* (2006), Daniel Craig suits up as secret agent James Bond for the first time. His first mission as 007 is to defeat a private banker to terrorists in a high stakes game of poker at Casino Royale, Montenegro, but he quickly finds out that things are not what they seem. The 21st-century film was the third screen adaption of Ian Fleming's 1953 *Casino Royale* novel. Filming took place at The Ocean Club, A Four Seasons Resort in the Bahamas.

SPLASH

In the 1984 fantasy/romance movie, Daryl Hannah plays a mermaid that saves a young boy from drowning. Twenty years later, the same young man (Tom Hanks) is reunited with the mermaid, not knowing who or what she is, and falls in love with her. The movie was filmed on the former Gorda Cay in the Bahamas, which now is known as Castaway Cay, the private island of Disney Cruise Line.

COCOON

Cocoon, a science-fiction/comedy and drama, is one of the most popular movies filmed in the Bahamas. The 1985 film follows senior citizens living in a Florida rest home when they stumble across an alien "fountain of youth" at the swimming pool of the home next door. Unbeknownst to them, aliens have been using the swimming pool in the house to store their cocooned brethren, giving the waters a powerful, rejuvenating quality. Parts of the film were shot in Nassau, Bahamas.

AFTER THE SUNSET

Having already stolen two from the set of three priceless Napoleon Diamonds, expert jewel thief Max Burdett (Pierce Brosnan) decides to retire on a tropical island with his girlfriend (Salma Hayek). When Max discovers the third and final diamond is sitting on a docked cruise ship on his very island, an FBI agent shows up to investigate him, which spells trouble for Max and his girlfriend. *After the Sunset* (2004) was shot in Paradise Island and Nassau.

GREAT WATER ADVENTURES

In an archipelago nation named for shallow seas that amaze even astronauts in space, don't miss having a close marine encounter. Water adventures range from a splash at the beach to shark diving. Or stay between the extremes with fishing

WHERE TO DIVE AND SNORKEL IN THE BAHAMAS

Although most water in the Bahamas is clear enough to see to the bottom from your boat, snorkeling or diving gets you that much closer to the country's true natives. Coral reefs, blue holes, drop-offs, and sea gardens abound.

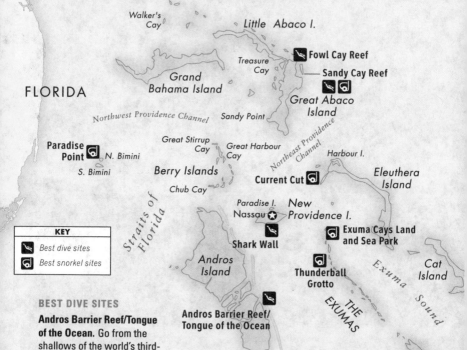

FLORIDA

Walker's Cay

Little Abaco I.

Treasure Cay

Grand Bahama Island

Northwest Providence Channel

Sandy Point

Fowl Cay Reef

Sandy Cay Reef

Great Abaco Island

Great Stirrup Cay

Great Harbour Cay

Paradise Point

N. Bimini

S. Bimini

Berry Islands

Chub Cay

Northeast Providence Channel

Harbour I.

Current Cut

Eleuthera Island

Straits of Florida

Paradise I.
Nassau

New Providence I.

Shark Wall

Andros Island

Exuma Cays Land and Sea Park

Thunderball Grotto

Exuma Sound

Cat Island

THE EXUMAS

Andros Barrier Reef/ Tongue of the Ocean

Great Exuma Island

KEY

Best dive sites

Best snorkel sites

BEST DIVE SITES

Andros Barrier Reef/Tongue of the Ocean. Go from the shallows of the world's third-largest barrier reef to the depths of the ocean.

Shark Wall, New Providence. Off southwest New Providence, this drop is a must for experienced divers. James Bond movies *Thunderball* and *Never Say Never Again* were filmed here.

The Wall, Crooked Island. The famed dive site about 50 yards off Crooked Island's coast drops from 45 feet to thousands.

Diving near New Providence Island

BEST SNORKEL SITES

The Current Cut, Eleuthera. Near the Current settlement in North Eleuthera there is great drift snorkel with the right tide.

Exuma Cays Land and Sea Park. This 176-square-mile park was the first of its kind. Since the park is protected and its waters have essentially never been fished, you can see what the ocean looked like before humanity.

Paradise Point, Bimini. Off northern Bimini, this area is rich in sea life and is famous for the underwater stone path some believe marks the road to the lost city of Atlantis. Dolphins and black coral gardens are just offshore.

Thunderball Grotto, the Exumas. This three-story limestone-ceiling cave at the northern end of the Exumas chain was featured in the James Bond movie of the same name.

Diving near Bimini

EXTREME DIVING ADVENTURES

Various outfitters on Grand Bahama and New Providence offer shark dives. With **Caribbean Divers** (☎ 242/373–9111 ⊕ *www.bellchannelinn.com*) and **UNEXSO** in Grand Bahama and **Stuart Cove's** in New Providence, you'll watch dive masters feed reef sharks which brush by you—no cage included. Dive masters control the ferocity and location of the frenzy, so the sharks' attention is on the food.

Incredible Adventures (☎ 800/644–7382 ⊕ *www.incredible-adventures.com*) in Grand Bahama offers cage diving with tiger sharks. You'll sit in the water as giant sharks come breathtakingly close, the only thing between you a few strips of metal.

Feeding sharks when humans are present make these dives controversial, especially when multiple sharks are involved and there's the possibility of a frenzy. Dive operators doing these extreme adventures are experienced and knowledgeable about shark-feeding patterns and signs of aggression, but partake in these dives at your own risk.

San Salvador

Rum Cay

Crooked Island Passage

Samana Cay

Long I.

The Wall

Crooked Island

Acklins Island

Mayaguana Passage

Mayaguana Island

0   50 mi
0   50 km

Little Inagua Island

Great Inagua Island

French Angelfish

Four-Eyed Butterflyfish

Grunt

Nassau Grouper

Parrotfish

Queen Triggerfish

Sergeant Major

Snapper

Tang

Barracuda*

Lionfish*

Shark*

*dangerous fish

WHAT YOU'LL SEE UNDER THE SEA

Reefs in the Bahamas are alive with colorful life. Vibrant hard corals—such as star, brain, staghorn, and elk—and waving purple sea fans are home to schools of myriad fish, some pictured above. Be on the lookout for lionfish; a prick from the fins of this poisonous fish is painful and could send you to the hospital. The most common sharks in the Bahamas are nurse sharks (typically non-threatening to humans) and Caribbean reef sharks. The deeper you dive, the bigger and more varied shark species get.

Generally, the further the reef is from a developed area the more abundant the marine life, but even sites around developed islands might surprise you.

TOUR THE EXUMA CAYS BY BOAT

The Bahamas is a boater's paradise, with shallow protected waters and secluded, safe harbors. In small island groups, travel takes just a few hours, even minutes.

THE EXUMA CAYS

To really get off the beaten path, the Exuma Cays are where it's at. This 120-mi archipelago is made up of small cays, many of which are still uninhabited or privately owned, and interspersed with sand banks and spits. Throughout is excellent diving and snorkeling. Boaters usually stock up and clear customs in Nassau, cross the yellow banks to the north of the chain, and slowly make their way south.

BOAT TOURS

If you don't have your own boat, these outfitters will take you on island-hopping adventures.

Exuma Water Sports
☎ 242/357-0770
⊕ www.exumawatertours. com. Come here for guided Jet Ski tours through the Exuma Cays, as well as a scenic boat cruise that includes snorkeling at Thunderball Grotto.

High Seas Private Excursions. ☎ 242/376-4234 ⊕ highseasexcursions.com. $3,500 for a full day excursion to the Exuma Cays from Nassau.

Highbourne Cay at the chain's northern end has a marina and food store. You can explore many of the surrounding cays by tender if you prefer to dock here. Nearby, **Allan's Cay** is home to hundreds of iguanas that readily accept food.

Norman's Cay has an airstrip and Norman's Cay Beach Club has a fantastic restaurant and bar. Just south is the 176-sq-mi **Exuma Cays Land and Sea Park.** It has some of the country's best snorkeling and diving. Warderick Wells Cay houses the park headquarters, which has nature trail maps and a gift shop. Just below, **Compass Cay** has a marina known for its friendly nurse sharks and a small convenience store. **Pipe Creek**, which winds between Compass and Staniel Cays, has great shelling, snorkeling, diving, and bonefishing. **Staniel Cay** is the hub of activity in these parts and a favorite destination of yachters. That's thanks to the Staniel Cay Yacht Club, the only full-service marina in the cays. It makes a good base for visiting **Big Major Cay**, where wild pigs swim out to meet you, and **Thunderball**

Ship Channel Cay
Allan's Cay
Highbourne Cay
Lang Cay
Norman's Cay
Shroud Cay
Hawksbill Cay   **Exuma Cays Land and Sea Park**
Cistern Cay
Waderick Wells Cay
Halls Pond Cay   O'Brian's Cay
Bells Cay   **Compass Cay**
Pipe Creek   Joe Cay
Thomas Cay
Big Major Cay   **Staniel Cay**
Thunderball Grotto

0   10 miles
0   10 km

Grotto, a beautiful marine cave that snorkelers (at low tide) and experienced scuba divers can explore.

SAILING

Sailing is popular in the Bahamas, and there are many regattas held here throughout the year. Various outfitters in New Providence and Paradise Island offer relaxing sailing cruises.

BONEFISHING

WHAT IS BONEFISHING?

Bonefishing is the fly-fishing sport of choice in the Bahamas. The country is full of pristine shallow flats and mangroves where stealthy "gray ghosts"—silvery white, sleek fish—school in large groups. Hooking one is a challenge, as the fish are fast, strong, and perfectly camouflaged to the sand and water.

To catch bonefish you need the right mix of knowledge, instinct, and patience. Guides are the best way to go, as their knowledge of the area and schooling patterns gives them an uncanny ability to find bonefish quickly.

EQUIPMENT

Basics include a fly-fishing rod and reel and the right lure. Experienced anglers, guides, and fishing-supply dealers can help you gear up with the best and latest technology. Bonefishing is catch and release, so always use barbless hooks and work quickly when removing them to avoid stressing the fish. Wear comfortable, light clothing that protects much of your body from the sun, as you'll be out for hours without shade.

In many places you can just walk offshore onto the flats. Some anglers use shallow draft boats with a raised platform in the back, where they pole into extremely shallow areas.

BEST PLACES TO BONEFISH

Bonefish hang out in shallow flats and mangrove areas. Andros, Bimini, and the Exumas have the best bonefishing; Abaco, Eleuthera, and Long Island also provide excellent adventures. If you have the time, visit the southernmost islands, like Crooked, Acklins, or Inagua, where these gray ghosts are "uneducated" to anglers.

OTHER TYPES OF FISHING

Make sure you are familiar with fishing regulations before you begin your adventure. Visit ⊕ *www.bahamas.com/things-do/fishing*.

DEEP-SEA FISHING

Deep water is just a few miles off most islands, where anglers try for large ocean fish—tuna, wahoo, mahi mahi, shark, and marlin. Like bonefishing, the fight is what most anglers are after; however, a day on the ocean can provide a great meal. The Abacos has great deep-sea fishing, and many tournaments are held there each year.

REEF/SHOAL FISHING

Fishing with a rod, or Bahamian "hand-lining" can be a great family fishing adventure. Anchoring near a shoal or reef, or even trolling with a lure, can be relaxing. The Out Islands are home to shoals, reefs, and wrecks that are less visited by fishing enthusiasts.

SPEARFISHING

Most reefs are okay for free-dive spear fishing, but spear guns (guns that fire spears) are illegal in the Bahamas. Spear is the traditional Bahamian fishing method, so reefs close to more developed islands tend to have fewer fish. The Out Islands still have lesser-known spots good for spearfishing.

WHERE TO STAY

Bonefishing lodges are common in the Bahamas and often include top-notch guides. Accommodations are usually basic. Here are our top bonefishing lodges:

■ Andros **Island** Bonefishing **Club**

■ **Crooked Island Lodge**

■ **Plus39** Peace **and Plenty
Bonefish Lodge, the Exumas**

■ **Small** Hope **Bay** Lodge, Andros

(left pg) Bonefishing in Andros.
(right) A prize catch.

Chapter 2

TRAVEL SMART

Updated by
Jessica Robertson

★ **CAPITAL:**
Nassau

POPULATION:
389,482

$ **CURRENCY:**
Bahamian dollar; pegged to
U.S. dollar

LANGUAGE:
English

☎ **COUNTRY CODE:**
1 242

⚠ **EMERGENCIES:**
919 or 911

🚗 **DRIVING:**
On the left

⚡ **ELECTRICITY:**
120v/60 cycles; plugs U.S.
2- and 3-prong

🕐 **TIME:**
EST

🌐 **WEBSITES:**
www.bahamas.com,
www.myoutislands.com,
www.bahamasvisitors
guide.com

FLORIDA

*Atlantic
Ocean*

BAHAMAS
✪ Nassau

*Caribbean
Sea*

CUBA

HAITI   *DOMINICAN
REPUBLIC*

JAMAICA

Know Before You Go

Before you head to the Bahamas for a vacation, there are a few things you should know that will make your visit even better. Here are the answers to the questions you're too afraid to ask, plus all the essentials.

DRIVE ON THE LEFT

One of many traditions left over from the Bahamas' days under British rule is driving on the left. This has its roots in medieval times when it was important to keep your right hand free to draw your sword if necessary. Today, the Bahamas is one of the few countries that still keeps left. The majority of the cars on the road here are imported from the United States, so the driver is on the left; rental cars usually have large 'Keep Left' stickers inside the windshield as a reminder. In late 2019 it became legal to turn left on red, but most drivers are still adjusting. For this reason it's important to be extra cautious of cars when you are a pedestrian.

VERY FRIENDLY AND POLITE

Bahamians are extremely polite and courteous so it's not unusual for locals to greet you in passing along the street or when you walk into a room. You'll make more friends if you return the courtesy and say 'Good Morning, Good Afternoon, or Good Evening' in return. You'll win extra points if you are the first to greet a local. In fact, if you need assistance, Bahamians are generally happy to lend a hand, but it's always best to offer a courteous greeting before rushing into your question or concern. To enjoy the real hospitality of Bahamians and get a true understanding of how they live, consider signing up with the Ministry of Tourism's People to People program that matches visitors with local families, couples, or individuals for some unique authentic experiences.

THERE ARE MORE THAN 700 ISLANDS

Although many of the country's 6 million annual visitors only get to New Providence, there are hundreds of other islands that make up the Bahamas. Sixteen of them are considered major islands with populations running from a few thousand to a few hundred thousand. The different islands and settlements have very different natural features: thick, towering pine forests and bonefish flats in the north, and low-lying scrubland in the south. There are also unique traits in the population from island to island.

Accents, physical features and last names often give clues as to which island or settlement a Bahamian or his or her parents or grandparents come from. The other 600-plus islands range from sizable land masses to rocks that jut out of the ocean at low tide.

THE BAHAMAS ISN'T TECHNICALLY A PART OF THE CARIBBEAN

Although the small country is considered part of the Caribbean from a touristic point of view, technically it is not. The islands are surrounded by the Atlantic Ocean and are situated hundreds of miles away from the Caribbean Sea. Politically the country does align with the other small countries in the English-speaking Caribbean and is a member of Caricom. Culturally the Bahamas is an interesting mix of Afro-Bahamian, English (it remained under British rule until July 1973), and American (due to its geographic proximity to the United States). The Bahamas is an independent country and a part of the Commonwealth.

THE U.S. DOLLAR IS ACCEPTED EVERYWHERE

If you are visiting from the United States, great news: there's no need to exchange your currency. The Bahamian dollar is on par with the U.S. dollar and American currency is accepted everywhere. If you are nearing the end of your trip, ask if they can give you any change in USD. If they have it, most cashiers are happy to comply. In highly frequented tourist areas you will also find ATMs that dispense U.S. cash, which can be handy as smaller shops and craft and food vendors are not set up to accept credit cards. Note that some stores and restaurants roll the 12% VAT service tax into the price of goods while others add it on at the cash register. Be sure to ask if there's no sign making it clear.

THE BAHAMAS IS A MELTING POT

While the majority of the country's residents are of African descent, this little island nation is a true melting pot, or as Bahamians like to say, they are mixed up like conch salad! You'll find Bahamians of English, Greek, Chinese, Filipino, Haitian, Jamaican, Canadian, and American descent as well as many other corners of the earth. These Bahamians share their islands with thousands of expatriate residents who also call the Bahamas home. Each October the various cultures that call the Bahamas home put on an incredible display to showcase the best of their homeland's food, culture, and entertainment at the International Culture, Wine & Food Festival.

PRE-CLEARANCE & CUSTOMS

When you arrive in the Bahamas, you will have to clear Bahamian immigration regardless of where you enter. You'll also go through customs. If you arrive at the Lynden Pindling International Airport, tourists are ushered through without

having to fill in forms or open their luggage for inspection. When flying out of the country's main airport, be sure to arrive at least two hours ahead of your scheduled flight. Depending on the time of day and the number of flights departing, security lines can be long. You will also need to allow extra time to go through the U.S. Customs and Immigration preclearance facility. The good news is that this process generally takes a lot less time than lining up at a U.S. airport to clear customs and immigration when you land.

IT'S PRONOUNCED *KONK*

Conch, that delicious sea snail you'll see on just about every menu, is pronounced "konk." The popular locally brewed beer is Kah-lik, not Kay-lick. As foreign as the Bahamian tongue may sound when you first arrive, it is indeed English. Like most other countries, the Bahamas has its own slang and ways of stringing words together that will likely take a bit of getting used to, especially when you are trying to follow a conversation between locals. When they speak to you, most Bahamians will use a very proper Queen's English.

HURRICANE SEASON

Hurricane season runs from June 1 through November 30, but there's no reason to avoid traveling there during this time. It is rare for storms to impact any part of the Bahama island chain in the initial summer months of the season, and the most likely time that

a storm will make its way to or through the Bahama island chain is in September and October. Even then, it is important to understand the country's unique archipelagic geography before changing or cancelling travel plans. As was the case with category 5 Hurricane Dorian, much of the island chain will be minimally impacted or not at all impacted even as one part is experiencing a storm, so pay attention to the path of the storm. Most hotels have hurricane policies that will allow you to cancel without penalty if your trip and a storm coincide.

ENVIRONMENTALLY SOUND

In January 2020, the Bahamas banned the consumption and sale of single-use plastic items, including straws, cutlery, grocery bags and styrofoam containers; it's also illegal to deliberately release balloons into the air. The Bahamas national Trust is the steward of more than a million acres of protected land and sea in a series of national parks that span the entire country. To further protect marine resources, the Bahamas has made it illegal to catch turtles and sharks and has closed seasons to give the popular Nassau Grouper and crawfish time to procreate.

Getting Here and Around

Air

Most international flights to the Bahamas connect through airports in Florida, New York, Charlotte, or Atlanta. The busiest airport in the Bahamas is in Nassau, which has the most connections to the more remote Out Islands. If you're traveling to these more remote islands, you might have to make a connection in both Florida and Nassau—and you still may have to take a ferry or a water taxi to your final destination.

A direct flight from New York City to Nassau takes approximately three hours. The flight from Charlotte to Nassau is two hours, and the flight from Miami to Nassau takes less than an hour. Most flights between the islands of the Bahamas also take less than an hour.

Boat

If you're adventurous and have time to spare, take a ferry or one of the traditional mail boats that regularly leave Nassau from Potter's Cay, under the Paradise Island Bridge. Although faster air-conditioned boats now make some of the trips, certain remote destinations are still served by slow, old-fashioned craft. Especially if you choose the mail-boat route, you may find yourself sharing company with goats or chickens, or piles of lumber and crates of cargo; on these lumbering mail boats, expect to spend 5 to 12 or more hours slowly making your way between island outposts. These boats operate on Bahamian time, which is a casual unpredictable measure, and schedules can be thrown off by bad weather. Mail boats cannot generally be booked in advance, and services are limited. In Nassau, check details with the dockmaster's office at Potter's Cay. One-way trips can cost from $35 to $100.

Within the Bahamas, Bahamas Ferries has the most (and most comfortable) options for island-hopping, with air-conditioned boats that offer food and beverages served by cabin attendants. Schedules do change rather frequently; if you're planning to ferry back to an island to catch a flight, double-check the departure times and planned routes. Ferries serve most of the major tourist destinations from Nassau, including Spanish Wells, Governor's Harbour, Harbour Island, Exuma, and Andros. The high-speed ferry that runs between Nassau and Spanish Wells, Governor's Harbour, and Harbour Island costs $81 one way, and takes about two hours each way.

Local ferries in the Out Islands transport islanders and visitors from the main island to smaller cays. Usually, these ferries make several round-trips daily and keep a more punctual schedule than the longer-haul ferry.

It's possible to get to Grand Bahama by ferry from Florida. Balearia Bahamas Express sails from Fort Lauderdale's Port Everglades (Terminal 1) and provides fast ferry service, making a day trip possible, while Bahamas Paradise Cruise Line sails from the Port of Palm Beach in Riviera Beach and is more like a small cruise ship. Some hotel packages include transportation to Grand Bahamas.

If you're setting sail yourself, note that cruising boats must clear customs at the nearest port of entry before beginning any diving or fishing. The fee is $150 for boats up to 35 feet and $300 for boats longer than 35 feet, which includes fishing permits and departure tax for up to three people. Each additional person above the age of three will be charged the $25 departure tax. Stays of longer than 12 months must be arranged with Bahamas customs and immigration officials.

🚗 Car

International rental agencies are generally in Nassau, and you will rent from privately owned companies on the small islands. Thoroughly check the vehicle before you leave as many are not in great condition. Bring your own car seats as companies do not often provide these.

To rent a car, you must be 21 years of age or older.

It's common to hire a driver with a van, and prices are negotiable. Most drivers charge by the half day or full day. Prices depend on the stops and distance, but the cost for a half-day tour is generally $50 to $100 for one to four people, and $100 to $200 for a full-day tour. It's customary to pay for the driver's lunch. All tour guides in the Bahamas are required to take a tourism course and pass an exam; they must also get a special license to operate a taxi.

GASOLINE

The cost of fuel in the Bahamas is usually at least twice that in the United States; be prepared to pay in cash. You can ask for a handwritten receipt if printed ones are not available. Stations are few and far between on the Out Islands, so keep the tank full. Gas stations may be closed on Sunday.

PARKING

There are few parking meters in the Bahamas, and none in downtown Nassau. Police are lenient with visitors' rental cars parked illegally and will generally just ask the driver to move it. Parking spaces are hard to find in Nassau, so be prepared to park on a side street and walk. Most hotels offer off-street parking for guests. There are few parking lots not associated with hotels.

ROADSIDE EMERGENCIES

In case of a road emergency, stay in your vehicle with your emergency flashers engaged and wait for help, especially after dark. If someone stops to help, relay information through a small opening in the window. If it's daylight and help does not arrive, walk to the nearest phone and call for help. In the Bahamas, motorists readily stop to help drivers in distress.

Ask for emergency numbers at the rental office when you pick up your car. These numbers vary from island to island. On smaller islands the owner of the company may want you to call them at their home.

RULES OF THE ROAD

Islanders drive on the left side of the road, though many cars here have a steering wheel on the left. Many streets in downtown Nassau are one-way. At roundabouts, keep left and yield to oncoming traffic as you enter the roundabout and at "Give Way" signs.

🚕 Taxi

There are taxis waiting at every airport and outside all the main hotels and cruise-ship docks. Beware of "hackers," drivers who don't display their license (and may not have one). Sometimes you can negotiate a fare, but you must do so before you enter the taxi.

You'll find that Bahamian taxi drivers are more talkative than their U.S. counterparts. When you take a taxi to dinner or to town, it's common for the driver to wait there and take you back at no additional cost. A 15% tip is suggested.

Essentials

Dining

The restaurants we list are the top-rated in each price category. You'll find all types, from cosmopolitan to the most casual restaurants, serving all types of cuisine. Unless otherwise noted, the restaurants *listed in this guide* are open daily for lunch and dinner.

PAYING

The U.S. dollar is on par with the Bahamian dollar and both currencies are accepted in restaurants. Most credit cards are also accepted in most restaurants, although more and more frequently local businesses are shunning American Express. Typically, you will have to ask for your check when you are finished.

WHAT IT COSTS in Dollars			
$	**$$**	**$$$**	**$$$$**
RESTAURANTS			
under $20	$20–$30	$31–$40	over $40

TIPPING

In the Bahamas, service staff and hotel workers expect to be tipped. The usual tip for service from a taxi driver or waiter is 15% and $1 to $2 a bag for porters. Most travelers leave $1 to $3 per day for their hotel maid, usually every morning since the maid may have a day off. Many hotels and restaurants automatically add a 15% gratuity to your bill; if not, a 15% to 20% tip at a restaurant is appropriate (more for a high-end establishment). Bartenders generally get $1 to $2 per drink. It's also customary to tip the gas station attendant who fills your rental car $1 to $2, especially if he cleans the windshield. Grocery store packing boys are also usually given a few dollars—more if you have lots of bags for him to pack and carry to the car.

RESERVATIONS AND DRESS

Reservations are recommended in Nassau and on the more remote islands, where restaurants may close early if no one shows up or has a table reserved. We mention dress only when men are required to wear a jacket or a jacket and tie. Otherwise, you can assume that dining out is a casual affair.

WINES, BEER, AND SPIRITS

Kalik and Sands beers are brewed in the Bahamas and are available at most restaurants for lunch and dinner.

Tours

Banks are generally open Monday–Thursday 9 or 9:30 to 3 or 4 and Friday 9 to 5. However, on the Out Islands banks may keep shorter hours—on the smallest cays, they may be open only a day or two each week. Some small islands and settlements no longer have a local bank, so it's always a good idea to take enough cash with you. Most Bahamian offices observe bank hours.

Hours for attractions vary. Most open between 9 and 10 am and close around 5 pm.

Though most drugstores typically abide by normal store hours, some stay open 24 hours.

Most stores, with the exception of straw markets and malls, close on Sunday, although a number of Bay Street stores will open if cruise ships are in port.

Generally, prices in the Bahamas are higher than in the United States. Businesses accept U.S. and Bahamian dollars as they are the same value, but they may not be able to give you change in U.S. currency. On the Out Islands, meals and simple goods can be expensive; prices are high due to the remoteness of the islands and the costs of importing.

🛏 Lodging

The lodgings we list are the top-rated in each price category. Depending on the island, top-rated could be a glitzy resort with spa and casino or a two-cottage secluded getaway with lots of charm but little in the way of amenities. We always list the facilities that are available—but we don't specify whether they cost extra: when pricing accommodations, always ask what's included.

WHAT IT COSTS in Dollars

$	$$	$$$	$$$$
HOTELS			
under $200	$200–$300	$301–$400	over $400

💲 Money

CREDIT CARDS
Some smaller hotels in the islands do not take plastic.

CURRENCY AND EXCHANGE
The U.S. dollar is on par with the Bahamian dollar and is accepted all over the Bahamas. Bahamian money runs in bills of $1, $5, $10, $20, $50, and $100. Because U.S. currency is accepted everywhere, there really is no need to change to Bahamian. You won't incur any transaction fees for currency exchange. Carry small bills when bargaining at straw markets.

TAXES
There's no sales tax in the Bahamas, but a 12% VAT is added to most goods and services; the $15 departure tax is included in the price of commercial airline tickets.

Tax on your hotel room is 6% to 12% in addition to VAT, depending on the island visited; at some resorts, a small service charge of up to 5% may be added to cover housekeeping and bellman service.

Comprehensive policies typically cover trip cancellation and interruption, letting you cancel or cut your trip short because of illness, or, in some cases, acts of terrorism in your destination. Such policies might also cover evacuation and medical care. (For trips abroad you should have at least medical-only coverage. *See Medical Insurance and Assistance under Health.*) Some also cover you for trip delays because of bad weather or mechanical problems, as well as for lost or delayed luggage.

Another type of coverage to consider is financial default—that is, when your trip is disrupted because a tour operator, airline, or cruise line goes out of business. Generally you must buy this insurance when you book your trip or shortly thereafter, and it's available to you only if your operator isn't on a list of excluded companies.

➕ Safety
FOOD AND WATER
The major health risk in the Bahamas is traveler's diarrhea. This is most often caused by ingesting fruits, shellfish, and drinks to which your body is unaccustomed. Go easy at first on new foods such as mangoes, conch, and rum punch.

If you're susceptible to digestive problems, avoid ice, uncooked food, and unpasteurized milk and milk products, and stick to bottled water, or water that

Essentials

has been boiled for several minutes, even when brushing your teeth.

Drink plenty of purified water or tea; chamomile is a good folk remedy. In severe cases, rehydrate yourself with a salt-sugar solution (½ teaspoon salt and 4 tablespoons sugar per quart of water).

DIVING

Do not fly within 24 hours of scuba diving. Always know where your nearest decompression chamber is before you embark on a dive expedition, and how you would get there in an emergency. The only chambers in the Bahamas are in Nassau and San Salvador, and emergency cases are often sent to Miami.

INSECTS

No-see-ums (sand fleas) and mosquitoes can be bothersome. Some travelers have allergies to sand-flea bites. To prevent the bites, use a recommended bug repellent. To ease the itching, rub alcohol on the bites. Some Out Island hotels provide sprays or repellents but it's a good idea to bring your own.

SUNBURN

Basking in the sun is one of the great pleasures of a Bahamian vacation, but take precautions against sunburn and sunstroke.

MEDICAL INSURANCE AND ASSISTANCE

The most serious accidents and illnesses may require an airlift to the United States—most likely to a hospital in Florida. The costs of a medical evacuation can quickly run into the thousands of dollars, and your personal health insurance may not cover such costs or require you to pay upfront and file for reimbursement later. If you plan to pursue inherently risky activities, such as scuba diving, or if you have an existing medical condition, check your policy to see what's covered.

Consider buying trip insurance with medical-only coverage. Neither Medicare nor some private insurers cover medical expenses anywhere outside the United States. Medical-only policies typically reimburse you for medical care (excluding that related to preexisting conditions) and hospitalization abroad, and provide for evacuation. You still have to pay the bills and await reimbursement from the insurer, though.

Another option is to sign up with a medical-evacuation assistance company. A membership in one of these companies gets you doctor referrals, emergency evacuation or repatriation, 24-hour hotlines for medical consultation, and other assistance. International SOS Assistance Emergency and AirMed International provide evacuation services and medical referrals. MedjetAssist offers medical evacuation.

There has been a significant spike in violent crime in Nassau, mostly in off-the-beaten-path locations. Exercise caution in these areas: be aware of your wallet or handbag at all times, and keep your jewelry in the hotel safe. Be especially wary in remote areas; always lock your rental vehicle, and don't keep any valuables in the car, even in the locked trunk.

Travel in groups at night in Nassau or in remote areas.

On the Calendar

See an expanded list of events in each chapter.

Winter

Bahamas International Film Festival. In early December, the Bahamas International Film Festival in Nassau celebrates cinema in paradise, with screenings, receptions, and movie-industry panels. ⊠ *Nassau* ⊕ *www.bintlfilmfest.com.*

Festival Noel. Since 1993, Festival Noel has marked the official start to the Christmas season. Traditionally held the first Friday evening in December at the Rand Nature Centre, this wine- and food-tasting event and art show displays local talent. Proceeds aid the Bahamas National Trust for the development and restoration of national parks on Grand Bahama Island. ⊠ *Rand Nature Centre, East Settler's Way, Freeport* ✛ *Across street from Sir Jack Hayward Junior High School* ☎ *242/352–5438.*

Junkanoo. Once Christmas dinner is over, the focus shifts to Junkanoo. The first major parade of the season starts just after midnight in downtown Nassau. There's a second parade on New Year's Day. ⊠ *Nassau.*

North Eleuthera Sailing Regatta. The North Eleuthera Sailing Regatta in October provides four days of exciting competition of Bahamian Class A, B, and C boats. Onshore activities based on Harbour Island include live bands playing Bahamian music, plus local food and drink.

Spring

Bahamian Music and Heritage Festival. March's Bahamian Music and Heritage Festival brings local and nationally known musicians to George Town, along with arts and crafts, Bahamas sloop exhibitions, storytelling, singing, poetry reading, and gospel music. ⊠ *George Town.*

Summer

Conch Fest. Deep Creek's annual, six-day Conch Fest in June means talent shows, Rake 'n' Scrape music, arts and crafts, and, of course, lots of conch. The event was designed to promote the Deep Creek settlement and to share its cultural heritage with the younger members of the community, descendants, and visitors. ⊠ *Rock Sound.*

Cat Island Rake 'n' Scrape Festival. The annual Cat Island Rake 'n' Scrape Festival celebrating the indigenous music is held in early June on the Bahamian Labour Day weekend. Each day the festivities begin with breakfast and lunch in the park with games of dominoes and checkers. At 7 pm the site is cleared for the Battle of the Rake 'n' Scrape Bands. You can also enjoy a gospel concert, cultural dance troupes, a children's corner with games, arts and crafts, and a fishermen and farmers' market. Nearby restaurants expand their menus for the after-parties. Between 1,000 and 2,000 people attend and fill local hotels, inns, and guesthouses, so book early. Two mail boats, Bahamasair, and private charters serve the festival, which takes place in the town square near Arthur's Town Airport. ⊠ *Arthur's Town Square, North Cat Island, Arthur's Town* 🖃 *$20.*

Great Itineraries

GRAND BAHAMA
IF YOU HAVE 3 DAYS

Rent a car for easy island touring at your own pace and schedule. Have breakfast and head out on your diving excursion at **UNEXSO**. Once back above water, head to Banana Bay on **Fortune Beach** to have lunch and unwind. For your evening's entertainment, stroll through **Port Lucaya Marketplace,** have drinks at Pelican Bay's Bones Bar, then dine on the dock at Flying Fish GastroBar. On Day 3, drive to **West End** for the day, stopping at Lover's Beach for sea glass, **Paradise Cove** for a good snorkel around Deadman's Reef, and on to West End's northeastern water's edge to sample a variety of fresh, made-in-front-of-you conch salads and fritters. End the night with dinner at East Sushi at Pier One to watch the sunset and feed the sharks.

IF YOU HAVE 5 DAYS

Book ecotours on Days 4 and 5 to kayak through the mangroves, snorkel around Peterson Cay, or go birding or feed sting-rays with Keith Cooper's West End Ecology Tours. Reserve one night's romantic dinner at the elegant Dolphin Clubhouse and wind down with a gourmet pizza or spicy curry at Pisces in Port Lucaya Marketplace the next.

IF YOU HAVE 7 DAYS

Save your last two days for more private, quiet relaxation away from the tourist crowds at Old Bahama Bay at the West End. If several days on a beach lounger or hammock is too slow for you, this spot has access to some of the best fishing on the island, plus the best fishing guides.

ELEUTHERA
IF YOU HAVE 3 DAYS

Fly into North Eleuthera and take the ferry to **Harbour Island**. Base yourself at a hotel near the famous 3-mile pink-sand beach or in historic Dunmore Town. Relax on the beach and have lunch at an oceanside restaurant. Stroll through **Dunmore Town** in the afternoon, stopping at crafts stands and fashionable shops, admiring colonial houses along Bay Street, and visiting historic churches. At night, dine at one of the island's fine restaurants, such as Sip Sip, Rock House, Pink Sands, or Acquapazza. On Day 2, go scuba diving or snorkeling, or hire a guide and try to snag a canny bonefish. Visit the conch shacks on Bay Street for a low-key beachside dinner. On Day 3 get some last-minute color on the beach or some in-room spa pampering; stop by Vic-Hum Club or Gusty's for late-night music.

IF YOU HAVE 5 DAYS

Head back to **Eleuthera** for the next two days. Rent a car at the North Eleuthera Airport (reserve in advance) and drive south past the **Glass Window Bridge,** where you can stand in one spot and see the brilliantly blue and often fierce Atlantic Ocean to the east and the placid Bight of Eleuthera to the west. Continue to **Governor's Harbour,** the island's largest town, and grab lunch at Tippy's or the Beach House. Stay at one of the beach resorts and enjoy the water views. Head into town for nightlife or dining options.

IF YOU HAVE 7 DAYS

On your last two days, drive back to **North Eleuthera,** base yourself at the Cove, and relax on the resort's two beaches. On your final day take the ferry to **Spanish Wells,** where you can rent a golf cart and spend a half day exploring the tiny town and relaxing on a white-sand beach with no tourists. Or stay put and explore Surfer's Beach.

EXUMA
IF YOU HAVE 3 DAYS

Fly into **George Town,** relax on the beach or at the pool, and if it's a Friday night drive to the Fish Fry, a collection of fish shacks and bars just north of George

Town; eat at a picnic table next to the beach. Finish the night at Club Peace and Plenty, the heart of George Town for more than 50 years. On Day 2, pick an activity: golfing at Sandals Emerald Bay; diving, snorkeling, or kayaking (make arrangements the night before at your resort); bonefishing; or driving to a beautiful secluded beach. Get gussied up (sundresses and linen shirts) for a nice dinner in town. On Day 3, head out to **Stocking Island** for some beach volleyball and that it's-five-o'clock-somewhere cocktail. Stay for dinner and sunset. If it's Sunday, a pig roast at noon brings all the islanders over.

IF YOU HAVE 5 DAYS

On Day 4, head to the **Exuma Cays** for some island-hopping: snorkel in Thunderball Grotto, feed swimming pigs and the rare Bahamian iguanas, or find your own secluded sandbar. Spend the night at Staniel Cay Yacht Club and enjoy a festive dinner at the bar. On Day 5, head to the Exuma Cays Land and Sea Park, and spend the day snorkeling, hiking, and relaxing on the beach.

IF YOU HAVE 7 DAYS

For the last two days, relocate to Grand Isle or Sandals Emerald Bay for a luxurious end to your vacation. Relax on the beach, go to the spa, and enjoy that gorgeous blue water one last time. Eat at some of the finer restaurants on the island, or at beach shacks off the resort property.

NEW PROVIDENCE AND PARADISE ISLANDS

IF YOU HAVE 3 DAYS

We're guessing you came to the Bahamas to get some sun, so don't waste any time. Decide whether you'd prefer a secluded stretch of sand or a beach right in the middle of the action, such as **Cable Beach**—New Providence has both. In the evening, check out the downtown bar-and-club scene. Spend Day 2 taking in the markets, gardens, and historic sites of **Nassau.** A good starting point is **Rawson Square,** in the heart of the commercial area. Do your shopping in the morning, hitting **Bay Street,** the capital's main street, and Festival Place at **Prince George Wharf.** To avoid the afternoon heat, visit the **National Art Gallery,** checking out the colonial architecture along the way. Head to Arawak Cay (the Fish Fry to locals) for an authentic Bahamian meal of grilled snapper (served whole) washed down with a cold Kalik or Sands beer. On your third day, tour Paradise Island. Try your luck at the **Atlantis** casino or explore the giant aquariums (non–resort guests will have to pay $39 for adults or $29 for kids under 12). For your final night, book a table at one of Atlantis's fancier restaurants; Nobu or Café Martinique will serve a last supper to remember. Alternately, head west and spend that final day exploring Baha Mar. You can play a round of golf, snorkel in the Sanctuary marine park, or book a massage at the impressive spa. With 40 restaurants and bars on-site, the hardest part of your day will be choosing one for that final meal.

IF YOU HAVE 5 DAYS

On Day 4, consider a day trip to one of the Out Islands. Quaint Harbour Island is two hours away on the Bohengy ferry (☎ 242/323–2166 ⊕ www.bahamasferries.com), or book seats on the large speedboats that will take you to a private island in the Exumas. If you want that private island experience closer to home, spend a day enjoying the VIP Beach Experience at Blue Lagoon Island, just off the northeast coast of New Providence. For your final day, rent a car or scooters and head to **Western New Providence,** stopping for fresh conch salad at **Dino's Gourmet Conch Salad** stall on your way to the **Clifton Heritage Park.**

Great Itineraries

Island-Hopping for 1 Week

The Bahamas is comprised of more than 700 islands, yet many visitors experience just one in a single visit. With limited scheduled transportation between the islands, it's difficult to island-hop without going back to Nassau for each leg, but this itinerary shows how you can use mail boats, speedboats, and scheduled flights to experience Nassau, Paradise Island, Rose Island, Sandals Island, mainland Exuma, and a handful of the Exuma cays in just a week, provided you arrive in Nassau on a Monday since the mail boat to George Town leaves on Tuesday.

1 DAY: NASSAU

Explore the sprawling marine habitat, face your fears on the exhilarating water-slides (including a clear acrylic slide that plunges through a shark tank), and get up close with sea lions and dolphins at the iconic Atlantis Resort. Aquaventure passes can be limited if occupancy is high, so guarantee access by booking a night at the sprawling resort or the Comfort Suites next door. Dine at one of the 21 restaurants on-property, and then dance the night away at Aura nightclub.

1 DAY: MAIL BOAT PASSAGE

On Day 2, head downtown and take in the history, architecture, culture, and (most importantly) the food of historic Nassau on the Bites of Nassau Food Tour. With your belly full, head to the eastern side of Potter's Cay Dock to the *Grand Master* mail boat (☎ 242/393–1041). Once you get your tickets (no need to book in advance), head over to the colorful stalls to enjoy a game of dominoes and an ice cold Sands or Kalik beer. The mail boat, which leaves port at 3 every Tuesday afternoon, will be your transportation, overnight accommodations, and dinner restaurant on your way to George Town, Exuma, all for $50 per person one

way. Don't expect anything fancy; you'll get only a basic bunk in one of two small and stark (yet air-conditioned) cabins. For dinner it's a plate full of the same hearty meal enjoyed by the crew.

1 DAY: GEORGE TOWN, EXUMA

Following your 14-hour overnight passage—complete with unbelievable sunsets, a strong possibility of dolphin spotting, and space shared with everything from cars to mail to sheep and goats—you'll arrive in George Town bright and early. Make Club Peace and Plenty your first stop for a Bahamian breakfast staple: boiled fish and johnnycake. Drop your bags at the hotel and take the water taxi from the Government Dock for a day of sun and fun at Chat 'N' Chill on Stocking Island, just a mile offshore. Swim with some wild stingrays that pop in daily for lunch, and treat yourself to tropical libations and conch salad prepared right before your eyes. After, head back over to the mainland for a restful night; evening activities are more or less limited to Fish Fry Friday or the annual Regatta.

1 DAY: EXUMA CAYS

The next day, island-hop the stunning Exuma cays on a half-day excursion with Four C's Adventures *(see Sports and the Outdoors in The Exumas)*. Skim through the azure, crystal-clear waters from island to island, feeding iguanas on Allan's Cay, petting the swimming pigs on Big Major Cay, taking the perfect selfie at one of the beautiful beaches, and snorkeling in ocean blue holes. Catch the last scheduled flight back to Nassau, where you'll spend another night.

1 DAY: ROSE ISLAND

Just 8 miles off the eastern coast of New Providence lies Rose Island. A popular weekend boating drop for locals, the long island is uninhabited. Book a night at the new Sandy Toes Retreat (☎ 242/363–8637 ⊕ www.sandytoesroseisland.com;

starting at $795 a night), a beautifully appointed two-bedroom cottage with unbelievable ocean views. Your boat transportation is included, and once the excursion day-trippers leave at 3:45, you'll have the island to yourself.

1 DAY: NASSAU

Catch the 20-minute boat ride back to Nassau, and head west to end your island-hopping week with a luxurious massage on the Sandals resort private island. A day pass gives you access to an array of restaurants, unlimited beverages, and all the amenities, including a private offshore island where you can be pampered in a tiki hut as the waves break on the northern shore, explore the three beaches, or lounge in the pool, and either head home late in the afternoon or early evening or spend one final night on New Providence.

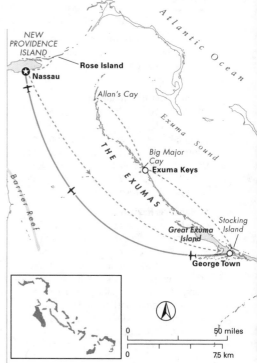

Tips

Because of the mail boat schedule, this itinerary should begin on a Monday.

The *Grand Master* departs Tuesday at 3 pm. Arrive a few hours early to buy your passenger ticket.

Mail boat has two rooms with six bunks each and no shower facilities on board.

Arrange provisioning for your meals on Rose Island, or stop at a food store in Nassau and stock up.

Tours

These are some of the best tour operators on the islands. See specific chapters for an expanded list of outfitters in each region.

Bahamas Out-Island Adventures

ADVENTURE TOURS | This tour operator offers day, half-day, and overnight kayaking, snorkeling, and surfing trips, and offers accommodations at its headquarters at Surfer's Beach. ⊠ *Gregory Town* ☎ *242/551–9635, 242/335–0349* ⊕ *www.bahamasadventures.com.*

★ **Bahamas Revisited**

GUIDED TOURS | Bahamas Revisited offers weeklong sailing excursions into the Exuma Cays aboard a 70-foot schooner. Guests can expect to feed iguanas, swim with pigs, snorkel with sharks, and lounge on sandbars all while giving to a great cause: a portion of each guest's payment funds free education excursions for underprivileged Bahamian youth. ☎ *242/427–6345* ⊕ *www.bahamasrevisited.com.*

★ **Harbour Safaris**

BOAT TOURS | If swimming with the pigs is on your bucket list, book well in advance with this tour operator. They have a fleet of saddle-style Parker RIB vessels to take you to the pigs in the Exuma Cays, or in Spanish Wells, Eleuthera. The full-day tours also include lunch and a stop at a deserted beach or sandbank. Passengers must be 10 or older for the Exuma trip and 8 or older for Spanish Wells. ⊠ *Nassau* ☎ *242/394–8687* ⊕ *www.harboursafaris.com* ⊠ *Exuma: $399; Spanish Wells: $288.*

Island Boy Adventures

ADVENTURE TOURS | Island Boy Adventures offers fishing charters, beach tours, snorkeling, and other ocean adventures in Exuma. ☎ *242/357–0459* ⊕ *www.islandboyadventures.com.*

★ **Powerboat Adventures**

EXCURSIONS | The company offers speed-filled day trips to the Exuma Cays on two custom-made powerboats. You can feed wild iguanas and stingrays, go on a snorkeling safari where you are pushed along by the ocean currents, and watch the daily shark-feeding. They even have some swimming pigs. Enjoy an open bar, a filling Bahamian lunch, and conch salad made fresh on the beach. For a true adventure, book an overnight stay on the company's island, Ship Channel Cay. ⊠ *Paradise Island* ☎ *242/363–2265* ⊕ *www.powerboatadventures.com* ⊠ *$219.*

★ **Seafari Dive Center at Club Med Columbus Isle**

SCUBA DIVING | The diving operation at Club Med is now run separately by Seafari International, and all dive trips and certifications (PADI and CMAS) are open to Club Med guests and other visitors to the island. This professional dive center consistently offers three dives a day except Thursday, in addition to a weekly night dive, to more than 35 dive sites with permanent moorings. Divers go out on one of two catamarans, 54 and 52 feet. A hyperbaric chamber is on-site, and the staff consists of 11 dive instructors and 4 dive masters. All necessary equipment is available for rent including udive computers, and Nitrox. ⊠ *Club Med, Cockburn Town* ☎ *242/331–2000, 242/331–2195* ⊕ *www.clubmed.us.*

★ **Tru Bahamian Food Tours**

SPECIAL-INTEREST | If you have three hours in Nassau, this is a great way to spend it. This ecofriendly walking tour combines the food, history, and culture of the Bahamas in a way that's sure to leave you satisfied. The six tasting stops include some popular hot spots as well as some off-the-beaten-path gems. Adults may opt for the two-hour-long food and cocktail tour offered on Sunday and public holidays. They have also partnered with five-star restaurant Graycliff to offer a private small group 3½-hour cooking class. ⊠ *George St. and King St., Nassau* ⊹ *Meet outside Christ Church Cathedral* ☎ *800/656–0713, 242/601–1725, 844/850–2318* ⊕ *www.trubahamianfoodtours.com* ✉ *Food tour $69; Food and Cocktail tour $79* ☞ *Not suitable for visitors in wheelchairs; must be at least 18 to join cocktail tour.*

★ **UNEXSO** (*Underwater Explorers Society*)

SCUBA DIVING | This world-renowned scuba diving facility provides rental equipment, guides, and boats. Facilities include a 17-foot-deep training pool with windows that look out on the harbor, changing rooms and showers, docks, an outdoor bar and grill, and an air tank filling station. Daily dive excursions range from one-day discovery courses and dives, to specialty shark, dolphin, and cave diving. Both the facility and its dive masters have been featured in international and American magazines for their work with sharks and cave exploration. UNEXSO and its sister company, the Dolphin Experience, are known for their work with Atlantic bottlenose dolphins. ⊠ *Port Lucaya, Lucaya* ⊹ *Next to Pelican Bay Hotel* ☎ *242/373–1244, 800/992–3483* ⊕ *www.unexso.com* ✉ *One-tank reef dives $59, Discover Scuba course $129, night dives $79, dolphin dives $219, shark dives $109.*

Contacts

✈ Air

AIRLINE SECURITY Transportation Security Administration. ⊕ www.tsa.gov.

MAJOR AIRLINES
American Airlines.
☎ 800/433–7300 ⊕ www.aa.com. **Delta Airlines.**
☎ 800/221–1212 ⊕ www.delta.com. **JetBlue.**
☎ 800/538–2583 ⊕ www.jetblue.com. **Southwest.**
☎ 800/435–9792 ⊕ www.southwest.com. **United.**
☎ 800/864–8331 ⊕ www.united.com.

SMALLER AIRLINES Apollo Jets. ☎ 954/239-7204 ⊕ www.apollojets.com.
Bahamasair. ☎ 242/702–4140, 800/222–4262 ⊕ www.bahamasair.com.
Cherokee Air. ☎ 242/367–1920 ⊕ www.cherokeeair.com. **Eastern Air Express.**
☎ 954/772–3363 ⊕ www.easternairexpress.com.
Flamingo Air. ☎ 242/351–4963, 954/839-8688 ⊕ www.flamingoairbah.com. **Glen Air.** ☎ 242/368–2116. **Golden Wings Charter.**
☎ 242/377–0039 ⊕ www.goldenwingscharter.com.
Island Air. ☎ 954/359-9942 ⊕ www.islandaircharters.com. **LeAir.** ☎ 242/377–2356 ⊕ www.flyleair.com. **Miami Seaplane.**
✉ 3401 Rickenbacker Causeway, Key Biscayne

☎ 305/361–3909 ⊕ www.miamiseaplane.com. **Monarch Air Group.** ☎ 954/359-0059, 877/281-3051 ⊕ monarchairgroup.com.
Pineapple Air. ☎ 242/328–1329 ⊕ www.pineappleair.com. **Silver Airlines.**
☎ 801/401–9100 in U.S. and Canada, 844/674–5837 toll-free from the Bahamas ⊕ www.silverairways.com. **Southern Air.**
☎ 242/323–7217 ⊕ www.southernaircharter.com.
Stella Maris Air Service.
✉ Stella Maris Airport ☎ 242/338–2050 reservations, 242/357–1182 pilot's cell phone ⊕ www.stellamarisresort.com/air-service. **Trans Island Airways.** ✉ Odyssey Aviation, Lynden Pindling International Airport, Nassau ☎ 242/362–4006 in Nassau, 954/727–3377 in Fort Lauderdale ⊕ www.tia.aero. **Triton Airways.**
☎ 844/359–8748 ⊕ www.tritonairways.com. **Tropic Ocean Airways.** ✉ Sheltair Aviation, 1100 Lee Wagener Blvd., Fort Lauderdale ☎ 954/210–5569, 800/767–0897 ⊕ flytropic.com. **Watermakers Air.**
✉ 2331 N.W. 55th Court, Hangar 19, Fort Lauderdale ☎ 954/771–0330 ⊕ www.watermakersair.com. **Western Air.**

☎ 242/377–2222 ⊕ www.westernairbahamas.com.

AIRPORT INFORMATION Grand Bahama International Airport. ☎ 242/352–6020.
Lynden Pindling International Airport. ☎ 242/702–1010 ⊕ www.nassaulpia.com.

⛴ Ferry

Bahamas Ferries.
☎ 242/323–2166 ⊕ www.bahamasferries.com.
Bahamas Paradise Cruise Line. ✉ 1 E. 11th St., Riviera Beach ☎ 800/995–3201 reservations, 800/374–4363 customer service ⊕ www.bahamasparadisecruise.com.
Balearia Bahamas Express.
✉ Port Everglades, Terminal 1, Fort Lauderdale ☎ 866/699–6988 ⊕ www.baleariacaribbean.com.
Potter's Cay Dockmaster.
☎ 242/393–1064.

⊙ Emergency

Bahamas Air Sea Rescue Association. ☎ 242/325–8864, 242/322–7412.

✚ Health

DECOMPRESSION CHAMBER Bahamas Hyperbaric Centre. ☎ 242/362–5765. **Bahamas Medical Center.** ☎ 242/302–4610 ⊕ www.doctorshosp.com.

🛏 Lodging

CONTACTS Bahamas Vacation Homes. ☎ 242/333–4080 ⊕ www.bahamasvacationhomes.com.

🌐 Passport

U.S. Customs and Border Protection. ⊕ www.cbp.gov. **U.S. Department of State.** ☎ 202/501-4444 ⊕ travel.state.gov/content/travel/en/contact-us/Emergencies-Abroad.html. **U.S. Embassy.** ☎ 242/322–1181 ⊕ www.nassau.usembassy.gov.

📍 Visitor Information

Bahamas Ministry of Tourism. ☎ 800/224–2627 ⊕ www.bahamas.com. **Bahama Out Islands Promotion Board.** ☎ 954/475–8315 ⊕ www.myoutislands.com. **Caribbean Tourism Organization.** ☎ 212/635-9530 ⊕ www.onecaribbean.org. **Grand Bahama Island Tourist Board.** ☎ 242/352–8356 ⊕ www.grandbahamavacations.com. **Harbour Island Tourism.** ⊕ www.harbourislandguide.com. **Nassau/Paradise Island Promotion Board.** ⊕ www.nassauparadiseisland.com.

Chapter 3

NEW PROVIDENCE AND PARADISE ISLANDS

Updated by
Jessica Robertson

● Sights	🍴 Restaurants	🛏 Hotels	🛍 Shopping	♉ Nightlife
★★★★★	★★★★★	★★★★★	★★★★☆	★★★★☆

WELCOME TO NEW PROVIDENCE AND PARADISE ISLANDS

TOP REASONS TO GO

★ **Beach-hop:** New Providence beaches, though less secluded than those on the Out Islands, still tempt travelers with their balmy breezes and aquamarine water. Choose between the more remote beaches on the island's western end, action-packed strips on Cable Beach, or public beaches in downtown Nassau.

★ **Dine with the best of 'em:** New Providence is the country's culinary capital. Eat at a grungy local dive for one meal, then feast in a celebrity-chef restaurant for the next.

★ **Experience Atlantis:** Explore the world's largest outdoor aquarium, splash around in the something-for-everyone water park, or dine at one of the 40-plus restaurants, all while never leaving the resort property.

★ **Celebrate Junkanoo:** This uniquely Bahamian carnival takes place the day after Christmas and again on New Year's Day. If you miss it, there are smaller parades in Marina Village on Paradise Island each Wednesday and Saturday at 9:30 pm.

New Providence Island is often referred to by the name of its historic capital city, Nassau. More than two dozen hotels and at least twice as many restaurants lure nearly 4 million tourists to the city, and nearby Paradise Island and Cable Beach, annually. The heart of commerce and government and the bulk of the country's 395,000 people are crammed onto the 21-mile by 7-mile island, less than 200 miles from Miami. Venturing outside the three main tourist areas will give you a better idea of true Bahamian life and a glimpse at some under-visited attractions that are worth the trek.

1 Nassau. Pink buildings dating back to the colonial era are interspersed with modern-day office complexes; horses pull their wooden carriages alongside stretch limousines; and tourists browse the local craft-centric straw market or shop for luxurious handbags at Gucci, all in this historic capital city.

2 Paradise Island. P. I. (as locals call the island) is connected to downtown Nassau's east end by a pair of bridges. Atlantis is a beachfront resort complete with a gamut of dining options, a huge casino, and some of the region's fanciest shops. Most memorable, however, are the water-based activities, slides, and aquariums, which make it a perfect family destination. Love it or hate it, it's today's face of paradise.

3 Cable Beach. The crescent-shape stretch of sand west of Nassau has been transformed into Baha Mar, a 1,000-acre

Northeast Providence Channel

Northwest Point
Old Fort Bay
West Bay St
Windsor
Lyford Cay
West Bay St
Pleasant Bay
Clifton Point
Clifton Heritage Park
4
Adelaide
South West Bay

0 — 2 miles
0 — 3 km

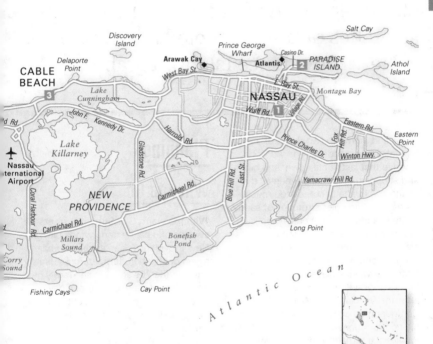

Discovery Island

Delaporte Point

CABLE BEACH 3

Lake Cunningham

Arawak Cay

Prince George Wharf

Salt Cay

Atlantis 2   PARADISE ISLAND

Casino Dr.

Athol Island

West Bay St.

E. Bay St.

Montagu Bay

NASSAU

Wulff Rd. 1

Village Rd.

Eastern Rd.

Eastern Point

d Rd.

John F. Kennedy Dr.

Harrold Rd.

Prince Charles Dr.

Fox Hill Rd.

Gladstone Rd.

Lake Killarney

Winton Hwy.

Nassau International Airport

NEW PROVIDENCE

Carmichael Rd.

Blue Hill Rd.

East St.

Yamacraw Hill Rd.

Coral Harbour Rd.

Carmichael Rd.

Millars Sound

Bonefish Pond

Long Point

Corry Sound

Fishing Cays

Cay Point

A t l a n t i c   O c e a n

destination to rival Paradise Island. Three brand-new resorts; a top-class golf course; the largest casino in the Caribbean; a sprawling upscale spa; a snorkeling sanctuary; and a vast array of restaurants, bars, and nightlife guarantee there is something to suit everyone. A short walk west of the resort complex is a smattering of restaurants and cafés.

4 Western New Providence. West of Cable Beach's high-rise hotels, New Providence becomes primarily residential, with small restaurants and bars along the way. West Bay Street hugs the coastline, providing spectacular ocean views. This part of the island is the least developed, so it's the perfect spot to find a secluded beach or go bird-watching.

An incongruous mix of glitzy casinos and quiet shady lanes, splashy megaresorts and tiny settlements that recall a distant simpler age, land development unrivaled elsewhere in the Bahamas, and vast stretches of untrammeled territory. This is New Providence Island, a grab-bag destination.

The island, home to two-thirds of all Bahamians, provides fast-paced living, nightlife that lasts until dawn, and high-end shopping strips. And when all the hustle and bustle becomes too much, it's easy to find quiet stretches of sandy white beach where the only noise is the waves rolling in. In the course of its history, the island has weathered the comings and goings of lawless pirates, Spanish invaders, slave-holding British Loyalists who fled the United States after the Revolutionary War, Civil War–era Confederate blockade runners, and Prohibition rumrunners. Nevertheless, New Providence remains most influenced by England, which sent its first royal governor to the island in 1718. Although Bahamians won government control in 1967 and independence six years later, British influence is felt to this day.

Nassau is the nation's capital and transportation hub, as well as its banking and commercial center. The fortuitous combination of tourist-friendly enterprise, tropical weather, and island flavor with a European overlay has not gone unnoticed: each year more than 2.5 million cruise-ship passengers arrive at Nassau's Prince George Wharf.

Planning

When to Go

With the warm Gulf Stream currents swirling and balmy trade winds blowing, New Providence is an appealing year-round destination. Temperatures usually hover in the 70s and 80s and rarely get above 90°F on a midsummer's day or below 60°F on a winter's night. June to October tend to be the hottest and wettest months, although rain is often limited to periodic afternoon showers.

The best time to visit the island is December to May, especially if you're escaping the cold. Don't mind the locals, who'll likely tell you it's too chilly to hit the beach in winter, but you may want to pack a light sweater if you plan on dining outdoors. Visitors from colder climates may find the humid summer days and nights a bit stifling. Be aware that tropical depressions, tropical storms, and hurricanes are a possibility in New Providence during the Atlantic hurricane season from early June to late November. Expect to pay between 15% and 30% less off-season at most resorts.

Festivals

WINTER

Bahamas International Film Festival

In early December, the Bahamas International Film Festival in Nassau celebrates cinema in paradise, with screenings, receptions, and movie-industry panels. ⊠ *Nassau* ⊕ *www.bintlfilmfest.com.*

★ Christmas Jollification

This ongoing arts-and-crafts fair with Bahamian Christmas crafts, food, and music is held at the Retreat in Nassau the third weekend in November. ⊠ *Nassau* ⊕ *www.bnt.bs.*

★ Junior Junkanoo Parade

The island's schoolchildren compete for bragging rights in the Junior Junkanoo Parade in late January along Bay Street. The parade starts at 6 pm and kids in preschool through high school dress up in crepe paper costumes and put on an exciting show. ⊠ *Nassau.*

★ Junkanoo

Once Christmas dinner is over, the focus shifts to Junkanoo. The first major parade of the season starts just after midnight in downtown Nassau. There's a second parade on New Year's Day. ⊠ *Nassau.*

SUMMER

Fox Hill Festival

The Nassau Fox Hill Festival in early August pays tribute to Emancipation with church services, Junkanoo parades, music, cookouts, games, and other festivities.

★ Junkanoo Summer Festival

Bay Street is transformed during the annual Junkanoo Summer festival held every Saturday afternoon until midnight from mid-July through mid-August. Watch some of the island's top Junkanoo groups and sample local foods. ⊠ *Nassau* ⊕ *www.bahamas.com/summerfestivals.*

FALL

International Cultural Weekend

Eat and drink your way around the world at the International Cultural Weekend, hosted at the Botanic Gardens the third weekend of October.

Getting Here and Around

AIR

Lynden Pindling International Airport (NAS) is 8 miles west of Nassau. Many major U.S. airlines fly to Nassau from several different gateways; in addition, the nation's flag carrier, Bahamasair, flies to Nassau from four airports in Florida: Fort Lauderdale (FLL), Miami (MIA), Orlando (MCO), and West Palm Beach (PBI). There is no public bus service from the airport to hotels. Many smaller airlines depart from Nassau to the other islands of the Bahamas. Major car-rental companies are represented at the airport. A taxi ride for two people from the airport to downtown Nassau costs $32; to Paradise Island, $38 (this includes the $2 bridge toll); and to Cable Beach, $25. Each additional passenger is $3, and excess baggage costs $2 a bag.

BOAT AND FERRY

Water taxis travel between Prince George Wharf and Paradise Island during daylight hours at half-hour intervals. The one-way cost is $3 per person, and the trip takes 12 minutes. Nassau is also the primary hub for Bahamas mail boats and ferries to the Out Islands.

BUS

The frequent jitneys are the cheapest choice on routes such as Cable Beach to downtown Nassau. Fare is $1.25 each way, and exact change is required. Hail one at a bus stop, hotel, or public beach. In downtown Nassau jitneys wait on Frederick Street and along the eastern end of Bay Street. Bus service runs throughout the day until 7 pm.

CAR

Rent a car if you plan to explore the whole island. Rentals are available at the airport, downtown, on Paradise Island, and at some resorts for $55–$120 per day. Gasoline costs between $5 and $6 a gallon. Remember to drive on the left. Virgo Car Rental, a local company, doesn't have a website or an airport rental desk, but it does offer a courtesy shuttle to its nearby office.

CONTACTS Avis Rent A Car. ⊠ *Lynden Pindling International Airport, Nassau* ☎ *242/377–7121* ⊕ *www.avis.com.* **Budget Rent-A-Car.** ⊠ *Lynden Pindling International Airport, Nassau* ☎ *242/377–9000* ⊕ *www.budget.com.* **Dollar/Thrifty Rent A Car.** ⊠ *Lynden Pindling International Airport, Nassau* ☎ *242/377–8300* ⊕ *www.dollar.com.* **Hertz Rent-A-Car.** ⊠ *Lynden Pindling International Airport, Nassau* ☎ *242/377–8684* ⊕ *www.hertz.com.* **Virgo Car Rental.** ☎ *242/377–1275.*

CRUISE SHIP

Cruise ships dock at one of three piers on Prince George Wharf. Taxi drivers who meet the ships may offer you a $2 "ride into town," but the historic government buildings and duty-free shops lie just steps from the dock area. As you leave the pier, look for a tall pink tower—diagonally across from here is the tourist information office. Stop in for maps of the island and downtown Nassau. On most days you can join a one-hour walking tour ($10 per person) conducted by a well-trained guide. Tours generally start every hour on the hour from 10 am to 4 pm; confirm the day's schedule in the office. Just outside, an ATM dispenses U.S. dollars.

As you disembark from your ship, you will find a row of taxis and air-conditioned limousines. Fares are fixed by the government by zones. Unless you plan to jump all over the island, taxis are the most convenient way to get around. The fare is $9 plus $2 bridge toll between downtown Nassau and Paradise Island, $20 from Cable Beach to Paradise Island (plus $2 toll), and $22 from Cable Beach to Nassau. Fares are for two passengers; each additional passenger is $3. It's customary to tip taxi drivers 15%.

Water taxis travel between Prince George Wharf and Paradise Island during daylight hours at half-hour intervals. The one-way cost is $3 per person, and the trip takes 12 minutes.

SCOOTER

Two people can rent a motor scooter for about $65 for a half day, $85 for a full day.

TAXI

Unless you plan to jump all over the island, taxis are the most convenient way to get around. The fare is $9 plus a $2 bridge toll between downtown Nassau and Paradise Island, $22 from Cable Beach to Paradise Island (plus $2 toll), and $22 from Cable Beach to Nassau. Fares are for two passengers; each additional passenger is $3. It's customary to tip taxi drivers 15%.

Restaurants

Find everything from shabby shacks to elegant eateries. You'll recognize celebrity chef names like Todd English, Jean-Georges Vongerichten, and Nobu Matsuhisa, all of whom have restaurants here. On a budget? Eat brunch at one of the myriad all-you-can-eat buffets at the larger hotels on Paradise Island and Cable Beach.

Note: A gratuity (15%) is often added to the bill automatically.

HOTEL AND RESTAURANT PRICES

Restaurant prices are based on the median main course price at dinner, excluding gratuity (typically 15%) and VAT (12%), which are automatically added to the bill. Hotel prices are for two people in a standard double room in high season, excluding service and 6%–12% hotel tax plus 12% VAT.

WHAT IT COSTS in Dollars			
$	$$	$$$	$$$$
RESTAURANTS			
under $20	$20–$30	$31–$40	over $40
HOTELS			
under $200	$200–$300	$301–$400	over $400

Hotels

If you want to mix with locals and experience a little more of Bahamian culture, choose a hotel in downtown Nassau. Its beaches are not dazzling; if you want to be beachfront on a gorgeous white strand, stay on Cable Beach or Paradise Island's Cabbage Beach. Reasons to stay in Nassau include proximity to shopping and affordability (although the cost of taxis to and from the better beaches can add up).

The plush Cable Beach and Paradise Island resorts are big and beautiful, glittering and splashy, and have the best beaches, but they can be overwhelming. In any case, these big, top-dollar properties generally have more amenities than you could possibly make use of, a selection of dining choices, and a full roster of sports and entertainment options. Stay in Cable Beach if you don't plan to visit Nassau or Paradise Island often; you need to take a cab, and the costs add up.

Beaches

New Providence is the Bahamas' most urban island, but that doesn't mean you won't find beautiful beaches. Powdery white sand, aquamarine waves, and shade-bearing palm trees are easy to come by.

Cable Beach and the beaches near Atlantis are where you'll typically find loud music, bars serving tropical drinks, and vendors peddling everything from parasailing and Jet Ski rides to T-shirts and hair braiding. Downtown Nassau only has man-made beaches, the best being Junkanoo Beach just west of the British Colonial Hilton. Yet the capital city's beaches can't compare to the real thing. For a more relaxed environment, drive out of the main tourist areas. You'll likely find stretches of sand populated by locals only, or, more likely, no one at all.

Shopping

Most of Nassau's shops are on Bay Street between Rawson Square and the British Colonial Hotel, and on the side streets leading off Bay Street. Some stores are popping up on the main shopping thoroughfare's eastern end and just west of the Cable Beach strip. Bargains abound between Bay Street and the waterfront. Upscale stores can also be found in Marina Village, in the Crystal Court at Atlantis, and at Baha Mar on Cable Beach.

You'll find duty-free prices—sometimes as much as 25% to 50% less than U.S. prices—on imported items such as crystal, linens, watches, jewelry, leather goods, and perfumes, but you really need to know the prices before you buy. Not everything is a bargain.

Activities

BOATING

From Chub Cay—one of the Berry Islands 35 miles north of New Providence—to Nassau, the sailing route goes across the mile-deep Tongue of the Ocean. The Paradise Island Lighthouse welcomes yachters to Nassau Harbour, which is open at both ends. The harbor can handle the world's largest cruise liners; sometimes as many as eight tie up at one time. Two looming bridges bisect the harbor connecting Paradise Island to Nassau. Sailboats with masts taller than

3

New Providence and Paradise Islands PLANNING

the high-water clearance of 72 feet must enter the harbor from the east end to reach marinas east of the bridges.

FISHING

The waters here are generally smooth and alive with many species of game fish, which is one of the reasons why the Bahamas has more than 20 fishing tournaments open to visitors every year. A favorite spot just west of Nassau is the Tongue of the Ocean, so called because it looks like that part of the body when viewed from the air. The channel stretches for 100 miles. For boat rental, parties of two to six will pay $600 or so for a half day, $1,600 for a full day.

SCUBA DIVING AND SNORKELING

DIVE SITES

Coral Reef Sculpture Garden. Created by the Bahamas Reef Environment Education Foundation (BREEF), this underwater art gallery is suitable for scuba divers and snorkelers. The highlight is the 17-foot-tall "Ocean Atlas" crouching on the ocean floor. The site is situated just off Clifton Heritage Park on southwestern New Providence and is accessible from land or boat. Be sure to take an underwater camera for a spectacular photographic souvenir.

Gambier Deep Reef. Off Gambier Village about 15 minutes west of Cable Beach, Gambier Deep Reef goes to a depth of 80 feet.

Lost Ocean Hole. The elusive (and thus exclusive) Lost Ocean Hole (east of Nassau, 40–195 feet) is aptly named because it's difficult to find. The rim of the 80-foot opening in 40 feet of water is studded with coral heads and teeming with small fish—grunts, margate, and jacks—as well as larger pompano, amberjack, and sometimes nurse sharks. Divers will find a thermocline at 80 feet, a large cave at 100 feet, and a sand ledge at 185 feet that slopes down to 195 feet.

Lyford Cay Drop-Off. Lyford Cay Drop-Off (west of Nassau, 40–200-plus feet) is

a cliff that plummets from a 40-foot plateau almost straight into the inky blue mile-deep Tongue of the Ocean. The wall has endless varieties of sponges, black coral, and wire coral. Along the wall, grunts, grouper, hogfish, snapper, and rockfish abound. Off the wall are pelagic game fish such as tuna, bonito, wahoo, and kingfish.

Rose Island Reefs. The series of shallow reefs along the 14 miles of Rose Island is known as Rose Island Reefs (Nassau, 5–35 feet). The coral is varied, although the reefs are showing the effects of the heavy traffic. Still, plenty of tropical fish live here, and the wreck of the steel-hulled ship *Mahoney* is just outside the harbor.

Sea Gardens. This site is off Love Beach on the northwestern shore beyond Gambier.

★ Stuart Cove's

SCUBA DIVING | Located on the island's south shore, this operator is considered by aficionados to be the island's leading dive shop. Although they're pros at teaching beginners (scuba instruction and guided snorkel tours are available), experienced thrill seekers flock to Stuart Cove's for the famous shark dives. The company runs dive trips to the south-shore reefs twice a day, weather permitting. The minisub adventure, which requires no experience, is $138; snorkeling expeditions cost $79 for adults and $39 for kids 11 and under. The shark dives are $182 for a three-hour dive. Complimentary shuttle service from all major hotels is included. ☎ *242/362-4171, 800/879-9832* ⊕ *www.stuartcove. com.*

DIVE OPERATORS

All recommended New Providence dive shops are PADI-affiliated (Professional Association of Diving Instructors) facilities. Expect to pay about $65 to $99 for a two-tank dive or beginner's course. Shark dives run $100 to $125, and certification costs $450 and up.

Bahama Divers Ltd.

SCUBA DIVING | This long-standing dive operator offers two-tank morning dives, single-tank afternoon dives, and twice-daily snorkeling excursions. Introduction to scuba and PADI certification courses are available, and there's a full line of scuba equipment for rent. It's also the only place on island to get your personal gear serviced or repaired. Destinations are drop-off sites, wrecks, coral reefs and gardens, and an ocean blue hole that teems with silky sharks early each summer. Bus pickup is scheduled twice daily from hotels throughout New Providence. ⊠ *Nassau* ☎ *242/393–5644, 954/602–7731, 954/602–7731* ⊕ *www. bahamadivers.com.*

Tours

DAY SAILS

Barefoot Sailing Cruises

BOAT TOURS | The company offers regularly scheduled half-day snorkeling trips, full-day sailing tours of New Providence, and sunset champagne trips, not to mention private charters. ⊠ *Bayshore Marina, E. Bay St.* ☎ *242/393–5817* ⊕ *www.bare-footsailingcruises.com* ⊠ *Half-day sail and snorkel $90; half-day sail, snorkel, and beach $115; full day $140.*

Flying Cloud

EXCURSIONS | This 57-foot catamaran based at the Paradise Island Ferry Terminal offers half-day sailing and snorkeling tours, full-day cruises with lunch included on some days, as well as sunset sails. Private charters can also be arranged. Price includes round-trip ground transportation from your hotel. ⊠ *Paradise Island Ferry Terminal, Paradise Island* ☎ *242/394–5067* ⊕ *www.flyingcloud. com* ⊠ *Half day (Mon.–Sat.) $85; full day (Thurs. and Sun.) $105; evening cruise (Mon., Wed., and Fri.) $75.*

OUT ISLANDS TRIPS

You can visit a number of islands and cays on a day trip by boat from Nassau. Bahamas Ferries does a day trip to Harbour Island: 2½ hours in an air-conditioned ferry (or with the ocean breeze blowing through your hair on the upper deck) and enough time onshore to explore the quaint island via golf cart, have lunch, and stroll the beautiful pink-sand beach. A number of operators offer daily powerboat trips to the upper cays in the Exuma chain where you can see wild iguanas, stingrays, sharks, and of course the world-famous swimming pigs up close and enjoy their private islands for the day, and there are also excursions to Blue Lagoon Island or Rose Island—both a short boat ride away from Nassau.

Bahamas Fast Ferries

EXCURSIONS | This isn't just a transportation company: Bahamas Fast Ferries also offers day trips from Nassau to Harbour Island, including lunch and pickups at major hotels. ⊠ *Potter's Cay, Nassau* ☎ *242/323–2166* ⊕ *www.bahamasferries. com* ⊠ *$234.*

★ Harbour Safaris

BOAT TOURS | If swimming with the pigs is on your bucket list, book well in advance with this tour operator. They have a fleet of saddle-style Parker RIB vessels to take you to the pigs in the Exuma Cays, or in Spanish Wells, Eleuthera. The full-day tours also include lunch and a stop at a deserted beach or sandbank. Passengers must be 10 or older for the Exuma trip and 8 or older for Spanish Wells. ⊠ *Nassau* ☎ *242/394–8687* ⊕ *www.harbour-safaris.com* ⊠ *Exuma: $399; Spanish Wells: $288.*

★ Powerboat Adventures

EXCURSIONS | The company offers speed-filled day trips to the Exuma Cays on two custom-made powerboats. You can feed wild iguanas and stingrays, go on a snorkeling safari where you are pushed along by the ocean currents, and watch the daily shark-feeding. They even have some swimming pigs. Enjoy an open bar, a filling Bahamian lunch, and conch salad made fresh on the beach. For a true adventure, book an overnight stay on the company's island, Ship Channel Cay. ⊠ *Paradise Island* ☎ *242/363–2265* ⊕ *www.powerboatadventures.com* 🖾 *$219.*

SPECIAL-INTEREST TOURS
★ Blue Lagoon Island
ADVENTURE TOURS | **FAMILY** | Learn about dolphins, sea lions, stingrays and sharks in their all-natural habitat at this American Humane Certified private island attraction. Three of their dolphins starred in the movie *Flipper* and their sea lions played the lead in a number of Hollywood films. Ferry transportation is included with departure from the Paradise Island Ferry Terminal. Make a day of it with the complimentary Beach Day and add on lunch and access to the largest inflatable aqua park in Nassau. Beach Day only or adults only VIP Beach Day packages are also available, as is a fun Segway Safari tour. ⊠ *Paradise Island* ☎ *242/363–1003* ⊕ *www.dolphinencounters.com* 🖾 *Dolphin Swim $190; Dolphin Encounter $120; Sea Lion Encounter $109; Beach Day $74; Segway Safari $85.*

Bowcar Bahamas
GUIDED TOURS | Rent a scooter, ATV, or buggy and head off on your own adventure or sign up for one of their guided tours—you'll drive your own buggy while following a tour guide to Nassau's hot spots. Headsets are provided so you can listen along to the narrative. Hotel pickup is included from most major hotels on the island. ⊠ *Nassau* ☎ *242/477–6778, 800/558–1364* ⊕ *www.bowcarbahamas. com.*

HORSEBACK RIDING
Happy Trails Stables
HORSEBACK RIDING | Happy Trails Stables gives guided 90-minute trail rides, including basic riding instruction, through remote wooded areas and beaches on New Providence's southwestern coast.

Two morning group rides are offered, but private rides can be arranged at any time. Courtesy round-trip bus transportation from hotels is provided (about an hour each way). Tours are limited to eight people. There's a 200-pound weight limit, and children must be at least 12 years old. Reservations are required. ☎ *242/362–1820* ⊕ *www.ridingbahamas. com* 🖾 *$150 per person.*

WALKING TOURS
★ Tru Bahamian Food Tours
SPECIAL-INTEREST | If you have three hours in Nassau, this is a great way to spend it. This ecofriendly walking tour combines the food, history, and culture of the Bahamas in a way that's sure to leave you satisfied. The six tasting stops include some popular hot spots as well as some off-the-beaten-path gems. Adults may opt for the two-hour-long food and cocktail tour offered on Sunday and public holidays. They have also partnered with five-star restaurant Graycliff to offer a private small group 3½-hour cooking class. ⊠ *George St. and King St., Nassau* ✦ *Meet outside Christ Church Cathedral* ☎ *800/656–0713, 242/601–1725, 844/850–2318* ⊕ *www. trubahamianfoodtours.com* 🖾 *Food tour $69; Food and Cocktail tour $79* ☞ *Not suitable for visitors in wheelchairs; must be at least 18 to join cocktail tour.*

Rum Runner's Passage
SPECIAL-INTEREST | This three-hour tour begins at Pirate Republic Brewing Company where you'll learn about rum from when pirates ran the town. Next, hear the history of the bootlegging era as you taste rums at Hillside House art gallery, then dive into rum lore and sample rum-infused chocolates at Graycliff. The sixth and final tasting takes place at the John Watling's Distillery. ⊠ *Nassau* ☎ *242 /698–2708* ⊕ *www.islandztours.com.*

Visitor Information

The Ministry of Tourism operates tourist information booths at the airport, open daily from 8:30 am to 11:30 pm, and at Festival Place, which is adjacent to Prince George Wharf and open daily from 9 am to 5 pm. The Ministry of Tourism's People-to-People Program sets you up with a Bahamian family with similar interests to show you local culture firsthand.

CONTACTS Ministry of Tourism.
☎ 242/302–2000 ⊕ www.bahamas.com. **People-to-People Program.**
☎ 242/324–9772 ⊕ www.bahamas.com/people-to-people.

Nassau

Nassau's sheltered harbor bustles with cruise-ship activity, while a block away Bay Street's sidewalks are crowded with shoppers who duck into air-conditioned boutiques and relax on benches in the shade of mahogany and lignum vitae trees. Shops angle for tourist dollars with fine imported goods at duty-free prices, yet you'll find a handful of stores overflowing with authentic Bahamian crafts, food supplies, and other delights.

With a revitalization of downtown ongoing, Nassau is trying to recapture some of its past glamour. Nevertheless, modern influences are completely apparent: fancy restaurants and trendy coffeehouses have popped up everywhere. These changes have come partly in response to the growing number of upper-crust crowds that now supplement the spring breakers and cruise passengers who have traditionally flocked to Nassau. Of course, you can still find a wild club or a rowdy bar, but you can also sip cappuccino while viewing contemporary Bahamian art or dine by candlelight beneath prints of old Nassau, serenaded by soft, island-inspired calypso music.

A trip to Nassau wouldn't be complete without a stop at some of the island's well-preserved historic buildings. The large, pink colonial-style edifices house Parliament and some of the courts, while others, like Fort Charlotte, date back to the days when pirates ruled the town. Take a tour via horse-drawn carriage for the full effect.

◉ Sights

Arawak Cay
RESTAURANT—SIGHT | Known to Nassau residents as "the Fish Fry," Arawak Cay is one of the best places to knock back a Kalik beer, chat with locals, watch or join in a fast-paced game of dominoes, or sample traditional Bahamian fare. The two-story Twin Brothers and Frankie Gone Bananas are two of the most popular places. Local fairs and craft shows are often held in the adjacent field. ✉ W. Bay St. and Chippingham Rd., Nassau ☜ Free.

★ Ardastra Gardens, Zoo, and Conservation Centre
GARDEN | FAMILY | Marching flamingos give a parading performance at Ardastra daily at 10:30, 2:15, and 4. Children can walk among the brilliant pink birds after the show. The zoo, with more than 5 acres of tropical greenery and ponds, also has an aviary of rare tropical birds including the bright-green Bahama parrot, native Bahamian creatures such as rock iguanas, the little (harmless) Bahamian boa constrictors, and a global collection of small animals. ✉ Chippingham Rd. south of W. Bay St., Nassau ☎ 242/323–5806 ⊕ www.ardastra.com ☜ $18.75.

Balcony House
HISTORIC SITE | A delightful 18th-century landmark—a pink two-story house named aptly for its overhanging balcony—this is the oldest wooden residential structure in Nassau and its furnishings and design recapture the elegance of a bygone era. A mahogany staircase,

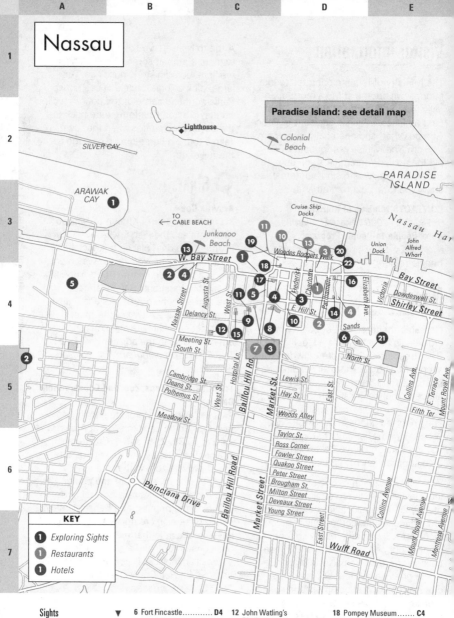

Nassau

Paradise Island: see detail map

SILVER CAY

Lighthouse

Colonial Beach

PARADISE ISLAND

Nassau Har

ARAWAK CAY **1**

TO
← CABLE BEACH

Junkanoo Beach

Cruise Ship Docks

Union Dock

John Alfred Wharf

13 W. Bay Street

Nassau Street

Augusta St.

Delancy St.

West St.

13 **4**

11 **5** **4**

9

12 **15**

Meeting St.

South St.

7 **3**

Hospital Ln.

Bailou Hill Rd.

Market St.

8

10

11

19

18

17

10

13

Woodes Rodgers Walk

Frederick St.

Charlotte St.

Parliament St.

2

E. Hill St.

14

Sands

6

20

22

16

4

North St.

21

Bay Street

Elizabeth Ave.

Victoria

Dowdeswell St.

Shirley Street

Collins Ave.

E. Terrace

Mount Royal Ave.

Fifth Ter.

Cambridge St.

Deans St.

Polhemus St.

Meadow St.

West St.

Lewis St.

Hay St.

Woods Alley

Taylor St.

Ross Corner

Fowler Street

Quakoo Street

Peter Street

Brougham St.

Milton Street

Deveaux Street

Young Street

East St.

Bailou Hill Road

Market Street

Poinciana Drive

Collins Avenue

East Street

Wulff Road

Mount Royal Avenue

Montrose Avenue

KEY

1 *Exploring Sights*

1 *Restaurants*

1 *Hotels*

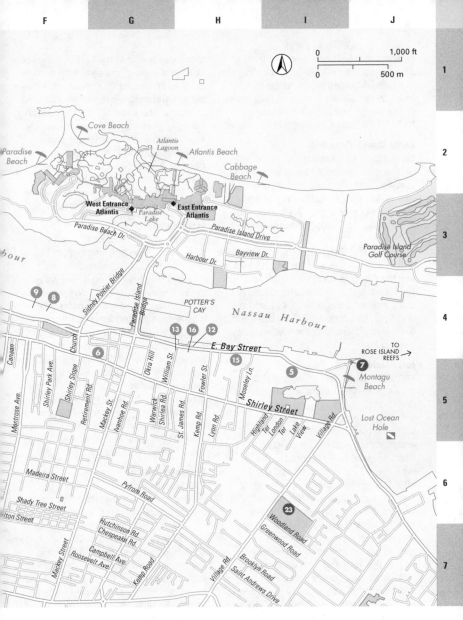

| F | G | H | I | J |

0   1,000 ft
0   500 m

Cove Beach

Paradise Beach

Atlantis Lagoon

Atlantis Beach

Cabbage Beach

West Entrance Atlantis   East Entrance Atlantis

Paradise Lake

Paradise Beach Dr.

Paradise Island Drive

Harbour Dr.   Bayview Dr.

Paradise Island Golf Course

bour

Sidney Poitier Bridge

Paradise Island Bridge

POTTER'S CAY

Nassau Harbour

Canaan

Shirley Park Ave.

Shirley Slope

Church

Retirement Rd.

Mackey St.

Ivanhoe Rd.

Okra Hill

William St.

Warwick

Shirlea Rd.

St. James Rd.

Kemp Rd.

Fowler St.

Lyon Rd.

Moseley Ln.

13   16   12

E. Bay Street

15

5

7

TO ROSE ISLAND REEFS

Montagu Beach

Shirley Street

Highland Ter.

London Ter.

Lake View

Village Rd.

Lost Ocean Hole

Montrose Ave.

Madeira Street

Shady Tree Street

ilton Street

Mackey Street

Pyfrom Road

Hutchinson Rd.

Chespeake Rd.

Campbell Ave.

Roosevelt Ave.

Kemp Road

Village Rd.

Saint Andrews Drive

Brooklyn Road

Woodland Road

Greenwood Road

23

Restaurants ▼

1 Athena Café and Bar... **D4**
2 Bahamian Cookin' Restaurant............... **D4**
3 The Bearded Clam Sports Bar **D4**
4 Café Matisse **D4**

5 East Villa Restaurant and Lounge.............. **I5**
6 Fifty-Fifty Grillers........ **G4**
7 Graycliff Restaurant.... **C4**
8 The Green Parrot **F4**
9 Luciano's of Chicago ... **F4**
10 Lukka Kairi............... **D3**

11 Never Say Never Again Bar & Grill........ **C3**
12 The Poop Deck.......... **H4**
13 Seafront Sushi **G4**
14 Sharkeez Bar & Grill.... **D3**
15 Syrah Cellar Cafe **H4**
16 Wild Thyme Restaurant............... **H4**

Hotels ▼

1 British Colonial Hilton Nassau **C4**
2 Courtyard Nassau Downtown/ Junkanoo Beach **B4**
3 Graycliff Hotel........... **C4**
4 Holiday Inn Express **C4**
5 Towne Hotel **C4**

believed to have been salvaged from a ship during the 19th century, is an interior highlight. A guided tour through this fascinating building is an hour well spent. ✉ *Market St. and Trinity Pl., Nassau* ☎ *242/302–2621* ✉ *Donations accepted.*

Christ Church Cathedral

RELIGIOUS SITE | It's worth the short walk off the main thoroughfare to see the stained-glass windows of this cathedral, which was built in 1837 when Nassau officially became a city. Don't miss the flower-filled Garden of Remembrance. Sunday Mass is held at 7:30 am, 9 am, 11:15 am, and 6 pm. Drop by the cathedral Christmas Eve and New Year's Eve to see the glorious church at night, and hear the music and choir. Call ahead to find out the time of the service. ✉ *George and King Sts., Nassau* ☎ *242/322–4186* ⊕ *www.christchurchcathedralbahamas. com* ✉ *Free.*

Fort Charlotte

HISTORIC SITE | FAMILY | Built in 1788, this imposing fort features a waterless moat, drawbridge, ramparts, and a dungeon with a torture device. Local guides bring the fort to life (tips are expected), and tours are suitable for children. Fort Charlotte was built by Lord Dunmore, who named the massive structure after George III's wife. The fort and its surrounding 100 acres offer a wonderful view of the cricket grounds, the beach, and the ocean beyond. On Wednesday and Friday enjoy fully regaled actors reenacting life as it was in the Bahamas in the 18th and 19th centuries. An historic military parade and canon firing takes place daily at noon. ✉ *W. Bay St. at Chippingham Rd., Nassau* ✛ *Opposite Arawak Cay* ✉ *Nonresidents $5.*

Fort Fincastle

HISTORIC SITE | Shaped like the bow of a ship and perched near the top of the Queen's Staircase, Fort Fincastle— named for Royal Governor Lord Dunmore (Viscount Fincastle)—was completed in 1793 to be a lookout post for marauders

trying to sneak into the harbor. It served as a lighthouse in the early 19th century. A 15- to 20-minute tour costs just $1 per person and includes the nearby Queen's Staircase. The fort's 126-foot-tall water tower is more than 200 feet above sea level (and the island's highest point). Unfortunately the tower remains closed pending restoration. ✉ *Top of Elizabeth Ave. hill, south of Shirley St., Nassau* ☎ *242/356–9085* ✉ *Nonresident adults $3; seniors, residents, and children $2.*

Fort Montagu

HISTORIC SITE | The oldest of the island's three forts, Montagu was built of local limestone in 1741 to repel Spanish invaders. The only action it saw was when it was occupied for two weeks by rebel American troops—among them a lieutenant named John Paul Jones— seeking arms and ammunition during the Revolutionary War. The small fortification is quite simple, but displays a lovely elevated view of Nassau Harbour. The second level has a number of weathered cannons. A public beach looks out upon Montagu Bay, where many international yacht regattas and Bahamian sloop races are held annually. ✉ *East of Bay St. on Eastern Rd., Nassau* ✉ *$2.*

Government House

GOVERNMENT BUILDING | The official residence of the Bahamas governor-general, the personal representative of the Queen since 1801, this imposing pink-and-white building on Duke Street is an excellent example of the mingling of Bahamian-British and American colonial architecture. Catch the changing of the guard ceremony, which takes place every second Saturday of the month at 11 am. The stars of the pomp and pageantry are members of the Royal Bahamas Police Force Band. There is a tea party open to the public from 3 to 4 pm on the last Friday of the month from January to June as part of the People-to-People program. ✉ *Duke and George Sts., Nassau* ☎ *242/356–5415 ceremony schedule,*

The Royal Bahamas Police Force Band performs in front of Government House.

242/397–8816 tea party, 242/322–2020
Government House.

Graycliff Chocolate Factory
TOUR—SIGHT | FAMILY | Go behind the scenes at this boutique chocolate factory where you can make your own sweet souvenirs. The tour lasts about an hour, and after watching master chocolatiers in action and learning the history of chocolate production around the world, guests enter the chocolate classroom where they get to design their own creations, including a signature Graycliff chocolate bar. There is also a kids' classroom for younger chocolate lovers as well as a chocolates and spirits pairing for adults. ✉ *Graycliff Hotel, W. Hill St., Nassau* ☎ *242/302–9150* ⊕ *www.graycliff.com* 🎫 *$49.95.*

Gregory's Arch
HISTORIC SITE | Named for John Gregory (royal governor 1849–54), this arch, at the intersection of Market and Duke streets, separates downtown from the "over-the-hill" neighborhood of Grant's Town, where much of Nassau's population lives.

Grant's Town was laid out in the 1820s by Governor Lewis Grant as a settlement for freed slaves. Visitors once enjoyed late-night mingling with the locals in the small, dimly lighted bars; nowadays you should exhibit the same caution you would if you were visiting the commercial areas of a large city. ✉ *Nassau* 🎫 *Free.*

Heritage Museum of The Bahamas
HOUSE | FAMILY | So many artifacts are on display in this small but interesting museum that you can easily spend an hour wandering. Opt for a guided tour, or use the audio tour to take in everything at your own pace. You'll learn about Bahamian history from the days of pirates through the days of slavery to the present. One of the best exhibits is the life-size replica of the old Bay Street General Store. Quite by a series of coincidences, the collection box from the oldest church ended up in this museum—right across the street from the remains of the very same church. ✉ *8–14 W. Hill St., Nassau* ☎ *242/302–9150* ⊕ *www.graycliff.com* 🎫 *$18.50 guided tour.*

John Watling's Distillery

MUSEUM | The former Buena Vista Estate, which featured in the James Bond film *Casino Royale,* has been painstakingly transformed and taken back to its glory days, emerging as the new home of the John Watling's Distillery. Parts of the home date back to 1789 and the actual production of the line of John Watling's artisanal rums, gins, vodkas, and liquors are handmade, hand bottled, and hand labeled just as they would have been in that era. Take a self-guided tour through the grounds and working estate to learn the fascinating history of the home and then walk out back to watch the rum production line from an overhead mezzanine. Sit in the Red Turtle Tavern with an internationally acclaimed Rum Dum or just a great mojito and pick up a unique Bahamian souvenir in the on-site retail store. ⊠ *17 Delancy St., Nassau* ☎ *242/322–2811* ⊕ *www.johnwatlings. com* 🗐 *Free.*

Junkanoo Beach

BEACH—SIGHT | Right in downtown Nassau, this beach is spring-break central from late February through April. The man-made beach isn't the prettiest on the island, but it's conveniently located if you only have a few quick hours to catch a tan. Food and drink shacks line the beach and you can rent lounge chairs, umbrellas and nonmotorized water-sports equipment. **Amenities:** food and drink; parking (no fee); toilets; water sports. **Best for:** partiers; swimming. ⊠ *Immediately west of British Colonial Hilton, Nassau* 🗐 *Free.*

Nassau Public Library and Museum

HISTORIC SITE | The octagonal building near Parliament Square was the Nassau Gaol (the old British spelling for jail), circa 1797. You're welcome to pop in and browse. The small prison cells are now lined with books. The museum has an interesting collection of historic prints and old colonial documents. ⊠ *Shirley St. between*

Pirates of the Bahamas 👁

Pirates roamed the waters of the Bahamas, hiding out in the 700 islands, but they especially liked New Providence Island. Edward Teach, or Blackbeard, even named himself governor of the island. He scared enemy and crew alike by weaving hemp into his hair and beard and setting it on fire.

Parliament St. and Bank La., Nassau ☎ *242/322–4907* 🗐 *Free* 🕐 *Closed Sun.*

★ **National Art Gallery of the Bahamas**

MUSEUM | Opened in 2003, the museum houses the works of esteemed Bahamian artists such as Max Taylor, Amos Ferguson, Brent Malone, John Cox, and Antonius Roberts. The glorious Italianate colonial mansion, built in 1860 and restored in the 1990s, has double-tiered verandas with elegant columns. It was the residence of Sir William Doyle, the first chief justice of the Bahamas. Don't miss the museum's gift shop, where you'll find books about the Bahamas as well as Bahamian quilts, prints, ceramics, jewelry, and crafts. ⊠ *West and W. Hill Sts., across from St. Francis Xavier Cathedral, Nassau* ☎ *242/328–5800* ⊕ *www.nagb.org.bs* 🗐 *$10* 🕐 *Closed Mon.*

Parliament Square

GOVERNMENT BUILDING | Nassau is the seat of the national government. The Bahamian Parliament comprises two houses—a 16-member Senate (Upper House) and a 39-member House of Assembly (Lower House). If the House is in session, sit in to watch lawmakers debate. Parliament Square's pink, colonnaded government buildings were constructed in the late 1700s and early 1800s by Loyalists who came to the Bahamas from North

Carolina. The square is dominated by a statue of a slim young Queen Victoria that was erected on her birthday, May 24, in 1905. ✉ *Bay St., Nassau* ☎ *242/322–2041* ✉ *Free* ⊘ *Closed weekends.*

Pirates of Nassau
MUSEUM | FAMILY | Take a self-guided journey through Nassau's pirate days in this interactive museum devoted to such notorious members of the city's past as Blackbeard, Mary Read, and Anne Bonney. Board a pirate ship, see dioramas of intrigue on the high seas, hear historical narration, and experience sound effects re-creating some of the gruesome highlights. It's a fun and educational (if slightly scary) family outing. ✉ *George and King Sts., Nassau* ☎ *242/356–3759* ⊕ *www.piratesofnassau.com* ✉ *$13.*

★ Pompey Museum
HISTORIC SITE | The building, where slave auctions were held in the 1700s, is named for a rebel slave who lived on the Out Island of Exuma in 1830. The structure and historic artifacts inside were destroyed by fire in December 2011, but have been painstakingly re-created and new exhibits have been acquired and produced. Exhibits focus on the issues of slavery and emancipation and highlight the works of local artists. A knowledgeable, enthusiastic young staff is on hand to answer questions. ✉ *Bay and George Sts., Nassau* ☎ *242/356–0495* ⊕ *www. ammcbahamas.com* ✉ *$5* ⊘ *Closed afternoon on Sun. and Thurs.*

Pompey Square
PLAZA | FAMILY | This open space at the western end of Bay Street overlooks the busy Nassau Harbour and is the spot to catch local festivals and events, live music, and Bahamian craft shows. With 24-hour security, public restrooms, an interactive water feature that delights kids of all ages, and a host of small restaurants and bars nearby, this square, which pays tribute to a slave who fought for his freedom, is part of a strategic

redevelopment of downtown Nassau. ✉ *Bay St., Nassau* ✉ *Free.*

Prince George Wharf
INFO CENTER | The wharf that leads into Rawson Square is the first view that cruise passengers encounter after they tumble off their ships. Up to a dozen gigantic cruise ships call on Nassau at any one time, and passengers spill out onto downtown, giving Nassau an instant, and constantly replenished, surge of life. Even if you're not visiting via cruise ship, it's worth heading to Festival Place, an outdoor Bahamian village–style shopping emporium. Here you'll find booths for Bahamian artisans; live music; vendors selling diving, fishing, and day trips; scooter rentals; and an information desk offering maps, directions, and suggestions for sightseeing. You can also arrange walking tours of historic Nassau here. A major overhaul and expansion of the port was expected to begin in late 2019. ✉ *Waterfront at Rawson Sq., Nassau* ✉ *Free.*

Queen's Staircase
MEMORIAL | A popular early-morning exercise regime for locals, "the 66 Steps" (as Bahamians call them) are thought to have been carved out of a solid limestone cliff by slaves in the 1790s. The staircase was later named to honor Queen Victoria's reign. Pick up some souvenirs at the ad hoc straw market along the narrow road that leads to the site. ✉ *Top of Elizabeth Ave. hill, south of Shirley St., Nassau* ✉ *Free.*

Rawson Square
PLAZA | This shady square connects Bay Street to Prince George Wharf. As you enter off Bay Street, note the statue of Sir Milo Butler, the first postindependence (and first native Bahamian) governor general. Horse-drawn surreys wait for passengers along Prince George Wharf (expect to pay about $30 for a half-hour ride through Nassau's streets). Between Rawson Square and Festival Place, check out (or perhaps stop inside) the open-air

hair-braiding pavilion, where women work their magic at prices ranging from $2 for a single strand to $100 for an elaborate do. Often-overlooked is the nearby Randolph W. Johnston's bronze statue, *Tribute to Bahamian Women.* The prime minister meets with his cabinet every Tuesday in the building that lines the eastern side of the square. ✉ *Bay St., Nassau* 🎟 *Free.*

The Retreat

GARDEN | Nearly 200 species of exotic palm trees grace the 11 verdant acres appropriately known as The Retreat, which serves as the headquarters of the Bahamas National Trust. Stroll in blessed silence through the lush grounds of this protected national park, and be on the lookout for native birds. It's a perfect break on a steamy Nassau day. The Retreat hosts the Jollification—the island's unofficial start to the Christmas season—the third weekend in November. Carols, festive food and drinks, a kids' holiday craft center, and local artisans selling native and Christmas crafts make this a must-do event. ✉ *Village Rd., Paradise Island* ☎ *242/393–1317* 🎟 *$2* 🕓 *Closed weekends.*

🍴 Restaurants

★ Athena Café and Bar

$$ | **GREEK** | You're greeted with a welcoming "Opa!" at this family-owned authentic Greek spot where they serve up tasty breakfasts and lunches at moderate prices seven days a week. This Greek restaurant provides a break from the Nassau culinary routine. **Known for:** the best Greek salad around; flaming cheese; the cries of "Opa!" as guests walk in. [$] *Average main: $20* ✉ *Bay St. at Charlotte St., Nassau* ☎ *242/326–1296* 🌐 *www.athenacafenassau.com* 🕓 *No dinner.*

★ Bahamian Cookin' Restaurant

$ | **BAHAMIAN** | Three generations of Bahamian women treat patrons as if they were guests in their own home. And the Bahamian food whipped up in the kitchen is as close to homemade as you can get in a restaurant. **Known for:** home-style cooking; tasty conch fritters; friendly service. [$] *Average main: $18* ✉ *Trinity Pl., Nassau* ✣ *Turn left off Bay St. onto Market St. toward Central Bank, then left onto Trinity Pl.* ☎ *242/328–0334* 🕓 *Closed Sun. No dinner.*

★ The Bearded Clam Sports Bar

$ | **AMERICAN** | Nestled in the middle of the International Arcade linking Bay Street and the wharf is this lively bar and restaurant serving up tasty appetizers and meals. There's the traditional Bahamian cracked conch or conch balls. **Known for:** daily happy hour 5–8; tasty bar fare; lively atmosphere. [$] *Average main: $15* ✉ *Nassau* ☎ *242/323–4455* 🌐 *www.beardedclamnassau.com.*

★ Café Matisse

$$$ | **ITALIAN** | Low-slung settees, stucco arches, and reproductions of the eponymous artist's works set a casual and refined tone at this restaurant owned by a husband-and-wife team. He's Bahamian, she's northern Italian, and the fare perfectly blends the two cultures. **Known for:** Italian cuisine with a Bahamian spin; biannually changing menu; delicious handmade cookies. [$] *Average main: $36* ✉ *Bank La. and Bay St., behind Parliament Sq., Nassau* ☎ *242/356–7012* 🌐 *www.cafematissenassau.com* 🕓 *Closed Sun., Mon., and Sept.*

East Villa Restaurant and Lounge

$$$ | **CHINESE** | In a converted Bahamian home, this is one of the most popular Chinese restaurants in town. The Chinese-Continental menu includes entrées such as conch with black-bean sauce, *hung shew* (walnut chicken), and steak *kew* (cubed prime fillet served with baby corn, snow peas, water chestnuts, and vegetables). **Known for:** traditional Chinese cuisine; broiled NY strip steaks; huge portions. [$] *Average main: $33* ✉ *E. Bay St. near Nassau Yacht Club, Nassau*

☎ *242/393–3377* 🌐 *www.eastvillabahamas.com* ⏲ *No lunch Sat. or public holidays.*

★ Fifty-Fifty Grillers

$ | BAHAMIAN | Follow the plume of smoke wafting onto Shirley Street to find this roadside spot with some of the best jerk chicken, pork, and slow grilled ribs around. Open Friday and Saturday for takeout only; meals come with a fresh baked roll as well as pasta salad or corn on the cob. **Known for:** best jerk pit around; great value for money; laid-back island vibe. [$] *Average main: $11* ✉ *opposite Ebenezer Methodist Church, Shirley Street, Nassau* ☎ *242/677–2833* ⏲ *closed Sun.–Thurs.* 💳 *No credit cards.*

★ Graycliff Restaurant

$$$$ | EUROPEAN | A meal at this hillside mansion's formal restaurant begins in the elegant parlor, where drinks are served over the sounds of a live piano. It's a rarefied world, where waiters wear tuxedos and Cuban cigars and cognac are served after dinner. **Known for:** only five-star rating in town; signature Kobe beef; third largest wine cellar in the world. [$] *Average main: $55* ✉ *Graycliff, W. Hill St. at Cumberland Rd., across from Government House, Nassau* ☎ *242/302–9150* 🌐 *www.graycliff.com* 👔 *Jacket required.*

The Green Parrot

$$ | AMERICAN | Two locations, at Harbourfront and Hurricane Hole, mean you get incomparable views of Nassau Harbour and a fresh breeze, whichever way the wind is blowing. The large burgers are a favorite at these casual, all-outdoor restaurants and bars. **Known for:** harbor views; simple but tasty American fare; large, lively bars. [$] *Average main: $28* ✉ *E. Bay St. west of bridges to Paradise Island, Nassau* ☎ *242/322–9248, 242/328–8382* 🌐 *greenparrotbar.com.*

Luciano's of Chicago

$$$ | ITALIAN | Green Roofs, the sprawling former residence of the late Sir Roland Symonette (the country's first premier), houses this harborside restaurant. The mansion's mahogany woodwork, gardens, and terraces create a romantic setting for enjoying Tuscan fare that features local seafood, including the fisherman's soup, grouper, and homemade pastas—try the delicious frutti di mare over linguine. **Known for:** Tuscan fare; views of Paradise Island at sunset; rum-soaked Bahamian-style bread pudding. [$] *Average main: $40* ✉ *E. Bay St., 2 blocks west of Paradise Island bridges, Nassau* ☎ *242/323–7770* 🌐 *www.lucianosnassau.com* ⏲ *No lunch Sat.*

Pop the Bubbly 🍸

A meandering maze underneath historic Graycliff's sprawling kitchen and dining area houses more than 200,000 bottles of wine and champagne, making this wine cellar one of the most extensive and impressive in the world. It costs $1,000 to book the elegant private cellar dining room, but tours are free.

★ Lukka Kairi

$$ | BAHAMIAN | Lukka Kairi means "people of the Islands," and at this hot spot you can experience the food, live music, and hospitality Bahamian people are known for. The tapas-style menu lets you sample a variety of traditional Bahamian dishes with a twist. **Known for:** some of the best conch fritters around; live Bahamian music on stage; great harbor views. [$] *Average main: $22* ✉ *Woodes Rodgers Walk, Nassau* ☎ *242/326–5254* 🌐 *www.lukkakairi.com.*

★ Never Say Never Again Bar & Grill

$$$ | ECLECTIC | For the best views of Nassau Harbour, dine at this 007-inspired bar and restaurant. A replica of the bar featured in the 1983 Bond film of the same name (and in the same location) references the espionage series on their menu. **Known for:** Bond-inspired martini menu; spectacular 180-degree harbor views; chef will prepare fish you caught. $ *Average main: $35* ✉ *Boardwalk behind Señor Frogs, Woodes Rodgers Walk, Nassau* ☎ *242/427–8886* 🕒 *Closed Mon.*

The Poop Deck

$$ | **BAHAMIAN** | Just east of the bridges from Paradise Island and a quick cab ride from the center of town is this favorite local haunt that is always busy. Start with the conch fritters, then move on to the fish (it's usually served head-to-tail, so if you're squeamish, ask your waiter to have the head cut off before it comes out on your plate). **Known for:** pick-your-own fish; calypso coffee made with secret ingredients (alcoholic); marina and harbor views. $ *Average main: $30* ✉ *E. Bay St. at Nassau Yacht Haven Marina, Nassau* ✥ *East of bridges from Paradise Island* ☎ *242/393–8175* 🌐 *www.thepoopdeck.com.*

★ **Seafront Sushi**

$$ | **SUSHI** | One of Nassau's hot spots, this simple restaurant has an extensive menu including traditional rolls, sushi, and sashimi, as well as more innovative options that incorporate conch and other local delicacies. The volcano roll topped with their special conch sauce is a favorite. **Known for:** volcano roll; sushi worth waiting for; traditional tatami rooms. $ *Average main: $20* ✉ *E. Bay St., Nassau* ☎ *242/394–1706* 🌐 *www.seafrontsushibahamas.com* 🕒 *Closed Sun. No lunch Sat.*

Sharkeez Bar & Grill

$$ | **BAHAMIAN** | If you arrive in Nassau aboard a cruise ship, you won't miss the sign for this second-floor bar and grill emblazoned atop its thatched roof. You may have a hard time picking your drink from the extensive menu of frozen concoctions. **Known for:** creative frozen concoctions; lively setting; theme nights. $ *Average main: $20* ✉ *Woodes Rodgers Walk, Nassau* ☎ *242/322–8519.*

★ **Syrah Cellar Cafe**

$$ | **ECLECTIC** | This intimate spot is usually packed with locals who reside on the eastern end of the island; be sure to call ahead to book a table. Dine surrounded by bottles of wine and, on some nights, live acoustic guitar. **Known for:** warm and friendly service and atmosphere; eclectic menu; impressive wine pairings. $ *Average main: $25* ✉ *Cotton Tree Traders Plaza, East Bay Street, Nassau* ☎ *242/676–0962* 🌐 *www.syrahvino.com* 🕒 *Closed Sun. and Mon.*

Wild Thyme Restaurant

$$$ | **ECLECTIC** | Dine inside or on the wraparound porches of a two story traditional wooden Bahamian home. The menu is small but there are lots of classic dishes to choose from, including golden beet and tomato salad with feta and goat cheese, or lobster salad with passion fruit mayo, avocado, and cassava chips. **Known for:** understated elegance; delicious generous portions; classic and unique signature cocktails. $ *Average main: $35* ✉ *east of Harbour Bay Shopping Plaza, 33 East Bay Street, Nassau* ☎ *242/393–4107* 🌐 *www.wildthyme-bahamas.com* 🕒 *Closed Sun.*

Hotels

British Colonial Hilton Nassau

$$ | **HOTEL** | This 1899 landmark hotel is the social heart of Nassau; it's the setting for political meetings and events, and offers sophisticated guest rooms with unmatched views of the harbor and old Nassau. **Pros:** right on Bay Street; quiet but trendy beach and pool area; centrally located. **Cons:** busy with local meetings and events; man-made beach; hard to access at peak traffic times. $ *Rooms from: $250* ✉ *1 Bay St., Nassau* ☎ *242/322–3301* 🌐 *www.bchiltonnassauhotel.com* 🛏 *288 rooms* 🍴 *No meals.*

Humidor Churrascaria Restaurant is in the Graycliff Hotel.

Courtyard Nassau Downtown/Junkanoo Beach
$ | **HOTEL** | Enjoy the hustle and bustle of downtown Nassau with a stay at this completely overhauled hotel overlooking Nassau Harbour. **Pros:** easy access to downtown Nassau shops and restaurants; recently renovated and upgraded property; great views of busy Nassau Harbour available. **Cons:** only basic breakfast and dinner restaurant on-site; located on a very busy street; beach is public access and extremely busy with cruise passengers. [$] *Rooms from: $148* ✉ *opposite Junkanoo Beach, West Bay St., west of Nassau St., Nassau* ☎ *242/302–2975* 🌐 *www.marriott.com/hotels/travel/nascy-courtyard-nassau-downtown-junkanoo-beach* 🛏 *118 rooms.*

★ **Graycliff Hotel**
$$$$ | **HOTEL** | The old-world flavor of this Georgian colonial landmark—built in the 1720s by ship captain Howard Graysmith—has made it a perennial favorite among both the rich and the famous (past guests have included the Duke and Duchess of Windsor, Winston Churchill, Aristotle Onassis, and the Beatles). **Pros:** exceptionally luxurious accommodations; lush tropical gardens; cigar and chocolate factories on-site. **Cons:** near busy restaurant and bar area; not easily accessible for handicapped; no beach. [$] *Rooms from: $435* ✉ *W. Hill St., Nassau* ☎ *242/322–2796, 800/476–0446* 🌐 *www.graycliff.com* 🛏 *20 rooms* 🍴 *Breakfast.*

Holiday Inn Express
$ | **HOTEL** | This simple and quiet six-floor hotel is a welcome addition to the New Providence budget-lodging market. **Pros:** walking distance from downtown; breakfast included; recently renovated. **Cons:** on two busy streets; popular with spring breakers; loud public beach is across the street. [$] *Rooms from: $150* ✉ *W. Bay St. and Nassau St., Nassau* ☎ *242/322–1515* 🌐 *www.ihg.com/holidayinnexpress* 🛏 *58 rooms* 🍴 *Free Breakfast.*

Towne Hotel
$ | **HOTEL** | For travelers hoping to do Nassau on a budget, this is one of the best options. **Pros:** cozy and quaint old Bahamian style; clean rooms; great location in historic downtown Nassau. **Cons:** only parking is public, street-side; dated decor; no additional amenities or activities. [$] *Rooms from: $104* ✉ *40 George Street, Nassau* ☎ *242/322–8450* 🌐 *www.townehotel.com* 🛏 *46 rooms* 🍴 *Free Breakfast.*

Nightlife

BARS AND CLUBS

Sharkeez Bar & Grill
BARS/PUBS | Every night brings a different theme and vibe to this popular restaurant and gathering spot. A DJ spins a range of music from Top 40 to reggae, soca, calypso, and Latin. Monday through Saturday they're open until midnight. The drinks menu is extensive, and includes Nassau's largest offering of frozen cocktails. ✉ *Woodes Rodgers Walk, Nassau* ☎ *242/322–8519.*

★ **Tiki Bikini Hut**
BARS/PUBS | Day or night you'll find a crowd of locals and tourists gathered around the largest beach bar on Junkanoo Beach. Pull up a bar stool or grab a table under the shaded dining area and enjoy views of Nassau Harbour and the sounds of live music. There are daily specials on drinks and shots, and packages that include beach chairs, umbrellas, and Wi-Fi access. ✉ *Junkanoo Beach, Nassau* ☎ *242/826–4053.*

Via Caffe
BARS/PUBS | Monday through Saturday, this lively restaurant and café is transformed into a lively locale for late-night entertainment with no cover charge. Depending on the night, you might find yourself learning salsa techniques while sipping a margarita, dancing to the hottest tunes spun by the house DJ, listening to a live band, or wowing the crowd at karaoke. For a late bite, the kitchen is open until the early morning hours. ✉ *Scotiabank Bldg., Corner of Parliament St. and Woodes Rogers Walk, Nassau* ☎ *242/322–3109.*

Shopping

CIGARS

Be aware that some merchants on Bay Street and elsewhere in the islands are selling counterfeit Cuban cigars—sometimes unwittingly. If the price seems too good to be true, chances are it is. Check the wrappers and feel to ensure that there's a consistent fill before you make your purchase.

Graycliff Hotel
TOBACCO | Graycliff carries one of Nassau's finest selections of hand-rolled cigars, featuring leaves from throughout Central and South America. Graycliff's operation is so popular that it has been expanded by the hotel to include an entire cigar factory, which is open to the public for tours, purchases, and even a cigar-rolling lesson. A dozen Cuban men and women roll the cigars; they live on the premises and work here through a special arrangement with the Cuban government. True cigar buffs will seek out Graycliff's owner, Enrico Garzaroli. In addition to the shop in the hotel, there's another Graycliff boutique at Lynden Pindling International Airport. ✉ *W. Hill St., Nassau* ☎ *242/302–9150* 🌐 *www.graycliff.com.*

CLOTHING AND ACCESSORIES

Brass and Leather
SHOES/LUGGAGE/LEATHER GOODS | Here you can find leather goods for men and women, including bags, shoes, and belts. Pick up one of the unique soft leather passport covers that come in an array of colors emblazoned with your country's coat of arms. ✉ *Charlotte St., off Bay St., Nassau* ☎ *242/322–3806.*

Cole's of Nassau

CLOTHING | This is a top choice for everything from ball gowns and cocktail dresses to resort wear and bathing suits with all the shoes and accessories for every look. ✉ *Parliament St., Nassau* ☎ *242/322–8393* ⊕ *www.colesofnassau. com.*

FOOD

Bahamas Rum Cake Factory

FOOD/CANDY | At the Bahamas Rum Cake Factory, delicious Bahamian rum-soaked cakes are made and packaged in tins right on the premises (peek into the bakery) and make a great souvenir. Just make sure you take one home for yourself. ✉ *602 E. Bay St., Nassau* ☎ *242/328–3750* ⊕ *thebahamasrumcakefactory.com.*

Mortimer Candies

FOOD/CANDY | Mortimer Candies whips up batches of uniquely Bahamian sweet treats daily. Pop in for a sno-cone on a hot day, or buy some bags of bennie cake, coconut-cream candy, or their signature Paradise Sweets in a swirl of the Bahamian flag colors. ✉ *E. St. Hill, Nassau* ☎ *242/322–5230* ⊕ *www.mortimercandies.com.*

GIFTS

★ Bahama Handprints

CLOTHING | Bahama Handprints fabrics emphasize local artists' sophisticated tropical prints in an array of colors. Also look for leather handbags, a wide range of women's clothing, housewares, and bolts of fabric. Ask for a free tour of the factory in back. A second location has opened up at the Island House near Lyford Cay. ✉ *Island Traders Bldg. Annex, off Mackey St., Nassau* ☎ *242/394–4111* ⊕ *www.bahamahandprints.com.*

★ The Craft Cottage

GIFTS/SOUVENIRS | This small shop situated in a traditional wooden structure is a great place to buy locally made souvenirs and gifts including soaps and oils, hand-painted glassware, jewelry, straw bags, and textiles. The artists and artisans are often on-site. ✉ *20 Village Rd., Nassau* ☎ *242/446–7373* ⊕ *www. craftcottagebahamas.com.*

Linen Shop

GIFTS/SOUVENIRS | This shop sells fine embroidered Irish linens and lace and has a delightful Christmas corner. ✉ *Bay St., Nassau* ☎ *242/322–4266.*

My Ocean

GIFTS/SOUVENIRS | Here you can find candles, soaps, salt scrubs, and lotions in island- and ocean-inspired scents and colors, all locally made. A second location can be found in Marina Village on Paradise Island. ✉ *Prince George Plaza, Nassau* ☎ *242/328–6167* ⊕ *myocean. com.*

JEWELRY, WATCHES, AND CLOCKS

Coin of the Realm

JEWELRY/ACCESSORIES | Coin of the Realm has Bahamian coins, stamps, native conch pearls, tanzanite, and semiprecious stone jewelry. ✉ *Charlotte St. off Bay St., Nassau* ☎ *242/322–4862, 242/322–4497* ⊕ *www.coinrealm.net.*

Colombian Emeralds International

JEWELRY/ACCESSORIES | Colombian Emeralds International is the local branch of this well-known jeweler; its stores carry a variety of fine jewelry in addition to its signature gem. There are also branches in Marina Village and at the Atlantis Paradise Island Royal Towers and Beach Towers. ✉ *Bay St. near Rawson Sq., Nassau* ☎ *242/322–2230* ⊕ *www.colombianemeralds.com.*

★ John Bull

JEWELRY/ACCESSORIES | Established in 1929 and magnificently decorated in its Bay Street incarnation behind a Georgian-style facade, John Bull fills its complex with wares from Tiffany & Co., Cartier, Mikimoto, Nina Ricci, and Yves Saint Laurent. The company has eight locations throughout Nassau and in Atlantis and Baha Mar Paradise Island and also owns a number of the better-known high-end boutique brand stores. ✉ *284 Bay St., Nassau* ☎ *242/302–2800* ⊕ *www.johnbull.com.*

LIQUOR

★ Pirate Republic Brewing Company

WINE/SPIRITS | When you spot a pirate hanging out on Woodes Rogers Walk, you know you've found the home of the Bahamas' only craft brewery. Inside the shop is Pirate Republic beer to sample—Long John Pilsner, Gold and Haze of Piracy, and the Island Pirate Ale—as well as live music most nights and a limited but tasty grub menu. For a look at how the brew is made, take one of the tours offered twice a day. ✉ *Woodes Rodgers Walk, Nassau* ☎ *242/328–0612* ⊕ *www. piraterepublicbahamas.com.*

MARKETS AND ARCADES

International Bazaar

SHOPPING CENTERS/MALLS | This collection of shops under a huge, spreading bougainvillea sells linens, jewelry, souvenirs, and offbeat items. There's often a small band playing all sorts of music along this funky shopping row. ✉ *Bay St. at Charlotte St., Nassau.*

Prince George Plaza

SHOPPING CENTERS/MALLS | Prince George Plaza, which leads from Bay Street to Woodes Rogers Walk near the cruise-ship docks, just east of the International Bazaar, has about two dozen shops with varied wares. ✉ *Bay St., Nassau.*

Straw Market

OUTDOOR/FLEA/GREEN MARKETS | This towering colonial-style marketplace houses hundreds of straw vendors selling straw bags, T-shirts, and other souvenirs. The Straw Market is one place in the Bahamas where bartering is accepted, so it's best to wander around and price similar items at different stalls before sealing a deal. Besides the wood-carvers on the western side of the market you're not likely to find any locally made items here. ✉ *Bay St., Nassau.*

PERFUMES AND COSMETICS

The Cosmetic Boutique

PERFUME/COSMETICS | This shop has beauty experts on hand to demonstrate the latest cosmetics offerings, including M.A.C., Clinique, Bobbi Brown, and La Mer. ✉ *Bay St. near Charlotte St., Nassau* ☎ *242/323–2731.*

Perfume Bar

PERFUME/COSMETICS | This shop carries the best-selling French fragrance Boucheron and the Clarins line of skin-care products, as well as scents by Chanel, Fendi, and other well-known designers. ✉ *Bay St., Nassau* ☎ *242/325–1258.*

🏃 Activities

BOATING

Bay Street Marina

BOATING | With 89 slips accommodating yachts up to 400 feet, this modern, centrally located marina on the Nassau side of the harbor has all the amenities you might need. The marina is within walking distance to Paradise Island as well as downtown Nassau and has a lively restaurant and bar on-site. ✉ *E. Bay St., Nassau* ☎ *242/676–7000* ⊕ *www. baystreetmarina.com.*

Brown's Boat Basin

BOATING | On the Nassau side, Brown's Boat Basin offers a place to tie up your boat, as well as on-site engine repairs. ✉ *E. Bay St., Nassau* ☎ *242/393–3331.*

Nassau Yacht Haven

BOATING | On the Nassau side of the harbor, the island's oldest marina, Nassau Yacht Haven, has 150 berths and also arranges fishing charters. ✉ *E. Bay St., Nassau* ☎ *242/393–8173* ⊕ *www.nassauyachthaven.com.*

Palm Cay Marina

BOATING | The easternmost marina on New Providence offers 194 slips and all the amenities, including a full restaurant, pool, and beach. ✉ *Palm Cay, Yamacraw*

Hill Rd., Nassau ☎ *242/676–8554*
⊕ *www.palmcay.com.*

FISHING

Born Free Charters

FISHING | This charter company has seven boats and guarantees a catch on full-day charters—if you don't get a fish, you don't pay. Pickup is included from various locations, and the company will make the arrangements for you. ✉ *Nassau* ☎ *242/698–1770, 954/526–1956 U.S. phone number* ⊕ *www.bornfreefishing. com.*

Chubasco Charters

FISHING | This charter company has four boats for deep-sea and light tackle sportfishing. Half- and full-day charters are available. Pickup is from Paradise Island Ferry Terminal or Nassau Harbour in front of the Straw Market. They guarantee you'll catch something when you go out fishing with them or you'll get your money back. ☎ *242/324–3474* ⊕ *www. chubascocharters.com.*

Nassau Yacht Haven

FISHING | Nassau Yacht Haven can put you in touch with one of the private fishing charter captains operating out of its 150-slip marina. ✉ *Nassau Yacht Haven, E. Bay St., Nassau* ☎ *242/393–8173* ⊕ *www.nassauyachthaven.com.*

SPAS

Baha-Retreat

SPA/BEAUTY | This spa, situated in an old wooden two-story Bahamian home, is popular with locals and offers a full range of spa and salon services seven days a week. Reservations are suggested, but walk-ins are welcome. Specialties include body sugaring and threading for hair removal, but massages are also good here. Book a Couples Spa Day for a complete pampering treat: aromatherapy body polish, aromatherapy massage, spa manicure and pedicure, and gourmet lunch with a glass of wine each. ✉ *E. Bay St., Nassau* ☎ *242/323–6711* ⊕ *www. baharetreat.com.*

Windermere Day Spa at Harbour Bay

SHOPPING OVERVIEW | This day spa offers a variety of spa treatments—such as hydrotherapy and salt glows—as well as facials, massages, manicures, and pedicures. They also have a location in Caves Village in Western New Providence. Get to the Lynden Pindling International Airport early for a final massage or manicure at their nail and massage bar in the departure lounge. ✉ *E. Bay St.* ☎ *242/393–8788* ⊕ *www.windermere-dayspa.com.*

TOURS

Bahama Barrels

SPECIAL-INTEREST | Right across the street from one of the world's largest wine collections is the country's only winery. Tour the space and enjoy samples in the tasting room, or try your hand at blending wine in a private class. ✉ *8-14 West Hill St., Nassau* ☎ *242/302–9150* ⊕ *www. graycliff.com.*

★ Blackbeard's Escape

SPECIAL-INTEREST | FAMILY | Nassau's only escape room features a pirate theme set in 1718 and is fun for all ages. The experience is limited to eight people at a time. You and your fellow pirates have an hour to solve the clues and escape before Woodes Rodgers and the British Army find you. ✉ *located upstairs at Pirates of Nassau, King & George Sts., Nassau* ☎ *242/813–3222* ⊕ *www.blackbeardsescape.com.*

★ Goombay House

SPECIAL-INTEREST | Learn to cook your favorite Bahamian dishes at this fun cooking school within an old Bahamian home on historic Queen Street. Da Conchin Tour includes a visit to a local fish market where you see how the conch shell is cracked to get the mollusk out. From there you'll return to the cooking studio where the chef will teach you how to prepare it. Enjoy your creation alongside a traditional local cocktail. There are a variety of classes (not all feature Bahamian cuisine) to choose from, including a boozy weekend brunch. ⊠ *Queen St., Nassau* ☎ *242/804–2665* ⊕ *www.goombayhousecookingstudio.com.*

Paradise Island

The graceful, arched bridges of Paradise Island ($2 round-trip toll for cars and motorbikes; free for bicyclists and pedestrians) lead to and from the extravagant world of Paradise Island. Until 1962 the island was largely undeveloped and known as Hog Island. A&P heir Huntington Hartford changed the name when he built the island's first resort complex. In 1994 South African developer Sol Kerzner transformed the existing high-rise hotel into the first phase of Atlantis. Many years, a number of new hotels, a water park, and more than $1 billion later, Atlantis has taken over the island. Home to multimillion-dollar homes and condominiums and a handful of independent resort properties, you can still find a quiet spot on Cabbage Beach or Paradise Beach, which is west of Atlantis.

◉ Sights

★ Aquaventure
AMUSEMENT PARK/WATER PARK | FAMILY | From near-vertical slides that plunge through shark tanks to a quarter-mile-long lazy river ride, this 141-acre water park allows you to both unwind and get your adrenaline pumping. Spend the day going from ride to ride, or relax under an umbrella on the white sand of three unique beaches, or one of 11 swimming pools. Three pools are designed especially for the youngest of guests, including Splashers, a Mayan-themed water playground. Day passes for nonresort guests are limited so be sure to plan well ahead. ⊠ *Atlantis Paradise Island, Paradise Island* ☎ *242/363–3000* ⊕ *www.atlantisbahamas.com* ⊠ *Day pass $161 high season, $150 low season; beach pass $70.*

★ Atlantis Paradise Island
AMUSEMENT PARK/WATER PARK | FAMILY | This pink fantasia with its sunstruck Royal Towers comes into view before you cross one of the Paradise Island bridges. With luxury shops, a glitzy casino, and many choices for dining and drinks (40 restaurants, bars, and lounges), Atlantis is as much a tourist attraction as a resort hotel. At Dolphin Cay you can interact with dolphins, sea lions, and stingrays. The 63-acre Aquaventure water park provides thrilling waterslides and high-intensity rapids as well as a lazy-river tube ride through the sprawling grounds. Celebrity sightings are frequent at both Nobu restaurant and Aura nightclub. The on-site comedy club, Joker's Wild, brings top comedians to the stage. Many of the resort's facilities, including the restaurants and casino, are open to nonguests, but the leisure and sports facilities are open only to resort guests and those who purchase a day pass. Atlantis has the world's largest man-made marine habitat, consisting of 11 lagoons. To see it, take the guided Discover Atlantis tour. ⊠ *Casino Dr., Paradise Island* ☎ *242/363–3000* ⊠ *Discover Atlantis tour $42; Aquaventure day pass $150–$161; beach day pass $70; lockers $15–$25 per day; casino free.*

Potter's Cay
MARKET | Walk the road beneath the Paradise Island bridges to Potter's Cay to watch sloops bringing in and selling loads of fish and conch . Along the road to the cay are dozens of stands where you can watch the conch being extracted from its glistening pink shell, straight from the sea.. If you don't have the know-how to handle the tasty conch's preparation—getting the diffident creature out of its shell requires boring a hole at the right spot to sever the muscle that keeps it entrenched—you can enjoy a conch salad on the spot, as fresh as it comes, and take notes for future attempts. Empty shells are sold as souvenirs. Many locals and hotel chefs come here to purchase

Paradise Island

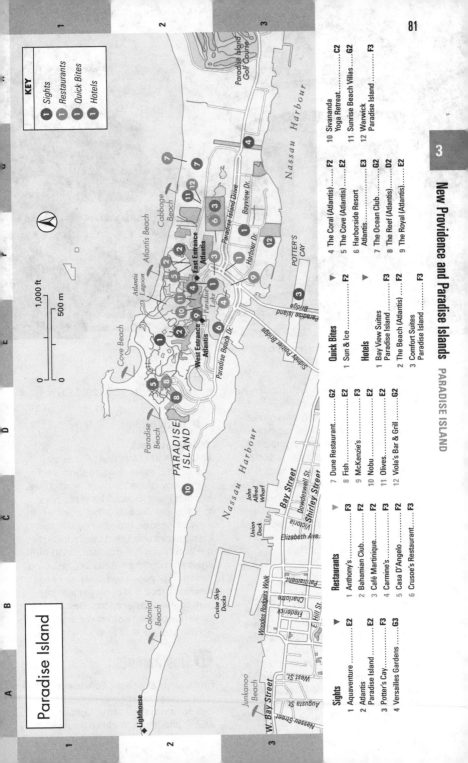

KEY

- Sights
- Restaurants
- Quick Bites
- Hotels

1,000 ft
500 m

3

New Providence and Paradise Islands
PARADISE ISLAND

Sights

1 Aquaventure	E2
2 Atlantis Paradise Island	E2
3 Potter's Cay	F3
4 Versailles Gardens	G3

Restaurants

1 Anthony's	F3
2 Bahamian Club	F2
3 Café Martinique	F2
4 Carmine's	F3
5 Casa D'Angelo	F2
6 Crusoe's Restaurant	F3
7 Dune Restaurant	G2
8 Fish	E2
9 McKenzie's	F3
10 Nobu	E2
11 Olives	E2
12 Viola's Bar & Grill	G2

Quick Bites

1 Sun & Ice	F2

Hotels

1 Bay View Suites Paradise Island	F3
2 The Beach (Atlantis)	F2
3 Comfort Suites Paradise Island	F3
4 The Coral (Atlantis)	F2
5 The Cove (Atlantis)	E2
6 Harborside Resort Atlantis	E3
7 The Ocean Club	G2
8 The Reef (Atlantis)	D2
9 The Royal (Atlantis)	E2
10 Sivananda Yoga Retreat	C2
11 Sunrise Beach Villas	G2
12 Warwick Paradise Island	F3

The Cloisters in Versailles Gardens is possibly the most peaceful spot on the island.

the fresh catches; you can also find vegetables, herbs, and such condiments as fiery Bahamian peppers preserved in lime juice, and locally grown pineapples, papayas, and bananas. Join in on a raucous game of dominoes outside many of the stalls. Some stalls are closed on Sunday. There's also a police station and dockmaster's office, where you can book an inexpensive trip on a mail boat headed to the Out Islands. Be aware that these boats are built for cargo, not passenger comfort, and it's a rough ride even on calm seas. ⊠ *Nassau* ⊠ *Free.*

Versailles Gardens
GARDEN | Fountains and statues of luminaries and legends adorn Versailles Gardens, the terraced lawn at the The Ocean Club, once the private hideaway of Huntington Hartford. At the top of the gardens stand the **Cloisters,** the remains of a stone monastery built by Augustinian monks in France in the 13th century, imported to the United States in the 1920s by newspaper baron William Randolph Hearst. ⊠ *The Ocean Club Four*

Seasons Resort, Paradise Island Dr., Paradise Island ☎ *242/363–2501* ⊠ *Free.*

🏖 Beaches

★ Cabbage Beach
BEACH—SIGHT | FAMILY | At this beach you'll find 3 miles of white sand lined with shady casuarina trees, sand dunes, and sun worshippers. This is the place to go to rent Jet Skis or get a bird's-eye view of Paradise Island while parasailing. Hair braiders and T-shirt vendors stroll the beach, and hotel guests crowd the areas surrounding the resorts, including Atlantis. For peace and quiet, stroll east. **Amenities:** food and drink; lifeguards; parking (fee); water sports. **Best for:** partiers; solitude; swimming; walking. ⊠ *Paradise Island* ⊠ *Free.*

🍽 Restaurants

Restaurants at Atlantis Paradise Island tend to close one or two nights a week (but not always the same nights each week), and their schedules vary with the resort's occupancy levels. Check with the reservations desk at Atlantis if you want to dine there. Reservations are essential at most of the upscale spots and a good idea at all restaurants that accept them.

Anthony's

$$ | **AMERICAN** | This lively, casual spot is one of the most affordable places for breakfast, lunch, or dinner this side of Nassau Harbour, but that doesn't mean it's cheap. The baby back ribs with a homemade barbecue sauce are among the most popular on this Bahamian and American fare menu. **Known for:** one of few nonresort restaurants on PI; extensive menu; affordable (by PI standards) dining. $ *Average main: $30* ⊠ *Paradise Village Shopping Plaza, Paradise Island* ☎ *242/363–3152* ⊕ *www.anthonysparadiseisland.com.*

Bahamian Club

$$$$ | **EUROPEAN** | Reminiscent of a British country club, this handsome restaurant has walls lined with dark oak, overstuffed chairs, and leather banquettes. Meat is the house specialty—rib-eye steak, Niman Ranch pork chop, Colorado lamb chops, and the prime rib trolley—but grilled, seared snapper fillets, classic Bahamian lobster thermidor, jumbo prawns, and other fresh seafood dishes are all prepared with finesse. **Known for:** upscale ambience; outstanding service; enough-to-share Mixed Grill. $ *Average main: $55* ⊠ *Atlantis Paradise Island, Coral Towers, Paradise Island* ☎ *242/363–3000* ⊕ *www.atlantisbahamas.com* ☯ *No lunch.*

★ Café Martinique

$$$$ | **FRENCH** | The original restaurant, which was made famous in the 1965 James Bond film *Thunderball*, has long been bulldozed, but with the help of renowned international chef Jean-Georges Vongerichten and New York designer Adam D. Tihany, this resurrected classic remains one of the hottest tables at Atlantis. **Known for:** white-glove service; superior cuts of meat; the chocolate lover's chocolate mascarpone. $ *Average main: $60* ⊠ *Atlantis Paradise Island, Marina Village, Paradise Island* ☎ *242/363–3000* ⊕ *www.atlantisbahamas.com.*

★ Carmine's

$$$$ | **ITALIAN** | **FAMILY** | This Italian restaurant is a great place to go with a small group. Appetizers, entrées, and desserts come in extra-large portions meant to feed a crowd and are served family-style, so the prices can be more affordable (by Paradise Island standards, at least) than they seem at first, especially if you share among several people. **Known for:** huge portions meant for sharing; Titanic (ice cream-laden chocolate torte); options for every member of the family. $ *Average main: $55* ⊠ *Atlantis Paradise Island, Marina Village, Paradise Island* ☎ *242/363–3000* ⊕ *www.atlantisbahamas.com* ☯ *No lunch.*

Casa D'Angelo

$$$$ | **ITALIAN** | At this restaurant, an outpost of the wildly popular Casa d'Angelo chain in south Florida, chef Angelo Elia brings his famous Tuscan-style cuisine to Paradise. The antipasti display whets the appetite for succulent seafood, hearty pasta dishes, and prime cuts of beef. **Known for:** wine pairings with every course; standard Italian fare; delectable pastries. $ *Average main: $50* ⊠ *Atlantis Paradise Island, Coral Towers, Paradise Island* ☎ *242/363–3000* ⊕ *www.atlantisbahamas.com* ☯ *No lunch.*

Crusoe's Restaurant

$$ | **BAHAMIAN** | **FAMILY** | This hidden gem is worth a visit even if you are not staying at the Comfort Suites. This casual and family-friendly, al fresco restaurant offers an enticing menu. **Known for:** casual setting with great service; nice alternative to the larger, fancier Atlantis offerings; guava brioche bread pudding. $ *Average main: $28* ⊠ *Comfort Suites, Paradise Island* ☎ *242/363–3680* ⊕ *www.comfortsuitespi.com/dining/cs-crusoe-restaurant.*

Did You Know?

Marina Village, an open-air marketplace at Atlantis, is a popular tourist destination. The bazaar features five restaurants, a crafts market, and upscale stores.

Dune Restaurant

$$$$ | **MODERN FRENCH** | Feast on Jean-Georges Vongerichten's intricately prepared dishes while overlooking Cabbage Beach at the renowned Four Seasons Ocean Club. Go for breakfast or lunch for the most (relatively) reasonable prices. **Known for:** chef Jean-Georges's signature dishes; fine dining overlooking the ocean; divine salted caramel banana cake. $ *Average main: $55* ⊠ *Four Seasons Ocean Club, Ocean Club Dr., Paradise Island* ☎ *242/363–2501* ⊕ *www. fourseasons.com/oceanclub/dining/ restaurants/dune.*

★ Fish

$$$$ | **SEAFOOD** | José Andrés is the latest celebrity chef to lend his name and global reputation to the restaurant offerings on Paradise Island. As you would expect from the name, seafood takes center stage on this restaurant's mouthwatering menu. **Known for:** fresh seafood; whole fried lionfish; tropical conch salad with dragonfruit. $ *Average main: $50* ⊠ *The Cove, Atlantis, Nassau* ☎ *888/526–0386* ⊕ *www.fishbyjoseandres.com/location/ fish-bahamas-atlantis-paradise-island.*

★ McKenzie's

$ | **BAHAMIAN** | You no longer have to venture over the bridge to get a bowl of authentic conch salad—this takeout shack in Marina Village makes conch salad to order. Pull up a bar stool and watch the dizzying display of knife skills it takes to make this local delicacy. **Known for:** only conch salad on Paradise Island; daiquiri bar; worth the long wait. $ *Average main: $15* ⊠ *Marina Village, Paradise Island* ⊕ *www.atlantisbahamas.com.*

★ Nobu

$$$$ | **SUSHI** | Sushi connoisseurs, celebrities, and tourists pack this Atlantis restaurant night after night. The rock shrimp tempura, yellowtail sashimi with jalapeño, and miso-glazed black cod are Nobu favorites, but this restaurant also takes advantage of fresh Bahamian seafood—try the lobster shiitake salad or the cold conch shabu-shabu with Nobu sauces. **Known for:** traditional Japanese sushi; sake cellar; delicious miso-glazed black cod. $ *Average main: $60* ⊠ *Atlantis Paradise Island, Royal Towers, Paradise Island* ☎ *242/363–3000* ⊕ *www. atlantisbahamas.com* ⊙ *No lunch.*

Olives

$$$$ | **MEDITERRANEAN** | Todd English has paired up with Atlantis to give his signature Mediterranean style a taste of the Caribbean. Enjoy the shellfish, clams, and oysters from the Raw Bar; pick the fish you want to see on your plate; or satisfy your meat craving with the huge Tomahawk rib eye—all steaks are 100% Akaushi Wagyu beef. **Known for:** late-night kitchen; extensive raw bar; homemade pasta dishes. $ *Average main: $50* ⊠ *Atlantis Paradise Island, The Royal, Paradise Island* ✛ *In casino* ☎ *242/363–3000* ⊕ *www.atlantisbahamas.com.*

★ Viola's Bar & Grill

$$ | **BAHAMIAN** | This unassuming bar and grill is a consistent Paradise Island favorite with locals and visitors. Their new menu has been upgraded from so-so pub fare to must-try Bahamian specialties as well as international options. **Known for:** lively vibe; delicious Bahamian cooking; frequented by locals and 'in the know' visitors. $ *Average main: $25* ⊠ *Casino Drive, Paradise Island* ☎ *242/363–2234* ⊕ *www.violasbarsunrisebeach.com.*

☕ Coffee and Quick Bites

★ Sun & Ice

$ | **BAHAMIAN** | **FAMILY** | Nothing beats ice cream to cool off after a hot day on the beach or by the pool. This local ice cream shop serving unique Bahamian flavors is located in the heart of The Coral lobby in Atlantis and often has a long line, but it's worth the wait. **Known for:** locally made ice cream; worth waiting in line for; native fruit flavors. $ *Average main: $10* ⊠ *The Coral lobby, Atlantis, Nassau* ☎ *242/363–3000* ⊕ *www.atlantisbahamas.com.*

Hotels

You'll find several hotels and apartment buildings on Paradise Island, but the sprawling Atlantis resort is the main attraction. It's a bustling fantasy world—at once a water park, entertainment complex, megaresort, and beach oasis. Other than the new Baha Mar resort complex in Cable Beach, it's the largest resort in the country. The public areas are lavish, with fountains, glass sculptures, and gleaming shopping arcades. There is plenty of nightlife on the premises; the casino, ringed by restaurants, is one of the largest in the Bahamas and the Caribbean. Some of these facilities can be visited by nonguests (restaurants, shops, the casino, and nightspots), but the famed Aquaventure Water Park is limited to guests of Atlantis, a handful of affiliated hotels, and cruise passengers.

Bay View Suites Paradise Island

$ | HOTEL | FAMILY | This 4-acre condominium resort has a lush, intimate character, and guests can socialize around three pools that are surrounded by tropical plants, including several hibiscus and bougainvillea varieties. **Pros:** children 12 and under stay free; private "at-home" vibe; suites are huge. **Cons:** long walk from beach; no restaurant serving dinner on property; no organized activities on-site. [$] *Rooms from: $148* ✉ *Bay View Dr., Paradise Island* ☎ *242/363–2555, 800/757–1357* 🌐 *www.bayviewsuitesparadiseisland.com* 🛏 *25 rooms* 🍴 *No meals.*

The Beach (Atlantis)

$$ | RESORT | FAMILY | Located at the easternmost edge of Atlantis, The Beach offers a bit of a reprieve from the activity of the rest of the megaresort, with a large inviting pool and lazy river that are less congested than Aquaventure. **Pros:** less congestion at beach and pools; close to kids' activities; best value for Atlantis Resort. **Cons:** far from the main attractions of Atlantis; no room service; only one restaurant in this section. [$] *Rooms from: $209* ✉ *Atlantis Paradise Island, Paradise Island* ☎ *242/363–3000, 888/877–7525 reservations* 🌐 *www.atlantisbahamas.com* 🛏 *487 rooms* 🍴 *No meals.*

Quick Bites

A quick snack or light lunch on the go can be picked up at most gas stations or bakeries on the island. Grab a hot patty—peppery chicken or beef is most popular—or a yellow pastry pocket filled with conch. One of these with a "coke soda"—the generic name for all brands of soft drink—will tide you over until your next real meal. On Paradise Island, there's a Dunkin' Donuts at Paradise Village and Starbucks at Marina Village.

★ Comfort Suites Paradise Island

$$$ | HOTEL | FAMILY | This all-suite hotel in the middle of Paradise Island is a great spot for families; guests have access to the features of nearby Atlantis, including Aquaventure and the Atlantis Kids Club. **Pros:** use of all Atlantis amenities; near shops, restaurants, and Cabbage Beach; breakfast included. **Cons:** not on a beach; busy traffic surrounds; activities are only at the Atlantis Resort. [$] *Rooms from: $350* ✉ *Paradise Island Dr., Paradise Island* ☎ *242/363–2581, 855/603–1105* 🌐 *www.comfortsuitespi.com* 🛏 *223 suites* 🍴 *Breakfast.*

The Coral (Atlantis)

$$ | RESORT | FAMILY | The newly renovated family-friendly Coral is at the heart of the Atlantis Resort, giving you good access to all the top amenities—including the casino and Aquaventure—at a moderate price point. **Pros:** on-site movie theater (included in resort fee); family-exclusive swimming pool; Marina Village steps away. **Cons:** always busy lobby area;

guest rooms lack some of the pizazz you might expect at Atlantis; many kids running around. [$] *Rooms from: $220* ✉ *Atlantis Paradise Island, Paradise Island* ☎ *242/363–3000, 888/877–7525 reservations* 🌐 *www.atlantisbahamas.com* 🛏 *609 rooms* 🍴 *No meals.*

★ **The Cove (Atlantis)**
$$$$ | **RESORT** | Worlds away from the other properties within the Atlantis Resort in terms of overall look, experience, and sophistication, this high-rise overlooking two stunning white-sand beaches is a true grown-ups' getaway. **Pros:** highly exclusive adult-only pool; incredible private beaches; amenities of Atlantis, but separated from the hustle and bustle. **Cons:** a long walk to Atlantis amenities; limited dining and bar options on-site; pricey. [$] *Rooms from: $465* ✉ *Atlantis Paradise Island, Paradise Island* ☎ *242/363–3000, 888/877–7525 reservations* 🌐 *www.atlantisbahamas.com* 🛏 *600 suites* 🍴 *No meals.*

★ **Harborside Resort Atlantis**
$$ | **RENTAL** | **FAMILY** | It you want more space to stretch out during your Paradise Island vacation, consider these one-, two-,and three-bedroom town-house-style villas that can accommodate up to nine guests and are fully equipped with separate living/dining areas, kitchens, and private laundry facilities. **Pros:** lots of space to stretch out; pool area is less crowded than Aquaventure; right next door to Nassau water taxi dock. **Cons:** Wi-Fi is extra; long walk to Atlantis restaurants and amenities; no room service. [$] *Rooms from: $300* ✉ *Paradise Beach Dr., Paradise Island* ☎ *242/363–3000* 🌐 *www.atlantisbahamas.com* 🛏 *392 villas* 🍴 *No meals.*

★ **The Ocean Club**
$$$$ | **RESORT** | Once the private hideaway of A&P heir Huntington Hartford, this exclusive Four Seasons Resort on magnificent Cabbage Beach's quietest stretch provides the ultimate in understated—and decidedly posh—elegance. **Pros:** ultra-exclusive; lovely beach; top-rated amenities. **Cons:** not within walking distance of Atlantis; limited (and very expensive) on-site dining; Crescent Wing room have ocean views, but no pool nearby. [$] *Rooms from: $750* ✉ *Ocean Club Dr., Paradise Island* ☎ *242/363–2501, 877/312–1211* 🌐 *fourseasons.com/oceanclub* 🛏 *107 rooms.*

The Reef (Atlantis)
$$$$ | **RESORT** | **FAMILY** | This 497-suite tower has exquisitely outfitted studios or one- and two-bedroom condominium-style accommodations. **Pros:** units fully equipped with kitchens or kitchenettes; quiet; cost-effective option with Atlantis benefits. **Cons:** no restaurants or bars on property; long walk to Atlantis amenities; no grocery stores nearby. [$] *Rooms from: $700* ✉ *Atlantis Paradise Island, Paradise Island* ☎ *242/363–3000, 888/877–7525 reservations* 🌐 *www.atlantisbahamas.com* 🛏 *497 apartments* 🍴 *No meals.*

★ **The Royal (Atlantis)**
$$$ | **RESORT** | **FAMILY** | At centrally located The Royal, spend your days riding the slides at Aquaventure, and your nights in the casino and the nightclub. **Pros:** access to top amenities including spa and Aquaventure water park; larger rooms than other Atlantis towers; plenty of on-site activities. **Cons:** full balconies only in suites; noisy; pricey on-site dining, subpar fast-food options. [$] *Rooms from: $400* ✉ *Atlantis Paradise Island, Paradise Island* ☎ *242/363–3000, 888/877–7525 reservations* 🌐 *www.atlantisbahamas.com* 🛏 *1201 rooms* 🍴 *Some meals.*

★ **Sivananda Yoga Retreat**
$ | **B&B/INN** | Accessible only by boat, this resort features guest rooms in the main house and one-room bungalows overlooking a gorgeous white-sand beach in a 5-acre compound that stretches from Nassau Harbour to the ocean; air-conditioning is an additional $10 per day. **Pros:** ideal for peace and quiet; inexpensive accommodations; free shuttle to and

Bond in the Bahamas

In *Casino Royale*, the 21st James Bond installment, Bond took on the bad guys at an embassy, which was, in reality, the lovely Buena Vista Restaurant and Hotel in Nassau, which closed shortly after filming and is now home to the John Watling's Distillery. Actor Daniel Craig also had the glamorous background of The Ocean Club resort on Paradise Island, where another Bond, Pierce Brosnan, frequently stays.

Bond and the Bahamas have a long relationship. Six Bond films have used the Bahamas as a backdrop, including *Thunderball*, filmed in 1965 with the original 007, Sean Connery. Connery loved the Bahamas so much he has chosen to live here year-round in the luxury gated community of Lyford Cay.

Thunderball was filmed at the Café Martinique, which, after being closed for more than a decade, reopened at Atlantis resort on Paradise Island in 2006. Scenes were also shot at the Mediterranean Renaissance–style British Colonial, built in the 1920s.

You can swim and snorkel in Thunderball Cave in the Exumas, site of the pivotal chase scene in the 1965 Sean Connery film. The ceiling of this huge, dome-shaped cave is about 30 feet above the water, which is filled with yellowtails, parrots, blue chromes, and yellow-and-black striped sergeant majors. Swimming into the cave is the easy part—the tide draws you in—but paddling back out can be strenuous, especially because if you stop moving, the tide will pull you back.

The Rock Point house, better known to 007 fans as Palmyra, the villain Emilio Largo's estate, was another Bond location, and Bay Street, where Bond and his beautiful sidekick Domino attended a Junkanoo carnival, is still the location of Junkanoo twice a year. The *Thunderball* remake, *Never Say Never Again*, was also shot in the Bahamas, using many of the same locations as the original.

Underwater shots for many of the Bond flicks were filmed in the Bahamas, including Thunderball Grotto, while Nassau's offshore reefs were the underwater locations for the 1983 film *Never Say Never Again*, the 1967 film *You Only Live Twice*, the 1977 film *The Spy Who Loved Me*, and *For Your Eyes Only*, released in 1981.

—Cheryl Blackerby

from Nassau. **Cons:** several night minimum stay during certain times of year; basic accommodations; no road access. $ *Rooms from: $140* ✉ *Paradise Island* 📞 *242/363–2902, 866/559–5167* ⊕ *www. sivanandabahamas.org* 🛏 *190 rooms* ⍾ *All meals.*

Sunrise Beach Villas
$$ | **HOTEL** | **FAMILY** | Lushly landscaped with crotons, coconut palms, bougainvillea, and hibiscus, this low-rise, family-run resort on Cabbage Beach has a tropical wonderland feel. **Pros:** on one of the best beaches on the island; lively bar on property; great for families. **Cons:** no activities; lots of walking to get to rooms; once-secluded spot on Cabbage Beach now busy due to an arrangement with the Warwick. $ *Rooms from: $265* ✉ *Casino Dr., Paradise Island* 📞 *242/698–7200, 800/451–6078* ⊕ *www.sunrisebeachclub. com* 🛏 *28 suites* ⍾ *No meals.*

Warwick Paradise Island

$$ | **ALL-INCLUSIVE** | Suitable for a friends getaway, romantic weekend, or even business trip, this 12-story, adults-only hotel overlooks Nassau Harbour. **Pros:** top-notch service; cocktails and dining options included in the rate; away from busy Atlantis. **Cons:** on-site beach is man-made; shuttle or walk to Cabbage Beach; not much by way of activities. $ *Rooms from: $271* ⊠ *Harbour Drive, Paradise Island* 🕾 *242/363–2560* ⊕ *www.warwick-hotels.com/warwick-paradise-island-bahamas/rooms* ➹ *250* ⦿ *All-inclusive.*

🍸 Nightlife

BARS AND CLUBS

Aura

DANCE CLUBS | Located upstairs from the Atlantis Casino, this is the place to see and be seen on Paradise Island, though many of the celebrities who frequent the club opt for the ultra-exclusive private lounge. Dancing goes on all night, and bartenders dazzle the crowd with their mixing techniques. The music varies from night to night. ⊠ *Atlantis Paradise Island Royal Towers, Paradise Island* 🕾 *242/363–3000 ext 65734* ⊕ *www.atlantisbahamas.com* ⊗ *Closed Sun.–Wed.*

CASINOS

Atlantis Casino

CASINOS | Featuring a spectacularly open and airy design, the 50,000-square-foot (100,000 if you include the dining and drinking areas) casino is ringed with restaurants and offers more than 1,100 slot machines, baccarat, blackjack, roulette, craps tables, and such local specialties as Caribbean stud poker. There's also a high-limit table area, and most of the eateries have additional games. The sports book with the massive video wall looks out over the luxury yachts in the marina. The casino is always open, with gaming tables available from 10 am to 4 am daily. ⊠ *Atlantis Paradise Island Royal Towers, Paradise Island* 🕾 *242/363–3000* ⊕ *www.atlantisbahamas.com/casino.*

Offshore Adventures

For a true beach getaway, head to one of the tiny islands just off the coast of Paradise Island. A 20-minute boat ride from Nassau, Blue Lagoon Island has a number of beaches, including one in a tranquil cove lined with hammocks suspended by palm trees. Enjoy a grilled lunch and then rent a kayak or water bike if you're feeling ambitious.

👜 Shopping

ARTS AND CRAFTS

Bahamacraft Centre

CRAFTS | Bahamacraft Centre offers some top-level Bahamian crafts, including a selection of authentic straw work. Dozens of vendors sell everything from baskets to shell collages inside this vibrantly colored building. You can catch a shuttle bus from Atlantis to the center. ⊠ *Paradise Island Dr., Paradise Island.*

🏃 Activities

BOATING

Atlantis Marina

BOATING | The marina at Atlantis has 63 megayacht slips and room for yachts up to 240 feet. Stay here and you can enjoy all the amenities at Atlantis, including Aquaventure. ⊠ *Atlantis Paradise Island, Paradise Island* 🕾 *242/363–6068.*

Hurricane Hole Marina

BOATING | Ninety-slip Hurricane Hole Marina is on the Paradise Island side of the harbor and accommodates yachts over 200 feet. ⊠ *Paradise Island* 🕾 *242/363–3600.*

Paradise Island's The Ocean Club has a scenic golf course.

GOLF

Ocean Club Golf Course

GOLF | Designed by Tom Weiskopf, the Ocean Club Golf Course is a championship course surrounded by the ocean on three sides, which means that the views are incredible but the winds can get stiff. Call to check on current availability and up-to-date prices. (Those not staying at Atlantis or The Ocean Club Four Seasons Resort can play at management's discretion and at a higher rate.) The course is open daily from 6 am to sunset. ✉ *One&Only Ocean Club, Paradise Island Dr., Paradise Island* ☎ *242/363–6682* ⊕ *www.oceanclub.oneandonlyresorts. com* ✆ *$230–$295 for 18 holes (discounted after 1 pm); club rentals $70* 🏌 *18 holes, 7100 yards, par 72.*

SPAS

★ Mandara Spa at Atlantis

SPA/BEAUTY | Located at Atlantis but open to the public, the expansive, multistory Indonesian-inspired Mandara Spa has treatments utilizing traditions from around the world. Plan to spend more time than your treatment or service requires to enjoy the unisex relaxation lounge, hot and cold plunge pools, and the sauna and steam room. Use of the 15,000-square-foot fitness center is complimentary for a day when you spend more than $99 on spa or salon services. The full-service salon offers hair and nail treatments as well as tooth whitening, hair extensions, and waxing. Men can get the works at the barbershop. Both the spa and fitness center are open until 8 pm daily. ✉ *Atlantis Paradise Island Royal Towers, Casino Dr.* ☎ *242/363–3000* ⊕ *www.mandaraspa.com.*

★ The Ocean Club Spa

SPA/BEAUTY | Paradise Island's Four Seasons Ocean Club has one of the island's most luxurious and indulgent spa retreats. For the ultimate relaxation, treat yourself to the signature Bahamas Rhythm Massage combining breathing techniques, percussive instruments, and deep tissue massage; finish it up with the Sea Lavender & Sapphire Polish and Wrap to replenish your skin. With just eight villas, it's a good idea to book well in advance, particularly during high season. You can also have the treatment in your hotel room. ✉ *Four Seasons Resort, Paradise Island* ☎ *242/363–2501* 🌐 *www.fourseasons.com/oceanclub/spa.*

Cable Beach

From downtown Nassau, West Bay Street follows the coast west, past Arawak Cay to the Cable Beach strip. If you're not driving, catch the No. 10 jitney for a direct ride from downtown. This main drag runs the length of the new Baha Mar resort development, separating the golf course and green space from the resorts and beach. Walk or drive west of the megaresort for a smattering of smaller restaurants and local neighborhoods.

👁 Sights

The Caves

ARCHAEOLOGICAL SITE | These large limestone caverns that the waves sculpted over the eons are said to have sheltered the early Arawak Indians. An oddity perched right beside the road, they're worth a glance—although in truth, there's not much to see, as the dark interior doesn't lend itself to exploration. Across the street is a concrete viewing platform overlooking the ocean. Just a short drive west beyond the caves, on an island between traffic lanes, is **Conference Corner,** where U.S. president John F. Kennedy, Canadian prime minister John Diefenbaker, and British prime minister Harold Macmillan planted trees on the occasion of their 1962 summit in Nassau. ✉ *W. Bay St. and Blake Rd., Cable Beach* 🎟 *Free.*

⛱ Beaches

Adelaide Beach

BEACH—SIGHT | **FAMILY** | Time your visit to this far-flung beach on the island's southwestern shore to catch low tide, when the ocean recedes, leaving behind sandbanks and seashells. It's a perfect place to take the kids for a shallow-water dip in the sea, or for a truly private rendezvous. Popular with locals, you'll likely have the miles-long stretch all to yourself unless it's a public holiday. **Amenities:** none. **Best for:** solitude; swimming; walking. ✉ *Adelaide* 🎟 *Free.*

Cable Beach

BEACH—SIGHT | Hotels, including the massive Baha Mar resort development, dot the length of this 3-mile beach, so don't expect isolation. Music from hotel pool decks wafts out onto the sand, Jet Skis race up and down the waves, and vendors sell everything from shell jewelry to coconut drinks right from the shell. Access via new hotels may be limited, but join the locals and park at Goodman's Bay park on the eastern end of the beach. **Amenities:** parking (no fee); water sports. **Best for:** partiers; sunset; swimming; walking. ✉ *Cable Beach.*

Love Beach

BEACH—SIGHT | If you're looking for great snorkeling and some privacy, drive about 20 minutes west of Cable Beach. White sand shimmers in the sun and the azure waves gently roll ashore. About a mile offshore are 40 acres of coral reef known as the Sea Gardens. Access is not marked, just look for a vacant lot. **Amenities:** none. **Best for:** solitude; snorkeling; sunset ✉ *Gambier Village.*

🍴 Restaurants

Black Angus Steakhouse & Grill

$$$$ | **STEAKHOUSE** | This steak house offers some of the best certified Angus beef on the island. Bring your appetite if you're going to try the gigantic cowboy steak (28 or 32 ounces), which is carved right in front of you. **Known for:** plate-sized steaks; melt-in-your-mouth mashed potatoes; live jazz. [$] *Average main: $50* ✉ *Meliá Nassau Beach Resort, W.*

Cable Beach

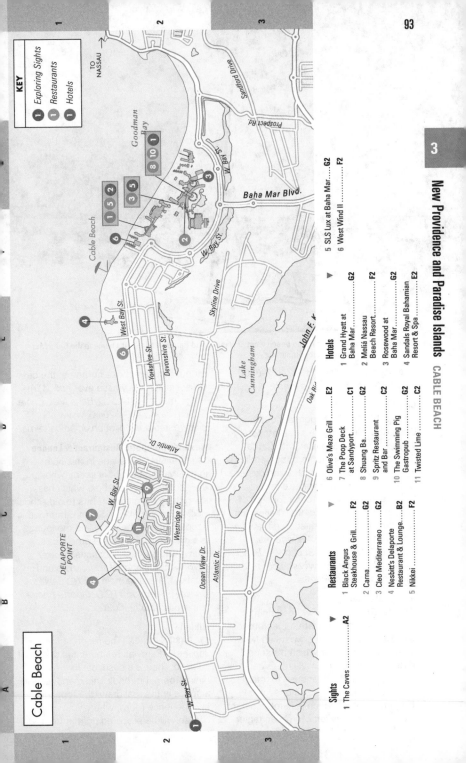

KEY
- 1 Exploring Sights
- 1 Restaurants
- 1 Hotels

TO NASSAU

Goodman Bay

Cable Beach

Baha Mar Blvd.

W. Bay St.

DELAPORTE POINT

Skyline Drive

Lake Cunningham

Oak Ri...

John F. K...

West Bay St.

Yorkshire St.

Devonshire St.

W. Bay St.

Atlantic Dr.

Westridge Dr.

Ocean View Dr.

W. Bay St.

Sandford Drive

Prospect Rd

3

New Providence and Paradise Islands CABLE BEACH

Sights ▶
1 The Caves A2

Restaurants ▶
1 Black Angus Steakhouse & Grill.......F2
2 Carna....................G2
3 Cleo Mediterraneo........G2
4 Nesbitt's Delaporte Restaurant & Lounge....B2
5 Nikkei F2

6 Olive's Meze Grill E2
7 The Poop Deck at Sandyport.............C1
8 Shuang Ba.............G2
9 Spritz Restaurant and Bar C2
10 The Swimming Pig Gastropub G2
11 Twisted Lime C2

Hotels ▶
1 Grand Hyatt at Baha Mar...............G2
2 Meliá Nassau Beach Resort...........F2
3 Rosewood at Baha Mar..............G2
4 Sandals Royal Bahamian Resort & Spa E2

5 SLS Lux at Baha Mar....G2
6 West Wind II F2

Cable Beach is the busiest island beach west of Nassau and Paradise Island. It's home to the Baha Mar resort, as well as several other resorts.

Bay St., Cable Beach ☎ *242/327–6200* 🌐 *www.melia.com* 🕓 *No lunch.*

Carna

$$$$ | **STEAKHOUSE** | Legendary butcher Dario Cecchini brings his contemporary steak house to Baha Mar with Carna. Start off with charcuterie or something from the raw bar: fresh shucked oysters with champagne mignonette or the seafood and shellfish tower for a bit of the best the sea has to offer. **Known for:** best cuts of beef; fresh-sourced raw bar; extensive wine list. [$] *Average main: $60* ✉ *Baha Mar near SLS, Cable Beach* ☎ *242/788–7250* 🌐 *www.sbe.com/restaurants/brands/carna.*

★ **Cleo Mediterraneo**

$$$ | **MEDITERRANEAN** | Award-winning chef Danny Elmaleh's latest Cleo outpost upholds the imaginative twists on Mediterranean cuisine for which his series of restaurants gained acclaim. Order hummus and baba ghanoush for starters, followed by grilled octopus or saganaki Halloumi cheese, which is flambéed right at the table. **Known for:** Moroccan tagine menu; tasty artichoke hummus; the best Brussels sprouts you've ever had. [$] *Average main: $40* ✉ *SLS, Baha Mar, Cable Beach* ☎ *242/788–8204* 🌐 *www.sbe.com/restaurants/locations/cleo-baha-mar.*

Nesbitt's Delaporte Restaurant & Lounge

$$ | **BAHAMIAN** | The vibe in this hole-in-the-wall restaurant is set by whoever controls the jukebox, which has everything from current hits to old-school R&B, to local Rake 'n' Scrape. The food is simple but hits the spot, and the lounge is a great place to meet some locals. **Known for:** late-night libations; greasy savory bites; hangout for tourists and locals. [$] *Average main: $20* ✉ *Cable Beach* ✣ *West of BTC Delaporte phone tower* ☎ *242/327–6036.*

Nikkei

$$$ | **ASIAN FUSION** | The menu at this Japanese-Peruvian restaurant is small but eclectic. There's a sushi bar in the main dining room, but book ahead and reserve a space in the real draw, the Teppanyaki Experience room, where your main course will be prepared right in front of you. **Known for:** hibachi experience; delicious conch ceviche; only local spot for Peruvian cuisine. $ *Average main: $35* ✉ *Meliá Nassau Beach Resort, W. Bay St., Cable Beach* ☎ *242/327–6000* ⊙ *No lunch.*

Olive's Meze Grill

$$$ | MEDITERRANEAN | Hip and trendy, this restaurant puts a fresh twist on Mediterranean classics. The fare is simple, but locally grown greens and fish caught in nearby waters make the meals special. **Known for:** flaming cheese lit table-side; all-you-can-drink mimosa or sangria weekend brunch; late-night weekend hot spot. $ *Average main: $35* ✉ *W. Bay St., Cable Beach* ☎ *242/676–5396* ⊕ *titanhospitalitygroup.com/meze-grill.*

The Poop Deck at Sandyport

$$$ | SEAFOOD | A more upscale version of the other Poop Deck in Nassau, this waterside restaurant has soaring ceilings, a pastel pink and aqua color scheme, and a dazzling view of the ocean. Seafood is the star on the menu here: shrimp, lobster, calamari, grouper, and, of course, conch. **Known for:** pick-your-own catch of the day; great ocean views; option to dine on the beach. $ *Average main: $36* ✉ *W. Bay St., Cable Beach* ☎ *242/327–3325* ⊕ *www.thepoopdecksandyport. com* ⊙ *Closed Mon.*

★ Shuang Ba

$$$ | CHINESE | With a team of chefs flown in from China, this is as close as you can get to authentic Chinese cuisine on the island. The menu includes dim sum for starters and the impressive Pork Pyramid, which is made with one piece of braised pork belly that is sliced into this strips and shaped into a pyramid. **Known for:** Peking duck; authentic Chinese dining experience; Baijiu Chinese liquor selection. $ *Average main: $40* ✉ *Baha Mar between Grand Hyatt and Rosewood, Cable Beach* ☎ *242/788–7867* ⊕ *bahamar.com/culinary/#dining* ⊙ *Closed Mon.–Tues. during the slow season.*

Spritz Restaurant and Bar

$$ | NORTHERN ITALIAN | FAMILY | This casual, open-air restaurant and bar overlooks the Sandyport Canal and the pedestrian-only streets of the Old Towne at Sandyport. Seating is limited, so reservations are recommended, especially for busy weekend nights. **Known for:** hand-tossed thin-crust pizzas; great spot for kids to run around; will cater to special dining needs. $ *Average main: $28* ✉ *Sandyport Olde Towne Marina Plaza, Cable Beach* ☎ *242/327–0762* ⊕ *www.spritzbahamas. com* ⊙ *No lunch Mon.*

The Swimming Pig Gastropub

$$ | AMERICAN | This bustling gastropub pays homage to the world-famous swimming pigs with its name and a few small paintings. The menu is mostly American-inspired—hearty burgers and flatbreads—with a few touches of English pub fare like the oxtail, Guinness pie, and fish-and-chips. **Known for:** 24 beers on tap; 24-hour kitchen service; hearty American and English bar and pub fare. $ *Average main: $28* ✉ *Baha Mar, Cable Beach* ☎ *242/788–7841.*

Twisted Lime

$$ | AMERICAN | This busy sports bar has something for everyone: indoors, the dining room and bar feature games on flatscreen TVs; outdoors, casual canal-front dining (think pub food like burgers and nachos) and drinks are available at high-tops or on plush sofas. The menu is quite extensive: fish tacos or nachos fiesta are good options for starters with local flair. **Known for:** dock and dine; sports fans' hangout; late-night food spot. $ *Average main: $30* ✉ *Sandyport Marina Village, Cable Beach* ☎ *242/327–0061* ⊕ *www. twistedlimebar.com.*

🛏 Hotels

Grand Hyatt at Baha Mar

$$ | RESORT | The largest property within the Baha Mar Resort is steps away from the ESPA spa and the Baha Mar

Casino—the largest in the Caribbean—and offers guests access to an array of other amenities even if it does lack some of the exclusivity of other hotels within the resort complex. **Pros:** plenty to do right on property; steps away from the casino, spa, and convention center; resort-view rooms face the nightly fountain show. **Cons:** long walk to the beach; hard to get away from it all; no access to upscale exclusive SLS and Rosewood pool areas. $ *Rooms from: $300* ✉ *Baha Mar Blvd., Cable Beach* ☎ *242/788–7800, 866/238–4218 reservations* ⊕ *bahamar.com/stay/#grand-hyatt* ⤳ *1800 rooms* ❍ *No meals.*

Meliá Nassau Beach Resort

$$$ | **RESORT** | Although the Meliá is not part of the Baha Mar resort next door, the property has embarked on a series of upgrades to keep pace with the changes to the neighborhood. **Pros:** easy access to Baha Mar amenities; lots of activities included; situated on a beautiful beach. **Cons:** large Baha Mar expansion construction site next door; standard rooms are in need of an upgrade; restaurants are hit-or-miss. $ *Rooms from: $360* ✉ *Cable Beach* ☎ *242/327–6000* ⊕ *www.melia.com* ⤳ *694 rooms* ❍ *All-inclusive.*

Rosewood at Baha Mar

$$$$ | **RESORT** | **FAMILY** | Luxurious touches abound at the most luxurious hotel within the sprawling Baha Mar Resort complex. **Pros:** access to all the Baha Mar amenities; situated on a stunning beach; luxurious accommodations. **Cons:** on the outer perimeter of the Baha Mar Resort complex; a long walk to some of the prime restaurants and amenities; sometimes too quiet. $ *Rooms from: $600* ✉ *Baha Mar Blvd., Cable Beach* ☎ *242/677–9000, 844/800–2242 reservations* ⊕ *www.rosewoodhotels.com/en/baha-mar* ⤳ *113 rooms, 87 suites* ❍ *No meals.*

★ Sandals Royal Bahamian Resort & Spa

$$$$ | **RESORT** | Cable Beach's most expensive all-inclusive has elegantly furnished rooms with views of the ocean, pool, or grounds replete with pillars and faux-Roman statuary, as well as personal butler service and a room that opens up to a private pool for the ultimate indulgence. **Pros:** no children; lovely setting; private offshore cay. **Cons:** couples only; need car or taxi to go into town; convention center popular for local functions. $ *Rooms from: $750* ✉ *W. Bay St., Cable Beach* ☎ *242/327–6400, 800/726–3257* ⊕ *www.sandals.com* ⤳ *404 rooms* ❍ *All-inclusive.*

★ SLS Lux at Baha Mar

$$$$ | **RESORT** | The first international property for the SLS brand—which emphasizes style, luxury, and service—constantly reminds you that you are in the Bahamas, starting with the magnificent ocean-view lobby. **Pros:** access to top Baha Mar amenities; luxurious SLS style and service; a variety of exclusive day and night entertainment locations. **Cons:** ongoing construction on west side of hotel; long walk to rest of Baha Mar property; service and style comes with a price. $ *Rooms from: $545* ✉ *Baha Mar Blvd., Cable Beach* ☎ *242/788–8200, 866/225–4561 reservations* ⊕ *www.slshotels.com/bahamar* ⤳ *299 rooms* ❍ *No meals.*

West Wind II

$$ | **RESORT** | **FAMILY** | Privacy is the lure of these time-share villas, with balconies and patios overlooking oceans and pools on Cable Beach's west end, 6 miles from downtown. **Pros:** fully stocked kitchens; condos sleep six; right on Cable Beach. **Cons:** no major activities; need car or taxi to go downtown; housekeeping, beach towels, and toiletries additional cost. $ *Rooms from: $300* ✉ *W. Bay St., Cable Beach* ☎ *242/327–7211, 242/327–7019* ⊕ *www.westwindii.com* ⤳ *54 villas* ❍ *No meals.*

Nightlife

Baha Mar Casino

CASINOS | With 100,000 square feet dedicated to gaming, this is the largest casino in the entire Caribbean. Out-of-the-ordinary, floor-to-ceiling windows keep gamers connected to the beautiful Bahamian ocean as they take a chance on 1,140 slot machines and 119 table games or bet in the state-of-art Baha Mar Race and Sports Book. There's also the option of gaming in the eclusive high limit-slot area or one of five reserved high roller gamng salons. ⊠ *Baha Mar Resort, Baha Mar Blvd., Cable Beach* ☎ *888/720–0923* ⊕ *www.bahamar.com/casino.*

Bond

DANCE CLUBS | The only nightclub this side of the island is located inside Baha Mar and keeps the party going all night long. International celebrity DJ's make sure the vibe is always on point and the team of mixologists offer specialty handcrafted cocktails. ⊠ *Baha Mar, Cable Beach* ⊕ *www.bahamar.com/bond.*

★ Monkey Bar

BARS/PUBS | The SLS lobby comes to life at night as this lively spot heats up and takes over. The drinks flow from 11 am until midnight during the week and until 1 am on weekends when there is also a DJ. This spot is popular with locals and hotel guests alike. ⊠ *SLS, Baha Mar, Cable Beach* ⊕ *www.slshotels.com/bahamar/day-nightlife.*

★ Skybar

BARS/PUBS | Enjoy some of the best views of the island, the Baha Mar Resort, and the ocean from the island's only rooftop bar. The open-air pavilion on top of the SLS hotel is a great spot to enjoy sundowners. World renowned DJ's ensure the vibe is just right. ⊠ *SLS, Baha Mar, Cable Beach* ⊕ *www.slshotels.com/bahamar/day-nightlife.*

🛍 Shopping

★ The Current

ART GALLERIES—ARTS | FAMILY | In addition to the largest collection of Bahamian art which is housed throughout various rooms and spaces on the property, there is an eclectic art gallery beneath the Grand Hyatt entrance. Exhibits change frequently and the shop is a great place to pick up unique souvenirs. You can also sign up for one of the art classes—acrylic pour, leaf prints, and landscape painting are just a few available. ⊠ *Baha Mar, Cable Beach* ☎ *242/788–8000* ⊕ *www.bahamar.com/art.*

🏃 Activities

GOLF

Royal Blue Golf Course

GOLF | You will get two different golf experiences in one golf course at Baha Mar, which was created from the island's oldest course. It has stunning ocean views on the front nine and a back nine taking players through a native forest all the way to the natural Lake Cunningham. Tee locations are placed each morning by the golf pros, ensuring a unique experience every time you hit the course. A bat cave on the course features a protected indigenous bat species, and more than 70 species of birds have been spotted on the course and surrounding lake. This new course is challenging for players at all levels. Nonresort guests are welcome to book a tee time. Rates vary for guests and nonguests and on weekdays versus weekends. ⊠ *Baha Mar Resort, Baha Mar Blvd., Cable Beach* ☎ *242/327–6000* ⊕ *www.bahamar.com* 🖅 *$250–$275 resort guests; $295–$325 nonresort guests* 🏌 *18 holes, 7189 yards, par 72.*

PADDLEBOARDING

★ Pappasurf

WATER SPORTS | FAMILY | There's no better way to explore the crystal-clear blue Bahamian ocean than gliding along the surface. Experienced paddlers can rent boards from this outfitter, or you can sign up for lessons. For a truly unique experience, book a sunset ($50) or nightglow ($65) tour. Both last for about 90 minutes and include all equipment and experienced guides. Launch locations change depending on weather conditions, but they'll let you know in advance where to meet. ⊠ *W. Bay St., Cable Beach* ☎ *242/327–3853* ⊕ *www.pappasurf.com.*

SPAS
ESPA at Baha Mar

SPA/BEAUTY | Encompassing 30,000 square feet, the only ESPA flagship spa in the Caribbean is also one of the largest spas in the region. Indulge in massages, facials, and body treatments using a variety of local products designed to soothe and relax. Treatments are done in one of 24 rooms, two of which are designed to accommodate couples. Plan some extra time before and after to relax in the sauna and steam rooms—there are male-and female-specific as well as unisex areas—or in the serene Relax Lounge, the social Chill Zone, or on the outdoor Ocean View Terraces. ⊠ *Baha Mar Casino & Hotel, Baha Mar Blvd., Cable Beach* ☎ *242/788–7800* ⊕ *www.bahamar.com/ experiences/spa.*

Western New Providence

Immediately west of Cable Beach, the hotel strip gives way to residential neighborhoods interspersed with shops, restaurants, and cafés. Homes become more and more posh the farther west you go; Lyford Cay—the island's original gated community—is home to the original 007, Sean Connery. Hang a left at the Lyford Cay roundabout, and you'll eventually come across the historic Clifton Heritage Park, the local brewery where Kalik and Heineken are brewed and bottled, a new upscale second home development whose financiers include

golfers Ernie Els and Tiger Woods, and finally the sleepy settlement of Adelaide.

The loop around the island's west and south coasts can be done in a couple of hours by car or scooter, but take some time for lunch and a swim along the way. Unless you're being taken around by a taxi or local, it's best to return along the same route, as internal roads can get confusing.

Sights

Adelaide Village
SCENIC DRIVE | The small community on New Providence's southwestern coast sits placidly, like a remnant of another era, between Adelaide Road and the ocean. It was first settled during the early 1830s by Africans who had been captured and loaded aboard slave ships bound for the New World. They were rescued on the high seas by the British Royal Navy, and the first group of liberated slaves reached Nassau in 1832. Today, there are two sides to Adelaide—the few dozen families who grow vegetables, raise chickens, and inhabit well-worn, pastel-painted wooden houses, shaded by casuarina, mahogany, and palm trees; and the more upscale beach cottages that are mostly used as weekend getaways. The village has a primary school, a few small grocery stores, and a few restaurants serving native foods. ⊠ *Adelaide* 🖾 *Free.*

Clifton Heritage Park
ARCHAEOLOGICAL SITE | **FAMILY** | It's quite a distance from just about any hotel you could stay at, but for history and nature buffs, this national park, rescued from the hands of developers, is worth the drive. Situated on a prehistoric Lucayan Village dating back to AD 1000–1500, Clifton Heritage Park allows you to walk through the ruins of slave quarters from an 18th-century plantation. The site can claim ties to pop culture as well because a number of hit movies have been

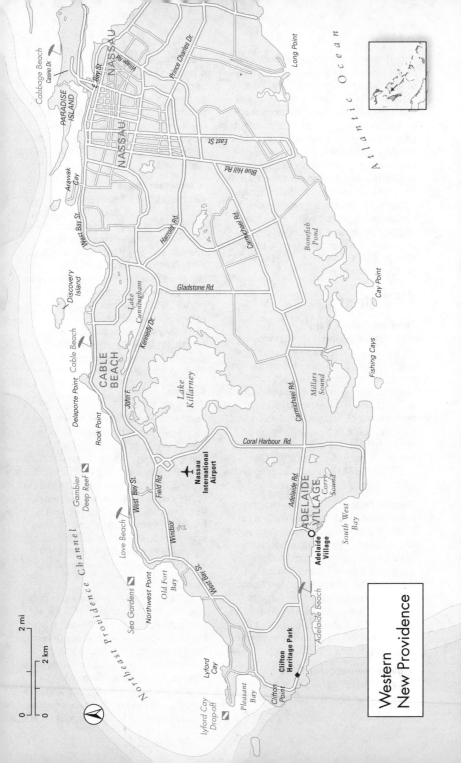

Western
New Providence

0 2 mi

0 2 km

Atlantic Ocean

Northeast Providence Channel

Cabbage Beach

Casino Dr.

PARADISE ISLAND

NASSAU

E. Bay St.

Village Rd.

Prince Charles Dr.

Long Point

Arawak Cay

West Bay St.

East St.

Blue Hill Rd.

Harrold Rd.

Carmichael Rd.

Bonefish Pond

Cay Point

Discovery Island

Gladstone Rd.

Lake Cunningham

Kennedy Dr.

CABLE BEACH

Cable Beach

Delaporte Point

Rock Point

John F.

Lake Killarney

Fishing Cays

Millars Sound

Carmichael Rd.

Coral Harbour Rd.

Gambier

Deep Reef

West Bay St.

Field Rd.

Nassau International Airport

Adelaide Rd.

ADELAIDE VILLAGE

Corry Sound

Love Beach

Windsor

South West Bay

Adelaide Village

Northwest Point

Old Fort Bay

West Bay St.

Sea Gardens

Adelaide Beach

Lyford Cay

Pleasant Bay

Clifton Point

Clifton Heritage Park

Lyford Cay Drop-off

filmed on land and sea here. Book one of the many tours ahead of time—they offer snorkeling out to the Coral Reef Sculpture Garden, nature walks, bush medicine and bird-watching tours, and ATV and buggy tours. Be sure to walk the path from the main parking lot toward the west, where you can enjoy the peace and quiet of the Sacred Space and admire the African women carved out of casuarina wood by local artist Antonius Roberts. Naturalists will enjoy walking along the paths lined with native flora and fauna that lead to wooden decks overlooking mangrove swamps. ✉ *Clifton Pier, W. Bay St., Clifton* ☎ *242/803–6870* 🌐 *cliftonheritage.net.*

🍴 Restaurants

Cocoplum Bistro & Bar

$$$ | **MEDITERRANEAN** | Whether you opt for indoor or outdoor seating, you'll find yourself in a cool, funky, tropical garden setting at this new Nassau hot spot. The food is an island twist on traditional French and Mediterranean cuisine. **Known for:** cool, sophisticated ambience; traditional beef tartare; welcoming service. [$] *Average main: $38* ✉ *Harbour Green Shopping Center, Lyford Cay* ☎ *242/677–6776* 🌐 *www.cocoplumbistro.com* 🕒 *Closed Sun. and Mon.*

Compass Point

$$$ | **AMERICAN** | This restaurant and bar is one of the best sunset-watching spots on the island. Sit indoors or out on the terrace overlooking the ocean and enjoy the simple Bahamian and island-style American fare for breakfast, lunch, and dinner. **Known for:** incredible sunsets; live music; late-night kitchen. [$] *Average main: $35* ✉ *W. Bay St., Gambier Village* ☎ *242/327–4500* 🌐 *www.compasspointbeachresort.com.*

★ Dino's Gourmet Conch Salad

$ | **BAHAMIAN** | Conch salad is the draw at the popular roadside joint; it might take half an hour or longer to get your made-to-order food, but you can grab a stool and order a refreshing (and intoxicating) gin and coconut water while you wait. If you're in a hurry, call ahead to place your order. **Known for:** cash only; great photo-op spot; signature tropical conch salad. [$] *Average main: $12* ✉ *Gambier Village* ☎ *242/377–7798* 💳 *No credit cards.*

★ Mahogany House

$$$$ | **ECLECTIC** | A favorite with the upscale Lyford Cay crowd, Mahogany House is sophisticated simplicity at its best. Whether you're dressed to the nines or sporting flip-flops, you're bound to feel both comfortable and welcome at this dining spot and lively bar. **Known for:** private wine cellar dining room; specialty ingredients like buffalo pork belly; vast selection of cured meats and cheeses. [$] *Average main: $45* ✉ *The Island House, Western Rd.* ☎ *242/698–6300* 🌐 *www.the-island-house.com/dining* 🕒 *No lunch weekends.*

★ Shima

$$$ | **ASIAN FUSION** | Enjoy authentic Southeast Asian–inspired cuisine at this popular restaurant and bar with views overlooking the ritzy Lyford Cay Marina. The little fire symbols peppered throughout the menu indicate their propensity for spice, but they're happy to tone things down if you ask. **Known for:** authentic Asian cuisine; happening weekend brunch; extremely spicy food. [$] *Average main: $34* ✉ *Upstairs at the Island House, Lyford Cay* ☎ *242/698–6300* 🌐 *www.the-island-house.com/dining.*

Studio Cafe

$$ | **ECLECTIC** | This cozy upstairs restaurant pays homage to its former life as Compass Point Studio where Bob Marley, the Rolling Stones, and James Brown used to record. In addition to Asian-fusion cuisine, they have a burger named after the B52s, open mic on Monday, an acoustic brunch on Sunday, and rich desserts. **Known for:** Guinness chocolate mousse cake; laid-back delicious brunch;

The cottages at Compass Point are known for their whimsical colors.

theme nights. $ *Average main: $20* ⊠ *Western New Providence* ☎ *242/677–3991* ⊕ *www.studiocafebahamas.com.*

☕ Coffee and Quick Bites

★ Louis and Steen's New Orleans Coffeehouse

$ | **CAJUN** | This relaxed, family-owned coffee shop offers pour-overs, cold brew, traditional macchiatos and cappuccinos made with beans that are roasted on-site and brewed with love. The pastries are made fresh each morning and the New Orleans-inspired menu includes a variety of sandwiches, salads, and beignets. **Known for:** treating customers like family; delicious coffee; incredible ocean views. $ *Average main: $18* ⊠ *West Bay Street, Western New Providence* ☎ *242/601–9907* ⊕ *www.louisandsteens.com* ⊘ *Closed mid-Aug.–early Sept.*

🛏 Hotels

Compass Point

$$$ | **RESORT** | This whimsical-looking hotel made up of brightly colored one- and two-story cottages offers a relaxing alternative to many of the area's major resorts. **Pros:** fun and funky accommodations; access to incredible private beach; romantic sunset views. **Cons:** in flight path; not ideal for children; expensive taxi ride to town. $ *Rooms from: $375* ⊠ *W. Bay St., Gambier Village* ☎ *242/327–4500* ⊕ *www.compasspointbeachresort.com* 🛏 *18 cottages* ⦿| *No meals.*

★ The Island House

$$$ | **B&B/INN** | The antithesis of the big resorts typically found in New Providence, The Island House delivers casual sophistication with high-end yet understated amenities and features at every turn. **Pros:** tranquil and private; near the airport; variety of amenities for sports and wellness enthusiasts. **Cons:** far from main attractions; no beach nearby; caters primarily to fitness-lovers.

[$] *Rooms from: $395* ✉ *Mahogany Hill, Western Rd., Western New Providence* ☎ *242/698–6300* 🌐 *www.the-island-house.com* 🛏 *30 suites* 🍴 *No meals.*

Orange Hill Beach Inn

$ | **B&B/INN** | If you prefer down-home coziness over slick glamour, then this basic hotel—on the site of a former orange plantation perched on a hilltop overlooking the ocean—is the place to stay. **Pros:** close to beach; family-friendly. **Cons:** long distance from town; not many activities; basic accommodations. [$] *Rooms from: $150* ✉ *W. Bay St., Gambier Village* ☎ *242/327–7157* 🌐 *www.orangehill.com* 🛏 *32 rooms* 🍴 *No meals.*

★ **A Stone's Throw Away**

$$ | **B&B/INN** | Featuring seaside comfort in fashionable surroundings, this hotel advertised as a bed-and-breakfast is actually a luxurious hideaway—the three-story colonial-style inn with wraparound verandahs is perched on a limestone cliff overlooking the beach, 13 miles west of Nassau. **Pros:** serene; secluded public-beach access; friendly staff. **Cons:** in flight path; long distance from anything else; hotel access up a steep staircase cut out of the limestone hill. [$] *Rooms from: $299* ✉ *Tropical Garden Rd. and W. Bay St., Gambier Village* ☎ *242/327–7030* 🌐 *www.astonesthrowaway.com* 🛏 *10 rooms* 🍴 *Free Breakfast.*

Activities

Lyford Cay

BOATING | At the western end of New Providence, Lyford Cay, a posh development for the rich and famous, has an excellent 74-slip marina, but there is limited availability for the humble masses. ☎ *242/362–4131.*

Chapter 4

GRAND BAHAMA ISLAND

4

Updated by
Jessica Robertson

👁 **Sights**
★★★★★

🍴 **Restaurants**
★★★★★

🛏 **Hotels**
★★★☆☆

🛍 **Shopping**
★★☆☆☆

🍸 **Nightlife**
★★★☆☆

WELCOME TO
GRAND BAHAMA ISLAND

TOP REASONS TO GO

★ **Take endless strolls on your own private beach.** Sprawling, reef-protected shoreline and cays offer more than 50 miles of secluded white-sand beaches along the southern shore.

★ **Go down under.** Between the shipwrecks, caves, coral reefs, and abundant marine life are some of the country's most varied and vivid snorkeling and diving.

★ **Get your green on.** Learn about the island's ecology underwater and among the mangroves where you can feed stingrays or catch sight of spotted dolphins and their calves.

★ **Party at the weekly fish fry or a beach bonfire.** Head to Smith Point to feast and party with locals, or dance around the bonfire at Taino by the Sea with all-you-can-eat authentic Bahamian cuisine and Bahama Mama cocktails.

★ **Swim with the dolphins or feed the sharks.** Several professional dive shops stand ready to introduce you to some of the ocean's most interesting characters.

Only 52 miles off Palm Beach, Florida, 96-mile-long Grand Bahama is one of the chain's northernmost islands. Freeport and Lucaya are its main cities, comprising the second-largest metropolitan area in the Bahamas. Lucaya sees the most action, as Freeport struggles to regain ground lost in the hurricanes and financial setbacks of the last decade. The town of West End, once a quiet, colorful fishing village, was nearly decimated during Hurricane Matthew in October 2016, but thankfully was spared the worst that Hurricane Dorian had to offer in 2019. The residents have pulled together to reconstruct their homes, and the conch shacks that lined the road along the coastline are slowly being rebuilt. Its upscale Old Bahama Bay Resort and marina are the extent of tourism on this end of the island. East of Freeport-Lucaya was leveled by Hurricane Dorian. Small fishing settlements experienced extensive damage and all of the rustic bars, restaurants, and hotels were destroyed. The storm left a mess

behind at the Lucayan National Park, but it was expected to be restored by the Bahamas National Trust. Secluded beaches and undeveloped forest stretching for 60 miles were all impacted by the hurricane and little was left, so if you do venture east, be sure to pack all that you will need for the day.

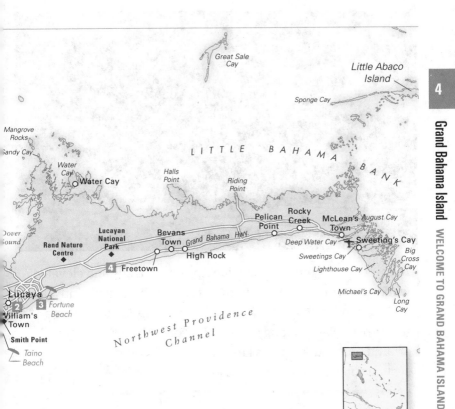

1 Freeport. The working end of Grand Bahama, Freeport is convenient to the airport and harbor for visitors in transit. Rand Nature Centre and The Bahamian Brewery make the area worth a visit, although downtown looks depressed and forlorn as developers await economic recovery.

2 Port Lucaya. Freeport's beachfront counterpart is dominated by two of the island's largest hotels and resorts and Port Lucaya Marketplace (the island's best shopping).

3 Greater Lucaya. Lucayan Beach along Port Lucaya can get crowded, but Taino Beach, Coral Beach, and Fortune Beach are nearby for those who prefer more space and solitude; you'll find additional hotels and restaurants here as well.

4 Greater Grand Bahama. The bulk of the island lies on either side of the neighboring metropolitan duo of Freeport and Lucaya. Escaping town means discovering treasures such as Paradise Cove and Lucayan National Park, in addition to remote beaches, time-stilled fishing villages, and wooded land the locals refer to as the "bush."

LUCAYAN NATIONAL PARK

In this extraordinary 40-acre land preserve, trails and elevated walkways wind through a natural forest of wild tamarind and gumbo-limbo trees, past an observation platform, over a mangrove swamp, along a postcard-worthy beach, and in and around one of the world's largest explored underwater cave systems (more than 6 miles long).

Twenty-five miles east of Lucaya, the park contains examples of the island's five ecosystems: beach, hardwood forest, mangroves, rocky coppice, and pine forest. From the designated parking lot, you can enter the caves at two access points; one is closed in June and July for the bat-nursing season. Across the highway from the caves, two trails form a loop. Creek Trail's boardwalk showcases impressive interpretive signage, and crosses a mangrove-clotted tidal creek to Gold Rock Beach, claimed by Grand Bahama's Ministry of Tourism to be the island's "welcome mat." A narrow strand of white sand at high tide, and an expansive white-sand playground at low tide, this lightly visited beach is edged by some of the island's highest dunes and a picturesque jewel-tone sea.

Visitors will find subtle treasures no matter what time of year they explore. Summer can be overbearingly hot for walking. However, that's also when certain orchids and other plants flower. Migrating birds and cooler temperatures make October–April optimal, especially mornings and low tide, when birds are most plentiful.

BEST WAYS TO EXPLORE

By Kayak. A kayak launch, near a beach where parts of the *Pirates of the Caribbean* movies were filmed, lies just east of the park's parking lot on the south side. From here paddlers can work their way through mangrove forest to the beach and Gold Rock Creek.

Underwater. Snorkeling is popular around Gold Rock Beach and its eponymous offshore Gold Rock. Certified cave divers can explore the intricate underwater network with Underwater Explorers Society (UNEXSO).

On Foot. Trails come in two parts. On the north side of the highway at the parking lot, one trail takes you into Ben's Cave and the Burial Mound Cave, where ancient Lucayan remains and artifacts have been discovered. A tricky spiral staircase descends into the dark depths of the former, and an easier wooden staircase to the latter. At both, observation platforms accommodate visitors who want to peer into the caves' clear depths. Across the highway, two flat, easy trails form a loop to the beach. Creek Trail (0.2 mile) is the easiest because its boardwalk is newer and more elevated. Birds are more abundant here in the tidal creek with its low forest of mangroves at your feet. Mangrove Swamp Trail (0.3 mile)

tends to be wet at high tide, and its boardwalk more difficult to negotiate (especially for small feet). Take one to the beach and the other to return to see the full range of environment here.

PETERSON CAY NATIONAL PARK

Only accessible by boat or a long swim, Peterson Cay National Park, one of the Bahamas' smallest national parks, takes up 1½ acres 1 mile offshore from Barbary Beach. The gorgeous, usually deserted beach and lively marine life make it worth the effort of snorkeling the reef or enjoying a quiet picnic. However, vegetation on the cay is salt-stunted and scrubby, so shade is scarce, but lively hermit crabs are abundant. All wildlife is protected in the park by the Bahamas National Trust, including ¼ mile of surrounding marine environment. Local ecotour operators lead kayak and snorkel excursions.

FUN FACT

A species of crustacean labeled *Speleonectes lucayensis* was discovered here and exists exclusively in the caverns of Lucayan National Park, where its population is protected. The rare, cave-dwelling Remipedia has no eyes or pigmentation.

4

Grand Bahama Island   LUCAYAN NATIONAL PARK

Natural beauty conspires with resort vitality to make Grand Bahama Island one of the Bahamas' most well-rounded, diverse destinations. In its two main towns, Freeport and Lucaya, visitors can find what the more bustling Nassau has to offer: resort hotels, a variety of restaurants, golfing, and duty-free shopping. But unlike New Providence, the touristy spots take up only a small portion of an island that, on the whole, consists of uninhabited stretches of sand and forest.

Prior to the development of Freeport, West End (the capital of Grand Bahama Island) was the epicenter of the Bahamas' logging industry and a playground for the wealthy in the 1920s. The fate of Grand Bahama changed in the 1950s when American financier Wallace Groves envisioned Grand Bahama's grandiose future as a tax-free shipping port. The Bahamian government signed an agreement that set in motion the development of a planned city, an airport, roads, waterways, and utilities as well as the port. From that agreement, the city of Freeport—and later, Lucaya—evolved. The past decade's hurricanes and economic downfall have demolished Freeport's resort glamour entirely and have left Lucaya struggling to stay afloat. That said, there are lots of gems, particularly for someone looking for relaxation on spectacular beaches or opportunities to explore nature.

Not much else on the island has changed since the early days, however. Outside of the Freeport-Lucaya commercial and resort area, fishing settlements remain, albeit now with electricity and paved roads. The East End is Grand Bahama's "back-to-nature" side, where Caribbean yellow pine-and-palmetto forest stretches for 60 miles, interrupted by the occasional small settlement. Unfortunately, most of these settlements were destroyed by Hurricane Dorian in September 2019, leaving little to see aside from the natural features, and even those have been altered by the storm. Little seaside villages with white churches and concrete-block houses painted in bright pastels once filled in the landscape between Freeport and West End, however a category 4 hurricane in 2016 nearly wiped them all out, and with the poor economy, rebuilding has been slow. Many of these settlements are more than 100 years old.

Planning

When to Go

As one of the northernmost Bahama Islands, Grand Bahama experiences temperatures dipping into the 60s with highs in the mid-70s in January and February, so you may need a jacket and wet suit. On the upside, the migrant bird population swells and diversifies during that time of year. High tourist season (which means seasonal crowds and increased room rates) runs from Christmas to Easter, peaking during spring break (late February to mid-April), when the weather is the most agreeable. October through mid-December can also exhibit good weather, so long as there hasn't been a particularly active hurricane season. Almost daily isolated thunderstorms never last more than a half hour, and the average temperatures steadily decrease from the high 80s at the beginning of October, to high 70s by mid-December.

Summers can get oppressively hot (into the mid and high 90s) and muggy; unless you're planning on doing a lot of snorkeling, diving, and other water sports, you may want to schedule your trip for cooler months. Afternoon thunderstorms and occasional tropical storms and hurricanes are also common in summer. The island averages around 20 days of rain per month from June to September, but it usually falls briefly in the afternoon. The good news is that hotel rates plummet and diving and fishing conditions are great.

Festivals

WINTER
Festival Noel

ARTS FESTIVALS | Since 1993, Festival Noel has marked the official start to the Christmas season. Traditionally held the first Friday evening in December at the Rand Nature Centre, this wine- and food-tasting event and art show displays local talent. Proceeds aid the Bahamas National Trust for the development and restoration of national parks on Grand Bahama Island. ⊠ *Rand Nature Centre, East Settler's Way, Freeport* ✛ *Across street from Sir Jack Hayward Junior High School* ☏ *242/352–5438.*

New Year's Day Junkanoo Parade

CULTURAL FESTIVALS | Junkanoo is the national festival of the Bahamas, named after an African tribal chief named "John Canoe," who demanded the right to celebrate with his people after being brought to the West Indies in slavery. Starting in the evening on January 1, and into the early morning hours, the downtown streets of Freeport come alive with larger-than-life costumed dancers jumping to the sounds of drums, whistles, and cowbells. At the end of January, watch local primary and secondary students take to the streets in the same colorful, cultural garb for Junior Junkanoo.

SPRING
Dog Days Half Marathon

RUNNING | FAMILY | Held every March, this fundraiser for the Grand Bahama Humane Society has grown in popularity since its inception in 2015. There's something for everyone: if you can't handle a half marathon, try out the 10k, 5k, or just the 1-mile fun run, where locals run, walk, and clown around with their dogs in tow. Stay after the race to swim at the beach beside the finish line, and to join the after-party. ⊠ *Bahamas Adventures, Jolly Roger Dr., Lucaya* ✛ *On Jolly Roger Dr., next to Taino Beach Resort* ⊕ *www. grandbahamadogdayshalfmarathon.com.*

SUMMER

BASRA's Bernie Butler Swim Race and Beach Party

FESTIVALS | Every summer a party crowd gathers for the Bahamas Air Sea Rescue Association's annual swim race and daylong beach bash. Grand Bahama residents of all ages swim the sea in honor and support of BASRA's volunteer force, who in conjunction with the Bahamas Defense Force and the U.S. Coast Guard help people in distress. Live music, food and drink tents, and a bikini-friendly, end-of-summer party atmosphere make this a memorable event. ⊠ *Coral Beach, off Royal Palm Way and Coral Rd.* ⊹ *Behind Coral Beach Bar* ⊕ *basragrandbahama. com.*

Grand Bahama Regatta and Heritage Festival

FESTIVAL | Sailing sloops from throughout the country meet in July for various sailing races, and crowd-pleasing favorite, the sculling competition. Onshore festivities take place at Smith's Point and include Junkanoo parades, dancing, live music, and food and drink. ⊠ *Smith's Point.*

FALL

Conchman Triathlon

FESTIVAL | The annual Conchman Triathlon at Taino Beach the first weekend in November is a swimming-running-bicycling competition for amateurs of all ages that raises funds for local charities. International applicants welcome. ⊠ *Taino Beach* ⊕ *www.conchmantriathlon.com.*

Getting Here and Around

AIR

Grand Bahama International Airport (FPO)

is about 6 minutes from downtown Freeport and about 10 minutes from Port Lucaya. Several international carriers offer direct service to Grand Bahama from various U.S. gateways, but you can also connect in Nassau on regional carriers, including Bahamasair. No bus service is available between the airport and hotels. Metered taxis meet all incoming flights, although most of the resorts can make arrangements ahead of time for you, for a fee. Rides cost about $15 for two to Freeport, or $22 to Lucaya; see posted signs for fixed rates. The price drops to $4 per person with larger groups. There's also an airport in **West End (WTD),** but it's strictly for private planes and charters.

CONTACTS Grand Bahama Airport Company (MYGF). ⊠ *Grand Bahama International Airport* ☎ *242/350–4233* ⊕ *www.free-portcontainerport.com.*

BOAT AND FERRY

Balearia Caribbean sails from Fort Lauderdale's Port Everglades and provides fast-ferry service, making a day trip possible, while Bahamas Paradise Cruise Line sails overnight from West Palm Beach, offering a more traditional cruise-ship experience, with two-night Grand Bahama hotel packages available. Taxis meet all ships.

BUS

Buses (usually minivans) are an inexpensive way to travel the 4 miles between downtown Freeport and Port Lucaya Marketplace daily until 8 pm. The fare is $1. Buses from Freeport to the West End cost $5 each way; to the East End, $15. Exact change is required. It should be noted that although this is a good way for the budget-conscious traveler to get around, these buses don't run on an exact schedule, and are often not in prime mechanical condition.

CAR

If you plan to drive around the island, it's cheaper and easier to rent a car than to hire a taxi. You can rent vehicles from local and major U.S. agencies at the airport. Calling ahead to reserve a car is recommended. Cars can range from $40/day to $125/day depending on the agency and length of rental.

CONTACTS AVIS. ⊠ *Grand Bahama International Airport, Freeport*

☎ *242/351–2847, 242/352–7666* ⊕ *www. avis.com.* **Brad's Car Rental.** ✉ *Grand Bahama International Airport, Freeport* ☎ *242/352–7930, 954/703–5246* ⊕ *www. bradscarrental.com.* **Hertz Rent-a-Car.** ✉ *Grand Bahama International Airport, Freeport* ☎ *242/352–9250, 242/352–3297* ⊕ *www.hertz.com.* **KSR Car Rental.** ✉ *Grand Bahama International Airport, Freeport* ☎ *242/351–5737* ⊕ *www.ksrrentacar.biz.*

SCOOTER

CONTACTS Island Jeep and Car Rentals. ☎ *242/373–4001, 242/727–2207* ⊕ *www. islandjeepcarrental.com.*

TAXI

Taxi fares are fixed (but generally you're charged a flat fee for routine trips; see posted trip fares at the airport) at $3 for the first ¼ mile and 40¢ for each additional ¼ mile. After two people, additional passengers are $3 each. Taxis are available outside of the big resorts or you can call the Grand Bahama Taxi Union for pickup.

CONTACTS Grand Bahama Taxi Union. ☎ *242/352–7101.*

Hotels

Grand Bahama accommodations remain some of the Bahamas' most affordable, especially those away from the beach. The majority of these provide free shuttle service to the nearest stretch of sand. The island's more expensive hotels are beachfront, with the exception of Pelican Bay. These include the all-inclusive Lighthouse Pointe at The Grand Lucayan; Viva Wyndham Fortuna Beach, an all-inclusive east of Port Lucaya; and West End's elegant Old Bahama Bay Resort & Yacht Harbour. Small apartment complexes and time-share rentals are economical alternatives, especially if you're planning to stay for more than a few days.

Rates post-Easter through December 14 tend to be 25%–30% lower than those charged during the rest of the year.

Restaurants

The Grand Bahama dining scene stretches well beyond traditional Bahamian cuisine. The resorts and shopping centers have eateries that serve everything from incredible curries and sushi to fine Continental and creative Pacific Rim specialties. For a true Bahamian dining experience, look for restaurants named after the owner or cook—such as Tony Macaroni's, Tanya's, or Bishop's.

A native fish fry takes place every Wednesday evening at Smith's Point, east of Port Lucaya (taxi drivers know the way). Here you can sample fresh fish, sweet-potato bread, conch salad, and all the fixings cooked outdoors at the beach. It's a great opportunity to meet local residents and taste real Bahamian cuisine—and there's no better place than seaside under the pines and palms.

Note: A gratuity or "service charge" (15%) is often added to the bill automatically; be sure to check your total before adding an additional tip. Restaurant prices are based on the median main course price at dinner, excluding gratuity, typically 15% and VAT, which is often automatically added to the bill. Hotel prices are for two people in a standard double room in high season, excluding service and 6%–12% of various taxes.

WHAT IT COSTS in Dollars			
$	**$$**	**$$$**	**$$$$**
RESTAURANTS			
under $20	$20–$30	$31–$40	over $40
HOTELS			
under $200	$200–$300	$301–$400	over $400

Nightlife

For evening and late-night entertainment, Port Lucaya is filled with restaurants and bars. Throughout the week there's live entertainment in the middle square; the best nights are Friday and Saturday. Other options include bonfire beach parties at Taino by the Sea, the Wednesday-night fish fry at Smith's Point, or taking a sunset cruise through the canals.

Shopping

In the stores, shops, and boutiques in Port Lucaya Marketplace you can find duty-free goods costing up to 40% less than what you might pay back home. At the numerous perfume shops, fragrances are often sold at a sweet-smelling 25% below U.S. prices. Be sure to limit your haggling to the straw markets.

Shops in Lucaya are open Monday–Saturday from 9 am to 6 pm. Stores may stay open later at the Port Lucaya Marketplace. Straw markets, grocery stores, some boutiques, and drugstores are open on Sunday.

Activities

BOATING CHARTERS

Private boat charters for up to four people average about $100 per person and up for half a day. Bahamian law limits the catching of game fish to six each of dolphinfish, kingfish, tuna, and wahoo per vessel.

Bonefish Folley & Sons at Blue Marlin Cove

BOATING | Committed to giving you the best fishing experience possible, Bonefish Folley & Sons will take you deep-sea fishing or through the flats for bonefish and permit. The late "Bonefish Folley" is a legend here, and delighted in taking people on bonefish tours for more than 60 years. He passed away in 2012 at the age of 91, but his two sons, Tommy and Carl, are continuing on in his footsteps. They offer a series of different packages from fishing and snorkeling to romantic sunset cruises. ⊠ *Blue Marlin Cove, West End* ☏ *242/646–9504, 242/349–4101* ⊕ *www.bluemarlincove.com.*

H2O Bonefishing

FISHING | Clients of this professional saltwater fly fishing outfitter book well ahead of their arrival on island. H2O's fleet of flats boats and professional guides are available as part of a prearranged multiday package that typically includes three to six days of fishing. They cater exclusively to their anglers both on and off the water for the length of their stay, including waterfront lodging at one of Grand Bahama's finest hotels. Fish year-round for trophy-sized bonefish and permit as well as seasonal tarpon, or fish offshore for yellowfin tuna and mahi-mahi from spring through summer. Light tackle and conventional fishing is also available. Check out their trendy clubhouse, Bones Bar. ⊠ *Lucaya* ☏ *242/359–4958, 954/364–7590* ⊕ *www.h2obonefishing.com.*

Reef Tours

BOATING | This family-owned company has been offering various tours on Grand Bahama since 1969. Deep sea and bottom-reef fishing tours are three to four hours in duration. Full-day trips are also available, as are paddleboard and kayak rentals, bottom-fishing excursions, glass-bottom-boat tours, snorkeling trips, wine and cheese evening cruises, parasailing, and even guided tours by Segway, Harley, and 4X4. Reservations are essential. ⊠ *Port Lucaya Marketplace, Lucaya* ☏ *242/373–5880, 242/373–5891* ⊕ *www.reeftoursfreeport.com.*

★ West End Ecology Tours

FISHING | FAMILY | You'll have fun while learning a lot about the marine life of the Bahamas when you take one of these ecotours run by Keith Cooper, whose family has lived in West End for generations. He provides educational fishing experiences focused on Grand Bahama's historical West End and the conservation and preservation of the area and its marine life. The private small group tours include deep-sea fishing, coral reef snorkeling, and the popular wild stingray interaction on beautiful Sandy Cay. Pricing is per tour for up to six people. ✉ *West End* ☎ *242/727–1156* ⊕ *www. westendecologytours.com.*

KAYAKING TOURS

★ Calabash Eco Adventures

ADVENTURE TOURS | FAMILY | This tour company, run by Grand Bahama local and avid diver Shamie Rolle, offers a variety of ecoexcursions to areas all over Grand Bahama for sport, history, and education. Options include kayaking, snorkeling, birding, bicycling, and cavern diving into some of the island's famous inland blue holes. All tours include pickup and drop-off at your lodging. ☎ *242/727–1974* ⊕ *www.calabashecoadventures.com.*

★ Grand Bahama Nature Tours

ECOTOURISM | One of the most well-known ecotour operators on the island for more than 20 years, Grand Bahama Nature Tours is continually updating and adding to their wide variety of excursions, run mostly by Grand Bahama natives who are both entertaining and full of island insight. Popular adventures include snorkeling around Peterson Cay, kayaking through the mangroves at Lucayan National Park, jeep safaris, off-road ATV tours, and birding through the Garden of the Groves. All tour prices include air-conditioned pickups at your lodging and any necessary equipment. ☎ *242/373–2485, 866/440–4542.*

SCUBA DIVING SITES

An extensive reef system runs along Little Bahama Bank's edge; sea gardens, caves, and colorful reefs rim the bank all the way from the West End to Freeport–Lucaya and beyond. The variety of dive sites suits everyone from the novice to the advanced diver, and ranges from 10 to 100-plus feet deep. Many dive operators offer a "discover" or "resort" course

where first-timers can try out open-water scuba diving with a short pool course and an instructor at their side.

A horseshoe-shaped ledge overlooks **Ben's Blue Hole,** which lies in 40 to 60 feet of water. Certified cavern divers can further explore the depths of the cave with guided groups from UNEXSO or Calabash Adventure Tours. Otherwise, interested visitors can view it aboveground when visiting the Lucayan National Park.

For moderately experienced divers, **Pygmy Caves** provides a formation of overgrown ledges that cut into the reef. The high-profile corals here form small caves.

One of Grand Bahama Island's signature dive sites, made famous by the UNEXSO dive operation, **Shark Junction** is a 45-foot dive where 4- to 6-foot reef sharks hang out, along with moray eels, stingrays, nurse sharks, and grouper. UNEXSO provides orientation and a shark feeding with its dives here.

Spid City has an aircraft wreck, dramatic coral formations, blue parrotfish, and an occasional shark. You'll dive about 40 to 60 feet down.

For divers with some experience, **Theo's Wreck,** a 228-foot cement hauler, was sunk in 1982 in 100 feet of water, and was the site for the 1993 IMAX film *Flight of the Aquanaut.*

Visitor Information

Tourist information centers are open weekdays at the Grand Bahama International Airport (9–5), Freeport Harbour (according to cruise ship arrivals), and Port Lucaya Marketplace (10–6). The People-to-People Program matches your family with hospitable locals who share like interests.

CONTACTS Ministry of Tourism Grand Bahama Office. ✉ *Fidelity Financial Center, Poinciana Dr., 1st fl., Freeport* ☎ *242/350–8600* ⊕ *www.*

bahamas.com. **People-to-People Program.**
☎ 242/302–2000 ⊕ www.bahamas.com/
people-to-people.

Freeport

Freeport, once an attractive, planned city of modern shopping centers, resorts, and other convenient tourist facilities, took a bad hit from the 2004 and 2005 hurricanes and subsequent economy downturn; its main resort and casino have not reopened. An Irish firm purchased the former Royal Oasis Resort & Casino but no plans have been made to rebuild or renovate. The International Bazaar next door is now a decrepit abandoned ghost town. Despite all this, Freeport's native restaurants, Rand Nature Centre, Bahamian Brewery, and beaches make it worth the visit. It's close to Lucaya (a 15-minute drive), and the airport and harbor are just a few minutes from downtown.

◉ Sights

The Bahamian Brewery

WINERY/DISTILLERY | One hundred percent Bahamian-owned, this 20-acre brewery opened in 2007, bringing to the Bahamian islands five new beers including Sands, High Rock Lager, Bush Crack, and Strong Back Stout. The brewery even makes a signature red ale served exclusively at the Atlantis Resort on Paradise Island. The brewery does everything on-site including bottling and labeling, and offers 45-minute to hour-long tours on weekdays that take you along each step in the brewing process. The tour ends in the tasting room where you can belly up to the bar or cocktail tables to sample each beer. Walk-ins are accepted. Beer, wine, and liquor can be purchased in the retail store; Bahamian Brewery souvenirs are available in the gift shop. ⊠ Just off Queen's Hwy., east of turn to West End, Freeport ☎ 242/352–4070 ⊕ www.

bahamianbrewery.com ⌨ $10 for tours ⊘ No tours on weekends, but liquor store open Sat. Closed Sun.

Bahamas National Trust Rand Nature Centre

NATURE PRESERVE | Established in 1939 on 100 acres just minutes from downtown Freeport, a half mile of self-guided botanical trails shows off 130 types of native plants, including many plants known for their use in bush medicine. The remaining tracts of land are left natural and undisturbed to serve as wildlife habitat. The center is also one of the island's birding hot spots, where you might spy a red-tailed hawk or a Cuban emerald hummingbird. Visit Donni, the one-eyed Bahama parrot the center has adopted, and the two Bahamian boas, a species that inhabits most Bahamian islands, but not Grand Bahama. The visitor center also hosts changing local art exhibits. The center survives on admissions, gift shop purchases, and donations alone, but has plans for a future face-lift and new exhibits. ⊠ E. Settlers Way, Freeport ☎ 242/352–5438 ⊕ www.bnt.bs ⌨ $5 ⊘ Closed weekends.

The Perfume Factory

STORE/MALL | Behind the now nearly defunct International Bazaar, the Perfume Factory occupies a replica 19th-century Bahamian mansion—the kind built by Loyalists who settled in the Bahamas after the American Revolution. The pink interior resembles an old-world tasteful drawing room. This is the home of Fragrance of the Bahamas, where you can find a large variety of perfumes, lotions, and colognes. Its biggest-selling Pink Pearl cologne actually contains conch pearls, and Sand cologne for men has a little sterilized Grand Bahama island sand in each bottle. Take a free 10-minute tour of the mixology laboratory and bottling area and get a free sample. For $30 an ounce, you can blend your own perfume using any of the 35 scents ($15 for 1½ ounces of blend-it-yourself body lotion). Sniff mixtures until they hit the right

More than 300 bird species call the Bahamas home, including this Bananaquit.

combination, then bottle, name, and take home the personalized potion. ⊠ *On the north side of the International Bazaar, W. Sunrise Hwy. and Mall Dr., Freeport* ☎ *242/352–9391, 800/628–9033* ⊕ *www. perfumefactory.com* ⊠ *Free.*

🏊 Beaches

Lucayan Beach and Coral Beach

BEACH—SIGHT | This stretch of sand divides into separately named beaches at the intersection of Sea Horse Road and Royal Palm Way. The eastern end is Lucayan Beach, monopolized by the broad spread of the Lighthouse Pointe at The Grand Lucayan resort, where nonguests can purchase day passes from the hotel which include use of pools, nonmotorized water equipment, and access to restaurants. Feed jackfish, snorkel at Rainbow Reef, parasail, or take a WaveRunner tour. Near the long-standing Ocean Motion Watersports, there is no admission fee for the beach. Go west from here along Coral Beach, where the shore widens for easier strolling

and the crowds thin considerably on the way to Coral Beach Bar. **Amenities:** food and drink; lifeguards; parking (no fee); water sports. **Best for:** partiers; snorkeling; sunrise; swimming, walking. ⊠ *Sea Horse Dr., Royal Palm Way, behind Grand Lucayan, and Coral Beach Bar, Freeport.*

William's Town Beach

BEACH—SIGHT | When the tide is high, this 1.9-mile slice of relatively hidden beach (from East Sunrise Highway, take Coral Road south, turn right onto Bahama Reef Boulevard, then left on Beachway Drive) can get a little narrow, but there's a wide area at its East End on Silver Point Beach near Island Seas Resort, where a food stand called Bernie's Tiki Hut serves fresh local delicacies such as cracked conch, fried snapper, or grilled lobster tail. Bernie's also hosts a bonfire on Tuesday nights. You can also grab a bite or a potent cocktail at Manta Ray Village nestled between Island Seas and Bernie's. Just west of here, a sidewalk runs the length of the beach along the road and at low tide the beach expands

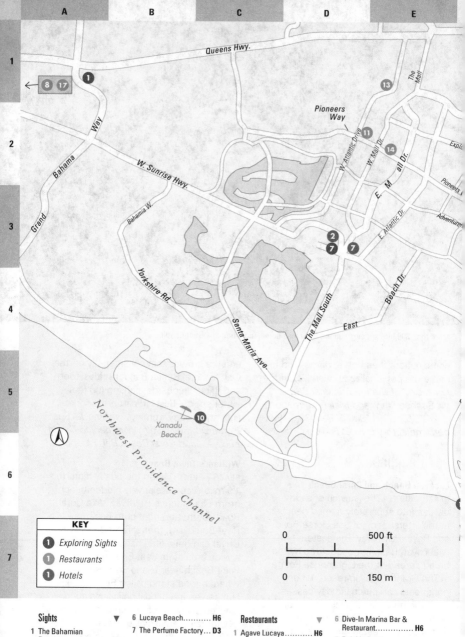

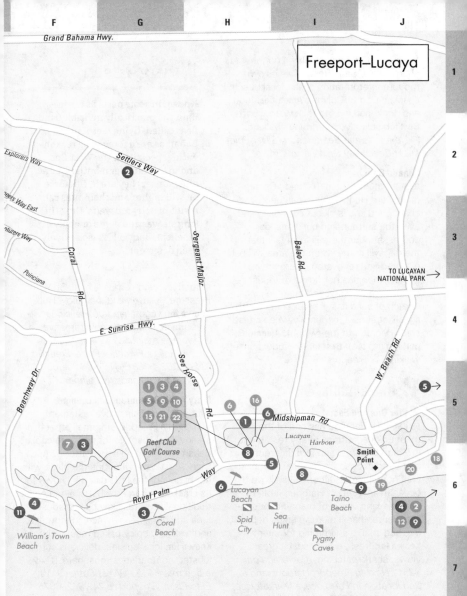

Freeport–Lucaya

TO LUCAYAN NATIONAL PARK →

Reef Club Golf Course

Lucayan Harbour

Midshipman Rd.

Smith Point

Lucayan Beach

Taino Beach

William's Town Beach

Coral Beach

Spid City

Sea Hunt

Pygmy Caves

Grand Bahama Hwy.

Settlers Way

Explorers Way

Adventurers Way East

Adventurers Way

Coral Rd.

Poinciana

Beachway Dr.

E. Sunrise Hwy.

Sergeant Major

Balao Rd.

W. Beach Rd.

Sea Horse Rd.

Royal Palm Way

far and wide for easy walking on the shore. Island Seas Resort has its own modern interpretation of the local beach shack, called CoCoNuts. **Amenities:** food and drink; parking (no fee); water sports. **Best for:** solitude; swimming; walking. ✉ *Next to Island Seas Resort, Silver Point Dr. at Beachway Dr., Williams Town.*

Xanadu Beach

BEACH—SIGHT | The old Xanadu Resort of Howard Hughes fame has been abandoned and is all but crumbling and even the surrounding buildings look depressed, but there is local talk that the day will come when the area will be restored and renovated. There are no longer amenities nor flocks of tourists on this beach. However, the mile-long stretch of sand is still serene and worth a walk at sunset, especially when cruise ships depart into the twilight. **Amenities:** parking (no fee). **Best for:** solitude; sunset; walking. ✉ *Freeport.*

🍴 Restaurants

★ Pier One and East

$$ | SUSHI | Pier One has one of the most unique settings of any restaurant in Grand Bahama, and two different menus to choose from: sushi or cooked continental fare. Built on stilts above the ocean near Freeport Harbour, it offers one-of-a-kind views of magnificent sunsets, larger-than-life cruise ships departing, and sharks swimming for chum. **Known for:** fresh, quality sushi; great views; shark-watching. [$] *Average main: $25* ✉ *Next to Freeport Harbour, and a 2nd location in Port Lucaya Marketplace, Freeport* ☎ *242/352–6674* ⏲ *No lunch weekends.*

Livity Vegetarian Juice Bar & Take-Out

$ | VEGETARIAN | Offering the healthiest food option on the island, this little shop (located in a shabby strip mall) doesn't look like much, but the quality of the food tells a different story. Livity blends up fresh fruit and vegetable juices and smoothies with names like Flu Shot, Pressure Reliever, and Incredible Hulk. **Known for:** vegetarian fare; delicious smoothies; healthy lunch alternatives. [$] *Average main: $8* ✉ *West Atlantic Dr. , in Rolle's Furniture Plaza, Freeport* ☎ *242/352–5483* 💳 *No credit cards* ⏲ *Closed weekends. No dinner.*

Flying Teeth

Known in some parts as no-see-ums, the practically invisible sand fleas called "flying teeth" in the Bahamas are a force to be reckoned with, especially at the West End and in the summer months. At and after sunset they are in full force on still nights, and their bites can result in itchy red welts. Dress in long sleeves and pants or apply a repellent. Baby oil is also a widely used deterrent.

Mary Ann's Restaurant and Lounge

$ | BAHAMIAN | This native restaurant tucked in a Freeport strip mall attracts a steady local clientele for its home-cooked Bahamian cuisine. Named after owner Mary Ann Ward, who runs the place with her husband, the little diner is known for its cracked or curried lobster, along with traditional favorites like chicken souse, tuna and grits, peas 'n' rice, johnnycake, and a slightly spicy baked mac 'n cheese. **Known for:** local cuisine; delicious curried lobster; nontouristy atmosphere. [$] *Average main: $12* ✉ *West Settler's Way, Elite Plaza, Freeport* ☎ *242/352–8875, 242/477–8040.*

★ Merport Bistro

$ | FRENCH FUSION | Offering French cuisine with a strong Bahamian influence, Merport Bistro is the spot in downtown Freeport for the local business crowd. Their weekly specials are worth checking out, and although the menu changes constantly, there is something for everyone, from seafood wraps and lobster bisque, to coq au vin, to stuffed snapper with corn and zucchini salsa. **Known for:** fresh ingredients; daily changing specials; friendly staff. [$] *Average main: $19* ✉ *3 Merport Bldg., Pioneer's Way, 1 Town Center, Freeport* ✣ *Across from BTC* ☎ *242/602–7506* ⏲ *Closed weekends.*

Senor Frog's Restaurant Bar & Souvenir Shop

$ | **MEXICAN** | This Mexican-themed party place fills with cruise-ship passengers in port for the day, and sends them back to the boat happy, fed, and full of rum drinks. The location at the Freeport Harbour is open-air and full of life, complete with a dance stage, large flat-screen TVs, a wraparound bar, and seating for more than 100 people. **Known for:** Mexican cuisine; party atmosphere; lots of tequila. [$] *Average main: $17* ✉ *Freeport Harbour, Freeport* ☎ *242/351–3764* 🌐 *www.senorfrogs.com* ⏲ *Closed when there are no docked cruise ships.*

Hotels

Castaways Resort and Suites

$ | **HOTEL** | In Freeport, this property is one of the nicer budget options in the area. **Pros:** free breakfast; nice array of services and facilities; close to the airport. **Cons:** the neighborhood is currently in a slump; lacking character; not much nearby. [$] *Rooms from: $115* ✉ *E. Mall Dr., Freeport* ☎ *242/352–6682* 🛏 *97 rooms, 21 suites* 🍴 *Free Breakfast.*

Island Seas Resort

$ | **HOTEL** | **FAMILY** | This time-share property also accommodates nonmembers looking for fun on the beach away from urban traffic; one- and two-bedroom suites with balconies overlook the flowery courtyard, where their thatch-roof CoCoNuts bar and restaurant and a free-form pool with waterfalls and swim-up bar are the centerpiece. **Pros:** on-site restaurant; fun pool and bar area; great beach. **Cons:** far away from everything; service can be slow; property is worn and room decor is outdated. [$] *Rooms from: $120* ✉ *123 Silver Point Dr., Williams Town* ☎ *242/373–1271, 800/801–6884* 🌐 *www.islandseas.com* 🛏 *190 rooms* 🍴 *No meals.*

Royal Islander

$ | **HOTEL** | Amenities without the sticker shock: this two-story, tin-roof, motel-style property provides free scheduled shuttle service to Xanadu Beach. **Pros:** affordable; convenient to airport; free beach shuttle. **Cons:** no beach on property; low on character; nothing much nearby. [$] *Rooms from: $90* ✉ *E. Mall Dr., Freeport* ☎ *242/351–6000* 🌐 *www.royalislanderhotel.com* 🛏 *100 rooms.*

Activities

HORSEBACK RIDING

★ **Pinetree Stables**

HORSEBACK RIDING | Horseback rides are offered on ecotrails and the beach twice a day, starting at 9 am. All two-hour rides are accompanied by a guide—no previous riding experience is necessary, but riders must be at least eight years old. Plan to bring a waterproof camera because you will get wet! Reservations are essential and drinks are available for purchase. Pinetree Stables offers free shuttles from hotels and the harbor. ✉ *N. Beachway Dr., Freeport* ☎ *242/602–2122* 🌐 *www.pinetree-stables.com* 🎟 *$165 for 2-hr ride.*

SPAS

La Belle Spa & Boutique

SPA/BEAUTY | This small but charming luxury day spa offers top-of-the-line treatments and specialty services such as gel manicures and pedicures, advanced facials and enzyme peels, microdermabrasion, reflexology, and hot stone massages. The technicians are knowledgeable and friendly, and you can relax with provided refreshments to the sounds of trickling water and meditative music. ✉ *W. Atlantic Blvd., Freeport*

Pinetree Stables can take you horseback riding on the beach.

☎ *242/351–3565* ⊙ *Closed Sun. and Mon.*

Renu Day Spa

SPA/BEAUTY | This simple yet elegant spa situated in the bright blue, statuesque Millenium House offers many general spa services including nail treatments, waxing, facials, body wraps and scrubs, massage, and Reiki. They use Essie and OPI nail products and Guinot skin products, in addition to several other organic lines. ⊠ *Millenium House, E. Mall Dr., Freeport* ☎ *242/352–7368* ⊕ *www. renudayspabahamas.com* ⊙ *Closed Sun. and Mon., except by appointment.*

Port Lucaya

On the beach and harbor of Grand Bahama's southern coast is resort center Lucaya, developed after its neighbor Freeport. Colorful Port Lucaya Market-place grew up along the safe harbor, known for its duty-free shops, bars, restaurants, straw market, and outdoor bandstand. This is also the home of UNEXSO, the island's famous diving and dolphin encounter attraction. Surrounding the port are the island's biggest hotels: Lighthouse Pointe at The Grand Lucayan, and Pelican Bay.

This quaint harborside shopping, dining, and entertainment village is one of the liveliest locales on the island. You can hop from bar to bar, find a variety of restaurants for breakfast, lunch, and dinner, and there is also a local chocolate factory and coffee shop. There's an extensive straw market and 20-plus local crafts vendors. Live music and entertainment bring the center bandstand to life on weekend nights, and additional entertainment is provided on busy cruise ship days. A few steps to the east and across the street you'll find more hotels and restaurants within walking distance.

Sights

Port Lucaya Marketplace

MARKET | Lucaya's capacious and lively shopping complex is on the waterfront across the street from the Grand Lucayan Hotel, and right in front of the Pelican Bay. The outdoor shopping center, whose walkways are lined with hibiscus, bougainvillea, and croton, has lots of well-kept, colorfully painted establishments, among them waterfront restaurants and bars, water-sports operators, and shops that sell clothes, silver, jewelry, perfumes, and local arts and crafts. The marketplace's centerpiece is **Count Basie Square,** where live entertainment featuring Bahamian bands appeals to joyful nighttime crowds every weekend. Lively outdoor watering holes line the square, which is also *the* place to celebrate the holidays: a tree-lighting ceremony takes place in the festively decorated spot at the beginning of December and fireworks highlight New Year's Eve, July 4, and Bahamian Independence Day, July 10. ✉ *Across from Grand Lucayan , Sea Horse Rd., Port Lucaya Marketplace* ☎ *242/373–8446* 🌐 *www.portlucaya.com.*

Restaurants

Most of the dining in Lucaya is in or around the Port Lucaya Marina or Port Lucaya Marketplace, which means that nearly all the restaurants are within walking distance of each other and of the hotels in the immediate vicinity.

Agave Lucaya

$$$ | **MEXICAN FUSION** | Popular for their $2 Taco Tuesdays where you get great deals on margaritas, mojitos, and martinis all night long, they also offer those cocktails half off from 4–7 daily. This Port Lucaya Marketplace offers Mexican staples with a unique Caribbean and Bahamian blend. **Known for:** Mexican-Caribbean fusion packed with flavor; taco Tuesdays and $2 margaritas; lively spot. [$] *Average main: $35* ✉ *Port Lucaya, Lucaya* ☎ *242/374–4887.*

Conching Out

Conch harvesting is illegal in the United States and closely regulated in other tropical locations to guard against overfishing. Currently, conch harvesting is limited to six per vessel in the Bahamas, but populations, while still plentiful, are slowly becoming depleted. The Bahamas National Trust launched a "Conchservation" campaign in 2013 in an effort to educate and preserve Queen Conch fishing in the Bahamas. Read more about it at 🌐 *www.bnt.bs/support/conchservation.*

★ **Bootleg Chocolates**

$ | **CAFÉ** | This cozy little café offers strong gourmet coffees, delicious pastries, and creative and delicious chocolates, handcrafted in-store. Try inventive flavors, such as black tea and ginger, goat pepper and balsamic caramel, or Bahamian seas salt and hibiscus caramel—a unique taste of the Bahamas to take home. **Known for:** strong coffee; inspired chocolate flavors; locally made chocolates. [$] *Average main: $10* ✉ *Port Lucaya Marketplace, on waterfront near main parking lot, Port Lucaya Marketplace* ☎ *242/373–6303* 🌐 *www.bootlegchocolates.com* 💳 *No credit cards.*

★ **Cappuccino's Italian Restaurant**

$$ | **ITALIAN** | This Italian family-run cozy restaurant offers consistently good food and great service. Traditional comfort pasta dishes adorn the menu, like pesto gnocchi and seafood linguine, in addition to steaks and daily fresh fish specials. **Known for:** delightful Italian cuisine; daily fresh fish specials; romantic atmosphere. [$] *Average main: $23* ✉ *Port Lucaya Marketplace, Sea Horse Rd., Lucaya*

☎ *242/373–1584* ⊗ *Closed Wed. No lunch.*

★ Da Conch Man (AKA Big Daddy Brown's)

$ | **BAHAMIAN** | Located in Port Lucaya Marketplace along the water, Big Daddy Brown's offers fresh conch salad and authentic Bahamian staples. Watch this family team put on a show as they prepare the salad right in front of you; they also serve conch fritters, fried fish, and fried lobster in this little bright-colored shack. **Known for:** authentic fried Bahamian staples; fresh conch salad; central location. $ *Average main: $15* ✉ *Port Lucaya Marketplace, Lucaya* ▭ *No credit cards.*

Dive-In Marina Bar & Restaurant

$ | **BAHAMIAN** | **FAMILY** | This relaxing outdoor poolside bar and grill at UNEXSO is great for lunch and weekend brunch, with delicious and creative menu items. Kids can splash in the pool (which has underwater windows to the marina, so bring goggles!) while adults sip spicy Bloody Marys and tropical drinks. **Known for:** casual lunches; weekend brunch; patrons can use the pool. $ *Average main: $17* ✉ *UNEXSO, Lucaya* ✛ *Next to Pelican Bay Hotel* ☎ *242/373–1244.*

★ Flying Fish GastroBar

$$$ | **ECLECTIC** | Flying Fish offers one of the finest culinary experiences in the Caribbean. You'll find quality service with an eclectic collection of seafood and Bahamian favorites, made with only the best, sustainable ingredients, and prepared in a way that gives you gourmet and comfort food on the same plate. **Known for:** eclectic and inspired menu; good wine list; casual Sunday evenings with live music. $ *Average main: $38* ✉ *1 Sea Horse Rd., Lucaya* ✛ *Next to Pelican Bay Hotel* ☎ *242/373–4363* ⊕ *www. flyingfishbahamas.com* ⊗ *Closed Tues. and all public holidays. No lunch Mon.* ☞ *Docking facilities for boaters.*

Giovanni's Cafe

$$ | **ITALIAN** | Tucked away under the bougainvillea at Port Lucaya Marketplace, this corner café evokes a bit of Italy. As you relax on the patio or study the giant mural of an Italian waterway inside the café, treat yourself to local seafood such as lobster in white-wine cream sauce and pan-fried grouper in lemon-wine sauce. $ *Average main: $25* ✉ *Port Lucaya Marketplace, Lucaya* ☎ *242/373–9107* ⊗ *Closed Sun.–Tues.*

★ Pisces Restaurant and Bar

$ | **ECLECTIC** | This well-established restaurant has moved to center stage in Port Lucaya Marketplace, filling an entire block with indoor and outdoor seating. Pisces is known for its seafood, West Indian–style curries, and thin crust pizza. **Known for:** delicious curries; substantial choice of pizzas; family-friendly. $ *Average main: $18* ✉ *Port Lucaya Marketplace, Sea Horse Rd., Lucaya* ☎ *242/373–5192* ⊗ *Closed Sun. and Sept. No lunch.*

Sabor Restaurant and Bar

$$ | **ECLECTIC** | The setting makes this restaurant the perfect place for an evening cocktail whether you sit overlooking the Port Lucaya Marina or nestled among the twinkling lights and palm trees around the pool deck. The lunch and dinner menu is a fun fusion of Bahamian and American favorites with tropical twists, such as O.M.G. jalapeño shrimp, cognac-infused lobster bisque, baked grouper with Thai coconut curry sauce, sesame spiced crusted tuna with an Asian salad, and steaks, burgers, and flatbreads to boot. **Known for:** unique twist on the usual island cuisine; friendly staff; pleasant, intimate atmosphere. $ *Average main: $28* ✉ *Harborside, Pelican Bay Hotel, Lucaya* ☎ *242/373–5588* ⊕ *www.sabor-bahamas.com.*

This sailboat is in front of Lighthouse Pointe at Grand Lucayan.

★ **Zorba's Cafe & Pastries**

$ | **CAFÉ** | Enjoy a great cup of coffee any time of day or night at this quaint café immediately adjacent to Zorba's Greek Restaurant. Try fresh-baked croissants, chocolate eclairs, and tiramisu, as well as a variety of other sweet treats. **Known for:** wide assortment of pastries; delicious coffee; authentic Greek specialties. [$] *Average main: $6* ✉ *Lucaya* ☎ *242/602–5500.*

Zorba's Greek Cuisine

$ | **GREEK** | Besides Greek favorites, this longtime Port Lucaya restaurant serves popular Bahamian dishes. Join the port's yacht-in clientele, shoppers, and locals, for breakfast, lunch, or dinner on the white-and-blue-trimmed sidewalk porch. Specialties include gyros, moussaka, Greek salad, pizza, conch fritters, fried snapper, and roasted leg of lamb. **Known for:** authentic Greek specialties; great value for money; casual dining and consistent service. [$] *Average main: $17* ✉ *Port Lucaya Marketplace, Lucaya* ☎ *242/373–6137.*

Hotels

Lighthouse Pointe at Grand Lucayan

$$ | **RESORT** | **FAMILY** | Lighthouse Pointe remains is a two-story structure that replicates Caribbean-style plantation manors with quiet ocean-view rooms and suites. **Pros:** across the street from Port Lucaya Marketplace; great beachfront activities; a number of on-site eateries and bars. **Cons:** service can be spotty; all-inclusive meals can be repetitive and lack choice; much of the sprawling resort complex remains closed. [$] *Rooms from: $210* ✉ *Sea Horse Rd., Lucaya* ☎ *242/373–1333, 855/708–6671* 🌐 *www.grandlucayan.com* 🛏 *196 rooms* 🍴 *All meals.*

★ **Pelican Bay Hotel**

$ | **RESORT** | Close to the beach with rooms overlooking Port Lucaya Marina or waterfront along the canal, Pelican Bay has a funky modern appeal, and suites overflow with character and decorative elements collected from around the world. **Pros:** stylish and comfortable;

water views; trendy on-site bars and restaurants. **Cons:** no beach; poolside/marina-front rooms can be noisy; no elevators to upper level rooms. $ *Rooms from: $180* ⊠ *Sea Horse Rd., Lucaya* ☎ *242/373–9550, 800/852–3702* ⊕ *www.pelicanbayhotel.com* ⇥ *90 rooms, 96 waterside suites* ¶⊙¶ *Breakfast.*

▼ Nightlife

BARS

★ Bones Bar

BARS/PUBS | This trendy spot on the waterfront at Pelican Bay Hotel is a popular evening and late-night watering hole with the local ex-pat crowd, with swim-up seating at the adjacent pool. Sip high-end tasting rums or fresh-squeezed cocktails like the Silver Fox (lime juice, homemade simple syrup, and vodka). The only food option is their savory meat pies. Call ahead to place your order as they tend to run out early. ⊠ *Pelican Bay Hotel, Sea Horse Rd., on the canal next to Flying Fish GastroBar, Lucaya* ☎ *242/602–2663* ⊕ *www.bones-bar.com.*

Market Square

CONCERTS | **FAMILY** | The stage at Market Square at the center of the Port Lucaya Marketplace becomes lively after dark, with live or piped-in island music and other performances (made all the more festive by surrounding popular watering holes: the Corner Bar, Pisces, and Rum Runners). Entertainment includes live Bahamian bands on weekend evenings, fire dancers, fashion shows, classic movie showings, and special holiday events. ⊠ *Port Lucaya Marketplace, Sea Horse Rd., Lucaya* ⊕ *www.portlucaya.com.*

Rum Runners

BARS/PUBS | This busy bar on the corner of Count Basie Square specializes in keeping bar hoppers young and old supplied with free Wi-Fi, tropical frozen drinks and punches, and piña coladas served in coconuts. Sit outside for people-watching or inside for cool air-conditioning and TVs

broadcasting sports events. The kitchen serves up basic American and Bahamian bar food. ⊠ *Port Lucaya Marketplace, Lucaya* ☎ *242/373–7233.*

🛍 Shopping

ART

★ Glassblower Shop

ART GALLERIES | The Glassblower Shop features the work of master artisan Sidney Pratt, who creates his blown glass masterpieces inside the small free-standing store. Order your name in glass or ask him to make whatever it is you want if you don't see it in the store. ⊠ *Free-standing booth outside John Bull, Lucaya* ☎ *242/442-3798.*

Leo's Art Gallery

ART GALLERIES | This little shop showcases the expressive Haitian-style paintings and colorful Bahamian impressionism of famed local artist Leo Brown, each piece with its own story. This storefront is both his studio and his showroom. This place is worth a visit, if only to meet the charming Leo and witness his inspiring work and creativity. ⊠ *Port Lucaya Marketplace, across from Zorba's, Lucaya* ☎ *242/373-1758.*

Treasure Nest

ART GALLERIES | In addition to displaying original artwork by well-known local watercolorist Sheldon Saint, this shop sells reproductions of his paintings on posters, postcards, and greeting cards. Treasure Nest also carries clothing, shoes, handbags, and accessories for ladies. Book a spot in the Saint n' Paint experience, where you'll create your own masterpiece under the expert guidance of this talented local artist. Every Friday at 7 pm. ⊠ Port Lucaya, #9 Port Lucaya Marketplace, Lucaya ⊹ Between Pisces and Giovanni's restaurants ☎ 242/352–1230 ⊕ sheldon-saint-studio-treasure-nest.business.site ☉ Closed Sat. after 2:30 and all day Sun.

FASHION
Bandolera

CLOTHING | Bandolera sells European-style women's fashions and accessories, such as classic Joseph Ribkoff designs. Find that perfect little chic dress, and everything from casual wear to gowns. ⊠ Port Lucaya Marketplace, Lucaya ☎ 242/373–7691.

JEWELRY AND WATCHES
Colombian Emeralds

JEWELRY/ACCESSORIES | Colombian Emeralds purveys a line of Colombian's famed gems plus other jewelry and crystal. ⊠ Port Lucaya Marketplace, Lucaya ☎ 242/373–8400 ⊕ www.colombianemeralds.com.

Freeport Jewellers

JEWELRY/ACCESSORIES | This jeweler caters to locals and visitors with watches, heavy gold and silver chains, larimar, and unique sea charms like conch shell jewelry. It also sells cigars, crystal, and Swiss-brand watches. ⊠ Port Lucaya Marketplace ☎ 242/373–2777 ⊕ www.freeportjewellers.com ☉ Closed after 3 pm on Sun.

John Bull

JEWELRY/ACCESSORIES | With locations throughout the Bahamas, this 85-year-old family business sells high-end items including gemstones; gold and designer jewelry like David Yurman and Antica Murrina; fine leather bags and accessories such as Dooney & Bourke and Michael Kors; and designer sunglasses by Maui Jim, Guccis, and Ray-Ban. John Bull has also been the official Rolex retailer in the Bahamas since 1955. ⊠ Port Lucaya Marketplace, Lucaya ☎ 242/374–6614 ⊕ www.johnbull.com.

MARKETS AND ARCADES
Arawak Crafts Center

CRAFTS | This independent collection of 27 small shops and booths on the west side of the Port Lucaya Marketplace is comprised of individual Bahamian artisans, each selling unique arts and homemade handicrafts, many customized on request. Items for sale include seashell ornaments, candles, soaps, straw goods, dolls, and more. ⊠ Port Lucaya Marketplace, across from Dominos Pizza, Lucaya ⊕ www.portlucaya.com.

Port Lucaya Straw Markets

CRAFTS | Come to this collection of 100 wooden stalls at Port Lucaya Marketplace's East and West ends to bargain for straw goods, T-shirts, and souvenirs. ⊠ Port Lucaya Marketplace, Sea Horse Rd., Lucaya.

MISCELLANEOUS
IIWII (It Is What It Is)

ART GALLERIES | It Is What It Is is an art gallery showcasing owner Matthew Wildgoose's paintings as well as the works of other local artists. It's also a

---

Hair Braiding

One of tourists' (especially children) favorite Bahamian souvenirs is braided hair. Licensed braiders, found wherever visitors shop, generally charge $3 per braid (up to 10 braids) and $160 for a full head. For the best of the best, head to Port Lucaya Marketplace.

These handwoven souvenirs can be purchased at Port Lucaya Marketplace.

spot to embrace your own inner Picasso under the guidance of Wildgoose by taking an art class, workshop, or a fun sip n' paint session. ⊠ *Across from Giovanni's restaurant, Port Lucaya Marketplace* ☎ *242/426–0329.*

Photo Specialist

CAMERAS/ELECTRONICS | Photo Specialist carries photo and video equipment, memory cards, rechargeable batteries, cell phone chargers, and any other electronic accessory you may have forgotten to bring with you. ⊠ *Port Lucaya Marketplace, Lucaya* ☎ *242/373–7858.*

★ Sun & Sea Outfitters at UNEXSO

CLOTHING | This retail shop at UNEXSO offers the biggest shopping selection in Lucaya, including water-sports equipment, toys, jewelry and accessories, home decor, brand-name apparel, and swimsuits for both men and women. Walk along the marina to enter poolside or enter at the front of the UNEXSO building. ⊠ *UNEXSO, next to Pelican Bay Hotel, Lucaya* ☎ *242/373–1244, 800/992–3483* ⊕ *www.unexso.com.*

Activities

BIKING

By virtue of its flat terrain, broad avenues, and long straight stretches of highway, Grand Bahama is perfect for bicycling. There's a designated biking lane on Midshipman Road.

Inexpensive bicycle rentals are available from some resorts, and the Viva Wyndham Fortuna Beach allows guests free use of bicycles. In addition to its other ecotouring options, Grand Bahama Nature Tours offers 10-mile biking excursions that include a visit to a native settlement and Garden of the Groves.

★ CocoNutz Cruisers

BICYCLING | CocoNutz is locally owned and operated and offers the only motorized (electric) bicycle experience on the island. Alfredo Bridgewater or one of his knowledgeable guides takes tourists along the southern shores of the island, offering island history and stops along the way for unique Grand Bahamian experiences. The 5½-hour ride can take up to 12 bikers, and includes bottled water and lunch. The guides even take photos along the way to send to you later. Find them behind the Port Lucaya Marketplace parking lot at the water's edge. If you're staying farther away, they'll arrange hotel pickup and drop-off at no additional charge. ⊠ *Port Lucaya Marketplace, Lucaya* ☎ *242/808-7292, 954/354–6889* ⊕ *www.coconutzcruisers. com.*

DIVE OPERATORS

★ **UNEXSO** (*Underwater Explorers Society*)

SCUBA DIVING | This world-renowned scuba diving facility provides rental equipment, guides, and boats. Facilities include a 17-foot-deep training pool with windows that look out on the harbor, changing rooms and showers, docks, an outdoor bar and grill, and an air tank filling station. Daily dive excursions range from one-day discovery courses and dives, to specialty shark, dolphin, and cave diving. Both the facility and its dive masters have been featured in international and American magazines for their work with sharks and cave exploration. UNEXSO and its sister company, the Dolphin Experience, are known for their work with Atlantic bottlenose dolphins. ⊠ *Port Lucaya, Lucaya* ✛ *Next to Pelican Bay Hotel* ☎ *242/373–1244, 800/992– 3483* ⊕ *www.unexso.com* 🍽 *One-tank reef dives $59, Discover Scuba course $129, night dives $79, dolphin dives $219, shark dives $109.*

SPAS

Dermalogica Skin Centre

SPA/BEAUTY | After an analysis of your skin, your therapist will advise which facials and products are best for your skin type. This small, clinical day spa also offers Swedish massages, face and body waxing, and brow and lash tinting. ⊠ *Port Lucaya Marketplace* ☎ *242/373–7546* ⊙ *Closed after 2 pm Sun. and Mon.*

Did You Know? ◉

Senses Spa at Grand Lucayan

SPA—SIGHT | This three-level spa offers a variety of luxury services including body wraps and scrubs, facials, various massage techniques, and manicures and pedicures, in addition to a full-service salon. On the top floor you will find state-of-the-art exercise equipment, including free weights and elliptical machines, a spin class studio, and daily exercise classes for every interest. Senses is open to nonguests as well, and a daily fee includes use of the locker room, lap pool, hot tubs, and sauna facilities. All spa services are by appointment. ⊠ *Grand Lucayan, Lighthouse Point, Lucaya* ☎ *242/350–5466* ⊕ *www.grandlucayan. com.*

Greater Lucaya

The lion's share of restaurants and resorts in Lucaya is located around Port Lucaya, but if you venture a bit farther you'll find a handful of attractions, eateries, and places to stay that are slightly removed from the crush of tourists.

◉ Sights

★ The Garden of the Groves

GARDEN | This vibrant, 12-acre garden and certified wildlife habitat with a trademark chapel and waterfalls, is filled with native Bahamian flora, butterflies, birds, and turtles. Interpretative signage identifies plant and animal species. First opened

Did You Know?

Grand Bahama is one of the most eco-oriented islands in the Bahamas. Kayaks are readily available across the island.

in 1973, the park was renovated and reopened in 2008; additions include a labyrinth modeled after the one at France's Chartres Cathedral, colorful shops and galleries with local arts and crafts, a playground, and a multideck indoor and outdoor café and bar. Explore on your own or take a half-hour-long guided tour at 10 am (Monday–Saturday). Enjoy the garden under twinkling lights on Friday nights only during the high season, with dinner specials and sometimes live music. ✉ *Midshipman Rd. and Magellan Dr., Freeport* ☎ *242/374–7778, 242/374–7779 Fri. night dinner reservations* 🌐 *www.thegardenofthegroves.com* 🎟 *$17* 🕓 *Cafe closed early July–early Oct. No dinner Sat.–Thurs.*

Beaches

Fortune Beach

BEACH—SIGHT | FAMILY | Fortune Beach lies between two canal channels, and in the middle sits the Wyndham Viva Fortuna all-inclusive resort, where visitors can purchase day passes to use water-sports equipment and resort facilities. Steps from the resort the secluded beach offers exceptional strolling, offshore snorkeling, and swimming. The western end backs the Margarita Villa Sand Bar and the private homes along Spanish Main Drive, known as "Millionaire Row." The eastern end is home to Banana Bay Restaurant, where at low tide a shallow lagoon forms alongside a drawn-out sandbar, allowing you to walk yards out to sea with cold drink in hand. **Amenities:** food and drink; parking near east end only (no fee). **Best for:** solitude; snorkeling; sunrise; swimming; walking. ✉ *Fortune Bay Dr., Greater Lucaya.*

Taino Beach

BEACH—SIGHT | FAMILY | A short walk down the long, gently coved beach takes you to Pirates Cove Water Park, where the kids can bounce to their hearts' content on giant trampolines in the water. Rent kayaks, paddleboards, and Jet Skis, or beach chairs and umbrellas. A bar with a small food menu is also available. Next door is the iconic Stoned Crab restaurant. A few steps farther is Outriggers Beach Club, home to the popular fish fry held every Wednesday night. This is also where you'll find the legendary Tony Macaroni's beach shack; be sure to give his roast conch a try. Plenty of green space edges the beach, and there's also a playground. **Amenities:** food and drink; parking (no fee); toilets; water sports. **Best for:** partiers; sunset; swimming; walking. ✉ *W. Beach Rd., near Smith's Point, Greater Lucaya.*

Restaurants

★ Banana Bay Restaurant

$ | BAHAMIAN | FAMILY | Directly on Fortune Beach, Banana Bay is a great place for lunch or daytime cocktails, whether you sit on the restaurant's shaded deck or on a lounger in the sand. As the tide rolls out the beach grows, creating a wonderful shallow lagoon and sandbar, perfect for wading and for frolicking kids. **Known for:** fresh fish daily specials; beautiful beach views; warm homemade banana bread. [$] *Average main: $18* ✉ *Fortune Beach, Fortune Bay Dr., Lucaya* ☎ *242/373–2960* 🕓 *No dinner.*

★ Dolphin Cove Clubhouse

$$$ | ECLECTIC | Each seat in this small but sophisticated old Bahamian manor home-styled dining room has a view into the open kitchen. With just 30 diners at a time, it's like the chef and his team are cooking dinner for an intimate group of friends as they watch. **Known for:** upscale island dining experience; warm and friendly service; bottomless mimosa brunch with many flavors to choose from. [$] *Average main: $40* ✉ *14 Swans Drive, Greater Lucaya* ☎ *242/602–4964* 🕓 *Closed Sun. eve and Mon.*

Did You Know?

Most dive operations in the Bahamas offer certification programs. If you are simply looking to try scuba on your vacation, opt for a resort course that provides enough instruction to get you into the water with equipment. If you find scuba is your new favorite adventure, get a full open-water certification. Initial certification in the Bahamas costs about $600. To save valuable vacation and bottom time, you can often begin your instruction at home or online.

★ **The Margarita Villa Sand Bar**

$ | **AMERICAN** | There is no flooring in this cozy little beach bar, just sand, along with a few bar-top tables and some stools along the bar. The bartender will treat you like an old friend. **Known for:** right on the beach; warm service; party atmosphere. [$] *Average main: $12* ✉ *Fortune Beach, off Spanish Main Rd., Mather Town, Lucaya* ☎ *242/373–4525* 🌐 *www.sandbarbahamas.com.*

★ **Smith's Point Fish Fry**

$ | **BAHAMIAN** | For Bahamian food fixed by Bahamians, head to Smith's Point for the famous weekly fish fry. Every Wednesday night this little settlement by Taino Beach comes to life with both locals and tourists, when the open-air beach shacks along the street serve up fried fish (with the head and tail still on), cracked conch (pounded and fried), lobster tail, fried grouper, and barbecue chicken down-home style. **Known for:** traditional Bahamian food; party atmosphere; on the beach. [$] *Average main: $10* ✉ *Smith's Point, Off W. Beach Rd., Lucaya* ✥ *Next to Taino Beach* 💳 *No credit cards.*

★ **The Stoned Crab**

$$$ | **ECLECTIC** | Back in the days when Freeport was Freeport, the Stoned Crab was one of the places to see and be seen. New owners have pumped millions into bringing it back to life and making it even better than before. **Known for:** spectacular ocean and beach-view dining; sophisticated beachy atmosphere; spend all day eating and drinking here. [$] *Average main: $38* ✉ *Greater Lucaya* ☎ *242/602–1010* 🌐 *www.thestonedcrabbahamas.com.*

★ **Tony Macaroni's Conch Experience**

$ | **BAHAMIAN** | **FAMILY** | For a taste of the local beach scene, follow the music to this weathered, thatch-roof shack at Taino Beach and get your fill of mouthwatering roast conch, the specialty of the "house." Operated by local personality Anthony "Tony Macaroni" Hanna, the popular eatery also sells conch salad, roast lobster and shrimp, and Gully Wash cocktails (fresh coconut water, sweetened condensed milk, a healthy dose of gin, and a sprinkle of nutmeg) for noshing en plein air on a stilted deck overlooking pristine sands and sea. **Known for:** fresh conch served many ways; incredible ocean views; memorable chats with Tony Macaroni. [$] *Average main: $12* ✉ *Taino Beach, Lucaya* ☎ *242/533–6766* 💳 *No credit cards.*

🛏 Hotels

Bell Channel Inn

$ | **HOTEL** | Right on the water and a short walk from Port Lucaya Marketplace, this charming family-run (through three generations) inn with simple-yet-spacious rooms has quick and easy access to the island's best down-under sites, making it perfect for scuba-oriented and budget-minded travelers. **Pros:** friendly, longtime staff; clean, affordable rooms; bar/restaurant on-site. **Cons:** no beach but on the canal; 10-minute walk from shopping and restaurant scene; rooms are not fancy but well maintained. [$] *Rooms from: $100* ✉ *Kings Rd., just off Midshipman, Lucaya* ☎ *242/373–1053* 🌐 *bellchannelinn.com* 🛏 *31 rooms* 🍴 *No meals.*

★ **Dolphin Cove**

$ | **HOTEL** | This adults-only apartment style resort situated on the Grand Bahama canals offers a quiet getaway perfect for a long weekend or an extended stay. **Pros:** stylish, upscale decor; one of island's best restaurants on property; friendly, personal service. **Cons:** not on the beach; limited amenities; shopping, entertainment, and other restaurants not walking distance. [$] *Rooms from: $129* ✉ *Greater Lucaya* ☎ *242/602–3346* 🌐 *www.dolphincovebahamas.com* 🛏 *52 rooms* 🍴 *Free Breakfast.*

Taino Beach Resort and Club

$$ | **RESORT** | **FAMILY** | One- and two-bedroom contemporary self-functioning suites, each with garden views, surrounding a large pool with a lazy river and waterslide, make this resort a haven for families. **Pros:** easy walk to Smith's Point for Wednesday night Fish Fry; on-site restaurant and swim-up bar; newly renovated room decor. **Cons:** no beachfront rooms; need a car, ferry, or taxi to get to main shopping and restaurant spots; Wi-Fi is spotty. [$] *Rooms from: $150* ✉ *Jolly Roger Dr., Greater Lucaya* ☎ *242/350–2200* 🌐 *www.tainobeach.com* 💳 *No credit cards* 🛏 *156 rooms* 🍴 *No meals.*

Viva Wyndham Fortuna Beach

$ | **RESORT** | Popular with couples, families, and spring breakers, this secluded resort provides a casual, all-inclusive getaway where one price covers meals, drinks, tips, nonmotorized water sports, and nightly entertainment. **Pros:** snorkeling and paddleboarding right offshore; trapeze lessons; beautiful, secluded beach. **Cons:** need a car or taxi to Port Lucaya or any other part of the island; rooms are small and need to be updated; resort bustles with spring breakers. [$] *Rooms from: $160* ✉ *Churchill Dr. at Doubloon Rd., Lucaya* ☎ *242/373–4000, 800/996–3426 in U.S.* 🌐 *vivafortunaresort.com* 🛏 *276 rooms* 🍴 *All-inclusive.*

Nightlife

Coral Beach Bar and Restaurant

BARS/PUBS | At the popular and long-standing condominium property Coral Beach Hotel, this spacious, open-air bar bustles with visitors and locals, too. Bartenders serve up tropical drinks and cold beer to a lively crowd with music in the background. The menu boasts Bahamian favorites like conch fritters along with burgers and sweet-potato fries. The kitchen closes at 7 pm Sunday through Thursday, and 8 pm on Saturday and Sunday evenings. Situated poolside and beachfront to Coral Beach, this spot is fun for lunch and a daytime drink, too. ✉ *Coral Rd., off Royal Palm Way, Lucaya* ☎ *242/373–2468* 🌐 *www.coralbeachonline.com.*

Activities

GOLF

Reef Club Golf Course

GOLF | The Reef Course is a par-72, 6,930-yard links-style course. Designed by Robert Trent Jones Jr., it features lots of water (on 13 of the holes), wide fairways flanked by strategically placed bunkers, and a tricky dogleg left on the 18th. While it is the most expensive and most pristine golf course on the island, budget constraints have left it comparable to an average municipal course in the States. Club rentals are available. Guests staying at the Pointe get special discounted rates. Cart rental is mandatory. ✉ *Sea Horse Rd., Lucaya* ☎ *242/373–2002, 866/870–7148* 🌐 *www.grandlucayan.com* ⛳ *18 holes, 6930 yards, par 72.*

DIVE OPERATORS

Caribbean Divers

SCUBA DIVING | This family-owned and -operated dive shop offers personalized and uncrowded trips to coral reefs, wrecks, tunnels, and caverns, as well as shark dives. They also rent equipment and offer NAUI, PADI, and SSI instruction. A resort course allows you to use equipment in a pool and then in a closely supervised open dive. The professionally trained dive staff has more than 30 years of experience and the boat resides right on the channel leading out to the sea, so rides to most major sites are about 5–10 minutes. Lodging packages with Bell Channel Inn are available, in addition to snorkeling trips and private charters. ✉ *Bell Channel Inn, King Rd., Lucaya* ☎ *242/373–9111, 242/373–9112* 🌐 *www.bellchannelinn.com.*

Sunn Odyssey Divers

SCUBA DIVING | This family-run shop has been on the island for more than 20 years. You'll dive with Nick Rolle, the owner himself, who caters to smaller dive groups for a more personalized experience. Full PADI certifications available. ⊠ *Beach Way Dr., Williams Town* ✛ *Near Island Seas Resort and Williams Town Beach* ☎ *242/373–4014, 866/652–3483* ⊕ *www.sunnodysseydivers.com.*

Viva Dive Shop, a Reef Oasis Diving Center

DIVING/SNORKELING | Part of the Reef Oasis Dive Club, this shop offers daily dives and snorkels to various reefs and wrecks on a large boat seating 21 divers straight off Fortune Beach at Viva Wyndham Fortuna Resort. This professional PADI-licensed shop also offers certifications for all levels (all equipment is included). ⊠ *Viva Wyndham Fortuna Resort, Churchill and Doubloon Rd., Lucaya* ☎ *242/441–6254* ⊕ *www.reefoasisdiveclub.com.*

WATER SPORTS

Lucaya Watersports and Tours

BICYCLING | Book a range of water-sports activities and tours inside the triangle-shaped building between Port Lucaya Marketplace and Pelican Bay. Choose from three daily snorkelling or glass-bottom boat excursions, rent a wave runner, or sign up for a wave runner tour. They also rent snorkel gear, kayaks, paddleboards, scooters and bicycles. ⊠ *Port Lucaya Marketplace* ☎ *242/373–6375.*

★ Ocean Motion Water Sports

DIVING/SNORKELING | In business since 1990, Ocean Motion Water Sports is one of the largest water-sports companies on Grand Bahama. Located on Lucayan Beach next to the public beach access across from Port Lucaya Marketplace, they offer everything from parasailing and Banana Boat rides to guided Waverunner tours through the canals and to Peterson Cay. They offer paddleboards, kayaks, Hobie Cat sailboats, waterskiing, and windsurfing instruction. Or, rent snorkel

equipment for the day, and regular ferries will take you to Rainbow Reef and back so you get more beach time. ⊠ *Lucayan Beach, Lucaya* ☎ *242/373–2139, 242/373–9603* ⊕ *www.oceanmotionwatersportsbahamas.com.*

Paradise Watersports

WATER SPORTS | This company offers a variety of tours and sports excursions from two locations, including glass-bottom boats, Waverunner tours, snorkeling cruises, and fishing trips. There's another location at Taino Beach Resort. ⊠ *Island Seas Resort, Lucaya* ☎ *242/373–4001, 954/237–6660 in U.S., 905/231–1689 in Canada.*

Pirate's Cove Zipline and Water Park

KAYAKING | FAMILY | Get your thrill on by whizzing along the overland zipline at this small water park. Be sure to keep your eyes open for views of the beach nearby. Your entrance fee includes use of kayaks and paddleboards, access to the water obstacle course, beach amenities, and games like volleyball. There's also a kids' corner with a shallow pool and swings. ⊠ *Taino Beach next to The Stoned Crab restaurant, Greater Lucaya.*

Greater Grand Bahama

Farther out on either side of the Freeport–Lucaya development, the island reverts to natural pine forest, fishing settlements, and quiet secluded beaches. Heading west from Freeport, travelers pass the harbor area, a cluster of shacks selling fresh conch and seafood at Fishing Hole, a series of small villages, and Deadman's Reef at Paradise Cove before reaching the historic fishing town of West End and its upscale resort at the very tip of the island. East of Lucaya lie long stretches of forest interrupted by the occasional small village, the Lucayan National Park, and myriad bonefishing flats along the eastern end. In September, 2019, Hurricane Dorian left extensive

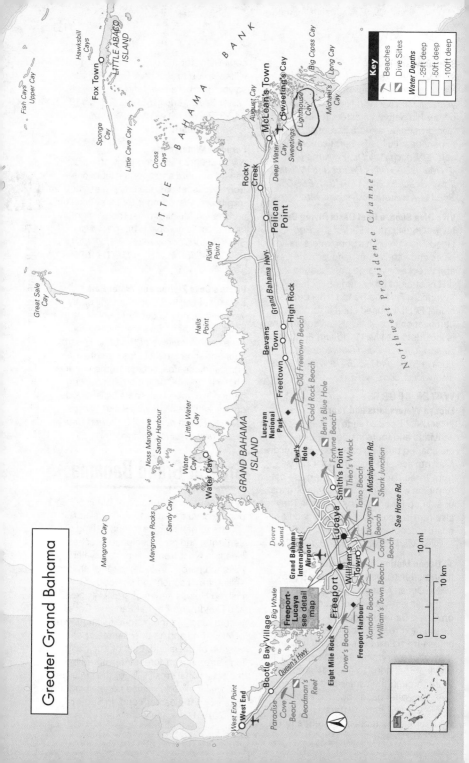

damage along the eastern end of the island, so apart from the beaches there is not much to see or do.

👁 Sights

Celebrity Eco Adventures
BOAT TOURS | FAMILY | Grand Bahama has its own swimming pigs on Crystal Beach. The only way to swim with these swine is to book a tour. Other activities include scooter and airboat tours, stingray feeding, ocean kayaking, and beach volleyball. You can also just grab a beach chair or hammock and relax. There's an on-site bar and restaurant serving local cuisine. Hotel pickup is available if you don't have a car. ✉ West End ☎ 242/351–1241, 242/727–4958 ⊕ www.celebecotours.com.

Eight Mile Rock
NEIGHBORHOOD | You have to get off the main road to get to what was once a real example of the heart and soul of Grand Bahama Island. This settlement is only 10 miles from Freeport Harbour, but now offers little to the tourist except for a few churches and the occasional conch stand. The string of brightly painted food shacks along the ocean, known as Sunset Village, was demolished by Hurricane Wilma in 2005, and has yet to fully recover its party atmosphere. Driving north through Eight Mile Rock will lead you to the West End, home to Paradise Cove and Old Bahama Bay resorts. ✉ Western Grand Bahama.

★ Lucayan National Park
BEACH—SIGHT | FAMILY | Considered the crown jewel of the four national parks on Grand Bahama, Lucayan National Park is the only place to find all six Bahamian ecosystems in a single, 40-acre expanse of land: pine forest, blackland coppice (ferns, bromeliads, orchids), rocky coppice (hardwoods), mangrove swamp, whiteland coppice (rich plant life, poisonwood), and beach/shoreline. Because

Island Dogs 👁

Island dogs, known as "potcakes"—a reference to the bottom of the rice pans they clean up—run wild, so be careful when driving. Efforts in recent years by the active Grand Bahama Humane Society have raised awareness of the need for neutering and spaying.

it is 25 miles east of Lucaya, booking a tour or renting a car is necessary in order to experience all the park has to offer. Explore two caves, hike around the nature trails, bird-watch across the raised boardwalks through the mangroves, or stroll along the spectacular Gold Rock Beach during low tide as the shoreline sets out its "welcome mat"—sand ripples created by tidal pools as the water recedes. ✉ Grand Bahama Hwy., Freetown ☎ 242/353–4149, 242/352–5438 ⊕ www.bnt.bs 💲 $5.

Owl's Hole
CAVE | Named for the mama owl who nests here every year, this vertical freshwater cave (a limestone sinkhole formed by the collapse of a section of a cavern's roof) is a popular local swimming hole. It's rimmed by a 24-foot cliff if you're up for taking a plunge. The less adventuresome can climb down a ladder into the cool but refreshing water. Take snorkel gear down with you to experience the beauty at its full potential, and if you're a certified cavern diver you can join local scuba diving excursions to explore even deeper. If your timing is right, you will see a nest full of fuzzy owlets (April and May) tucked under the ledge as you descend the ladder. The drive here feels a bit like a ride on a Bahamian bush roller coaster but it's worth it—finding the hole is half the adventure. ✉ Off Grand Bahama Hwy. ✛ From Grand Bahama Hwy., turn right on last dirt road

before "Dangerous Curve" sign (before Lucayan National Park). Drive 1.6 miles to tiny parking area on left. You've gone too far if you reach beach.

West End

NEIGHBORHOOD | Once a rowdy, good-time resort area, West End was nearly leveled by Hurricane Matthew in 2016, and is slowly rebuilding. It still attracts small crowds on Sunday evenings for friendly, casual street gatherings, and small fish fry shacks on weekend afternoons, offering up some of the island's best traditional Bahamian fare. Today's visitors stop at Paradise Cove for snorkeling, and farther west at the bay-front conch shacks for conch salad straight from the shell (try Tanya's) or at other tiny eateries along the way like Chicken' Nest, known for having the best conch fritters on island. Overnighters stay at Old Bahama Bay Resort & Yacht Harbour, an upscale gated resort. Nonguests are welcome at the hotel's beachside Tiki Bar for breakfast and lunch, or at the West Side Grille for dinner. ⊠ *Western Grand Bahama, West End.*

🌊 Beaches

★ Gold Rock Beach

BEACH—SIGHT | Located just off the Grand Bahama Highway 26 miles outside town, this secluded beach is accessible via a lovely 10-minute walk through the Lucayan National Park, spanning for yards into the sea when the tide is low. The turquoise water is exceptionally clear, calm, and shallow. Occasional cruise-ship tours visit for a couple of hours around midday, but there is enough space that you will never feel crowded. The beach is almost nonexistent when the tide is high and shade is sparse, but when the tide rolls out, it's one of the most spectacular beaches around, so time your visit accordingly. **Amenities:** none. **Best for:** solitude; swimming; walking. ⊠ *Grand Bahama Hwy., Freetown.*

Here's Where 👁

The last time locals spotted pirates on Grand Bahama Island was in 2005, when Johnny Depp and his crew were filming the second and third installments in the *Pirates of the Caribbean* series. They used a special device in Gold Rock Creek at one of the world's largest open-water filming tanks to give the illusion that the pirate ship was pitching and yawing. You can view the set near Gold Rock Beach.

Lover's Beach

BEACH—SIGHT | This beach on the island's west side is relatively unknown and rarely visited by tourists, and its sand is far less fine and powdery than what's found along the southern shores. However, it's the only spot on Grand Bahama to find sea glass. Adding to its uniqueness is its view of the large tanker and container ships anchored at sea for the island's industrial businesses, and the pastel-painted heavy-equipment tires planted in the sand for seating. **Amenities:** parking (free). **Best for:** walking. ⊠ *Hepburn Town, across the channel from Freeport Harbour, West End.*

Old Freetown Beach

BEACH—SIGHT | This lightly visited beach will take you far from the tourist crowds and resorts. Considered one of the prettiest beaches on the island, with a wide scattering of sea biscuits, blinding white sand, and shallow turquoise water, you will most likely have the whole stretch of sand to yourself. **Amenities:** none. **Best for:** solitude; swimming; walking. ⊠ *Off Grand Bahama Hwy., just west of Ol' Freetown Farm* ✛ *Turn south on dirt road that lies just east of Grand Bahama Hwy.'s "Dangerous Curve" sign. Road to Owl's Hole will also land you at this beach.*

Continued on page 142

JUNKANOO IN THE BAHAMAS

by Jessica Robertson

It's after midnight, and the only noise in downtown Nassau is a steady buzz of anticipation. Suddenly the streets erupt in a kaleidoscope of sights and sounds—Junkanoo groups are parading down Bay Street. Vibrant costumes sparkle in the light of the street lamps, and the revelers bang on goatskin drums and clang cowbells, hammering out a steady celebratory beat. It's Junkanoo time!

Junkanoo is an important part of the Bahamas' Christmas season. Parades begin after midnight and last until midday on Boxing Day (December 26), and there are more on New Year's Day. What appears to be a random, wild expression of joy is actually a well-choreographed event. Large groups (often as many as 500 to 1,000 people) compete for prize money and bragging rights. Teams choose a different theme each year and keep it a closely guarded secret until they hit Bay Street. They spend most of the year preparing for the big day at their "shacks," which are tucked away in neighborhoods across the island. They practice dance steps and music, and they design intricate costumes. During the parade, judges award prizes for best music, best costumes, and best overall presentation.

Junkanoo costume, Grand Bahama

JUNKANOO HISTORY

Junkanoo holds an important place in the history and culture of the Bahamas, but the origin of the word *junkanoo* remains a mystery. Many believe it comes from John Canoe, an African tribal chief who was brought to the West Indies as a slave and then fought for the right to celebrate with his people. Others believe the word stems from the French gens *inconnus*, which means "the unknown people"—significant because Junkanoo revelers wear costumes that mask their identities.

The origin of the festival itself is more certain. Though its roots can be traced back to West Africa, it began in the Bahamas during the 16TH or 17TH century when Bahamian slaves were given a few days off around Christmas to celebrate with their families. They left the plantations and had elaborate costume parties at which they danced and played home-made musical instruments. They wore large, often scary-looking masks, which gave them the freedom of anonymity, so they could let loose without inhibition.

Over the years, Junkanoo has evolved. Costumes once decorated with shredded newspaper are now elaborate, vibrant creations incorporating imported crepe paper, glitter, gemstones, and feathers.

MUSIC'S ROLE

There's something mesmerizing about the simple yet powerful beat of the goat-skin drum. Couple that steady pounding with the "kalik-kalik" clanging of thousands of cowbells and a hundreds-strong brass band, and Junkanoo music becomes downright infectious.

Music is the foundation of Junkanoo. It provides a rhythm for both the costumed revelers and crowds of spectators who jump up and down on rickety bleacher seats. The heavy percussion sound is created by metal cowbells, whistles, and oil barrel drums with fiery sternos inside to keep the animal skin coverings pliant. In the late 1970s, Junkanoo music evolved with the addition of brass instruments, adding melodies from Christmas carols, sacred religious hymns, and contemporary hits.

If you're in Nassau anytime from September through the actual festival, stand out on your hotel balcony and listen carefully. Somewhere, someone is bound to be beating out a rhythm as groups practice for the big parade.

DRESS TO IMPRESS

Each year, talented artists and builders transform chicken wire, cardboard, Styrofoam, and crepe paper into magnificent costumes that are worn, pushed, or carried along the Junkanoo parade route. Dancers and musicians tend to wear elaborate head dresses or off-the-shoulder pieces and cardboard skirts completely covered in finely fringed, brightly colored crepe paper—applied a single strip at a time until every inch is covered. Gemstones, referred to as "tricks" in the Junkanoo world, are painstakingly glued onto costumes to add sparkle. In recent years, feathers have been incorporated, giving the cardboard covered creations an added level of movement and flair.

In order to wow the crowd, and more importantly, win the competition, every member of the group must be in full costume when they hit Bay Street. Even their shoes are completely decorated. Massive banner pieces so big they graze the power lines and take up the entire width of the street are carried along the route by men who take turns. Every element, from the smallest costume to the lead banner, as well as the entire color scheme, is meticulously planned out months in advance.

EXPERIENCE JUNKANOO

SECURE YOUR SEATS

■ Junkanoo bleacher seat tickets ($10–$50) can be hard to come by as the parade date approaches. Contact your hotel concierge ahead of time to arrange for tickets.

■ Rawson Square bleachers are the best seats. This is where groups perform the longest and put on their best show.

■ If you don't mind standing, make your way to Shirley Street or the eastern end of Bay Street, where the route is lined with barricades. Judges are positioned all along the way so you'll see a good performance no matter where you end up.

■ Junkanoo groups make two laps around the parade route. Each lap can take a few hours to complete, and there are many groups in the lineup, so most spectators stay only for the first round. Head to Bay Street just before dawn, and you'll be sure to score a vacant seat.

BEHIND THE SCENES

■ During the parade, head east along Bay Street and turn onto Elizabeth Avenue to the rest area. Groups take a break in the parking lot here before they start round two. Costume builders frantically repair any pieces damaged during the first rush (Bahamian slang for parading), revelers refuel at barbeque stands, goatskin drums are placed next to a giant bonfire to keep them supple, and in the midst of all the noise and hubbub, you'll find any number of people taking a nap to ensure they make it through a long and physically demanding night.

■ If star-stalking is your thing, scour the crowds in the VIP section in Parliament Square or look across the street on the balcony of the Scotiabank building. This is where celebrities usually watch the parades.

■ When the parade ends, wander along the route and surrounding streets to score a one-of-a-kind souvenir. Despite the many hours Junkanoo participants spend slaving over their costumes, by the time they're done rushing the last thing they want to do is carry it home. Finders keepers.

■ If you're in Nassau in early December, watch the Junior Junkanoo parade. School groups compete for prizes in various age categories. The littlest ones are usually offbeat and egged on by teachers and parents, but are oh-so-cute in their costumes. The high school groups put on a show just as impressive as the groups in the senior parade.

JUNKANOO TRIVIA

■ Kalik beer, brewed in the Bahamas, gets its name from the sound of clanking cowbells.

■ An average costume requires 3,000 to 5,000 strips of fringed crepe paper to completely cover its cardboard frame.

■ During the height of sponge farming in the Bahamas, a major industry in the early 1900s, many Junkanoo participants used natural sponge to create their costumes.

JUNKANOO ON OTHER ISLANDS

Nassau's Junkanoo parade is by far the biggest and most elaborate, but most other islands hold their own celebrations

Junkanoo parade in Nassau

on New Year's Day. Nassau's parades are strictly a spectator sport unless you are officially in a group, but Out Island parades are more relaxed and allow visitors to join the rush.

JUNKANOO YEAR-ROUND

Not satisfied with limiting Junkanoo to Christmastime, the Bahamas Ministry of Tourism hosts an annual **Junkanoo Summer Festival**. Smaller scale parades are held on alternating weekends in June and July on most major islands, including Nassau. In addition to the traditional Junkanoo rush, these festivals offer arts and crafts demonstrations, conch cracking, crab catching, coconut-husking competitions, concerts featuring top Bahamian artists, and of course, lots of good Bahamian food. ☎ 242/302–2000.

Marina Village on Paradise Island hosts **Junkanoo rushouts** on Wednesday and Saturday (9:30 pm). There are no big stand-alone pieces, but dancers and musicians wear color-coordinated costumes and headpieces. The parade is much less formal, so feel free to jump in and dance along.

The **Educulture Museum and Workshop** in Nassau gives a behind-the-scenes look at Junkanoo. Some of each year's best costumes are on display, as well as costumes from years gone by when newspaper and sponges were used as decoration. The diehard Junkanoo staff will help you make your own Junkanoo creations. Be sure to arrange your visit ahead of time. ☎ 242/328–3786.

★ Paradise Cove Beach

BEACH—SIGHT | **FAMILY** | A 20-minute drive from Freeport, this beach's spectacular swim-to reef (called Deadman's Reef) is its best asset. Close to shore, you'll also find the longest man-made reef (composed of a long line of concrete reef balls) in the Bahamas, with spectacular marine life that includes various rays, sea turtles, and barracudas. Paradise Cove is a small native-owned resort with many different adventure packages, which all include return transportation from Freeport and Lucaya. The beach is short but wide with scrubby vegetation and swaying palm trees. Snorkel equipment and kayaks are available to rent, and refreshments flow at the Red Bar. Beaches are public access up to the high water mark in the Bahamas so you can go and explore, but if you want to use any of their amenities, you must pay a small fee at the bar. **Amenities:** food and drink; parking (no fee); showers; toilets; water sports. **Best for:** snorkeling. ✉ *Warren J. Levarity Hwy., between Eight Mile Rock and West End, West End* ☎ *242/349-2677 Paradise Cove tour reservations number* 🌐 *www.deadmansreef.com.*

Hotels

★ Old Bahama Bay Resort & Yacht Harbour

$$ | **RESORT** | **FAMILY** | Fishing enthusiasts, yachters, and families can relax in relative seclusion at this West End resort, made up of colorful beachfront and poolside suites individually decorated with island charm. **Pros:** top-shelf marina; quiet and secluded; on-site activities including tennis and basketball courts. **Cons:** limited dining choices; far from main airport, shopping, and other restaurants; need a car to explore the rest of the island. [$] *Rooms from: $275* ✉ *West End* ☎ *242/350–6500, 888/800–8959* 🌐 *www.oldbahamabayresorts.com* 🛏 *76 rooms* 🍴 *No meals.*

Paradise Cove

$ | **RENTAL** | **FAMILY** | Devoted snorkelers and peace-lovers will like this offbeat location (owned and operated by a local family), offering two two-bedroom stilted cottages overlooking the beach. **Pros:** on the beach; superb snorkeling; quiet in the off-hours. **Cons:** far from restaurant options, nightlife, and shopping; sometimes swarmed with bused-in visitors during the day; fee to rent snorkeling gear and kayaks. [$] *Rooms from: $175* ✉ *Warren J. Levarity Hwy., 8 miles east of West End turnoff, West End* ☎ *242/349–2677* 🌐 *www.deadmansreef.com* 🛏 *2 cottages* 🍴 *No meals.*

Chapter 5

ANDROS, BIMINI, AND THE BERRY ISLANDS

Updated by
Noelle Nicolls

⊙ Sights	🍴 Restaurants	🛏 Hotels	🛍 Shopping	🍸 Nightlife
★★★★★	★★★☆☆	★★★★☆	★★☆☆☆	★☆☆☆☆

WELCOME TO ANDROS, BIMINI, AND THE BERRY ISLANDS

TOP REASONS TO GO

★ **Bonefish:** Andros, Bimini, and the Berry Islands have world-class reputations for bone-fishing. Hire a guide to show you how to fly-fish, then hunt the bights of Andros or the shallow flats of Bimini and the Berries in pursuit of the elusive "gray ghost."

★ **Day Trips:** These islands are closest to both Nassau and South Florida, making them ideal for day trips by ferry or air for gaming, beaching, dining, and fun shore excursions.

★ **Dive Andros or Bimini:** Go with the diving experts at Small Hope Bay or Kamalame Cay and drop "over the Andros wall" or at Neal Watson's Bimini Scuba Center to explore magnificent wrecks and reefs.

★ **Fish for big game:** Charter a boat and experience the thrill of catching deep-sea prizes such as marlin, mahi-mahi, tuna, and wahoo.

1 Andros. Vast fishing flats, blue holes, vibrant reefs, and the Tongue of the Ocean wall make fishing, diving, and snorkeling the main reasons adventurers travel to Andros. The island is mostly flat, lush with pine forests and mangroves, rimmed with white-sand beaches, and laced with miles of creeks and lakes.

2 Bimini. Year-round, boaters and tourists from Florida cross the Gulf Stream seeking fish and fun. Many visit North Bimini via the Bimini fast ferry to enjoy Resorts World Bimini with its new Hilton hotel, casino, dining, and fun excursions. Fishing and yachting fans frequent Alice Town's quaint hotels, bars, and Bahamian food shacks. South Bimini appeals more to the nature-minded and adventurous visitor.

3 The Berry Islands. For the ultimate remote island getaway, fly and stay on the small capital of Great Harbour Cay in the north or on semiprivate Chub Cay in the south. In between lies a necklace of beautiful island gems accessible only by boat. Both hubs have clubs, affordable villas, and full-service marinas, and both are celebrated for bone-, deep-sea, and bottom-fishing.

Alice Town · North Bimini
South Bimini
Turtle Rocks · *Bimini* 2
Holm Cay
North Cat Cay
South Cat Cay
Ocean Cay

Great Stirrup Cay

Great Harbour Cay

Hoffman's Cay

Comfort Cay

Berry Islands
3

Bond's Cay

Chub Cay

Whale Cay

Joulters Cays

Lowe Sound

Morgan's Bluff

Red Bays

Nicholl's Town

Mastic Point

San Andros

NASSAU

Barrier Reef

Kamalame Cay

Staniard Creek

New Providence Island

Small Hope Bay

Fresh Creek

Tongue of the Ocean

Williams Island

Andros Town

Gold Cay

Andros Island
1

Cargill Creek

Behring Point

Barrier Reef

Big Wood Cay

GRAND

Moxey Town

Lisbon Creek

Wood Cay

Driggs Hill

BAHAMA

Yellow Cay

Mangrove Cay

Congo Town

The Bluff

Kemps Bay

BANK

Poptop Cay

Barrier Reef

Deep Creek

Mars Bay

20 mi

Water Cays

Curley Cut Cays

30 km

Legends loom large (and small) on these northwestern Bahamas islands. On Bimini, you'll hear about the lost underwater city of Atlantis, Ernest Hemingway's visits, and the Fountain of Youth. Tiny birdlike creatures known as chickcharnies are said to inhabit the pine forests of Andros Island. On both islands, along with the Berry Islands, bonefishing has made legends of mere men.

Andros, Bimini, and the Berries remain a secret mostly known to avid divers, boaters, and fishermen—fishing and commercial diving sustain the economies here, though Andros also thrives on farming fruit and vegetables. Local produce from a demonstration and training farm is available for sale at The Bahamas Agriculture and Marine Science Institute (BAMSI) located in Central Andros. These islands stash their reputation for superlative blue holes and other natural phenomena away from the glamour of Nassau, just minutes away by plane but a world apart, yet you'll still find some of the Bahamas' most admired resorts here. North Bimini has been transformed into a busier island by Resorts World; its casino and new Hilton hotel feed the island with hundreds of golf-carting tourists that buy packages on the fast ferry from Fort Lauderdale. Although Andros is the largest Bahamas island and a favorite of nature-lovers, most of its land is far from any settlement and hardly habitable. All resorts, inns, and lodges lie on a narrow east-coast strip, adjoining beautiful beaches and the barrier reef.

The 30-some cays of the Berry Islands are lesser known still.

Planning

When to Go

Traveling to all islands by boat is easiest in summer when seas are calmer. Fishing and diving are good year-round, although cold fronts from December to February can cause rough seas. November, March, and April are often the most pleasant months. Temperatures are more comfortable in winter and spring and, during these drier months, mosquitoes and sand flies are fewer. Temperatures usually remain steady enough to enjoy the beaches year-round, but they occasionally drop into the 60s in cold fronts. Hurricane season runs from June through November. August and September, the most likely months for hurricanes, can be hot and steamy, and many resorts and restaurants are closed. Among Andros, Bimini, and the Berries, it seems each hotel or lodge has its own high, low, and shoulder seasons and respective rates. Some hotels, such as the Hilton at Resorts World Bimini peak in summer, while others such as bonefish lodges, peak in winter. Highest rates are invariably in the holiday seasons between late December and early January, around Easter in March and April, and U.S. Labor Day in early September. Bargains can be found in late January, February, October, and early December.

Festivals

WINTER

Junkanoo Celebrations occur all over the islands on **Boxing Day** (December 26) and **New Year's Day,** with festivities that include traditional People's Rush mini-Junkanoo parades, music, dancing, and food. They take place in Fresh Creek, Central Andros; Nicholl's Town, North Andros; Moxey Town, Mangrove Cay; Driggs Hill, South Andros; Alice Town, North Bimini; and Bullock's Harbour Park in Great Harbour Cay, Berry Islands. In February, Resorts World Bimini hosts its annual **Wahoo Challenge** fishing tournament and the Bimini Wahoo Mahem in November.

SPRING

In Andros, though bonefishing is the name of the game, in May the town of Red Bays, North Andros, hosts a Snapper Tournament. Mangrove Cay in mid-May comes alive with its own local Mother's Day Homecoming and Regatta with islander sloop sailing races, food, drinks, and entertainment.

SUMMER

During the second weekend in June, three days of crab races, cook-offs, live Rake 'n' Scrape music, and national musical artists comprise the **All Andros CrabFest** in Fresh Creek, held at Queen's Park. Expect wild street parties across the Bahamas on July 10, **Independence Day.** The Regattas are often the Bahamas Out Islands' most attended festivals featuring passionate rivalry and multiple races of one or more of the A, B, and C class Bahamian sailing sloops. Around The Bahamas' Labour Day in early June, South Andros holds its regatta at The Bluff. The largest sailing festival in the region is the **All Andros & Berry Islands Regatta,** on Morgan's Bluff Beach on the second weekend in July. In Nicholl's Town, at the end of July you can also catch the **Junkanoo Summer Festival.** Every Saturday in July Fresh Creek's Queen's Park hosts **Andros Nights** where locals and visitors gather until midnight to dance and enjoy Bahamian food prepared by women in the community. In Andros, on the third weekend in July, the **Goombay Summer Festival** is held on Friday (noon to midnight) at Morgan's Bluff in North Andros and on Saturday night (6 pm to midnight) at Cargill Creek, south Central Andros. Both feature live local bands, Junkanoo, food, drinks, and fun contests such as onion-peeling, watermelon-eating, and sack races. Every Saturday in July, the Berry Island's Great Harbour Cay Marina hosts the **Junkanoo Summer Fest** with a Junkanoo miniparade, and on the second August weekend, it hosts the **Lobster & Lionfish Derby,** a fishing tournament with prizes and entertainment including Junkanoo, limbo, fire-dancing, and a lobster cook-off contest. In June and July, Bimini hosts the **Bahamas Boating Flings,** guided flotillas of motor yachts wishing to cross the Gulfstream with piloting help organized by the Bahamas Ministry of Tourism's Boating Department. Participating boats gather at a marina in Fort Lauderdale. (See Boating Flings at ⊕ *www.bahamas.com.*)

In mid-October, South Andros hosts the three-day **Andros ConchFest** on Mars Bay Blue Hole Beach and Community Center where locals and a few lucky visitors are entertained with myriad ways to cook and eat conch amid fun contests including dancing and crack-conching. In

November, the famous deep-sea fishing resort Bimini Big Game Club hosts its **Annual Wahoo Smackdown** fishing tournament. Conviviality abounds when the boats arrive back at the dock and at the evening parties. All are welcome to enter.

Getting Here and Around

AIR

Scheduled nonstop and direct flights from the United States to the Bahamas' northwestern islands are growing in frequency with small, reliable operators from Miami International Airport (MIA), Miami's Watson Island Seaplane Base (XX4), Fort Lauderdale-Hollywood International (FLL), and Fort Lauderdale Executive (FXE) airports. Western Air operates direct flights from Nassau (NAS) to San Andros Airport (SAQ) and Nassau to Bimini (BIM). Flamingo Air flies direct from Nassau to Mangrove Cay (MAY), Andros and Freeport to Bimini (BIM).

FROM NASSAU Flamingo Air. ☎ *242/377–0354* ⊕ *flamingoairbah.com.* **GlenAir.** ☎ *242/368–2116, 242/471–1860.* **LeAir.** ☎ *242/377–2356* ⊕ *www.flyleair.com.* **Randolph Holdings.** ☎ *242/368–2922, 242/477–1335* ⊕ *www.flycharterbahamas.com.*

FROM FORT LAUDERDALE AND MIAMI Air Flight Charters. ☎ *954/359–0320* ⊕ *www.airflightcharters.com.* **Silver Airways.** ☎ *801/401–9100* ⊕ *www. silverairways.com.* **Tropic Ocean Airways.** ☎ *800/767–0897* ⊕ *www.flytropic. com.* **Watermakers Air.** ☎ *954/771–0330* ⊕ *www.watermakersair.com.*

BOAT AND FERRY

Visiting private boaters must clear Bahamas Customs and Immigration at the nearest port-of-entry, found in Bimini on both South and North Bimini, in the Berry Islands on Great Harbour Cay and Chub Cay, and in Andros at Nicholl's Town (Morgan's Bluff Harbour) in North Andros, Fresh Creek Harbour and Drigg's

Hill Harbour in South Andros. Customs officers are stationed at the nearest airport—San Andros, Andros Town, and Congo Town airports, respectively—so call the airports ahead of time to inform them you are coming in. Once cleared, you can explore other islands, marinas, and anchorages. You can also clear at gorgeous private island and marina Cat Cay Yacht Club, a few miles south of Bimini. Except for Morgan's Bluff, all ports-of-entry have full-service marinas with amenities, lodging, dining, beaches, and fun activities. From Florida, North Bimini is the only island reachable by ferry. From the Port of Miami, FRS Caribbean has a fast ferry that speeds in two hours to Resorts World Bimini's pier, costing from $130 to $200 round-trip. From Nassau's Potter Cay Dock, each main island is served weekly or three times a month by ferry or mail boat. Note that mail boats may make several stops, and due to weather, you may be marooned on your chosen island for days until the next mail boat arrives. Between South and North Bimini a ferry runs the 15-minute harbor ride every half hour or so and even until 11 pm. Boating between other islands requires a boat rental or charter. *See Boat and Ferry for each island.*

CONTACTS Bahamas Customs. ☎ *242/347–3100 Alice Town, North Bimini, 242/347–3101 South Bimini airport, 242/325–5788 Chub Cay airport, 242/367–8116 Great Harbour Cay airport, 242/329–2140 San Andros airport (for Nicholl's Town, Morgan's Bluff), 242/368–2030 Andros Town airport (for Fresh Creek), 242/369–2640 Congo Town airport (for Drigg's Hill and Kemp's Bay), 242/377–7030 Nassau Airport customs, answers call all hrs, 242/326–4401 through 6 Customs HQ Nassau, business hrs only* ⊕ *www. bahamas.gov.bs/customs.* **Bahamas Ferries.** ✉ *From Potter's Cay Dock, Nassau* ☎ *242/323–2166* ⊕ *www.bahamasferries.com.* **Balearia Caribbean Bimini Fast Ferry.** ☎ *866/699–6988 toll-free* ⊕ *www.*

balariacaribbean.com. **Potter's Cay Dock-master's Office.** ☎ *242/393–1064.*

CAR

Blessedly devoid of rental cars, most of Bimini is accessed on foot or by golf cart. Car rentals are available on Andros and on Great Harbour Cay in the Berry Islands. Don't expect major companies; rentals are done through microenterprises and are usually arranged directly by the hotel or lodge. Most take credit cards but cash is handy. Rates range between $60 and $120 per day and average $85 per day. Especially in Andros, make sure to call in advance to have a rental car waiting upon arrival. Some Andros hotels and lodges offer free airport transfers.

TAXI

Taxis are readily available at airports to meet incoming flights and for sightseeing. On Andros's larger islands, most mail boats and ferries are greeted with one or two taxis. If not, you can often hitch a ride with a friendly islander going your way.

Hotels

Find everything from luxury properties to boutique hotels, rentals on private cays (pronounced "keys"), and simple fishing lodges. Comfortable lodge and motel-style accommodations are most common, and usually have a restaurant and bar. Some lodges don't have in-room telephones, TVs, or Internet. Most have a phone for guest use on the property, and some will have a computer with Internet in the lounge or lobby. Almost all take credit cards, though very small lodges and non-hotel restaurants may accept cash only. Although places advertise Internet services, connection can be spotty. Rates typically vary between high and low seasons. In the smaller Out Islands, rates are often expressed per cabin, room, or cottage (usually with double occupancy).

Hotel prices are for two people in a standard double room in low season, excluding service and 6%–12% tax and 12% VAT.While most properties also charge gratuities, not all are registered to charge VAT. All businesses that charge VAT should be registered and certified to do so. The highest rates and busiest times vary with each resort, usually occurring around the Thanksgiving, Christmas, and Easter holidays and from February to June. High season is usually February to April, but these islands can also be busy through June.

Restaurants

With a few notable exceptions, dining here is a casual experience. Most restaurants, lodges, and inns serve traditional Bahamian fare. Call ahead to make sure a restaurant is open. Except for roadside and seaside conch shacks, almost all require you to order dinner ahead of time. Resort restaurants have à la carte sit-down meals. Some lodges have all-inclusive meal plans with stays and offer day or night passes for dining nonguests. Many of the favored Bahamian food outlets are takeout places with picnic tables. A common practice is to take food back to your room to enjoy air-conditioned and fly- and mosquito-less comfort. Thatched conch stands and colorful roadside bars are a great way to mingle with the locals.

Restaurant prices are based on the median main course price at dinner, excluding gratuity, typically 10% to 15%, coupled with the new Bahamas Valued Added Tax (VAT) of 12% (on food but not gratuities)—which are usually automatically added to the bill.

WHAT IT COSTS in Dollars

	$	$$	$$$	$$$$
RESTAURANTS				
	under $20	$20–$30	$31–$40	over $40
HOTELS				
	under $200	$200–$300	$301–$400	over $400

Visitor Information

CONTACTS Andros Tourist Offices.
☎ 242/368–2286 Central Andros, 242/369–1688 South Andros, 242/368–2286 North Andros ⊕ www.bahamas.com/islands/andros. **Association Of Bahamas Marinas.** ☎ 844/556–5290 toll-free, 954/462–4591 U.S. and Canada ⊕ www.bahamasmarinas.com. **Bahama Out Islands Promotion Board.** ☎ 954/740–8740 U.S. and Canada, 242/322–1140 Nassau office ⊕ www.myoutislands.com. **Berry Islands Tourism Administrator.** ✉ Great Harbour Cay Airport, Great Harbour Cay ☎ 242/367–8291 office, 242/451–0404 cell, 242/225–2563 toll-free within Bahamas ⊕ www.bahamas.com/islands/berry. **Bimini Tourist Office.** ✉ Alice Town ☎ 242/347–3528 or 29 ⊕ www.bahamas.com/islands/bimini.

Andros

The Bahamas' largest island (100 miles long and 40 miles wide) and one of the least explored, Andros's landmass is carved up by myriad channels, creeks, lakes, and mangrove-covered cays. The natural **Northern, Middle,** and **South bights** cut through the width of the island, creating shallow boating access between both the east and west coasts. Andros' high concentration of inland blue holes also polka-dot the land. Nestled inside the island's pine and coppice forests, blue-hole exploration, nature hikes, sea kayaking, and snorkeling are draws to this glorious ecotourism island. Above all, Andros is best known for its vast bonefishing flats and diverse diving, particularly the high-quality reef dives, wreck dives, blue holes, and spectacular wall dives at the edge of the continental shelf.

The Spaniards who came here in the 16th century called Andros *La Isla del Espíritu Santo*—the Island of the Holy Spirit—and it has retained its eerie mystique. The descendants of Seminole Indians and runaway slaves who left Florida in the mid-19th century settled in the North Andros settlement of **Red Bays** and remained hidden until a few decades ago. They continue to celebrate the tribal heritage, making a living by weaving straw goods, along with fishing and harvesting sea sponge. The Seminoles originated the myth of the island's legendary (and elusive) chickcharnies—red-eyed, bearded, green-feathered creatures with three fingers and three toes that hang upside down by their tails from pine trees. These mythical characters supposedly wait deep in the forests to bestow good luck upon the friendly passersby and vent their mischief on the hostile trespasser. The rest of Andros's roughly 8,000 residents live in a dozen settlements on the eastern shore. Farming and commercial fishing sustain the economy.

Andros's undeveloped **West Side** adjoins the Great Bahama Bank, a vast shallow-water haven for lobster, bonefish, and tarpon. Wild orchids and dense pine and mahogany forests cover the island's lush green interior. The marine life–rich **Andros Barrier Reef**—the world's third largest—is within a mile of the eastern shore and runs for 140 miles. Sheltered waters within the reef average 6 to 15 feet, but on the other side ("over the wall") they plunge to more than 6,000 feet at the **Tongue of the Ocean.**

GETTING HERE AND AROUND
AIR

Consult your hotel to figure out which airport to fly into. From north to south: serving North Andros is the **San Andros Airport (SAQ),** serving Central Andros and Fresh Creek is **Andros Town Airport (ASD)**; **Mangrove Cay Airport (MAY)** serves the island of the same name, and serving South Andros is **Congo Town Airport (TZN).** All except Mangrove Cay are ports of entry, enabling customs clearance for private flights or charters directly from the United States. San Andros (SAQ) is best for hotels between Nicholl's Town to Stafford Creek, and is reachable from the United States via Watermakers Air four times a week and from Nassau via Western Air twice daily. Best for all other hotels in North and Central Andros is Andros Town airport, which sees the most traffic and is reachable from the United States by Watermakers Air four times a week. Le Air operates a twice daily service from Nassau's domestic terminal and Randolph Holdings Air Charters usually flies twice a day from Nassau Airport's General Aviation base, a short taxi ride from the main Nassau airport. Mangrove Cay Airport is reachable from Nassau twice daily via Le Air and Flamingo Air. Congo Town in South Andros is served by Watermakers Air from Fort Lauderdale Executive and Western Air from Nassau twice daily.

For groups and families, private charters from Miami, Fort Lauderdale, or Nassau can be an affordable, convenient option. From the United States are numerous charter services to all Andros airports including Watermakers Air and Air Flight Charters. If you're willing to splash out on luxurious travel, a floatplane via Tropic Ocean Airways or a helicopter from Florida can be an exotic highlight.

CONTACTS Andros Town Airport.
☎ *242/368–2134.* **Congo Town Airport.**
☎ *242/369–2270.* **Mangrove Cay Airport.**

☎ *242/369–0270.* **San Andros Airport.**
☎ *242/329–4401.*

CAR RENTAL

All airports have jeeps or cars for rent from $70 to $120 a day, plus gas, depending on size and vehicle condition. Note that some resorts or lodges may also offer cars-plus-stay packages and free transfers to and from the airport. Lodges will often offer you a ride to wherever you want to go.

FERRY

Andros is divided by water into three parts: North and Central Andros, Mangrove Cay, and South Andros. Each is serviced by either a ferry or mail boat from Potter's Cay Dock in Nassau. Mail boats are good options for budgeting backpackers, adventurous students, or groups carrying lots of luggage such as film crews. Passage costs vary between mail boats from $40 to $70 one way and may include a meal. The journey is often overnight and each vessel sails three or four times a month. Nicholl's Town and The Bluff in North Andros is served by M/V *Lady Rosalind*; Fresh Creek by Bahamas Ferries and the M/V *KCT*, Mangrove Cay and South Andros by the M/V *Capt. Moxey* and M/V *Lady Katherine*. Note that mail boats may make several stops, and due to their infrequency you may be marooned on your chosen island for days, if not weeks, until the next mail boat arrives. For the most up-to-date information on mail boat schedules, passengers should always consult the dockmaster in Potter's Cay in Nassau, weekdays 9 to 5. Once on North and Central Andros you have to fly or charter a boat to reach its southerly sister islands, but you can take the *Capt. Moxey* mail boat or the free twice-daily government ferry between Mangrove Cay and South Andros. The ferry is run by Frederick Major in a 30-foot outboard from Driggs Hill on South Andros to Lisbon Creek on Mangrove Cay, at 8 am and 4 pm. The journey takes around six minutes.

CONTACTS Frederick Major's Ferry Service.
☎ 242/376–8533, ⊕ www.bahamas.
com/vendor/south-andros-tourist-of-
fice. **Potter's Cay Dockmaster's Office.**
☎ 242/393–1064. **South Andros Tourist
Office.** ☎ 242/369–1688 ⊕ www.baha-
mas.com/andros.

TAXI

Confirm with the hotel to see if your taxi
will meet airplanes and ferries. Rates
run around $1.50 per mile, though most
fares are set and generally known. In
North or South Andros fares can be quite
a surprise; always ask your hotel and
always agree on a fare before you set
foot in a taxi. Taxis are also available for
touring around the islands and, because
of their friendliness, local knowledge,
and insight, they often become vacation
highlights. Tours will take you to shops,
farms, restaurants, beaches, historic
ruins, and blue holes—giving you a sense
of the scene and recommendations on
where to dine and more. Tour rates vary:
for five passengers and up they start
from $50 per person for a half day and
$100 per person for a full day.

North Andros

The northern part of Andros spreads
from the settlements of **Morgan's Bluff,
Nicholl's Town, Lowe's Sound,** and **Red
Bays,** and ends at **Stafford Creek.** North
Andros consists of long stretches of
pine forests, limestone bluffs, and fields
and gardens of ground crops. Seminole
Indians, American slaves, and Mennon-
ites settled this land along with the West
Indian population. White-sand beaches,
mostly deserted, line the island's eastern
face, interrupted by creeks, inlets, and
rock outcroppings. Logging supported
North Andros in the 1940s and 1950s,
and laid the foundation for its roads. Tourism, farming, and commercial fishing,
especially in the west and the northernmost Joulters Cays, drives the economy
today.

San Andros is home to North Andros's
airport, but **Nicholl's Town** is the port
and largest settlement here and in all of
Andros. Once home to a vogue resort in
the 1960s (Andros Beach Hotel), today
it is mostly residential, inhabited in part
by snowbirds who own the adorable
Bahamian-style, brightly painted cottages
that were once part of the iconic resort.
Although recent repaving has improved
the main highway, you'll often encounter potholes. Near the airport, road
conditions are good; don't worry about
traffic—you'll be lucky if you see more
than 20 vehicles on the highway in a
single day.

GETTING HERE AND AROUND

The San Andros airport (SAQ) has flights
from Nassau through SkyBahamas and
Western Air. Taxis meet incoming flights.
You can get around on foot in Nicholl's
Town; car rentals are available for exploring the island's 65 miles of Queen's Highway and feeder roads in the north. They
run about $85 to $130 a day. Main roads
in Central Andros are in good shape, but
watch out for potholes in North Andros.
If you're renting a car, call in advance to
make sure your car is available at the
airport.

CAR RENTALS CJ's Car Rental. ☎ 242/471–
3386. **Executive Car Rentals.** ☎ 242/471–
5259, 242/329–4081. **Gaitor's Car Rental.**
☎ 242/471–1550, 242/464–3151 ✉ an-
dreadaphne@yahoo.com.

◉ Sights

Morgan's Bluff & Beach

BEACH—SIGHT | Three miles north of
Nicholl's Town is a crescent beach, a
headland known as Morgan's Bluff, and
a set of caves named after the 17th-cen-
tury pirate Captain Henry Morgan, who
allegedly dropped off some of his stolen
loot in the area. The beach and park is
the site of Regatta Village, a colorful
collection of stands and stalls used in
July when the big event, the All Andros

Did You Know?

Andros is the largest yet one of the most sparsely developed islands in the Bahamas. Putting the first footprints of the day on an empty beach might become your favorite activity.

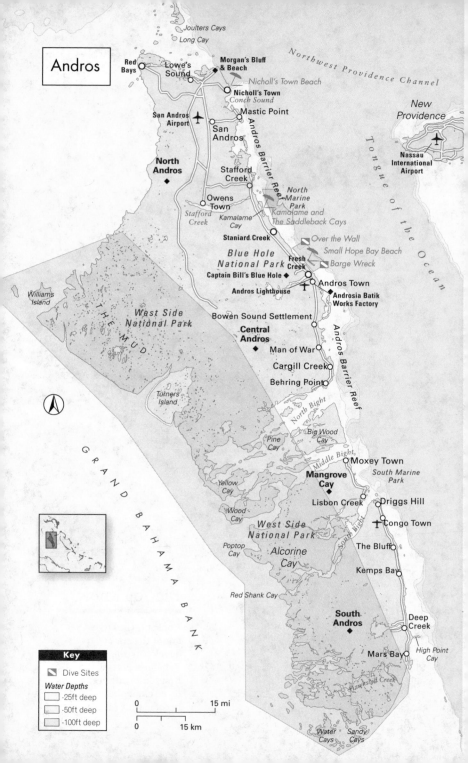

& Berry Islands Regatta, takes place. Adjacent is the Government Dock and a safe harbor, with a small, popular island bar and restaurant. ✉ *Nicholl's Town.*

Nicholl's Town

TOWN | Nicholl's Town, on Andros's northeastern corner, is a spread-out settlement with its eastern shore lying on a beautiful beach and its northern shore on Morgan's Bluff beach. It is the island's largest settlement, with a population of about 600. (Interestingly, the name used to be spelled Nicoll's Town, without the h.) This friendly community, with its agriculture- and fishing-based economy, has grocery and supplies stores, a few motels, a public medical clinic, government offices, and more. Adorable cottages, a throwback from the town's big resort era of the 1960s, house the island's wintering population from the United States, Canada, and Europe. ✉ *Nicholl's Town.*

Red Bays

TOWN | Fourteen miles west of Nicholl's Town, Red Bays is the sole west-coast settlement in all of Andros. The town was settled by Seminole Indians and runaway African slaves escaping Florida pre–Civil War and was cut off from the rest of Andros until a highway connected it to Nicholl's Town in the 1980s. Residents are known for their craftsmanship, particularly straw basketry and wood carving. Tightly plaited baskets, some woven with scraps of colorful Androsia batik, have become a signature craft of Andros. Artisans have their wares on display in front of their homes (with fixed prices). Despite opening their homes to buyers, Red Bays locals don't seem very used to visitors. Expect a lot of curious stares and occasional smiles. ✉ *Red Bay Settlement.*

Uncle Charlie's Blue Hole

TOUR—SIGHT | Mystical and mesmerizing, blue holes pock Andros's marine landscape in greater concentration than anywhere else on Earth—an estimated 160-plus—and provide entry into the islands' network of coral-rock caves. Offshore, some holes drop off to 200 feet or more. Inland blue holes reach depths of 120 feet, layered with fresh, brackish, and salt water. Uncle Charlie's Blue Hole is one of Andros's most popular with a 40-feet diameter, lined with picnic benches and a ladder. ✉ *North Andros, north of San Andros airport, 300 yards off main highway after turnoff for Owen Town.*

🏖 Beaches

If solitude is what you're searching for, you'll definitely find it on the beaches of North Andros. Long and secluded, you might find each beach with just one small resort or bar close by—and a few reefs for snorkeling.

Conch Sound & Ocean Hole

BEACH—SIGHT | South of Nicholl's Town's eastern shore, Conch Sound is a wide bay with strands of white sand and tranquil waters where you can also find Conch Sound Ocean Hole, a sea-filled blue hole where you can snorkel around and see the rich marine life. The flats are a convenient wading spot for bonefishermen who can wade for hours. Commercial fishermen bring their catches to a little beach park nearby. You can buy fresh catch and dine at a couple of shacks. **Amenities**: only at nearby restaurants. **Best for**: solitude; fishing; snorkeling. ✉ *Nicholl's Town.*

Nicholl's Town Beach

BEACH—SIGHT | Two-and-a-half miles east of Nicholl's Town commercial center, the settlement reaches the east-facing coast along beautiful and long Nicholl's Town Beach, which catches the easterly breezes and is by far the preferred beach in this area. It adjoins Conch Sound to the south. You might be on your own except for guests at the renovated Andros Island Beach Resort with its tiki bar and restaurant, where you can rent kayaks or snorkeling gear. **Amenities:** resort nearby. **Best for:** solitude; swimming; walking. ✉ *Nicholl's Town.*

🍴 Restaurants

F&H Take Away

$ | **BAHAMIAN** | This tiny shack on the water in Lowe's Sound is the quintessential Bahamian conch shack experience where owner will wade out in the water, select, and hammer out the conch before your eyes. Ask him to eat the extraneous pistile or bibby for a laugh. **Known for:** authentic Bahamian experience; extremely fresh catches; delicious seafood. [$] *Average main: $10* ✉ *Nicholl's Town* ✣ *Lowes Sound, 2 miles north of Nicholl's Town* ☎ *242/329–7143* 💳 *No credit cards.*

Lil' Anchor Restaurant

$ | **BAHAMIAN** | On the water at Conch Sound this cute shack of a restaurant is a great place for island-fresh fish, conch, and lobster in season. View the fishermen come in with their catches. **Known for:** local patronage; fresh fish and conch. [$] *Average main: $12* ✉ *Nicholl's Town* ☎ *242/464–3049, 242/429–4387* 💳 *No credit cards.*

🛏 Hotels

Andros Island Beach Resort

$ | **RESORT** | **FAMILY** | Facing east on long, pristine Nicholl's Town Beach, this palm tree–festooned property offers three secluded beachfront cottages, four villas, and a beachside tiki bar and restaurant with beautiful views. **Pros:** gorgeous beach and water activities; on-site restaurant and bar; spacious villas with kitchens; gym and car rentals. **Cons:** breakfast usually self-catered; bug spray in summer and fall; rental car necessary. [$] *Rooms from: $185* ✉ *Nicholl's Town* ☎ *242/329–1009* 🌐 *www.androsislandbeachresorts.com* 🔑 *4 villas and 3 suites from 1 to 3 bedrooms* 🍽 *No meals.*

Love at First Sight

$ | **B&B/INN** | At the mouth of Stafford Creek, self-sufficient anglers and do-it-yourself vacationers can sit on the sundeck or at the bar, sip a cold local beer or a cocktail, and contemplate the superb fishing and diving in Central Andros. **Pros:** restaurant and bar overlooking creek; quiet and clean. **Cons:** rental car necessary; basic rooms with amenities; not on beach. [$] *Rooms from: $130* ✉ *On main highway at mouth of Stafford Creek* ☎ *242/368–6082* 🌐 *www.loveatfirstsights.com* 🔑 *10 rooms.*

Pineville Motel

$ | **B&B/INN** | This truly one-of-a-kind, eye-popping plot of land fits in 16 rooms, a petting zoo, a small disco, a movie theater, a bar, and a DIY gift shop—made mostly of recycled materials such as tires, reclaimed wood, and seashells. **Pros:** unique experience; cheap rates; enthusiastic owner. **Cons:** not near beach; basic accommodations; overcrowded petting zoo. [$] *Rooms from: $80* ✉ *Nicholl's Town* ☎ *242/329–2788, 242/557–4354* 🔑 *16 rooms* 🍽 *No meals.*

Red Bay Sunset Lodge

$$$$ | **B&B/INN** | Owner and flats guide Benry Smith built this humble three-room lodge with a dining room for visitors eager to go bonefishing in North Andros. **Pros:** owner is a flatfishing guide; right on the water; complimentary beer and wine in dining room. **Cons:** very modest accommodations; only if you're a serious angler; three-night minimum. [$] *Rooms from: $750* ✉ *North Andros* ☎ *242/368–2833, 242/471–6319 for the bonefishing guide* 🌐 *www.redbaysunset.com* 🔑 *3 rooms* 🍽 *All-inclusive.*

🍸 Nightlife

Da Big Shop

BARS/PUBS | Overlooking Nicholl's Town Beach, Da Big Shop is as local as it gets. The 200-year-old building used to be Andros's only trading post for the sponge harvesters; unfortunately, the building has not aged well, but the interior bar, open daily from noon until late, is a good time. On the weekends it has DJs and on some holidays, a live band. For lunch or dinner, try Da Big Shop's island dinners, sandwiches, burgers, and pastas. It tends to attract local anglers and North Andros's younger demographic. You might be the only tourists here. ⊠ *Nicholl's Town* ☎ *242/225–2947, 242/329–2047* 🖰 *Free.*

Activities

Bonefishing

FISHING | North Andros's north coast and the string of Joulter Cays lying 5 to 10 miles offshore, are among the country's richest fly-fishing grounds for bonefish and permit. Conch Sound and Lowes Sound are reachable by car and good for DIY fishing by wading, but to have full scope of the best fishing spots and to learn about this tricky craft of catching spooky bonefish, hire a skiff and Bahamian guide. Some of the country's leading guides operate in North Andros, and visiting enthusiasts flock to the local lodges to fish with them. They can also arrange diving and snorkeling tours. ⊠ *North Andros* ☎ *242/471–5299 Elias Griffin, 242/471–1535 Keith Russell, 242/357–2781 Phillip Rolle, 242/329–2661 North Andros Flyfishing* ⊕ *www.northandrosflyfishing.com.*

Deep Sea and Bottom Fishing

FISHING | From Morgan's Bluff Harbour, Craig Curry takes out fishing charters to the reefs and shelfs for grouper and snapper bottom-fishing and to the deep ocean Tongue of the Ocean for bill- and game fish. His 35-foot open fisherman comfortably accommodates 6; the larger 55-foot yacht can fit 10. Craig can also arrange snorkeling and scuba-diving tours. Call for rates. ⊠ *North Andros* ☎ *242/558–3799, 242/471–3339.*

Wild Boar Hunting

TOUR—SPORTS | Perhaps oddly for such a passionate animal-lover, Eugene Campbell of Pineville Hotel offers sometimes-thrilling guided wild boar hunting in the scrub forests of mid-west North Andros. With a vast National Park to escape to and live in, they have a similarly vast non-park habitat. They are not endangered and often hard to track down. Eugene closely guides up to three hunters and, because hunting the tusk-bearing boars is dangerous, he gives a mandatory safety lecture. Prices include hunting gear, transportation, and lunch. ⊠ *North Andros* ☎ *242/329–2788, 242/557–4354* 🖰 *$350 for half day and $600 for full day, with gear, transportation, and lunch included.*

Central Andros

Those arriving in **Central Andros** by Bahamas Ferries from Nassau will arrive in the village of **Fresh Creek**; those arriving by plane will arrive in neighboring **Andros Town** (the petite transportation and governmental hub). Both Fresh Creek and Andros Town, joined by a small bridge over the creek, are found midisland, on the east coast of North and Central Andros.

Heading north from Andros Town and Fresh Creek, Central Andros extends as far north as Stafford Creek, near Kamalame Cay, where the land officially becomes North Andros (though it's debated exactly where Central ends). As you head south from Andros Town airport, scrub pine forests and brush give way to mangroves and hardwood coppice. Long beaches scallop the eastern shoreline and the sole road, Queen's Highway, will bring you to the bonefishing villages of **Cargill Creek** and **Behring Point.** Here, along the bonefish sweet spot of **Northern Bight,** you'll find nice homes with flowering gardens, palm trees, and sea grapes that overlook the ocean or the wide estuary.

Central Andros accounts for 60% of Andros's entire hotel inventory. Those expecting the glitz and glamour of the Bahamas' megaresorts and more touristy islands should look elsewhere. Here the glamour is the romantic, natural type with open vistas of the beaches, tidal estuaries, pine forests, and distant barrier reef. However rustic it may seem, you'll find pockets of extraordinary excellence and success, notably the award-winning, luxurious private island resort **Kamalame Cay,** as well as the more homey, family-friendly, all-inclusive **Small Hope Bay Lodge,** and private villa **KettleStone.** This part of Andros has many simpler home rentals and bonefishing lodges with lodging, dining, and fishing packages. All lodging types attract many repeat visitors who come year after year (or a couple times every year) to savor Andros's beautiful beaches, reefs, and world-class diving and fishing.

Central Andros's famed and remote **West Side** is a national park that teems with mangrove estuaries, rich with marine life, including conch, lobster, bonefish barracuda, and small sharks. Flocks of West Indian Pink Flamingos, more commonly associated with the Southern Islands, also find habitat in the Andros West Side National Park. This uninhabited region is accessible only by private boat. Central Andros has several national parks, two marine parks offshore, Blue Hole National Park north of Fresh Creek and a Crab Reserve south of it.

GETTING HERE AND AROUND
Fly into Andros Town airport (ASD) with LeAir from Nassau, with Watermakers Air from Fort Lauderdale Executive (FXE) or Tropic Ocean Airways from Miami's Seaplane base at Watson Island or Fort Lauderdale International Airport (FLL). Randolph Holdings and Glen Air fly here regularly, even a couple times a day. Alternatively, take the three-hour Sealink

ferry with Bahamas Ferries from Nassau to Fresh Creek. Taxis meet airplanes and ferries. The fare from the airport to Fresh Creek is about $20; to Cargill Creek area, some 20 miles south of the airport, it costs about $50.

A number of car-rental operators are available (rentals start at $85 a day), but if you're staying in the Cargill Creek area, you'll probably be doing most of your traveling by boat. Many lodges will pick you up at the airport. In Andros Town and Fresh Creek you can easily get around to the local restaurants, beaches, and blue holes by bike and on foot. Good advice is to take a taxi tour early in your stay to get the lay of the land and meet a well-informed local. They know all the places to go, and where to shop and dine.

CAR RENTAL CONTACTS Adderley's Car Rental. ⊠ *Fresh Creek* ☎ *242/357–2149.* **Rooney's Auto Car Rental.** ☎ *242/471–0346, 242/368–2255.*

⊙ Sights

Andros Lighthouse
BEACH—SIGHT | As you enter Fresh Creek Harbour, you'll see this historical lighthouse built circa 1892 to navigate boats into the southern entrance of Fresh Creek Channel. No longer in use, the lighthouse and a brace of rusty cannon near a delightful small beach is an island landmark and a picturesque view including a large, rusty old shipwreck. ⊠ *Andros Town* 🆓 *Free.*

Androsia Batik Works Factory
LOCAL INTEREST | The Androsia Batik Works Factory in Andros Town is home to the famous Androsia batik that has been adopted as the official fabric of the Bahamas. Small Hope Bay Lodge's Birch family established it in 1973 to boost employment in Andros. The brightly colored hand-dyed cotton batik has designs inspired by Andros's flora, fauna, and culture. You can prearrange a batik lesson ($25) and make your own design

on a choice of fabric, garment, or bag. Self-tours are free. The unique brand is seen and sold throughout the Bahamas, the Caribbean, and online. The outlet store (with different opening times) offers bargains on shirts, skirts, wraps, fabric, jewelry, books, crafts, and souvenirs. ⌧ *Andros Town* ☎ *242/368–2020* ⊕ *www. androsia.com.*

Captain Bill's Blue Hole

NATIONAL/STATE PARK | One famous Andros sight that nature lovers should catch is Captain Bill's Blue Hole, one of hundreds in Andros and in the Bahamas National Trust's Blue Hole National Park. Blue holes are the top of extensive water-filled underground cave systems formed in the ice age. Located northwest of Small Hope Bay, the National Trust has made Captain Bill's popular and comfortable with a boardwalk and a shady gazebo. Steps allow you to jump 30 feet down to cool off and there's a nature trail around the hole's 400-foot diameter. Accessible by car or bike, Captain Bill's is included on most guided tours. ⌧ *Fresh Creek* ✛ *Go 2 miles north from Small Hope Bay, turn left (west) in Love Hill, and take white road 2.7 miles west* ⊕ *www.bnt. bs/parks/andros* ✉ *Free.*

Fresh Creek

TOWN | Fresh Creek is an estuary, a hamlet, and a harbor, forming the north side of Andros Town and the south side of Fresh Creek settlement, both joined by a small bridge. The north Fresh Creek side is more built up with a few docks, stores, churches, motels, and restaurants, including Hank's Place, a local hot spot. On the south Andros Town side, the ferry and mail boats off-load at the dock next to the closed Andros Lighthouse Beach Club & Marina. You can still walk around the resort's point to get close to the lighthouse, small beach, and shipwreck. The Andros Tourist Office and some shops are a short walk away. The creek itself cuts over 16 miles into the island, creating tranquil bonefishing flats

and welcoming mangrove-lined bays that boaters and sea kayakers can explore. Upstream, there's even a remote Sunset Point houseboat where you can stay surrounded by the flowing water and scintillating views. ⌧ *Fresh Creek* ⊕ *www. bahamas.com/islands/andros* ✉ *Free.*

Staniard Creek

TOWN | Sand banks that turn gold at low tide lie off the northern tip of Staniard Creek, a small island settlement 9 miles north of Fresh Creek, accessed by a bridge off the main highway. Coconut palms and casuarinas shade the oceanside beaches, and offshore breezes are pleasantly cooling. Kamalame Cove, part of nearby luxurious resort and private Kamalame Cay, are at the northern end of the settlement. Three creeks snake into the mainland, forming extensive mangrove-lined back bays and flats, good for wading and bonefishing. ⌧ *Staniard Creek.*

🕄 Beaches

Because they're famous for their off-the-chart fishing and diving, the islands of Andros often get shorted when talk turns to beaches. This is a great injustice, especially in the case of the long, deserted beaches defining Central Andros's east coast and the abandoned white-sand beaches of Central Andros's outlying cays.

Kamalame and The Saddleback Cays

BEACH—SIGHT | East of Staniard Creek lies a series of serene cays, idyllic for beach drops or consummating the ultimate Robinson Crusoe fantasies. The first is Kamalame Cay, home to the luxurious resort of the same name. Just past Kamalame, uninhabited Big and Little Saddleback Cay boast sparkling, white-sand beaches and crystal-clear waters. You'll need a small, private boat to reach either (note that these cays are a regular drop point for guests of Kamalame Cay). Little Saddleback is tiny with no shade, so bring plenty of sunblock. Big Saddleback has a wider crescent beach, and plenty of shade from the pine trees. Also nearby is Rat Cay, which offers excellent snorkeling especially around the adjacent blue hole. **Amenities:** none. **Best for:** solitude; snorkeling; swimming; walking. ✉ *Staniard Creek.*

Small Hope Bay Beach

BEACH—SIGHT | Small Hope Bay Lodge is planted squarely on this long, coved beach where the near-shore snorkeling is excellent and the sand is white. Sign up for a resort course, a dive excursion, or simply enjoy a $55 beachside lunch buffet (with advance notice). A full day of beach fun with breakfast, lunch, and dinner, and all drinks and water sports included, is $199. Nonguests can also enjoy the dinner buffet with its open bar and music. **Amenities:** food and drink; showers; toilets; water sports. **Best for:** snorkeling; swimming; walking. ✉ *Small Hope Bay Lodge* ☎ *855/841–6966 toll-free U.S. and Canada, 242/368–2014 office* 🌐 *www.smallhope.com.*

Somerset Beach

BEACH—SIGHT | Two miles south of Andros Town airport, off a long beaten-up bare road through an arch of Australia pines, is Somerset Beach, a stunning, long, and wide beach with offshore sandbars that let you walk offshore for half a mile. The pines offer shade and there's a picnic table built by the workers from AUTEC, the nearby U.S. Navy's submarine testing base. Bring a camera as this is one of the most beautiful beach sights in the Bahamas. **Amenities:** none. **Best for:** photography; shelling; swimming; walking.

🍴 Restaurants

Hank's Place Restaurant and Bar

$ | **BAHAMIAN** | On the north side of Fresh Creek, near the bridge, this restaurant and bar juts out into the harbor and is graced with sweeping views. Locals, visitors, and workers from the nearby naval base enjoy Hank's for decent Bahamian dinners (chicken, fish, lobster, and pork), and for the popular dance parties on Saturday night. **Known for:** Hanky Panky frozen cocktail; dance parties. [$] *Average main: $18* ✉ *Fresh Creek* ☎ *242/368–2447* 🌐 *www.hanksplace2.com* 🕒 *Closed Sun. and Mon.*

★ Kamalame Cay

$$$ | **CARIBBEAN** | If you're not a guest on Kamalame Cay's private island resort you might have to travel miles to enjoy this casual but luxurious dining experience, which is every bit worthwhile. Reservations are required. **Known for:** romantic setting; fixed menu; innovative dishes. [$] *Average main: $33* ✉ *Kamalame Cay Resort, Staniard Creek.*

Small Hope Bay Lodge

$$$$ | **BAHAMIAN** | Unless you're a lucky all-inclusive guest at this resort famous for its diving and fishing, the best way to enjoy it is to buy an all-inclusive $199 day pass allowing you breakfast, lunch, dinner, and bar drinks (starting at lunchtime). From 7 am to 10 pm you can enjoy all the facilities and equipment on Small Hope's gorgeous beach: kayaks, windsurfers, sailboats, snorkeling, paddleboards, and the fresh whirlpool on the gorgeous beach. Just dinner and wine is $90 per person, and does not include bar drinks. **Known for:** communal dining experience. [$] *Average main: $99* ✉ *Small Hope Bay* ☎ *242/368–2014* 🌐 *www.smallhope.com.*

🛏 Hotels

Andros Island Bonefish Club (*AIBC*)

$$$$ | **B&B/INN** | If you're a dedicated bonefisher, AIBC is the place for you. **Pros:** outdoor deck and bar idyllic for fishing stories; prime location on Cargill Creek; waterslide. **Cons:** not much for nonanglers; basic accommodations. [$] *Rooms from: $485* ✉ *Cargill Creek* ☎ *242/368–5167* 🌐 *www.androsbonefishing.com* 🔑 *12 rooms* 🍽 *All meals.*

Big Charlie's & Fatiha's Fishing Lodge

$$$$ | B&B/INN | On the banks of Cargill Creek, this small and charming bonefishing lodge is run by Charlie Neymour, a bonefishing legend, and his wife, Fatiha, who serves deliciously aromatic Moroccan and Mediterranean cuisine in the dining room—with tasty fresh seafood Bahamian-style as well. **Pros:** pristine facilities; fridges, satellite TV, and Wi-Fi in rooms; unusually good cuisine for a lodge. **Cons:** beach is some distance; only for fishing fans. $ *Rooms from: $500 ⊠ Cargill Creek ☎ 242/368–4297 ⊕ www.bigcharlieandros.net ⇥ 4 rooms, 8 guests maximum ¶◯¶ All-inclusive.*

Hank's Place & Boat Rentals

$$ | B&B/INN | Hank's Place, with its restaurant and bar next door, offers four spacious, comfy rooms on the water for $95 double occupancy. **Pros:** central convenience; on the water; on-site restaurant. **Cons:** basic but clean; loud music Saturday night; three-night minimum. $ *Rooms from: $95 ⊠ Fresh Creek ☎ 242/357–2214 cell, 242/368–2447 ⇥ 4 standard rooms ¶◯¶ All meals.*

★ Kamalame Cay

$$ | RESORT | An all-inclusive resort with individual villas spaced along a 3-mile beach, the breathtaking and private 96-acre Kamalame Cay occupies a Bahamian pinnacle in luxury island retreats—and is surprisingly affordable. **Pros:** private white-sand beaches; quiet, remote location; discreet pampering; delicious, innovative food; on-site overwater spa. **Cons:** Wi-Fi only in reception area; eye mask needed for sleeping past sunrise; round-trip airport transfers are costly. $ *Rooms from: $250 ⊠ Staniard Creek ✛ At north end of Staniard Creek ☎ 242/368–6281, 800/768–9423 ⊕ www.kamalame.com ⊙ Closed Aug. 10–Oct. 7 ⇥ 5 cottages, 5 villas, 9 rooms ¶◯¶ All-inclusive.*

★ KettleStone Luxury Villa

$$$$ | RENTAL | FAMILY | Perched on a small bluff overlooking Andros's Barrier Reef, this dreamy newly constructed luxury villa provides a consummate private getaway. **Pros:** oceanfront luxury; very private; near town; freshwater pool and free snorkeling. **Cons:** must drive to beach; self-catered or hired chef; not a resort. $ *Rooms from: $857 ⊠ Fresh Creek ☎ 242/357–2746 cell, 800/827–7048 toll-free in U.S. and Canada ⊕ www. kettlestoneluxuryvilla.com ⇥ 3 bedrooms sleeping 6 standard guests (Maximum 2 additional guests at $50 per person) ¶◯¶ No meals.*

★ Small Hope Bay Lodge

$$$$ | HOTEL | FAMILY | This casual, lusciously palm-shaded beach and oceanfront property is more than 50 years strong and offers 17 private cottages, a main dining clubhouse, lounge, and waterfront terrace and bar. **Pros:** best dive operation on Andros; air-conditioning; free Wi-Fi in public areas; all-inclusive options; camaraderie; friendly service. **Cons:** in summer you'll need insect repellent; hot tub instead of pool. $ *Rooms from: $572 ⊠ Small Hope Bay ☎ 242/368–2014 resort, 800/223–6961 toll-free ⊕ www.smallhope.com ⇥ 17 cottages ¶◯¶ All-inclusive.*

Sunset Point House Boat

$$ | B&B/INN | If you're into nature and relaxation, this B&B on Fresh Creek lets you snorkel under your lodge and view birds, fish, rays, and maybe even dolphins passing mere feet away. **Pros:** private, serene, and ecoimmersed; self-catered or cook for hire; expert Andros tourism guide. **Cons:** too quiet for some; children must be eight years or older and able to swim; car rental often needed. $ *Rooms from: $300 ⊠ Fresh Creek ✛ 1¼ miles west of Fresh Creek Bridge, on southern side of estuary ☎ 242/357–2061 cell ⊕ www.sunsetpointhouseboat.*

com ⟳ 3 beds, 3 baths, available for 2 to 6 persons ⟨○⟩ No meals.

▽ Nightlife

Hank's Place

BARS/PUBS | The overwater bar at Hank's Place Restaurant and Bar is *the* place to be on Saturday and some Fridays. Sunset is more of a relaxed scene; but come late night the music gets louder, people get "happier," and the dancing begins! It's also enjoyed by mostly young workers from the nearby AUTEC U.S. Navy base. It's open from 2 pm to 10 pm Tuesday to Friday, and until 3 am on Saturday. ✉ *Fresh Creek* ☎ *242/368–2447, 242/357–2214 cell* ⊕ *hanksplace2.com.*

⊖ Shopping

★ **Androsia Store**

CLOTHING | Adjacent to the Androsia Batik Works Factory is the Androsia Store, where you can buy original fabrics, clothing, bags, souvenirs, and stuffed toys. Designed with island-inspired natural and cultural motifs, Androsia is popular nationwide and has been adopted by many as the official fabric of the Bahamas. ✉ *Andros Town* ☎ *242/368–2080* ⊕ *www.androsia.com* ⊙ *Closed Sun.*

🏃 Activities

BOATING AND FISHING

Andros fishermen claim the island is the world's best bonefishing location, and legends at Central Andros's south end are famed for pioneering the field of fly-fishing and island fishing lodges. The four main fishing regions are the hard-to-reach West Side flats, the creeks (Stafford, Staniard, and Fresh), the Joulters Cays north of Andros, and the bights between Central and South Andros. Fishermen will find a wealth of knowledgeable bonefishing guides in the **Cargill Creek–Behring Point** area who

---

Did You Know? ⊙

In the Bahamas, mail is still delivered by mail boats, and has been for decades. Mail boats leave Nassau's Potter's Cay carrying mail, cars, produce, consumer goods, and passengers on trips to more than 30 Bahamian islands, including Andros, a four-hour cruise.

---

will take you into the Northern Bight and West Side for some of the world's best bonefishing. Full-day fishing excursions cost about $500 to $600 for two. Better value are the lodges' guided bonefishing, lodging, and dining packages that work out to range from $400 to $660 per person per day at the half dozen lodges in the area.

Reef and deep-sea fishing excursions are secondary although you can catch snapper, and in season, grouper, along with game fish mahi-mahi, wahoo, and tuna.

Andra "Andy" Smith

BOATING | Andy is a living legend and highly recommended for guiding anglers through Andros's bights and to the bonefish-rich West Side, for both novices and professionals. Andy now has his own exclusive fishing lodge at Broad Shad Cay, located in the middle of North Bight, accessible from either Andros Town airport with a 25-mile taxi ride (about $60) to the dock and a further 25-minute boat ride with Andy, or from Mangrove Cay's Moxey Town airport, with a 5-minute taxi ride and 25-minute boat ride. ✉ *Behring Point* ☎ *242/368–4261, 242/225–0082.*

Charlie Neymour

BOATING | Legend and expert guide Charlie Neymour is popular for guided fishing expeditions; now he and his wife Fatiha own a cute new bonefishing lodge with excellent island and Moroccan cuisine, plus fishing, dining, and lodging packages. The lodge is in Behring Point near the expansive flats. ✉ *Behring Point* ☎ *242/368–4297* ⊕ *www.bigcharlieandros.net.*

Rupert Leadon

FISHING | Led by owner Rupert, expert fishing guides have modern flats skiffs to whisk you to nearby or distant fishing grounds in the North Bight, the famed West Side for bonefish and permit, or to the barrier reef and the shelf off Tongue of the Ocean for grouper, snapper, marlin, sailfish, mahi-mahi, or wahoo, with all the gear you need. The Leadon family operate the Andros Island Bonefish Club, one of Andros's best specialty lodges where prices include all meals and guided fishing on skiffs. ✉ *Cargill Creek* ☎ *242/368–5167* ⊕ *www.androsbonefishing.com.*

★ Small Hope Bay Lodge

BOATING | A famous and popular Andros diving and bonefishing resort, Small Hope Bay Lodge has bone-, deep-sea, fly-, and reef-fishing, as well as vast flats rich in bonefish and tarpon in the 20-mile-long Fresh Creek and more on the West Side. Small Hope offers more variety than regular fishing lodges: a fabulous beach with free kayaks, paddleboards, and bikes, superb diving, sumptuous buffets, open bar, and a strong sense of camaraderie. Rates for bonefishing in Fresh Creek and reef-fishing are $385 for a half day and $550 for a full day. Deep-sea rates are $500 for half a day and $700 for a full day (with all gear and lunch). Small Hope books seven of the top bonefishing guides in Andros including Glaister Wallace, known for his magical casting skills. Book in advance. ✉ *Small Hope Bay* ☎ *242/368–2014* ⊕ *www.smallhope.com.*

SCUBA DIVING AND SNORKELING

Divers can't get enough of the sprawling **Andros Barrier Reef,** the world's third largest, stretching the length of the island's east coast, ½ to 3 miles offshore. Boats from local lodges and resorts bring

guests to beautiful parts of the reef to relish in underwater rapture. Snorkelers can explore such reefs as the Trumpet Reef, where visibility is clear 15 feet to the sandy floor and jungles of elkhorn coral snake up to the surface. Divers can delve into the 60-foot-deep coral caves of the Black Forest, beyond which the wall slopes down to depths of 6,000 feet. Anglers can charter boats to fish offshore or over the reef, and bonefishers can wade the flats on their own. While the marine life is not as rich nor as diverse as one would expect from such a vibrant, healthy reef, the assemblies of coral are breathtaking.

★ Kamalame Cay

DIVING/SNORKELING | The luxury, all-inclusive resort on private Kamamale Cay offers bespoke diving, dive certification, and snorkeling tours on top of its all-inclusive rates. For the four- to five-day PADI Open Water Certification with nine dives you can practice theory at home or, with the cay's instructors, either online or at the resort starting from $1,027 (with multiple divers). Two-hour resort courses are from $197 to $292 depending on group size. Fabulous snorkeling tours are also available when booked in advance. Half day tours are $399, full day at $699. With all that it offers on the cay and the barrier reef, it's probably one of the nicest places in the world to gain certification. ✉ *Central Andros* ☎ *876/632–3213, 800/790–7971* ⊕ *www.kamalame.com.*

★ Small Hope Bay Lodge

SCUBA DIVING | Andros's top dive center is full-service with resort dives, PADI certification courses, one- and two-tank dives, specialty dives such as shark and night, and snorkeling. One-tank dives are $90, and two-tanks are $110. Rental equipment is available for Small Hope Bay Lodge excursions only. Lodging dive packages are offered. Hot showers await after long days at sea. ✉ *Small Hope Bay* ☎ *242/368–2014, 800/223–6961* ⊕ *www.smallhope.com.*

Mangrove Cay

Home to 800 resilient, friendly locals, remote Mangrove Cay is sandwiched between two sea-green bights, separating it from Central and South Andros and creating an island of shorelines strewn with washed-up black coral, gleaming deserted beaches, and dense pine forests. **Moxey Town,** known locally as Little Harbour, is historically based on commercial fishing and conch and sponge harvesting and rests on the northeast corner in a coconut grove. Pink piles of conch shells and mounds of porous sponges dot the small harbor. Anglers come on a mission, in search of giant bonefish on flats called "the promised land" and "land of the giants." A five-minute boat ride takes fly-fishers to Gibson Cay to wade hard sand flats sprinkled with starfish.

GETTING HERE AND AROUND

From Nassau twice daily, Flamingo Air and LeAir fly a scheduled service to Mangrove Cay Airport (MAY), located in Moxey Town. Through many services you can charter from Nassau or from Fort Lauderdale with Tropic Ocean Airways's floatplanes or Watermakers Air. Taxis meet airplanes and mail boats from Nassau, and taxi tours are a great way to get to know the island with all its shops, restaurants, and attractions.

Rent a car from Gaitor's or PB's car rentals at the airport from $80 to $100 a day. The cay's main road runs south from Moxey Town, past the airport, then along coconut-tree-shaded beaches to the settlement of Lisbon Creek.

Frederick Major runs the free government ferry linking Mangrove Cay with South Andros. In his 30-foot outboard, it takes a few minutes to run from Lisson Creek to Drigg's Hill—or a few more minutes to reach Tiamo Resort and a lodge along the Southern Bight's north shore. The ferry leaves Drigg's Hill twice a day at 8 am and 4 pm. The proposed ferry link from Mangrove Cay to Central Andros Island (Behring Point) has been put on hold.

TRANSPORT CONTACTS Frederick Major Ferry Services. ☎ 242/376–8533, 242/323–6111 Nassau office, 242/554–1880 cell phone. **Gaitor's Car Rental.** ☎ 242/471–1550, 242/464–3151. **Henson "Harry" Saunders Taxi & Tours.** ☎ 242/357–2365. **Patrick King Taxi & Tours.** ☎ 242/471–1126.

◉ Sights

With its beautiful wildlife along its coastline, tidal flats, and limestone caves, Mangrove Cay offers days of adventuresome exploring and sightseeing. Ask your local lodge about guided tours. Patrick King or Harry Saunders will take you around the cay's 8 miles to see Little Harbour and the fisherman's dock with its fresh catches of lobster, conch, grouper, and snapper. You can also explore caves, myriad churches, and small souvenir stalls replete with Mangrove Cay sponges. Ask to visit Ralph Moxey, another kind of Andros legend, in his case, in the crafts of boat-building and carving. Ralph has built many island sloops, won many races, and, today, carves miniatures out of local woods like Andros Mahogany and Sapodilla along with shell crafts. He can also teach you about bush medicine and the healing qualities of local plants such as Noni, Naked Wood, Strongback, and more. Visit Diane Cash's souvenir and craft store to browse her raffia-and-shell-decorated straw dolls, hats, bags, billfolds, and fish- and star-shaped bags. Dine and sample tropical homemade breads from Rosa Bullard's Four Kid's Bakery & Restaurant.

Victoria Point Blue Hole

REEF | On an island known for magical blue holes, the Victoria Point Blue Hole is Mangrove Cay's superb ocean hole for snorkeling and diving. Just ask the folks at Swain's Cay Lodge or Seascape Inn—or any local—to point out where to find it. ✉ *Mangrove Cay.*

🍴 Restaurants

If you stay at one of Mangrove Cay's lodges, you're sure to be served fresh, delicious island fare, usually as part of your lodging and fishing package. You can, however, also explore other lodges. It's a great way to get to know them, so long as you book a day ahead. Swain's Cay Lodge is a wonderful dining spot on the beach, 3 miles south of the airport on the main road. Enjoy fresh catches, conch, lobster, and more island dishes either alfresco on the beachfront porch or in the cool inside. The island's famous conch stand is Shine's One-Stop Conch Shack north and then west of the airport road, sitting on the edge of Middle Bight. Here, enclosed in air-conditioning and away from flies, enjoy conch and fresh fish myriad ways. Some snowbirds and second-home owners treat themselves to Tiamo Resort's finer dining by taking the Tiamo's free ferry from Lisbon Creek (south Mangrove Cay) to the resort on South Andros. Explore other eateries as you bike, drive, or walk around other settlements on the 7-mile-long cay.

Seascape Inn's Barefoot Bar and Grill
$ | **BAHAMIAN** | Every table has a nice ocean view at this warm and friendly beachfront restaurant and bar at the Seascape Inn. Owners Mickey and Joan McGowan do the baking and cooking themselves. **Known for:** homemade ice cream; chocolate ganache; fresh catch of the day. [$] *Average main: $18* ✉ *Seascape Inn* ☎ *242/369–0342* 🌐 *www.seascapeinn.com.*

Shine's One-Stop Conch Shack
$ | **BAHAMIAN** | Also known as Greene's after its owner Ornald "Shine" Greene, this waterfront spot on Little Harbour is as close to nightlife as you'll get on Mangrove Cay—live music is rare (certainly there during homecoming and regatta festivals) but if the island's busy or a big group requests it, they'll arrange a live band. Dominoes and backgammon with reggae and calypso tunes add to the upbeat ambience as you view the harbor, sip a beer of Goombay Smash, and tuck into the daily catch of fish, conch, and lobster. **Known for:** lively ambience; outstanding hospitality; excellent fresh ceviche. [$] *Average main: $12* ✉ *Mangrove Cay* ☎ *242/369–0078* 🅿 *Free* 💳 *No credit cards.*

Swain's Cay Reefside Restaurant
$$ | **BAHAMIAN** | Swain's Cay Lodge's beachside Reefside Restaurant & Bar is a local dining and cocktail-sipping hot spot serving delicious authentic Bahamian cuisine for breakfast, lunch, and dinner, supported with a well-stocked bar. (Nonguests are welcome, but book in advance.) The decor is modern contemporary and big windows and glass doors give it a bright ambience. Dine inside in air-conditioned comfort or on the beachside deck. **Known for:** extensive drinks menu; warm hospitality; authentic cuisine. [$] *Average main: $22* ✉ *Mangrove Cay* ☎ *242/422–5018 cell* 🌐 *www.swainscaylodge.com.*

🛏 Hotels

Seascape Inn
$ | **B&B/INN** | One of Andros's few lodging options catering to more than fishermen, Seascape Inn is a small, rustic beachfront gem; five individual, well-maintained cottages with private decks overlook the glass-clear ocean. **Pros:** quiet beachfront location; outstanding food; great snorkeling, kayaking, and bird-watching on-site. **Cons:** no air-conditioning; no TV; insect repellent a must. [$] *Rooms from: $159* ✉ *Mangrove Cay* ☎ *242/369–0342* 🌐 *www.seascapeinn.com* 🛏 *5 cottages* 🍽 *Breakfast.*

Undersea Adventures in Andros

Andros probably has the largest number of dive sites in the country. With the third-longest barrier reef in the world (behind those of Australia and Belize), the island offers about 100 miles of drop-off diving into the Tongue of the Ocean.

Uncounted numbers of **blue holes** are forming in the area. In some places these constitute vast submarine networks that can extend more than 200 feet down into the coral (Fresh Creek, 40–100 feet; North Andros, 40–200-plus feet; South Bight, 40–200 feet). Blue holes are named for their inky-blue aura when viewed from above and for the light-blue filtered sunlight that is visible from many feet below. Some of the holes have vast interior chambers with stalactites and stalagmites, offshoot tunnels, and seemingly endless corridors. Others have distinct thermoclines (temperature changes) between layers of water and are subject to tidal flow.

The dramatic Fresh Creek site provides an insight into the complex Andros cave system. There isn't much coral growth, but there are plenty of midnight parrotfish, big southern stingrays, and some blacktip sharks. Similar blue holes are all along the barrier reef, including several at Mastic Point in the north and the ones explored and filmed off South Bight.

Undersea adventurers can also investigate wrecks such as the *Potomac*, a steel-hulled freighter that sank in 1952 and lies in 40 feet of water off Nicholl's Town. And off the waters of Fresh Creek, at 70 feet, lies the deteriorated 56-foot-long World War II LCM (landing craft mechanized) known only as the **Barge Wreck**, which was sunk in 1963 to create an artificial reef. Newer and more intact, the *Marian* wreck lies in 70 feet. Both are encrusted with coral and are home to a school of groupers and a blizzard of tiny silverfish. You'll find fish-cleaning stations where miniature cleaning shrimp and yellow gobies clean grouper and rockfish by swimming into their mouths and out their gills, picking up food particles. It's an excellent subject matter for close-up photography.

The multilevel **Over the Wall** dive at Fresh Creek takes novices to depths of 65–80 feet and experienced divers to 120–185 feet. The wall is covered with black coral and all kinds of tube sponges. **Small Hope Bay Lodge** is the most long-respected dive resort on Andros. It's a friendly, informal place where the only thing taken seriously is diving and fishing. There's a fully equipped dive center with a wide variety of specialty dives, including customized family-dive trips with a private dive boat and dive master. If you're not certified, check out the lodge's morning resort course and be ready to explore the depths by afternoon. If you are certified, don't forget to bring your C card.

If you are leery of diving but want to view the spectacular undersea world, try snorkeling. Shallow reefs, beginning in 6 feet of water, and extending down to 60 feet or more, are ideal locations for spotting myriad brightly colored fish, sea urchins, and starfish. Don't forget your underwater camera.

Winter water temperatures average about 74°F. In summer, water temperatures average about 84°F.

Tiamo Resort is the most luxurious resort in South Andros.

Swain's Cay Lodge

$ | **B&B/INN** | This petite, beachfront resort is a gem for bonefishing fans and escape artists who want to enjoy Andros's natural beauty in peace and quiet. **Pros:** beachfront; excellent island food; free transfers to airport and tours. **Cons:** sleeps only 22; beach is shallow for swimming. [$] *Rooms from: $188* ✉ *Mangrove Cay* ☎ *242/422–5018* 🌐 *www.swainscaylodge.com* *3 ocean-view units, 3 beachfront units, and 1 3-bed apartment with kitchenette* 🍴 *Breakfast.*

South Andros

South Andros's road stretches 25 miles from **Drigg's Hill**—a small settlement of pastel houses, a tiny church, a grocery store, the government dock, and the Emerald Palms Resort—to Mars Bay. Eight miles farther south, the Bluff settlement sprawls atop a hill overlooking miles of golden beaches, lush cays, and the Tongue of the Ocean. Here skeletons of Arawak peoples were found huddled together. A local resident attests that another skeleton was found—this one of a 4-foot-tall, one-eyed owl, which may have given rise to the legend of the mythical, elf-like chickcharnie. South Andros is laced with an almost continuous set of beaches on the northwest and east coast, and more than 15 boutique resorts, bonefishing lodges, inns, and rentals are scattered along the island's many small settlements. It's a magnet for serious anglers and divers alike.

GETTING HERE AND AROUND

The Congo Town Airport (TZN) is 4 miles south of Drigg's Hill and receives flights four times a week from Fort Lauderdale Executive Airport (FXE) via Watermakers Air and daily flights from Nassau (NAS) via Western Air. Nassau-based Golden Wings Charters is a respected charter company that can be used to reach South Andros. For the ultimate thrill and the convenience of flying direct to your resort's beach or dock, charter a seaplane either with Miami Seaplane Tours & Charters or Safari Seaplanes from Nassau. Taxis and many lodges and hotels meet incoming flights and ferries.

A free government ferry operated by Frederick Major's Ferry Services makes the quick trip between Mangrove Cay and South Andros twice daily. It departs from South Andros at 8 am and 5 pm and from Mangrove Cay soon after. Schedules (and weather) are subject to change.

TRANSPORT CONTACTS Frederick Major Ferry Services. ☎ *242/376–8533, 242/323–6111 Nassau office, 242/554–1880 cell phone.* **Lee Meadows Taxi Service.** ☎ *242/369–5029.* **Lenglo Car Rental.** ⊠ *South Andros, Congo Town* ☎ *242/369–1702.* **Rahming's Rental Car** . ☎ *242/369–1608.* **Shirley Forbes Taxi Service.** ☎ *242/369–2930.*

 Hotels

Andros Beach Club

$$$$ | **ALL-INCLUSIVE** | In Kemp's Bay, 10 miles south of Congo Town Airport, Andros Beach Club lies on a beach of powder soft sand that stretches uninterrupted for almost 4 miles north. **Pros:** on fabulous beach; excellent diving and instructing; includes delicious meals; safe and secluded. **Cons:** remote and petite; fairly basic. $ *Rooms from: $550* ⊠ *Deep Creek* ✛ *10 miles south of Congo Town Airport* ☎ *954/681–4818, 242/369–1454 resort* ⊕ *www.androsbeachclub.com* ↝ *7 rooms* ❍l *All meals.*

The Pointe Resort & Marina

$$$ | **HOTEL** | This modern, smart, two-story resort with six suites, a restaurant, bar, and small marina makes great use of the views on a breathtaking point south of Kemp's Bay. Favoring bonefishing and diving fans, the rooms all have air-conditioning, fans, kitchenettes, free Wi-Fi, and DIRECTV. **Pros:** clean and modern ambience; gorgeous views; popular on-site restaurant good for groups. **Cons:** long taxi ride from airport; call in advance for dining; not on beach. $ *Rooms from:*

$350 ⊠ *Deep Creek* ↝ *4 rooms with kitchettes* ❍l *No meals.*

★ **Tiamo Resort & Spa**

$$$$ | **RESORT** | At this chic hideaway for jet-setters in-the-know you might feel like you're in French Polynesia, yet it is one of the Atlantic's last great secrets. **Pros:** 1½-to-1 staff-to-guest ratio; spectacular private beachfront location; great cuisine and water sports. **Cons:** alcohol not included in rates; insect repellent a must; only accessible by resort's ferry. $ *Rooms from: $1,155* ⊠ *South Bight, Driggs Hill* ✛ *3-mile boat ride from Driggs Hill or Lisbon Creek (Mangrove Cay)* ☎ *242/225–6871 within Bahamas, 786/374–2442 in U.S. and Canada* ⊕ *www.tiamoresorts.com* ❍ *Closed Sept. and Oct.* ↝ *2 small rooms, 11 villas (3 large, 8 medium; 9 with pools, 2 without)* ❍l *All-inclusive.*

⚡ **Activities**

FISHING

Reel Tight Charters

FISHING | Usually operated by Jesse from Abaco Beach Club, an experienced diving instructor, this renowned charter company is often hired by other resorts and lodges on South Andros. With its 25-foot 300HP catamaran and 14-foot skiff, they offer a variety of excursions, mostly in South Andros but also farther afield such as Green Cay on the other side of Tongue of the Ocean. Tours, including deep-sea, reef, and spearfishing, plus diving, snorkeling, private island picnics, and blue hole exploring tours. They also rent water-sports gear and kayaks. ⊠ *Drigg's Hill Marina, Driggs Hill* ☎ *242/369–1454 Bahamas, 954/681–4818 in U.S. and Canada.*

Bimini

Bimini has long been known as the Bahamas' big game-fishing capital. Bimini's strong tourist season falls from spring through summer, when calmer seas mean the arrival of fishing and pleasure boats from South Florida. The nearest of the Bahamian islands to the U.S. mainland, Bimini consists of two main islands and a few cays just 50 miles east of Miami, across the Gulf Stream that sweeps the area's western shores. Most visitors spend their time on bustling North Bimini; South Bimini is quieter and more eco-oriented. Except for the vast new Resorts World Bimini development that occupies the island's northern third, most of the hotels, restaurants, churches, and stores in Bimini are in capital **Alice Town** and neighboring **Bailey Town** and **Porgy Bay,** along North Bimini's King's and Queen's highways. Along the east coast of North Bimini are long beaches; on the west, the protected harbor, docks, and marinas. Most of the islands' 3,000 inhabitants reside in South Bimini although they travel to North Bimini daily to attend school and to work. Although the local communities in North Bimini are walkable, the preferred (and fun) way to scoot around is by golf cart. Resorts World Bimini has increased North Bimini's bustle and economy. Three times a week, the Balearia Fast Ferry takes up to 650 passengers to Bimini in two hours from Fort Lauderdale, who spread around the island enjoying its beaches, eateries, bars, nightclubs, and casino.

Sparsely populated **South Bimini** is where Juan Ponce de León allegedly looked for the Fountain of Youth in 1513, and a site with a well and natural trail memorialize it. More engaging, however, is the island's biological field station, known as the Sharklab for its study of lemon-, hammerhead-, and nurse-shark behavior and tracking, among other things. The main resort on this island is the modern, marina-based, Bimini Sands Resort & Marina that sits atop of a gorgeous mile-long beach. South Bimini is much more low-key than North Bimini, a slower pace loved by hundreds of visiting residents (and some visiting boating partiers) who have built nearly 80 homes in Port Royal on the island's southern tip.

Salvagers, gunrunners, rumrunners, and the legendary Ernest Hemingway peopled the history of Bimini. Hemingway wrote much of *To Have and Have Not* and *Islands in the Stream* here between fishing forays and street brawls. Finding solace and inspiration in the natural environment, civil rights icon Dr. Martin Luther King Jr. penned one of his last speeches in Bimini.

GETTING HERE AND AROUND
AIR
South Bimini's teensy airport (BIM) was enlarged and improved in 2015 thanks to help from Resorts World Bimini, to cope with the extra traffic it brings. Silver Airways, with its feeder network of many Florida cities, flies in from Fort Lauderdale (FLL) twice a day. Tropic Ocean Airways with its floatplanes flies from Miami's Watson Island Seaplane base (MPB) and Fort Lauderdale International (FLL) straight to North Bimini Harbour (NSB), docking at Resort World. From Nassau, Western Air and Flamingo Air fly to South Bimini daily and Flamingo also has a daily schedule from Grand Bahama Airport (FPO). Numerous operators from Florida and Nassau fly into South Bimini. More than six charter airlines fly from Fort Lauderdale: Apollo Jets from FLL, Island Air Charters, and Watermakers Air and Bahamas Express from FXE. To reach North Bimini (Alice Town) from South Bimini Airport, you take a short taxi ride ($3) from the airport and a five-minute ferry ($2). The ferry runs until 10 pm or so for staff and guests who live on South Bimini.

CONTACTS Bimini Airport.
☎ *242/347–4111.*

BOAT AND FERRY

Three times a week (Wednesday, Friday, and Sunday) Balearia Bimini's fast ferry whisks visitors and day-trippers to North Bimini, docking at Resorts World's new ocean-side pier. Accommodating more than 600 passengers in relative spacious comfort, the high-speed catamaran *Jaume II* departs Terminal 21 in Port Everglades, Florida, and covers the 49 nautical miles in only two hours. Business Class includes everything in Economy Class but adds a light lunch and snack and discounts at the duty-free store. You can choose day trips from $75 plus taxes, giving you seven hours on Bimini. (Oddly, if you book a ferry ticket for longer, such as three days, the price rises to $198 per person.) You can book a ferry-and-stay at the Hilton, which, for the lodging, works to be around $235 per night, double occupancy. RWB's website, however, usually offers great ferry-and-stay specials as well as exciting party weekends with live bands and more. Of course, with a ferry-only ticket, you don't have to stay at the Hilton; you can choose any of Bimini's hotels or inns.

Although rarely chosen, you can also sail to Bimini by old-fashioned mail boat. Contact the Dockmaster in Potter's Cay in Nassau at or the Bimini mail boat office at ☎ *242/347–3203* for an up-to-date schedule. M/V *Sherice M* usually leaves Potter's Cay, Nassau, on Thursday afternoon for Chub Cay, North Bimini, and Cat Cay, and returns on Monday morning. The one-way trip takes about 12 hours and costs $50. Going between North and South Bimini requires a five-minute ferry crossing, managed by the local government ($2 each way but, combined with the airport taxis' $3, totals $5). It runs from early morning to fairly late at night.

Bimini's eight marinas accommodate private yachts and fishing boats in droves with most crossing the Gulf Stream from Florida, a distance of around 48 nautical miles. As you enter port, fly the yellow quarantine flag. Coming into North Bimini, you have to clear Customs and Immigration in Alice Town at the Bimini Big Game Club or at the government buildings in Bailey Town. Coming into South Bimini, dock at Bimini Sands Resort & Marina and take a taxi to clear at Customs and Immigration at the airport, 2 miles away.

Once docked, only the captain can leave the boat in order to clear with local Customs and Immigration. All crew are required to remain on board until the captain returns having cleared. The clearance fee is $150 for boats up to 30 feet in length and $300 for boats over 30 feet, and covers the cruising permit, fishing permit, Customs and Immigration charges, and the $25-per-person departure tax for up to three persons. Additional persons over the age of six are charged a $25 departure tax.

CONTACTS Bimini Customs Office. ✉ *Alice Town* ☎ *242/347–3100.* **Balaeria Bimini Fast Ferry.** ☎ *866/699–6988* ⊕ *www.baleariacaribbean.com.* **Nassau Dockmaster's Office.** ☎ *242/393–1064.*

CONTACTS Bimini Tourist Office. ✉ *Alice Town* ☎ *242/347–3528, 242/347–3529* ⊕ *www.bahamas.com/bimini.*

North Bimini

Bimini's capital, **Alice Town,** is at North Bimini's southern end. It's colorful, painted in happy Caribbean pastels, and by night and day is buzzing with golf-carting visitors from Resorts World and the marinas along the main road of King's Highway. In a prominent location stand the ruins of the Compleat Angler Hotel, Ernest Hemingway's famous haunt, which burned down in 2006. A short walk away on the west coast is Radio Beach (aka Alice Town Beach) and in the

Sunsets in Bimini can be otherworldly.

center of town is the Bimini Native Straw and Craft Market, the tourist office, the government dock, the marinas, and many restaurants and bars.

In quick succession, Alice Town turns into **Bailey Town,** then **Porgy Bay**. Going north you'll see conch stands, restaurants, and the pink-color government center and clinic. The beaches here are less frequented. Beyond Porgy Town, the north third of the island is the expansive Resorts World Bimini development.

GETTING HERE AND AROUND
If arriving by plane, catch a taxi ($3) at the South Bimini Airport and a ferry ($2) to the new government dock in Alice Town. The entire process costs $5. You can walk, take a taxi, or hire a golf cart to reach your accommodations. From Resorts World you can hire a golf cart or taxi, or take the free hourly tram into Alice Town.

Most people get around North Bimini on gas-powered golf carts, available for rent from various vendors from $70 to $100 per day. At smaller rental companies, try bargaining. Note that the speed limit is 25 mph and that the roads follow the British system—driving on the left.

GOLF CART RENTAL CONTACTS ABC Rentals. ✉ *King's Hwy., Alice Town* ☎ *242/473–0286 cell* ⊕ *www.biminigolf-carts.com.* **Elite Golf Carts At Resorts World.** ☎ *242/464–5025.* **Sue & Joys Rentals.** ✉ *Alice Town* ☎ *242/347–6081.*

⊙ Sights

Ansil Saunder's Boat Building Shop
MUSEUM | In Bailey Town, near the government park, is Ansil Saunder's boat-building shop where you can see his beautiful flats fishing boat called the *Bimini Bonefisher,* handcrafted from oak, mahogany, and island horseflesh. Ansil is firstly a bonefisherman of some repute, having scared up a 16-pound, 3-ounce bonefish for Jerry Lavenstein in 1971— the still-standing bonefish world record. Ansil is equally famous for taking Dr. Martin Luther King Jr. on a guided boat

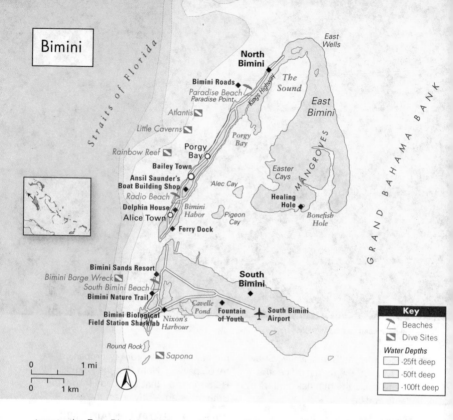

Bimini

Straits of Florida

East Wells

North Bimini

Bimini Roads
Paradise Beach
Paradise Point

The Sound

King's Highway

East Bimini

Atlantis

Little Caverns

Rainbow Reef

Porgy Bay

Porgy Bay

Bailey Town

Ansil Saunder's
Boat Building Shop

Radio Beach

Dolphin House
Alice Town

Bimini Habor

Alec Cay

MANGROVES

Easter Cays

Healing Hole

Pigeon Cay

Bonefish Hole

● Ferry Dock

Bimini Sands Resort
Bimini Barge Wreck
South Bimini Beach
Bimini Nature Trail

South Bimini

Bimini Biological
Field Station Sharklab

Nixon's Harbour

Cavelle Pond

Fountain of Youth

South Bimini Airport

Round Rock

Sapona

GRAND BAHAMA BANK

0 ___ 1 mi
0 ___ 1 km

Key	
⬐	Beaches
◥	Dive Sites
Water Depths	
☐	-25ft deep
☐	-50ft deep
☐	-100ft deep

tour to the East Bimini wilderness. Dr. King wanted inspiration for an upcoming speech to be given for striking sanitation workers in Memphis. He found it in the mangroves, so rich in life and full of God's Creation, says Ansil, who recited his Creation Psalm to King. Three days after the Memphis speech, Dr. King was killed. At the time, with some foreboding, Ansil says that Dr. King mentioned to him that he didn't think he would live very long. To those who inquire, Ansil proudly shows memorabilia from Dr. King's wife and various VIPs. Saunders became an active member of the Bahamas independence movement, and met Margaret Thatcher and Queen Elizabeth of England twice. Saunders is regarded as one of the Bahamas' living legends— and a consummate ambassador. You probably can't find, in all the country, a more historically rich guide to take you fishing or to the Healing Hole in one of the boats he crafted. ⊠ *Bailey Town, on harbor front, Alice Town* ☎ *242/347–2178 shop* 🖃 *Donations accepted.*

Bailey Town

TOUR—SIGHT | Most of the island's residents live in Bailey Town in small, pastel-color concrete houses, just off King's Highway, north of the Bimini Big Game Club and before Porgy Bay. Bailey Town has two of Bimini's biggest grocery stores, where goods and produce come in by mail boat usually on Thursday; Friday is the best day to shop. It's also a good place to find a home-cooked meal or conch salad from shacks along the waterfront. Don't miss a bite at Joe's Conch Stand; it's a local institution. ⊠ *North Bimini.*

Bimini Museum

MUSEUM | The Bimini Museum, sheltered in the restored (1921) two-story original post office and jail—a two-minute walk from the ferry dock, across from the island straw market—showcases varied artifacts, including Adam Clayton Powell's domino set and photos, a fishing log, and rare fishing films of Ernest Hemingway with artifacts from the old Rod & Gun Club. Also view photos from Bimini's Prohibition rum-running era, rum kegs, old cannonballs, and Martin Luther King Jr.'s immigration card from 1964. The exhibit includes films shot on the island as early as 1922. The museum is privately managed. ⊠ *King's Hwy., Alice Town* ☎ *242/347–3038, 242/473–1252 cell* ☞ *$2 donation requested.*

Bimini Roads

NATURE SITE | Avid divers shouldn't miss a trip to underwater Bimini Roads, aka the Road to Atlantis. This curious rock formation under about 20 feet of water, 500 yards offshore at Bimini Bay, is shaped like a backward letter J, some 600 feet long at the longest end. It's the shorter 300-foot extension that piques the interest of scientists and visitors. The precision patchwork of large, curved-edge stones forms a perfect rectangle measuring about 30 feet across. A few of the stones are 16 feet square. It's purported to be the "lost city" whose discovery was predicted by Edgar Cayce (1877–1945), a psychic with an interest in prehistoric civilizations. Archaeologists estimate the formation to be between 5,000 and 10,000 years old. Carvings in the rock appear to some scientists to resemble a network of highways. ⊠ *North Bimini.*

Dolphin House

MUSEUM | Bimini historian and poet laureate Mr. Ashley Saunders has spent decades constructing this eclectic home and guesthouse from materials salvaged from local construction sites and the sea, and writing a two-volume set on Bimini's history. Mr. Saunders offers walking tours of Alice Town, which begin with a tour of his structure—named for the 27 mosaic, sculpted, and painted dolphins throughout—then continues through Alice Town to tell the island's history. His books on the history of Bimini make for a fascinating read and souvenir. You'll see intricate conch shell and coconut crafts for sale. ⊠ *Alice Town between King's and Queen's Hwys., Alice Town* ☎ *242/347–3201* ☞ *Tours $20/hr.*

⤢ Healing Hole

Hidden in the west coast mangroves of East Bimini is the Healing Hole—a cold spring of freshwater amid the hot sea saltwater with, some say, real, and others, mythical, healing powers. Hard to get to and find, it's best to hire a guide in a shallow boat, or, if you want exercise, in a kayak. You can only get there in mid-to-high tide, and make sure to take insect repellent. You'll see much life above and below water. For ecolovers and adventure-seekers only. ⊠ *North Bimini.*

🏖 Beaches

Luna Beach at Resorts World

BEACH—SIGHT | On Resorts World's long Paradise Beach, Luna Beach brings chic luxury to fun-in-the-sun and beach parties at night. Upscale food, exquisite cocktails, mod music, and beach toys are all part of the mix, centered on the open-air clubhouse. The solar-powered private cabanas even have phone charging ports. For more action jump on a Jet Ski, paddleboard, or kayak, or simply sun bake on a float. You can even book stingray and snorkeling tours here. During Sunset Sessions Happy Hour DJ Arlette reverbs the beach with danceable tunes. On special full-moon weekends, Luna Beach imports live bands for its moonlight beach parties, also featuring Bahamian bands and mini-Junkanoo breakouts. Cocktails are half price from 8 to 9 pm. Open Sunday to Wednesday noon–7 pm; Friday and Saturday, noon–11

You can kayak in North Bimini's mangrove flats.

pm. **Amenities:** food and drink; lifeguards. **Best for:** partiers; snorkeling; swimming ✉ *Resort World* ⊕ *www.rwbimini.com.*

Radio Beach/ Blister Bay

BEACH—SIGHT | Alice Town's Radio Beach and Bailey Town's Blister Bay form a continuous stretch of beach off Queen's Highway, easily accessible in many places. Also called Alice Town Beach, its southern part is often busier and where spring breakers and the young like to party together. CJ's bar and grill, among other stands, is the default HQ, serving affordable beers, drinks, burgers, and island dinners. Eat inside (away from the flies), on the deck, or on the beach. **Amenities:** food and drink. **Best for:** partiers; swimming. ✉ *Alice Town.*

South Bimini Beach

BEACH—SIGHT | Many would say Bimini's finest beach is on South Bimini, stretching about a mile from Bimini Sands Resort & Marina to South Bimini Beach Club (now closed) at Port Royal where the sand loops round the point and collects in a wide crescent—a favorite of spring breakers and Florida boaters. At South Bimini Beach Club is a protected anchorage and docks, but if you have a boat it's best to slide into the marina at the north end of the beach. There you have amenities and an infinity pool with a bar serving food and drinks. From North Bimini, take a $8 ferry plus taxi to reach the resort—it's well worth the trip to get away from it all. ✉ *South Bimini* ☎ *242/347–3500* ⊕ *www.thebiminisands. com.*

Spook Hill Beach

BEACH—SIGHT | North of Radio Beach and named for its proximity to the local cemetery and Bimini's memorial park, Spook Hill Beach is quieter than Radio and Blister Bay beaches and caters mostly to families looking for quiet sands and calm waters. Shallow shores are ideal for wading and the crystal-clear waters make for great snorkeling. There is a permanent snack bar here and usually a few pop-up beach bars add to the fun.

The beach is heavily lined with pine trees and is narrow at high tide. **Amenities:** food and drink. **Best for:** solitude; snorkeling; swimming. ✉ *North Bimini.*

🍴 Restaurants

Bimini Big Game Bar & Grill

$$ | **BAHAMIAN** | A favorite place for boaters and anglers, this popular restaurant has a large, cool (and insect-free) interior and patio deck with excellent second-story views of the marina, boats passing in the harbor, and shimmering flats beyond. Enjoy beers, cocktails, and island and American fare at reasonable prices. **Known for:** great place to watch sports; great views; camaraderie and atmosphere. [$] *Average main: $26* ✉ *Alice Town* ☎ *242/347–3391* 🌐 *biggameclubbimini.com.*

Captain Bob's

$ | **BAHAMIAN** | Across from the Sea Crest Marina, centrally located in Alice Town, this casual cafeteria-style joint starts serving rib-sticking American and Bahamian breakfasts at 7 am (try the conch or lobster omelet), seven days a week. Bob's is now serving lunches and dinners, closing at 4 pm on Monday and Tuesday and at 11 pm other days. **Known for:** family-owned; people-watching; hearty dinners in summer. [$] *Average main: $15* ✉ *King's Hwy., Alice Town* ☎ *242/347–3260, 242/473–4665* 💳 *No credit cards* ⏲ *No dinner fall–spring.*

Joe's Conch Shack

$ | **BAHAMIAN** | This small island-style open-air conch stand lies on a tiny beach between Bailey Town and Resorts World. Both locals and visitors swear the salad has more conch and is more tender here and his fritters and lobster salad are favorites. Joe personally extracts conch (with his eyes on you) while serving with a big smile. **Known for:** genuine Bahamian experience; fresh conch; harbor views. [$] *Average main: $12* ✉ *North Bailey Town* ☎ *242/554–5183* 💳 *No credit cards.*

🛏 Hotels

Bimini Big Game Club Resort & Marina (*BBGC*)

$$ | **HOTEL** | This king of Alice Town's marina-based resorts has an illustrious fishing history since 1936, and in 2015 enjoyed a $10 million upgrade. **Pros:** spacious rooms; excellent marina for fishing boats; great base with good restaurant. **Cons:** only fishing and diving oriented; most rooms ground level; not on the beach. [$] *Rooms from: $211* ✉ *King's Hwy., Alice Town* ☎ *242/347–3391 resort, 800/867–4764 reservations* 🌐 *www.biggameclubbimini.com* 🔑 *35 rooms, 12 cottages, 4 penthouses* 🍽 *No meals* ☞ *On-site is Bimini Scuba Center, a top Bahamas dive operator. Also on-site are Bahamas Customs & Immigration for quick clearing for yachts.*

★ **Resorts World Bimini Hilton & Marina**

$$ | **RESORT** | **FAMILY** | This pastel-splashed luxury resort now boasts a boutique casino and a stunning new Hilton hotel with a rooftop infinity pool, a luxury spa, and a fitness center. **Pros:** top-quality marinas with all services; children's activity center; shuttle service around the property. **Cons:** restaurant opening times irregular; north-end units are long walk from town; beach can get crowded. [$] *Rooms from: $239* ✉ *King's Hwy., North of Bailey Town* ☎ *888/930–8688 reservations, 242/347–8000 Hilton, 242/347–2900 front desk, 305/374–6664 marina* 🌐 *rwbimini.com* 🔑 *374 units with 200 rooms and suites at the Hilton* 🍽 *No meals.*

Sea Crest Hotel & Marina

$ | **HOTEL** | Near Radio Beach, this small marina has two buildings: one with three stories down a little lane leading to the beach and one with two stories on the marina. **Pros:** free Wi-Fi; central location;

welcoming service. **Cons:** rooms are motel style; rooms lack decor; no restaurant. $ *Rooms from: $120* ⊠ *King's Hwy., Alice Town* ☎ *242/347–3071* ⊕ *www.seacrestbimini.com* ⤸ *25 rooms, 2 suites.*

▼ Nightlife

Big John's Bar & Grill
BARS/PUBS | This waterside sports bar, restaurant, and tiny marina, patronized by the younger set, is one of the most popular places on-island to party, dance, and grab a cold beer, burger, or island snack. It's open from 11:30 am until late. It now sports a snazzy humidor with authentic Cuban cigars. Come nightfall Thursday to Saturday, a fabulous local Bimini band plays live music combining pop, Bahamian hits, reggae, and soca. At midnight, a local DJ takes over and spins until 3 am. If you want to book a room in the boutique hotel upstairs be mindful of the loud vibes. ⊠ *King's Hwy., Alice Town* ☎ *239/347–3117* ⤸ *$10 cover for live music.*

● Shopping

Bimini Craft Centre & Straw Market
CRAFTS | Near the Government Public Dock in Alice Town, this craft center features the original straw, wood carving, and craft works of myriad islanders. Products are showcased over 17 stalls. A great place for tie-dye resort wear and T-shirts, there's also some amazing food to be had. Make sure to stop at Nathalie's Thompson's Bread stand to try a loaf of decadent Bimini Bread. Think hot challah with sugar glaze. ⊠ *Next to a big pink government building and government dock, Alice Town* ☎ *242/347–3529.*

Fisherman's Village Marina
SHOPPING NEIGHBORHOODS | This 136-slip full-service marina, one of two marinas at Resorts World Resort & Marina, doubles as North Bimini's main touristic shopping village. Adjacent to the reception area, the "village" houses Bimini Undersea

dive shop, a liquor and grocery store, an ice-cream shop, a gourmet pizzeria, a café and deli, a clothing boutique, and the surprisingly affordable and good-value Healing Hole Rum Bar & Grill (only open 11 am–4 pm, Monday, Wednesday, and Friday). ⊠ *North Bimini* ☎ *242/347–2900, 242/347–2941 Bimini Undersea Tours* ⊕ *rwbimini.com/dining/on-island-dining.*

Trev Inn Marketplace
CONVENIENCE/GENERAL STORES | Trev Inn has probably the largest selection of groceries and produce on North Bimini. It's located four buildings south of the pink-color Bimini Clinic in Porgy Bay, a short distance from Resorts World. (Also, Brown's is nearby and farther south is Roberts' Grocery Store near the big power station in Bailey Town, and Jontra's near the Bimini Big Game Club.) The mail boat comes in Thursday, so best to shop for fresh produce Thursday evening, Friday, and Saturday. Exploring local grocery stores is quaint and amusing except when you get to the cash register: with costly freight, import duties, and 7.5% VAT, expect to pay about double. To save money, bring coolers packed with fresh and frozen food. ⊠ *King's Hwy., Porgy Town, Alice Town* ☎ *242/347–2452* ⤸ *patricia-roberts@hotmail.com.*

▲ Activities

BOATING AND FISHING
Bimini is not only one of the big game fishing capitals of the world, it also holds six bonefishing world records. Hire one of the island's famous guides—and great characters—to hunt for the spooky "gray ghost." Full-day fishing excursions cost upwards of $600. Reef and deep-sea fishing excursions are also available from $400 for a half day. The best bonefishing guides must be booked well in advance.

Bimini Big Game Club Resort & Marina
DIVING/SNORKELING | Bimini Big Game Club Resort & Marina is a great base for fishing, diving, and snorkeling charters.

They book the island's top bonefish guides and bottom and deep-sea fishing captains. You can also rent a small boat here, as well as kayaks, paddleboards, and snorkeling gear, and you can buy bait. There's a convenience store on property for mid-dive and mid-tour snacks (and liquor)—along with a Bahama Customs and Immigration office for port-of-entry clearance for boats. It's also the new home of the famous Neal Watson's PADI Bimini Scuba Center. At this writing, BBGC offers $250 credit off your airline or ferry tickets with a stay of four nights or more. ⊠ *Alice Town* ☎ *800/867–4764 toll-free, 954/615–1011 Florida, 242/473–8816 dive center.*

"Bonefish" Ebbie David

BOATING | With his personality-plus, you'll get more laughs out of Ebbie David than fish—or will you? He's one of Bimini's most famous and highly recommended bonefishing guides. In 2015 he won a coveted Ministry of Tourism Cacique Award for his excellence in the sport and in hospitality. Ebbie now runs his own bonefishing lodge. ⊠ *Alice Town* ☎ *242/347–2053, 242/359–8273 cell* ⊕ *www.bahamas.com.*

Captain Carson Saunders

DIVING/SNORKELING | For snorkeling and sightseeing tours in relatively calm weather, Captain Carson, based at Bimini Big Game Club, is a great choice for his value. Half days are $400 and full days are $800 in his 25-foot Proline center console. Although it lacks the luxury of bigger cabin cruisers, you'll save time and money. Bring a hat and sunblock. ⊠ *Bimini Big Game Club Resort & Marina, Alice Town* ☎ *242/464–5810.*

Golden Dream Charters

FISHING | Ex-commercial fisherman and island-born Captain Stephen Knowles has a special insight when and where the fish are biting. His Ocean Yachts 46-foot Convertible *Golden Dream* is purpose-made for comfortable, fun fishing. Stephen heads to the Gulf Stream, trolling for big

game: blue marlin, sailfish, mahi-mahi, wahoo, and tuna. Bimini abounds with bottom-fishing spots where he'll set you on groupers, snappers, porgies, and yellowtails. In his 46-foot luxury sportfishing cabin cruiser it's $800 for a half day, and $1,600 for a full day. ⊠ *Alice Town* ☎ *242/727–8144 cell, 242/347–3391 Bimini Big Game Club marina* ✉ *stephenknowles57@hotmail.com.*

SCUBA DIVING AND SNORKELING

The **Bimini Barge Wreck** (a World War II landing craft) rests in 100 feet of water. **Little Caverns** is a medium-depth dive with scattered coral heads, small tunnels, and swim-throughs. **Rainbow Reef** is a shallow dive popular for fish gazing. **Moray Alley** teems with captivating moray eels and **Bull Run** is famous for its profusion of sharks. And, of course, there's **Bimini Road (aka, Road to Atlantis),** thought to be the famous "lost city." Dive packages are available through most Bimini hotels. You can also check out the best diving options through the **Bahamas Diving Association** (☎ *954/236–9292 or 800/866–3483* ⊕ *www.bahamasdiving.com).*

Bimini Undersea

SCUBA DIVING | Headquartered in Fisherman's Village at Resorts World, the highly rated Bimini Undersea tour operator offers myriad excursions and experiences, including scuba diving, shark dives and stingray adventures, scuba, nature boat tours, fishing, and snorkeling with wild spotted dolphins. They run Sunset Celebration Cruises, and near the marina and on Paradise Beach at the new Luna Beach Club they offer Jet Skis, kayaks, and paddleboards. You can also rent or buy snorkel and diving gear. They offer two, two-tank dives a day and introductory scuba lessons. Dive packages with accommodations at Resorts World are available, and day-trippers are also welcome to join. ⊠ *Resorts World Bimini & Marina* ☎ *242/347–2941, 786/462–4641 in U.S. and Canada* ⊕ *www.biminiundersea.net.*

This large bonefish was caught on Bimini's shallow flats.

Neal Watson's PADI Bimini Scuba Center
DIVING/SNORKELING | The PADI-certified
Bimini Scuba Center, located at Bimini
Big Game Club Resort & Marina, offers
two-tank dives in the morning and one-
tank dives in the afternoon. Besides
exciting Great Hammerhead Shark
dives (from October to March), Bull
Shark dives near Cat Cay, and Caribbean
Reef and Lemon Shark dives, BSC also
offers Wild-Spotted Dolphin snorkeling
excursions. (You may need patience
and understanding; after all, these are
free and wild creatures.) The operator
visits all of Bimini's popular dive spots:
the Sapona Wreck, the Bimini Barge,
Atlantis Road, Tuna Alley, Victory Reef,
the Nodules, the Strip, Rainbow Reef,
and much more. They offer a full range
of rentals and tank fills, as well as kayaks
and paddleboards for exploring the
harbor and flats beyond. You can also
arrange for small boat rentals and all
types of fishing charters. Novices can
safely train in the resort's pool, then grab
a quick bite and drink. With everything
so convenient, Bimini Scuba Center is
an excellent choice for a diving or fishing
vacation. ✉ *Alice Town* ☏ *242/347–3391
resort, 800/867–4764 toll-free in U.S. and
Canada, 242/473–8816 cell.*

South Bimini

Bigger, with nicer beaches and higher
elevation than low-lying North Bimini,
South Bimini is nonetheless the quieter
of the two islands. Home to the island's
only airport, it has a smattering of shops
near the ferry landing where boats make
regular crossings between the two
islands, a short five-minute ride. Bimini
Sands Resort is the biggest property on
the island with its safe-harbor marina,
condos, and nature trail. South of the
main resort in Port Royal are 80-plus
vacation homes, some docks, and a scal-
loped beach that's a favorite of visiting
boaters. The resort also helps preserve
the island's ecofocus by staying low-key
and keeping much of its land undeveloped. It helps maintain the little Fountain

of Youth Park, the Sharklab, and beautiful beaches.

GETTING AROUND

Visitors do not need a car on Bimini, and there are no car-rental agencies. A taxi from the airport to Bimini Sands Resort is $3. Hitching a ride is common.

⊙ Sights

Bimini Biological Field Station Sharklab

NATURE PRESERVE | The Bimini Biological Field Station Foundation's Sharklab was founded more than 25 years ago by Dr. Samuel Gruber, a shark biologist at the University of Miami. Visitors can tour the lab at low tide. The highlight is wading into the bay where the lab keeps several lemon sharks. The hands-on presentation, done by the research assistants or researchers themselves, is entertaining and educational. Tours are offered daily but visitors must call in advance. ⊠ *South Bimini* ✛ *End of long road to south of island, turn left* ☎ *242/347–4538* ⊕ *www. biminisharklab.com* ✍ *$10 donation desirable.*

Bimini Nature Trail

TOUR—SIGHT | FAMILY | Developed by Bimini Sands Resort on undeveloped property, this mile-loop trail is one of the best of its kind in the Bahamas. Its slight rise in elevation means a lovely shaded walk under hardwood trees such as gumbo-limbos, poisonwood (marked with "Don't Touch" signs), and buttonwood. Check out the ruins of the historic Conch House, a great place for sunset-gazing. There is also a pirate's well exhibit devoted to the island's swashbuckling history. Excellent signage guides you through the island's fauna and flora if you prefer doing a self-guided tour. However, for the best interpretation and learning experience, book a guided tour through Bimini Sand's front desk. Kids always love petting the indigenous Bimini boa on the guided tour. The trail was recently improved by Bahamian bird-watchers such as Erika

Gates of Freeport's famous Garden of the Groves reserve. ⊠ *South Bimini* ☎ *242/347–3500 resort* ✍ *Free. Guided tours $12.*

Fountain of Youth

HISTORIC SITE | Famous explorer Juan Ponce de León heard from Indians about a Fountain of Youth possibly located in Bimini, so in 1513, on his way to discovering Florida and the Gulf Stream, he landed on Bimini but never found the fountain. The historical result? Somehow Biminites adopted a freshwater natural well that was carved out of limestone by groundwater thousands of years ago and used it to commemorate Ponce de León's search. Now there's a plaque to celebrate the myth. So, nonetheless, go there and make a wish (without casting a penny—this is an ecoisland). You'll find the Fountain of Youth on the road to the airport. ⊠ *South Bimini* ☎ *242/347–3500 Bimini Sands Resort & Marina* ✍ *Free.*

⊙ Beaches

South Bimini claims Bimini's prettiest beaches, with a pristine, mile-long stretch on the western side and near Port Royal, a sandy cove and point on the southern side, with some of the best from-shore snorkeling around. In the far south, the South Bimini Beach Club was closed after a hurricane in 2016, but the point's gorgeous beach is there to enjoy for all and sundry. It's a favorite beach for boaters, with a couple of docks and safe anchorages from northerly or easterly winds. The partiers tend to congregate here leaving the northern beaches relatively secluded. At the north end of the long beach is Bimini Sands Resort & Marina. Dock there and you can use their infinity pool and other amenities (and a fuel dock, too). The Pool Bar, with its refreshments and food, is welcome to all beach walkers.

Bimini Sands Beach

BEACH—SIGHT | Patrons of Bimini Sands Resort & Marina are not the only ones who love Bimini Sands's mile-long beach. This gorgeous stretch of white-sand powder, with its offshore snorkeling, is so enticing that vacationers from North Bimini and even Floridians often take the quick ferry over or boat across the Gulf Stream for the day. The southern cove and point once had facilities which are, at press time, closed, but the beach and beautiful waters are still a magnet for boaters. To clear Bahamas Customs, who are stationed at the airport, it's best to slide into Bimini Sands's marina where you have access to amenities including the Pool Bar and freshwater pool. The southern beach gets particularly busy during spring break but the northern stretch stays relatively secluded. ✉ *South Bimini* ☎ *242/347–3500 Bimini Sands Resort & Marina* 🌐 *www.thebiminisands.com* 🎟 *Free. Ferry plus taxi from North Bimini $5.*

🍴 Restaurants

The Petite Conch

$ | BAHAMIAN | This second-story cozy little diner/café overlooks Bimini Sands Marina, and although they don't serve fancy cuisine, it does have excellent and comforting Bahamian dishes at a reasonable cost. Very convenient for the resort's and marina's guests, The Petite Conch serves breakfast, lunch, and dinner with American and local favorites. **Known for:** cozy ambience; convenient for resort and marina guests; fast and friendly service. [$] *Average main: $10* ✉ *South Bimini* ☎ *242/347–3500* 🌐 *www.thebiminisands.com.*

Plan Ahead

Even though you're going to the laid-back islands, you need to reserve your guides, boats, cars, and golf carts in advance. And if you ask, these friendly islanders might include an airport greeting and transfer to your hotel.

🛏 Hotels

Bimini Sands Resort & Marina

$$ | RESORT | FAMILY | Overlooking the Straits of Florida on a stunning beach, this well-designed property rents one- to three-bedroom condominiums with direct marina access. **Pros:** self-catering condos; full-service marina with customs nearby; small restaurant with pool bar and café; good tour operations. **Cons:** limited nightlife on South Bimini (party is daytime here); sometimes shortage of lounge chairs; somewhat remote. [$] *Rooms from: $250* ✉ *South Bimini* ☎ *242/347–3500 resort, 888/588–2464 in U.S. and Canada* 🌐 *www.thebiminisands.com* 🛏 *206 condominiums* 🍴 *No meals.*

🏃 Activities

BOATING, FISHING, AND DIVING

Bimini Sands Resort & Marina

BOATING | Bimini Sands Resort & Marina arranges and has access to all the tours and excursions offered by the excursion and dive operators in North Bimini including the shark, stingray, wreck, reef, and wild spotted dolphin tours offered by Neal Watson's Bimini Scuba Center. You can join those tours either by taking the $5 ferry plus taxi to Alice Town or by asking the tour boat to pick you up at the Bimini Sands Marina. The resort itself offers kayaks, snorkeling gear, and boat rentals so you can go and discover Bimini's many reefs and wrecks on your own. ✉ *Bimini Sands Resort & Marina* ☎ *242/347–3500* ⊕ *www.thebiminisands. com.*

SCUBA DIVING AND SNORKELING

Bimini has excellent diving opportunities, particularly for watching marine life. Off the shore of South Bimini the concrete wreck of the SS *Sapona* attracts snorkelers as well as partiers.

The Berry Islands

The Berry Islands consist of more than two dozen small islands and almost a hundred tiny cays stretching in a thin crescent to the north of Andros and Nassau. Although a few of the islands are privately owned, most of them are uninhabited—except by rare birds who use the territory as their nesting grounds, or by visiting yachters dropping anchor in secluded havens. The Berry Islands start in the north at **Great Stirrup Cay** and **Coco Cay** where thousands of cruise passengers enjoy Bahama-island experiences. and the Stingray City Bahamas attraction on neighboring Goat Cay. The Berries end in the south at **Chub Cay,** only 35 miles north of Nassau.

Most of the islands' 700 residents live on the tranquil, 10-mile-long **Great Harbour Cay,** the largest of the Berry Islands. Its main settlement, **Bullock's Harbour,** aka "the Village," has a couple of good restaurants, grocery and liquor stores, and small shops. A mile west, the Great Harbour Cay's beach area was developed in the early 1970s. More homes, condos, and villas have been built or remodeled since. The 65-slip protected marina has also been renovated and is once again popular with yachties. There are no big resorts on Great Harbour; instead, there's a delightful, world-class boutique hotel called Carriearl, a former house of a famous Hollywood star matchmaker who invited his guests here to party within their tight circle. There's a small hotel

at the marina, and homes and villas for rent on the marina and beaches. The GHC Property Owners Association is active and provides many fun activities and events, including the partial upkeep of 9 holes of the original golf course. Many private pilots have homes and fly in here. The Berries are reputed to have one of the world's highest concentrations of millionaires per square mile, but, surprisingly, there are no banks or ATMs, so make sure you bring some cash with your credit cards.

In recent years, family, wedding, honeymoon, and beach-seeking vacations and bonefishing have become more popular. In the south, Chub Cay is close to a deep-sea pocket where the Tongue of the Ocean meets the North West Providence Channel—a junction that traps big game fish. Remote flats south of Great Harbour, from Anderson Cay to Money Cay, are excellent bonefish habitats, as are the flats around Chub Cay. Deeper-water flats hold permit and tarpon.

Chub Cay, a popular halfway point for boaters crossing to and from Florida, is also experiencing a comeback with millions having been recently invested in the Chub Cay Resort & Marina, which is soon to become private, catering more to investors who own or build homes on the island. On Chub, you'll certainly connect with your friends and young ones but make sure you have a boat to give you freedom to explore, dive, and fish. Bring food, drinks, and snacks for your stay. The luxury-looking new clubhouse has a well-stocked convenience store. Most rental units come with kitchens.

AIR

In the Berry Islands, Great Harbour Cay (GHC) Airport receives regular flights from Fort Lauderdale airport (FLL) through Tropic Ocean Airways, with their land-capable floatplanes, on Friday and Sunday. Four times weekly Makers Air flies to Chub Cay (CCZ) and GHC from Fort Lauderdale Executive Airport (FXE).

From Nassau (NAS), two flights a day come in via LeAir. Many other charter operators with props, jets, and helicopters fly in from Florida. For a full list of schedule and charter flights see ⊕ www.bahamas.com/islands/berry-islands/getting-here.

BOAT

Great Harbour Cay and Chub Cay are popular yachting destinations and stop-offs for boats going farther afield. Both are ports of entry with friendly service by Customs and Immigration for entry clearance and gaining the mandatory cruising permits. Both have excellent marinas with fuel and full services. From Nassau, the mail boat M/V *Capt. Gurth Dean* sets sail twice or three time a month from Potter's Cay Dock on Wednesday night, arriving Thursday morning to supply the GHC with groceries, supplies, and general cargo. Fuel for boaters is also available at Alder Cay and Little Whale Cay, halfway down the chain.

Take a boat or hire a guide and island hop to explore the cays' splendid turquoise serenity and wildlife on land and undersea. The Berries are favored among bone- and deep-sea fishermen in-the-know and who want to get away from crowds. World-class fishing tournaments used to be held here and at the start of the crawfish season on August 1, many boats from Nassau chose to spearfish here for its westerly lee-side shelters, its proximity, and the lucrative bounty. On Little Harbour Cay, 16 miles southeast of Great Harbour, is the famous outpost Flo's Conch Bar, now run by Flo's family. Visit the Stingray City Bahamas' tour to snorkel with stingrays off Goat Cay by catching the company's staff boat from Great Harbour Cay.

CONTACTS Chub Cay Resort & Marina. ☎ *242/325–1490 resort and marina, 786/209–0025 in U.S. and Canada* ⊕ *www.chubcayresortand-marina.com.* **Great Harbour Cay**

Marina. ☎ *242/367–8005 marina* ⊕ *www.greatharbourcay.com.*

ISLAND TRANSPORTATION

On Great Harbour Cay, you can get most places on foot, which is convenient as there are not a lot of ground transportation options. There is one car rental provider with vehicles ranging from $75 up to $90. On Chub Cay you can rent golf carts at the marina and elsewhere. On both islands, transport may be included in your villa rental. Hopefully you'll get on to the water and sightsee some Berry magic by renting a small boat or doing some fishing. Make sure you have a reliable VHF radio and plot your course on a good chart that you can buy at the marinas: these islands have many hazardous reefs and sandbars. Gas is around $5 a gallon.

CONTACTS Happy People Rentals. ⊠ *Great Harbour Cay Marina, Great Harbour Cay* ☎ *242/367–8117 shop, 242/359–9052 cell.* **Krum's Rentals.** ☎ *242/367–8370.*

🔱 Beaches

Off these always secluded, immaculate beaches, the clarity of Bahamian waters is especially evident when you reach the Berry Islands. Starfish abound, and you can often catch a glimpse of a gliding stingray, eagle ray, barracuda, and needle fish. You'll find ocean beaches with gentle lapping waves, sultry beaches with sandbar flats where you can walk half a mile, and private coves enclosed by cliffs for ultraprivate experiences.

Chub Cay Beach

BEACH—SIGHT | As well as the 400-yard beach right at the marina, Chub Cay has a splendid 1¼-mile strand with great swimming and nearby snorkeling. The Club House with its pool is a mere 400 yards away for refreshments. **Amenities:** none. **Best for:** swimming; snorkeling. ⊠ *Chub Cay's southern coast* ☎ *242/325–1490 clubhouse and marina office.*

Great Harbour Cay Beach

BEACH—SIGHT | Two crescents scoop Great Harbour Cay's east coast with 5 miles of almost unbroken powder. Travel north to discover Sugar Beach with its bluff-surrounding romantic private coves. Progressing south, the beach becomes Lover's Beach, thinning out until Hotel Point Beach where the strand widens and you can see waves clash from two directions. Farther south still is famous Great Harbour Beach itself, where you'll encounter the fabulous boutique hotel Carriearl and its fine pool, restaurant, and bar. On the south end of Great Harbour Beach near the airport, you'll find The Beach Club, a popular daytime bar and grill with a gift shop. Play beach volleyball, or take a yoga class. (They may ask for a small donation.) At the extreme south are the shallow, simmering sandbars of Shelling Beach that let you wade out for yards. At low tide, you can cross the tidal Shark Beach Creek to the pristine Haines Cay that, hidden from the north by a hill, offers an even more splendid, long beach. Along Great Harbour Cay's powdery 5-mile stretch, nearby reefs beckon snorkelers and gin-clear waters invite kayakers and paddleboarders. **Amenities:** food and drink. **Best for:** shelling; swimming; walking; snorkeling. ⊠ *Great Harbour Cay* ✛ *5 miles long with varying names* ☎ *242/367–8005 marina and resort* ⊕ *www.greatharbourcay.com.*

Haines Cay Beach

BEACH—SIGHT | At low tide, walk across from Shelling Beach estuary, round the point, and walk south a half mile and you'll discover one of the Bahamas' most unspoiled, beautiful beaches. It's 2 miles long with excellent snorkeling on its north end and swimming all along. Wear some sturdy footwear for the land walk. It's also reachable by kayak. There are no trees for shade, so an umbrella, lots of fluids, and sunscreen are advisable. **Amenities:** none. **Best for:** swimming; walking; snorkeling;

Early-Bird Dinners

Dinner is commonly served in most restaurants starting at 6 pm and can be over by 8:30. It is always best to call ahead for reservations, and to let the restaurant know you are coming as hours can be irregular; they may decide to close if they think they aren't going to be busy. Some like to have your order ahead of time.

solitude. ⊠ *Great Harbour Cay* ✛ *½ mile west of Shelling Beach.*

Sugar Beach

BEACH—SIGHT | Sugar Beach is the northernmost of the island's beaches, where rock bluffs divide the sand into romantic "private" coves of various lengths. Explore the caves or snorkel in calm waters. On top of one of the hills are the ghostly remains of the Sugar Beach Hotel, a 1950s lair built by the Hollywood Rat Pack—Sammy Davis Jr., Dean Martin, Frank Sinatra, Peter Lawford, and Joey Bishop. Female stars invited there included Marilyn Monroe, Shirley MacLaine, Lauren Bacall, Angie Dickinson, and Judy Garland. This was their scenic escape from paparazzi. The hilltop ruins are decrepit and surrounded by bush and cliffs, so explore with caution. ⊠ *Great Harbour Cay.*

🍴 Restaurants

★ Carriearl Restaurant

$$$ | **BAHAMIAN** | Guests who discover Carriearl Restaurant are pleasantly stunned that a restaurant of such charm and caliber just happens to be on their tiny island. The warm and capable couple from Manchester, restaurateur Martin "Dronzi" Dronsfield and former British

Kayaks line the beach at Little Stirrup Cay in the Berry Islands.

Airways flight attendant Angie Jackson, have managed to fashion one of the Bahamas' most illustrious beachside mansions into a gem of culinary and visual delight. **Known for:** tropical chic atmosphere; outstanding pizzas. [$] *Average main: $35* ✉ *Great Harbour Cay Beach, Great Harbour Cay* ☎ *242/367–8785, 242/451–8785 cell* 🌐 *www.carriearlhotel.com* 🕓 *For nonguests: closed Mon. and Tues., no lunch Wed., no dinner Sun.* ☞ *Breakfast, lunch, and dinner daily for hotel guests.*

Coolie Mae's Sunset Restaurant

$$ | **BAHAMIAN** | In the island food category, expats, locals, and visitors rate Mae's food as true-true excellent. Her bright sign makes the casual 60-seat restaurant, on Bullock's Harbour's central seafront, easy to find. **Known for:** conch salad; Bahamian specialties; reservations recommended. [$] *Average main: $22* ✉ *In middle of Bullock's Harbour's west peninsula, Great Harbour Cay* ☎ *242/367–8730* 💳 *No credit cards* 🕓 *Closed Sun.*

The New Beach Club

$ | **BAHAMIAN** | This is the island's cool locale for breakfast and lunch, across the road from the airport, overlooking the beach and turquoise water. At breakfast, go for the eggs and ham with home grits, and at lunch, have a grilled cheeseburger or whatever fresh fish is on the menu for the day. **Known for:** group dinners available on request; yoga and volleyball at club; fresh fish. [$] *Average main: $14* ✉ *On Great Harbour Cay Beach, near airport, Great Harbour Cay* ☎ *242/367–8108* 💳 *No credit cards* 🕓 *No dinner unless requested by group.*

🛏 Hotels

★ **Carriearl Boutique Hotel**

$$ | **B&B/INN** | An unassuming front entrance hides what many say is one of the Bahamas' top small vacation retreats, and guests love having 7 miles of powdery beach to themselves. **Pros:** right on 7 miles of silky sand beach; superb restaurant and bar; excellent, attentive,

and friendly service. **Cons:** only four rooms; rooms only for 18 years or older. $ *Rooms from: $245* ✉ *Great Harbour Cay* ☎ *242/367–8785 hotel, 242/451–8785 cell* ⊕ *www.carriearlhotel.com* ⤴ *4 rooms* ⦿ *No meals.*

★ Chub Cay Resort & Marina
$$$$ | HOTEL | Chub Cay Resort & Marina has been speedily and most beautifully restored to what is a luxury oasis on an otherwise rustic cay. **Pros:** excellent location for flats and offshore fishing; quality bar and restaurant serves three meals; luxury-style clubhouse and well-appointed rooms with balconies. **Cons:** construction may occur but away from hotel; not much to do on land but plenty on the sea. $ *Rooms from: $425* ✉ *Chub Cay* ☎ *242/325–1490 hotel, 786/209–0025 in U.S. and Canada* ⊕ *www.chubcay.com* ⤴ *11 rooms and suites, 8 1-bedroom beach cabanas, 12 villas with 2–4 bedrooms, largest sleeps 10* ⦿ *All-inclusive.*

🏃 Activities

BOATING
The water's depth is seldom more than 20 feet here. Grass patches and an occasional coral head or flat coral patch dot the light-sand bottom. You might spot the odd turtle, and if you care to jump over the boat's side with a mask, you might also pick up a conch or two in the grass. Good snorkeling and bonefishing, and peaceful anchorages, can be found on the lee shores of the Hoffmans and Little Harbour cays. **Flo's Conch Bar,** at the southern end of Little Harbour Cay serves fresh conch prepared every way.

Great Harbour Cay Marina
BOATING | In the upper Berry Islands, the full-service Great Harbour Cay Marina has 65 slips for yachts up to 150 feet. This is the island's touristic nerve center where you can book fishing and snorkeling charters and arrange boat rentals. Accessed through an 80-foot-wide channel from

the west, the marina has almost no motion even in rough weather: it's a top hurricane hole. (Matthew in 2016 went right over it.) This sleepy and crime-free island on a gorgeous beach still has plenty to do: join a game of pétanque in the street with free rum punch on Wednesday evening or the Chill 'N' Grill ($10–$15) get-together on Friday night, or weekly yoga, fitness classes, and beach volleyball at The Beach Club. You can even play nine holes of golf on the rather weedy course. The marina is a great base for boating, snorkeling, and fishing. HeuBoo's Deli on the dock is a good place for ice cream and pastries. Fuel is at a separate dock west of the marina. The marina's management company also rents out town houses. ✉ *Great Harbour Cay* ☎ *242/367–8005 dock, 242/457–4216 cell* ⊕ *www.greatharbourcay.com.*

Happy People Boat Rental
BOATING | At Great Harbour Cay Marina, Elon Rolle, located in a small convenience store on the dock, hires for the day, half day, or hour, an unsinkable 20-foot Boston Outrage with 200HP for $250 a day plus gas (using about $150 for 30 gallons for a day). Snorkeling, spear, and fishing gear are extra. It also comes with VHF radio. ✉ *Great Harbour Cay Marina, Great Harbour Cay* ☎ *242/367–8117 marina, 242/367–8761 home, 242/359–9052 cell.*

FISHING
Percy Darville's Bonefishing
BOATING | Percy Darville and his family and crew know the flats of the Berries better than anyone. The fleet comprises four skiffs. Percy has a speedy 26-foot Mako with 400HP, speedy and ideal for bottom-fishing and taking tours to highlights such as Hoffman's Cay Blue Hole. From GHC, Five Hearts also travels the 1½ hours to Chub Cay when clients request them, or anywhere in the Berries. Worldly fishermen say the Berries have a higher percentage of larger fish.

A half day with Five Hearts is $400 and a full day is $600, with gas included; you only pay extra for gas on longer trips. Contact this top crew well in advance as they are much in demand. In 2007, Capt. Percy was awarded the Cacique Award for Sports and Leisure, the Bahamas' prestigious award for hospitality, and for his contribution to tourism. ✉ *Great Harbour Cay* ☎ *242/464–4149 cell, 242/367–8119 home.*

SNORKELING

Stingray City

DIVING/SNORKELING | FAMILY | A snorkel trip by boat to this spot on Goat Island is a favorite experience of both cruise passengers and anyone staying in Great Harbour Cay. Visitors interact in the pristine, sparkling, and shallow water with southern rays and swimming pigs. ✉ *Great Harbour Cay* ☎ *242/364–1032 Nassau office* ⊕ *www.stingraybahamas. com.*

Chapter 6

ELEUTHERA AND HARBOUR ISLAND

Updated by
Sheri-kae McLeod

⊙ Sights	🍴 Restaurants	🛏 Hotels	🛍 Shopping	🍸 Nightlife
★★★★★	★★★☆☆	★★★★☆	★★☆☆☆	★☆☆☆☆

WELCOME TO ELEUTHERA AND HARBOUR ISLAND

TOP REASONS TO GO

★ **Play in pink sand:** Glorious, soft pink sand, the ethereal shade of the first blush of dawn, draws beach connoisseurs to Harbour Island. Plenty of pretty pink beaches also dot Eleuthera's east and north coasts.

★ **Ogle island architecture:** Historic homes with storybook gables and gingerbread verandahs are the norm on Harbour Island and Spanish Wells. Picturesque Victorian houses overlook Governor's Harbour in Eleuthera.

★ **Savor soulful sounds:** Nights here rock with the Bahamian group Afro Band, the hip-hop of TaDa, the traditional sound of Jaynell Ingraham, and the calypso of Dr. Sea Breeze.

★ **Indulge in alfresco dining:** Harbour Island's intimate restaurants have reinvented regional cuisine. On Eleuthera, Governor's Harbour has a number of laid-back spots with memorable menus and magnificent views.

1 Gregory Town and North Eleuthera. Eleuthera's undeveloped, serene north holds some of the island's most iconic natural wonders: the Glass Window Bridge, a heart-racing span between 80-foot cliffs often buffeted by a raging Atlantic; the 17th-century Preacher's Cave; and the thrilling waves of Surfer's Beach.

2 Hatchet Bay. "The Country's Safest Harbour" is Hatchet Bay's claim to fame. The naturally protected harbor is a popular place to anchor sailboats and fishing vessels.

3 Governor's Harbour. The administrative capital of Governor's Harbour is a pretty, Victorian town, with a lively harbor that's a frequent stop for mail boats, ferries, and yachts. The town offers upscale restaurants and down-home conch cafés, boutique inns, and inexpensive apartments.

4 Rock Sound and South Eleuthera. Rock Sound, the original capital of Eleuthera, is a quaint seaside settlement with 19th-century homes. Thirty miles away, yachties stop at Cape Eleuthera

peninsula for a few nights of luxury in elegant town houses. Environmentalists also come here from around the world to learn about the self-sustaining Island School.

5 Harbour Island. Dunmore Town, the first capital of the Bahamas, has historic Loyalists' houses, fronted by white picket fences, some with cutouts of pineapples and boats, and festooned with red bougainvillea and tumbling purple morning glories. Luxurious inns, renowned restaurants, and the magnificent pink beach attract celebrities.

6 Spanish Wells. A quaint town of tidy clapboard white houses is on windswept St. George's Cay, a destination for those who don't want to bump elbows with other tourists. Idyllic white- and pink-sand beaches are the main attractions.

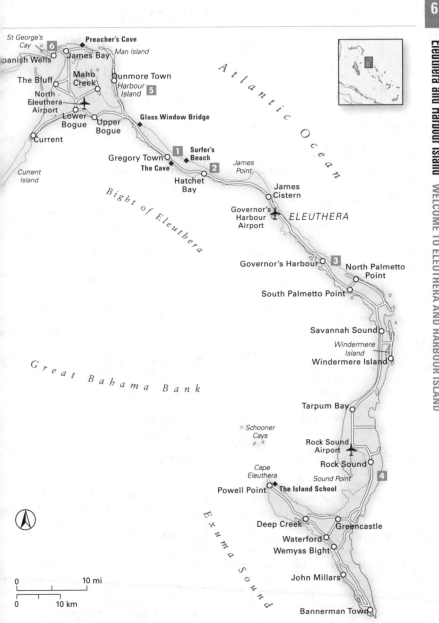

You haven't experienced a real escape until you've vacationed in Eleuthera. Simple luxury resorts are the norm, deserted expanses of white- or pink-sand beaches are your playground, and islanders are genuinely friendly. Seclusion, sun, and starry skies are abundant here.

Eleuthera was founded in 1648 by a British group fleeing religious persecution; the name is taken from the Greek word for freedom. These settlers, who called themselves the Eleutheran Adventurers, gave the Bahamas its first written constitution. "Adventurers" has taken on new meaning as a clarion call to sailors, tourists, and, more recently, retirees looking for adventures of their own.

Largely undeveloped rolling green hills and untrammeled sandy coves, along with sleepy 19th-century towns, offer an authentic Bahamas experience that is quickly disappearing. Try not to notice the ubiquitous HG Christie and Sotheby's "For Sale" signs unless, of course, you're so smitten you want to stay. Rent a car—or even better, an SUV—for washboard back roads, and explore the island's secluded beaches and sandy coves fringing turquoise and aqua water that rivals anything in the Caribbean. The island is among the prettiest in the Bahamas, with gentle hills, unspoiled "bush" (backwoods), and gardens of tumbling purple lantana and sky-blue plumbago. Hotels and inns are painted in the shades of Bahamian bays and sunset, which is best watched from the comfort of inviting verandas and seaside decks.

If you're looking for all of this and a bit more action, ferry over to Harbour Island, Eleuthera's chic neighbor. With its uninterrupted 3-mile pink-sand beach, top-notch dining, and sumptuous inns, the island has long been a favorite hideaway for jet setters and celebrities. For splendid beaches with few, if any, tourists, head to Spanish Wells, a quiet, secluded island, located approximately 500 meters off the northern tip of Eleuthera island. Eleuthera and Harbour Island beaches are some of the best in the world, thanks to their pristine beauty and dazzling variety.

Planning

When to Go

High tourist season in Eleuthera runs December through April. Low temperatures might dip into the 60s, and the water can be chilly. Bring a sweater and a jacket, especially if you plan on boating. Expect to pay higher rates for rooms, boat rentals, and airfare during this time. For the cheapest hotel rates and some of the best deals on water-sports packages, visit in summer or fall when the ocean is generally calm and warm. Be aware, however, that hurricane season runs June through November, with the highest risk of storms from August to October. During this time weather can be steamy and rainy.

The liveliest times to visit Eleuthera are when island-wide festivals and celebrations are held like the annual Junkanoo celebration during Christmas, the Pineapple Festival and Conch Fest in June, the Rock Sound Homecoming during Easter, and the North Eleuthera Sailing Regatta in October. Reserve hotel rooms early.

Festivals

FALL AND WINTER

The North Eleuthera/Harbour Island Sailing Regatta in October is an exciting five-day boat competition, with onshore activities like live Bahamian bands plus food and drink. **Junkanoo** is celebrated in Rock Sound and Harbour Island on December 26. Celebrations start around 7 pm.

SUMMER

The Eleuthera Pineapple Festival is celebrated at the beginning of June in Gregory Town. If you like a little competition during your vacation, time your trip around the Pineappleman Sprint Triathalon. **Conch Fest** with live Rake 'n' Scrape promoting Deep Creek's cultural heritage takes place in June in Rock Sound.

Conch Fest
Deep Creek's annual, six-day Conch Fest in June means talent shows, Rake 'n' Scrape music, arts and crafts, and, of course, lots of conch. The event was designed to promote the Deep Creek settlement and to share its cultural heritage with the younger members of the community, descendants, and visitors. ⊠ Rock Sound.

North Eleuthera Sailing Regatta
The North Eleuthera Sailing Regatta in October provides four days of exciting competition of Bahamian Class A, B, and C boats. Onshore activities based on Harbour Island include live bands playing Bahamian music, plus local food and drink.

Pineapple Fest
In June, Gregory Town hosts the four-day Pineapple Festival, with a Junkanoo parade, crafts displays, tours of pineapple farms, the annual 40-mile Cycling Race—as well as an opportunity to sample what Eleuthera natives proclaim to be the sweetest pineapple in the world. ⊠ Gregory Town.

Getting Here and Around

AIR
Eleuthera has three airports: **North Eleuthera (ELH),** midisland **Governor's Harbour (GHB),** and **Rock Sound International (RSD)** in the south. Taxis usually wait for scheduled flights at the airports. Taxi service for two people from North Eleuthera Airport to the Cove is $35 ($60 from Governor's Harbour Airport); from Governor's Harbour Airport to Pineapple Fields, $40; from Rock Sound Airport to Cape Eleuthera, $75. Visitors going to Harbour Island and Spanish Wells should fly into North Eleuthera Airport.

CONTACTS Governor's Harbour Airport. ☎ 242/332–2321. **North Eleuthera Airport.** ☎ 242/335–1242. **Rock Sound Airport.** ☎ 242/334–2125.

BOAT AND FERRY
Mail boats leave from Nassau's Potter's Cay for the five-hour trip to Eleuthera. One-way tickets cost $30. M/V Current Pride sails to Current Island, Hatchet Bay, the Bluff, and Long Bay Cay on Thursday, returning Tuesday to Nassau. M/V Bahamas Daybreak III leaves Nassau on Monday and Wednesday for Harbour Island, Rock Sound, and Davis Harbour, returning to Nassau Tuesday and Sunday. The Eleuthera Express sails for Governor's Harbour, Rock Sound, Spanish Wells, and Harbour Island on Monday

and Thursday, returning to Nassau on Tuesday and Sunday. Contact the **Dockmaster's Office. Bahamas Ferries,** high-speed catamarans, connect Nassau to Harbour Island, Governor's Harbour, and Spanish Wells. The trip takes three hours and costs $161 round-trip.

CONTACTS Bahamas Ferries. ☎ 242/323–2166 ⊕ www.bahamasferries.com. **Dockmaster's Office.** ☎ 242/393–1064.

CAR

Rent a car if you plan to travel around Eleuthera. You can drive north to south in about three hours. Daily rentals run about $70. Request a four-wheel drive if you plan to visit Preacher's Cave or Surfer's Beach.

CONTACTS Big E's Eleuthera Car Rentals. ☎ 242/470–0467 ⊕ www.bigescarrental. com. **Central Auto Rentals.** ☎ 242/552–5460 ⊕ www.careleuthera.com. **Eleuthera Car Rental.** ☎ 242/470–0844 ⊕ www. eleutheracars.com. **Major's Car Rental & Taxi Service.** ☎ 242/359–7163. **Turnquest Car Rentals.** ☎ 242/332–2467 ⊕ www. turnquestcarrentals.com. **Taylor and Taylor Car Rentals.** ☎ 242/332–1665 ⊕ www. eleutheracarrentals.com.

GOLF CART

You'll want a golf cart if you spend more than a couple of days on Harbour Island or Spanish Wells. Four-seater carts start at about $60 a day. Carts can be rented at most hotels and at the docks.

CONTACTS Dunmore Rentals. ☎ 242/333–2372 ⊕ www.dunmorerentalsgolfcarts. com. **Harbourside Rentals.** ☎ 242/333–5022 ⊕ www.harboursidebahamas.com. **Major's Golf Cart Rentals.** ☎ 242/470–5065 ⊕ www.majorsrentals.com. **Ross Golf Cart Rentals.** ☎ 242/333–2122 ⊕ www. rossgolfcartrentals.com.

TAXI

Taxis are almost always waiting at airports and at the North Eleuthera and Harbour Island water taxi docks. Your hotel can call a taxi for you; let them know a half hour before you need it.

CONTACTS Arthur Nixon Taxi and Rentals. ☎ 242/359–7879. **Fine Thread Taxi Service.** ☎ 242/359–7780. **J.Q. Taxi Service.** ☎ 242/553–6781. **Royal Williams Taxi Service.** ☎ 242/335–1175.

Hotels

Harbour Island, more than any other Out Island, is where the cognoscenti come to bask in ultraluxurious inns and atmospheric small resorts. Follow the celebrities to $600-a-night cottages with views of the beach, or to elegant rooms in Dunmore Town. Eleuthera offers elegant, intimate, beach-adjacent resorts pleasantly empty of crowds. You'll also find plenty of friendly, tidy, and affordable inns, a few on the beach, for around $200 a night. For urbanites who want all-out American luxury, there are modern town houses with stainless-steel appliances and granite in the kitchens, and bedrooms for the entire family. Whether you spend a lot or a little, the staff on this friendly island will know your name after a day. Many hotels are closed in September and October.

Restaurants

Don't let the outdoor dining on rustic wood tables fool you—Harbour Island and Eleuthera offer sophisticated cuisine that rivals that of any restaurants in Nassau. Although the place is usually casual and you never have to wear a tie, food is taken seriously. Island specialties such as cracked conch, barbecued pork, or chicken, and the succulent Bahamian lobster (known locally as crawfish) still abound, but you'll also find cappuccinos, steak, and lobster ravioli. For delicious conch, stop by one of the seafood restaurants on Bay Street, north of Government Dock, where you can eat fresh conch salad on decks next to the water.

Most eateries are closed Sunday in addition to seasonal closure during the hurricane season. During the months of September and October, call before visiting restaurants on the island. Many restaurants have entertainment on regular nights so plan your dining schedule accordingly.

Restaurant prices are based on the median main course price at dinner, excluding gratuity, typically 15%, which is often automatically added to the bill. Hotel prices are for two people in a standard double room in high season, excluding service and 6%–12% tax.

WHAT IT COSTS in Dollars			
$	$$	$$$	$$$$
RESTAURANTS			
under $20	$20–$30	$31–$40	over $40
HOTELS			
under $200	$200–$300	$301–$400	over $400

Visitor Information

CONTACTS Eleuthera Tourist Office.
📞 242/332–2145 ⊕ www.bahamas.com. **Harbour Island Tourist Office.** ✉ Dunmore St. 📞 242/333–2621 ⊕ www.bahamas. com. **Bahama Out Islands Promotion Board.** 📞 242/322–1140 ⊕ www.myoutislands. com.

Gregory Town and North Eleuthera

Gregory Town is a sleepy community, except on Friday nights when people are looking for music, whether that is speakers blasting reggae or a local musician playing Rake 'n' Scrape at a roadside barbecue. There's action, too, at Surfer's Beach, where summer and winter waves bring surfers from around the world. The famous Glass Window Bridge is north of town, and Preacher's Cave, landing of the earliest settlers, is on the northern tip of the island. Gregory Town is home to a little more than 600 people, residing in small houses on a hillside that slides down to the sea. The town's annual Pineapple Festival begins on the Thursday evening of the Bahamian Labor Day weekend, at the beginning of June, with live music continuing into the wee hours.

GETTING HERE AND AROUND

The North Eleuthera Airport is closer to Gregory Town hotels than the airport in Governor's Harbour. The taxi fare from the North Eleuthera Airport to the Cove Eleuthera, the area's most upscale inn, is $35 for two people. Rent a car at the airport unless you plan to stay at a resort for most of your visit.

⊙ Sights

★ **Glass Window Bridge**
BRIDGE/TUNNEL | At a narrow point of the island a few miles north of Gregory Town, a slender concrete bridge links two sea-battered bluffs that separate the island's Central and North districts. Sailors going south in the waters between New Providence and Eleuthera supposedly named this area the Glass Window because they could see through the natural limestone arch to the Atlantic on the other side. Stop to watch the northeasterly deep-azure Atlantic swirl together under the bridge with the southwesterly turquoise Bight of Eleuthera, producing a brilliant aquamarine froth. Artist Winslow Homer found the site stunning, and painted *Glass Window* in 1885. The original stone arch, created by Mother Nature, was destroyed by a combination of storms in the 1940s. Subsequent concrete bridges were destroyed by hurricanes in 1992 and 1999. Drive carefully, because there is frequent maintenance

Great Itineraries

If You Have 3 Days

Fly into North Eleuthera and take the ferry to **Harbour Island**. Base yourself at a hotel near the famous 3-mile pink-sand beach or in historic Dunmore Town. Relax on the beach and have lunch at an ocean-side restaurant. Stroll through **Dunmore Town** in the afternoon, stopping at crafts stands and fashionable shops, admiring colonial houses along Bay Street, and visiting historic churches. At night, dine at one of the island's fine restaurants, such as Sip Sip, Rock House, Pink Sands, or Acquapazza. On Day 2, go scuba diving or snorkeling, or hire a guide and try to snag a canny bonefish. Visit the conch shacks on Bay Street for a low-key beachside dinner. On Day 3 get some last-minute color on the beach or some in-room spa pampering; stop by Vic-Hum Club or Gusty's for late-night music.

If You Have 5 Days

Head back to **Eleuthera** for the next two days. Rent a car at the North Eleuthera Airport (reserve in advance) and drive south past the **Glass Window Bridge,** where you can stand in one spot and see the brilliantly blue and often fierce Atlantic Ocean to the east and the placid Bight of Eleuthera to the west. Continue to **Governor's Harbour,** the island's largest town, and grab lunch at Tippy's or the Beach House, upscale, laid-back beach bistros overlooking the Atlantic Ocean. Stay at one of the beach resorts and enjoy the incredible water views. Head into town if you're looking for some nightlife or dining options.

If You Have 7 Days

On your last two days, drive back to **North Eleuthera**, base yourself at the Cove, and relax on the resort's two beaches. On your final day take the ferry to **Spanish Wells**, where you can rent a golf cart and spend a half day exploring the tiny town and relaxing on a white-sand beach with no tourists. Or stay put and explore Surfer's Beach.

---

work going on. ✉ *Queen's Hwy., North of Gregory Town, Gregory Town.*

★ Preacher's Cave

NATURE SITE | At the island's northern tip, this cave is where the Eleutheran Adventurers (the island's founders) took refuge and held services when their ship wrecked in 1648. Note the original stone altar inside the cave, done by Captain William Sayles in the 1600s. Across from the cave is a long succession of deserted pink-sand beaches. ✉ *North Eleuthera* ✛ *Follow Queen's Hwy. to T-intersection at north end of island. Turn right and follow signs to cave.*

The Queen's Baths

NATURE SITE | Much like natural hot tubs or "moon pools" (as the locals call them), the Queen's Baths are a warm collection of tidal pools which were formed from the erosion of nearby rocks. The clear, dark-blue waters of the Atlantic Ocean, which fill the pools, are warmed by the Bahamian sun, providing a warm and calming alternative to a crowded and sometimes chilly beach. The best time to visit the pools is during low and medium tides, so be sure to check before going to take a dip. Wear hard-bottom shoes to avoid slipping on rocks. ✉ *Queen's Hwy., Gregory Town* ✛ *Located between the Glass-window Bridge and Daddy Joe's restaurant. A 'Queen's Bath' sign marks the entrance.*

Beaches

Gaulding's Cay Beach

BEACH—SIGHT | Snorkelers and divers will want to spend time at this beach, 3 miles north of Gregory Town. You'll most likely have the long stretch of white sand and shallow aqua water all to yourself, and it's great for shelling. At low tide, you can walk or swim to Gaulding's Cay, a tiny rock island with a few casuarina trees. There's great snorkeling around the island; you'll see a concentration of sea anemones so spectacular it dazzled even Jacques Cousteau's biologists. **Amenities:** none. **Best for:** snorkeling; sunset. ⊠ *Queen's Hwy., across from Daddy Joe's restaurant, Gregory Town* ☎ *242/332–2142.*

Surfer's Beach

BEACH—SIGHT | This is Gregory Town's claim to fame and one of the few beaches in the Bahamas known for surfing. Serious surfers have gathered here since the 1960s for decent waves from December to April. If you don't have a jeep, you can walk the ¾ mile to this Atlantic-side beach—take a right onto the paved road past the Hatchet Bay silos, just south of Gregory Town. Look for a young crowd sitting around bonfires at night. **Amenities:** water sports. **Best for:** surfing. ⊠ *Queen's Hwy., Gregory Town.*

Tay Bay Beach

BEACH—SIGHT | Steps from historical Preacher's Cave, this beach offers a long expanse of pink powdery sand. The area is remote, so you're likely to have the beach to yourself. There are plenty of palmetto trees to relax underneath for a quiet afternoon. Just offshore is Devil's Backbone, where the Eleutheran Adventurers shipwrecked and sought shelter in the cave. **Amenities:** parking. **Best for:** solitude; walking. ⊠ *North Eleuthera* ⊹ *Follow Queen's Hwy. to T-intersection at north end of island. Turn right and follow signs to Preacher's Cave.*

🍴 Restaurants

⭐ The Cove Eleuthera Restaurant

$$$ | **EUROPEAN** | The spacious, window-lined dining room serves three meals a day, blending classic Continental with fresh Bahamian fare. An extensive cocktail list from the Freedom Bar includes the Glass Window Bridge—the exquisite landmark of the same name is just a short drive away. **Known for:** excellent sushi; stone crab; delicious vegan dishes on the menu. Ⓢ *Average main: $36* ⊠ *Queen's Hwy., Gregory Town* ☎ *242/335–5142, 888/776–3901* ⊕ *www. thecoveeleuthera.com* ☯ *Closed Sept.*

Daddy Joe's

$$ | **BAHAMIAN** | Located just south of the Glass Window Bridge, this restaurant serves up what it describes as "Bahamian Soul Food" along with hosting local bands every Sunday. Order conch bites as a starter to complement the long list of tropical concoctions, including the aptly named "Da Glass Window." In addition to wings and wraps, Daddy Joe's also offers grilled options like fresh seafood and chicken. **Known for:** live music; in-season guava duff dessert; delicious chicken wings. Ⓢ *Average main: $28* ⊠ *Queen's Hwy., Gregory Town* ☎ *242/335–5688* ▭ *No credit cards* ☯ *Closed Mon. and Sept.*

El Karaka Glass Window Bar & Grill

$$ | **BAHAMIAN** | Just a stone's throw away from one of Eleuthera's most popular natural treasures is this casual, open-air restaurant offering classic Bahamian dishes and stunning views of the sea. This restaurant provides the perfect rest stop for travelers that want to relax and have a cold beer or enjoy one of the special featured dishes like grilled pineapple or the El Karaka Salad—a signature dish named in honor of the owner's father. **Known for:** stunning sea views; secluded beach nearby; curry grouper. Ⓢ *Average main: $26* ⊠ *Queen's Hwy., Gregory Town* ⊹ *about ½ mile north of Glass Window*

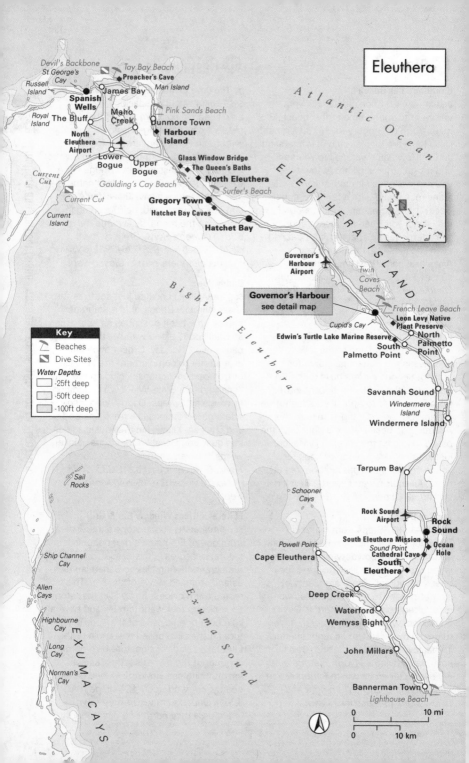

Eleuthera

Atlantic Ocean

ELEUTHERA ISLAND

Devil's Backbone
St George's Cay
Tay Bay Beach
Russell Island
Preacher's Cave
James Bay
Man Island
Spanish Wells
Royal Island
Maho Creek
The Bluff
Pink Sands Beach
Dunmore Town
North Eleuthera Airport
Harbour Island
Lower Bogue
Upper Bogue
Glass Window Bridge
The Queen's Baths
North Eleuthera
Gaulding's Cay Beach
Surfer's Beach
Current Cut
Gregory Town
Current Cut
Hatchet Bay Caves
Current Island
Hatchet Bay

Governor's Harbour Airport

Bight of Eleuthera

Twin Coves Beach

Governor's Harbour
see detail map

French Leave Beach

Cupid's Cay
Leon Levy Native Plant Preserve
Edwin's Turtle Lake Marine Reserve
North Palmetto Point
South Palmetto Point

Key

- Beaches
- Dive Sites

Water Depths
- -25ft deep
- -50ft deep
- -100ft deep

Savannah Sound

Windermere Island
Windermere Island

Sail Rocks

Tarpum Bay

Rock Sound Airport
Rock Sound
South Eleuthera Mission
Ocean Hole
Sound Point
Cathedral Cave
South Eleuthera

Ship Channel Cay

Schooner Cays

Powell Point
Cape Eleuthera

Allen Cays

Exuma Sound

Deep Creek
Waterford
Wemyss Bight

Highbourne Cay

John Millars

Long Cay

EXUMA CAYS

Norman's Cay

Bannerman Town
Lighthouse Beach

0   10 mi

0   10 km

Bridge, on the left ☎ *242/809–4673* ⊕ *www.glasswindowbar.com* ⊙ *Closed mid-Sept.–mid-Nov.*

Surf Shack

$ | **SEAFOOD** | As the name implies, the Surf Shack is a casual, open-air restaurant that serves Bahamian seafood dishes prepared with fresh ingredients. The restaurant is small, but what it lacks in size it makes up for in meal portions and delicious flavors. **Known for:** mahi fingers; baked stuffed crab; special banana ice-cream dessert. $ *Average main: $18* ✉ *Queen's Hwy., Gregory Town* ⚓ *Opposite the Gregory Town gas station* ☎ *242/828–9541* ⊙ *Closed Mon. and Tues.* ▭ *No credit cards.*

Unca Gene's Seafood Restaurant & Bar

$ | **BAHAMIAN** | Some of the most delicious Bahamian meals are what you'll find at Unca Gene's casual, seaside restaurant. The restaurant has a homey feel, painted in light blue, with an outside dining patio where guests can enjoy the cool sea breeze while they eat. **Known for:** sea views; fettuccine Alfredo (shrimp, lobster, conch); cracked conch. $ *Average main: $14* ✉ *Queen's Hwy., Gregory Town* ⚓ *Beside Rebecca's Beach Shop* ☎ *242/335–5060* ⊙ *Closed Sun.* ▭ *No credit cards.*

🛏 Hotels

★ The Cove Eleuthera

$$$ | **RESORT** | Forty secluded acres studded with scenic beach cottages set the tone for this relaxing island escape; a rocky promontory separates two coves, each with a sandy beach and calm water, perfect for snorkeling. **Pros:** sandy beaches; top-rated amenities; one of the most luxurious places to stay on the island. **Cons:** need a car if you want to do anything outside the property; limited dining options; some lower-budget rooms lack the privacy of the bungalows and villas. $ *Rooms from: $354* ✉ *Queen's Hwy., Gregory Town* ⚓ *1½ miles north*

Pineapple Express 👁

Pineapples remain Eleuthera's most famous product, even though the industry has been greatly reduced since the late 1800s, when the island dominated the world's pineapple market. These intensely sweet fruits are still grown on family farms, primarily in northern Eleuthera. Don't miss Gregory Town's Pineapple Festival in June.

of Gregory Town ☎ *242/335–5142, 888/776–3901* ⊕ *www.thecoveeleuthera. com* ⊙ *Closed Sept.* ⇥ *57 rooms* ⦾ *No meals.*

Daddy Joe's Hotel

$ | **B&B/INN** | Daddy Joe's is already quite popular among locals of Eleuthera for its delicious food, but traditional Bahamian hospitality and a friendly staff draw visitors to Daddy Joe's Hotel. **Pros:** quiet location; near Gaulding's Cay Beach; live entertainment every Sunday. **Cons:** not many amenities; limited dining options; might be too remote. $ *Rooms from: $120* ✉ *Queen's Hwy., Gregory Town* ☎ *242/335–5687* ⇥ *15 rooms* ⦾ *No meals.*

Surfer's Manor

$ | **RESORT** | Near Surfer's Beach is a quaint, brightly painted resort that provides a great escape for those who want to relax in the tropics. **Pros:** near Surfer's Beach; car and bicycle rentals available on property; quiet and clean grounds. **Cons:** no meal plans; basic rooms and amenities; away from any restaurants or sights. $ *Rooms from: $150* ✉ *Queen's Hwy., Gregory Town* ⚓ *½ mile away from Surfer's Beach* ☎ *242/335–5300* ⇥ *9 rooms* ⦾ *No meals.*

Did You Know?

Deserted Island: It's not difficult to find an empty cay to call your own. Schooner Cays are just off the island's southern coast.

☕ Nightlife

Champion's Sports Bar and Grill

BARS/PUBS | For afternoon or nighttime fun in Gregory Town, head to Champion's Bar on Queen's Highway. The bar hosts live bands and parties on weekends, along with karaoke and pool games. There's a restaurant serving local Bahamian food and a bar stocked with assorted beers and cocktails. The outdoor tiki bar also opens in the afternoon, serving drinks and bar snacks. ⊠ *Queen's Hwy., Gregory Town* ☎ *242/551–1178.*

🛍 Shopping

★ Island Made Gift Shop

CRAFTS | This shop, run by Pam and Greg Thompson, is a good place to shop for Bahamian arts and crafts, including Androsia batik (made on Andros Island), driftwood paintings, Abaco ceramics, Neem products and prints. Look for the old foam buoys that have been carved and painted into fun faces. ⊠ *Queen's Hwy., Gregory Town* ☎ *242/335–5369* ☉ *Closed Sun.*

🏃 Activities

ADVENTURE TOURS

Bahamas Out-Island Adventures

ADVENTURE TOURS | This tour operator offers day, half-day, and overnight kayaking, snorkeling, and surfing trips, and offers accommodations at its headquarters at Surfer's Beach. ⊠ *Gregory Town* ☎ *242/551–9635, 242/335–0349* ⊕ *www.bahamasadventures.com.*

ISLAND TOURS

Arthur Nixon Tours

DRIVING TOURS | The caretaker and keeper of the North Palmetto Sound Lighthouse offers tours of the lighthouse and the island. ☎ *242/359–7879.*

Eleuthera Adventure Tours

ADVENTURE TOURS | Eleuthera Adventure Tours provides guided tours throughout Eleuthera. Spend the day at Schooners Cay or go swimming with the pigs on an epic Exuma adventure. They offer a range of ocean and outdoor adventure tours and also provide water equipment rentals. ☎ *242/334–2356, 242/470–8212.*

Freedom Vacation Tours

DRIVING TOURS | Freedom Vacation Tours offers a range of tours throughout Eleuthera, Harbour Island, and Spanish Wells. They also provide accomodation and dining. ☎ *242/335–1700* ⊕ *www.freedomvacationtours.com.*

SCUBA DIVING AND SNORKELING

The **Current Cut,** a narrow passage between North Eleuthera and Current Island, is loaded with marine life and provides a roller-coaster ride on the currents. You'll want a boat and, most importantly, a guide, as the fast current can be dangerous.

Current Cut

SCUBA DIVING | This narrow passage between North Eleuthera and Current Island is loaded with marine life and provides a roller-coaster ride on the currents. You'll want a boat and, most importantly, a guide, as the current is very fast. ⊠ *End of Current road, Current* ☎ *242/448–1609 Mr. Foster, the Current Cut guide.*

SURFING

Rebecca's Beach Shop

SURFING | In Gregory Town, stop by Rebecca's Beach Shop, a general store, crafts shop, and, most important, a surf shop, where local surf guru "Ponytail Pete" rents surfboards, fishing and snorkel gear, and more. A chalkboard lists surf conditions and tidal reports. He also gives surf lessons. ⊠ *Queen's Hwy., Gregory Town* ☎ *242/335–5436.*

Hatchet Bay

"The Country's Safest Harbour," Hatchet Bay (also known as "Alice Town"), which has one of mid-Eleuthera's few marinas, is a good place to find a fishing guide and friendly locals, or to anchor sailboats and fishing vessels when storms are coming. Take note of the town's side roads, which have such colorful names as Lazy Road, Happy Hill Road, and Smile Lane. Just south of town, the Rainbow Inn and restaurant is the hub of activity for this stretch of the island. Don't miss James Cistern, a seaside settlement to the south.

GETTING HERE AND AROUND

Hatchet Bay is equidistant between the Governor's Harbour and North Eleuthera airports. The taxi fare from either airport is about $60 for two people. Rent a car at the airport unless you plan to stay at a resort for most of your visit.

Sights

Hatchet Bay Caves

NATURE SITE | North of Hatchet Bay lies a subterranean, bat-populated tunnel complete with stalagmites and stalactites. Pirates supposedly once used it to hide their loot. An underground path leads for more than a mile to the sea, ending in a lofty, cathedral-like cavern. Within its depths, fish swim in total darkness. The adventurous may wish to explore this area with a flashlight (follow the length of guide string along the cavern's floor), but it's best to inquire first at one of the local stores or the Rainbow Inn for a guide. ✉ *Queen's Hwy.* ✣ *2 miles north of Hatchet Bay, turn left at sign for "Hatchet Bay Caves".*

Restaurants

The Front Porch

$$ | **SEAFOOD** | This little roadside restaurant features a beautiful view of the bay, particularly at sunset when the orange horizon is freckled with the silhouettes of moored sailboats. The menu is island-inspired European cuisine and always includes fresh seafood. **Known for:** Caesar salad with a twist; sunset views; stone crab Wednesdays. [$] *Average main: $28* ✉ *Queen's Hwy.* ☎ *242/335–0727.*

The Rainbow Inn Seafood & Steakhouse

$$$ | **EUROPEAN** | With a classy but no-fuss aura and exhibition windows that face gorgeous sunsets, this restaurant is well-known for its steaks, which are flown in daily. Grouper, conch, mahi-mahi, and cobia are also fresh, caught daily. **Known for:** fresh fish; wood-fired pizzas; live music. [$] *Average main: $35* ✉ *Queen's Hwy.* ✣ *2½ miles south of Hatchet Bay* ☎ *242/335–0294* 🌐 *www.rainbowinn.com* 🕒 *Closed Sept. and Oct. No lunch Wed.*

Twin Brothers

$$ | **BAHAMIAN** | This brightly painted restaurant is famous for its frozen daiquiris and range of local cuisine. Icy mixes of strawberry and piña colada are swirled into a striking (and delicious) dessert cocktail. **Known for:** fruit daiquiris; alfresco dining; Bahamian specialties like conch fritters and steamed grouper. [$] *Average main: $25* ✉ *West off Queen's Hwy.* ☎ *242/335–0730* 🌐 *www.twinbrothersbahamas.com* 🕒 *Closed Mon.*

Hotels

★ **Rainbow Inn**

$ | **RENTAL** | Immaculate, generously sized cottages, some octagonal—all with large private porches—have sweeping views of the ocean. **Pros:** super-spacious cottages at reasonable prices; great water views; friendly service. **Cons:** not on the beach; not close to a town or shops; rustic accommodations. [$] *Rooms from: $150* ✉ *Queen's Hwy.* ✣ *2½ miles south of Hatchet Bay* ☎ *242/335–0294* 🌐 *www.rainbowinn.com* 🕒 *Closed Sept. and Oct.* 🛏 *4 rooms* 🍴 *No meals.*

Nightlife

Dr. Sea Breeze

MUSIC CLUBS | The debonair, one-man band Cedric Bethel, better known as Dr. Sea Breeze, strums his acoustic guitar while singing island songs at the Rainbow Inn in Hatchet Bay and Sky Beach Club in Governor's Harbour. Call

A Governor's Harbour home

beforehand to confirm his schedule.
☎ *242/470–0504.*

Governor's Harbour

Governor's Harbour, the capital of Eleuthera and home to government offices, is the largest town on the island and one of the prettiest. Victorian-era houses were built on Buccaneer Hill, which overlooks the harbor, bordered on the south by a narrow peninsula and Cupid's Cay at the tip. To fully understand its appeal, you have to settle in for a few days and explore on foot—if you don't mind the steep climb up the narrow lanes. The town is a step into a gentler, more genteel time. Everyone says hello, and entertainment means wading into the harbor to cast a line, or taking a painting class taught by Martha's Vineyard artist Donna Allen at the 19th-century pink library on Monday mornings. You can see a current movie at the balconied Globe Princess, the only theater on the island, which also serves the best hamburgers in town. Or,

swim at the gorgeous beaches on either side of town, which stretch from the pink sands of the ocean to the white sands of the Bight of Eleuthera. There are three banks, a few grocery stores, and some of the island's wealthiest residents, who prefer the quiet of Eleuthera to the fashionable party scene of Harbour Island.

GETTING HERE AND AROUND

Fly into Governor's Harbour Airport north of town, or arrive by mail boat from Nassau. You will want to rent a car at the airport, even if you plan to stay in Governor's Harbour, to best explore the beaches and restaurants.

⊙ Sights

Edwin's Turtle Lake Marine Reserve

NATURE PRESERVE | This 43-acre, deep-blue saltwater lake is the perfect place to see much of Bahamas' beautiful marine life up close. The marine reserve was established in 1954 by the Burrows Family to protect the endangered green sea turtles, various kinds of fish, lobster, and other marine life that call the lake home. One-hour guided kayak and paddleboard tours are available at the Reserve at $70 for two people. Call to book reservations before visiting. ✉ *Queen's Hwy.* ☎ *242/422–9109* 🕓 *Closed weekends.*

Haynes Library

HISTORIC SITE | The heart of the community, this 19th-century building has a local book club, offers art classes and Tuesday-morning coffee hours for visitors and residents. The library has a wide selection of books and computers, with gorgeous views of the harbor. ✉ *Haynes Ave.* ☎ *242/332–2877* 🕓 *Closed weekends.*

Leon Levy Native Plant Preserve

GARDEN | Walk miles of scenic trails in this 25-acre nature preserve located on Banks Road. Funded by the Leon Levy Foundation and operated by the Bahamas National Trust, the preserve serves as an environmental education center with a focus on traditional bush medicine. Follow the boardwalk over a small waterfall and take the path to the Observation Tower to see hundreds of indigenous trees, plants, and wildlife such as mangroves, five-finger plants, and bullfinches. Group tours are available, or if you'd prefer to tour the preserve on your own, the welcome center will provide you with a map and a plant identification guide. ✉ *Banks Rd.* ☎ *242/332–3831* 🌐 *www.levypreserve.org* 🎟 *$10.*

Beaches

French Leave Beach

BEACH—SIGHT | This stretch of pink sand was Club Med's famed beach before the resort was destroyed by a hurricane in 1999, and is now home to the new French Leave Marina Village. The gorgeous Atlantic-side beach is anchored by fantastic bistros like the Beach House and Tippy's. The wide expanse, ringed by casuarina trees, is often deserted and makes a great outpost for romantics. **Amenities:** food and drink. **Best for:** solitude; swimming; walking. ✉ *Banks Rd.* 🌐 *www.frenchleaveeleuthera.com.*

Twin Coves Beach

BEACH—SIGHT | This unique beach got its name because of its interesting geography; being split into two coves by a narrow sand bridge. Frequent sightings of nurse sharks, lobster, various kinds of fish, rays, and other marine life are what you'll find on either side of the beach. Not many people visit here during the week so it's the perfect place to relax and go swimming or snorkeling. **Amenities:** parking (free). **Best for:** swimming; snorkeling; solitude. ✉ *Twin Cove.*

Why Is the Sand Pink?

Contrary to popular belief, pink sand comes primarily from the crushed pink and red shells of microscopic insects called foraminifera, not coral. Foraminifer live on the underside of reefs and the sea floor. After the insects die, the waves smash the shells, which wash ashore along with sand and bits of pink coral. The intensity of the rosy hues depends on the slant of the sun.

Restaurants

Buccaneer Club

$$ | BAHAMIAN | On the top of Buccaneer Hill overlooking the town and harbor, this mid-19th-century farmhouse is now a must-try restaurant which serves three meals a day. The outdoor dining area is located under a huge tree, with candlelit tables and soft jazz music playing in the background. **Known for:** close to beach; scenic dining; coconut rum–infused French toast. [$] *Average main: $26* ✉ *Haynes Ave.* ☎ *242/332–2000* 🌐 *www.hwadventures.com* 🕓 *Closed Sept. and Oct.*

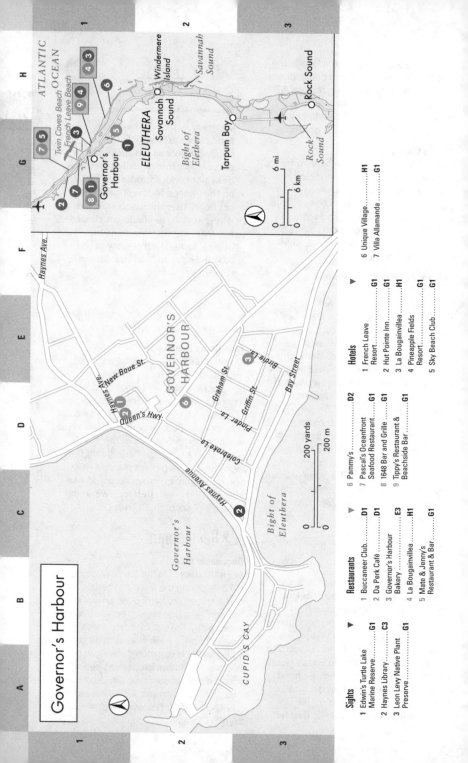

Governor's Harbour

ATLANTIC OCEAN

Twin Coves Beach
French Leave Beach

ELEUTHERA

Savannah Sound
Windermere Island
Savannah Sound

Bight of Elethera

Tarpum Bay

Rock Sound
Rock Sound

6 mi
6 km

GOVERNOR'S HARBOUR

Haynes Ave.
New Boue St.
Queen's Hwy.
Haynes Avenue
Colebroke La.
Pinder La.
Graham St.
Griffin St.
Birdie La.
Bay Street

Bight of Eleuthera

Governor's Harbour

CUPID'S CAY

200 yards
200 m

Sights ▶

1 Edwin's Turtle Lake Marine Reserve.............**G1**
2 Haynes Library..........**C3**
3 Leon Levy Native Plant Preserve...............**G1**

Restaurants ▶

1 Buccaneer Club...........**D1**
2 Da Perk Café...............**D1**
3 Governor's Harbour Bakery...................**E3**
4 La Bougainvillea..........**H1**
5 Mate & Jenny's Restaurant & Bar...........**G1**

6 Pammy's.....................**D2**
7 Pascal's Oceanfront Seafood Restaurant......**G1**
8 1648 Bar and Grille......**G1**
9 Tippy's Restaurant & Beachside Bar...........**G1**

Hotels ▶

1 French Leave Resort.......................**G1**
2 Hut Pointe Inn.............**G1**
3 La Bougainvillea..........**H1**
4 Pineapple Fields Resort.....................**G1**
5 Sky Beach Club...........**G1**

6 Unique Village...........**H1**
7 Villa Allamanda.........**G1**

Da Perk Café

$ | **CAFÉ** | This tidy restaurant offers free Wi-Fi and is an excellent place to catch up on emails over a homemade quiche and Lavazza coffee. The café is located in the middle of town, making it a convenient spot for a quick bite at breakfast or lunch. **Known for:** breakfast bagels; delicious deli sandwiches; pastries and desserts. [$] *Average main: $13* ✉ *Queen's Hwy.* ☎ *242/332–2620* 💳 *No credit cards* 🕓 *Closed Sun. No dinner.*

Governor's Harbour Bakery

$ | **BAKERY** | A Governor's Harbour staple since 1989, this bakery serves delicious pastries and breads, baked fresh daily. Stop in to pick up come of the popular Danish coffee cake, or sample johnnycakes and hot patties—Bahamian favorites. **Known for:** homemade baked goods; fresh doughnuts; conch and beef patties. [$] *Average main: $5* ✉ *Tucker Lane* ✥ *South past Burrow's Grocery Store* ☎ *242/332–2071* 💳 *No credit cards* 🕓 *Closed Sun.*

La Bougainvillea

$$$ | **ITALIAN** | Enjoy an electric fusion of classic Italian dishes and Bahamian cuisine served at the stunning oceanfront La Bougainvillea property. The resort has a luxurious ambience, but the restaurant is calm and inviting, while simultaneously maintaining a fine dining experience. **Known for:** views of the ocean; seafood pasta; wood-fired homemade pizza. [$] *Average main: $32* ✉ *North Palmetto Point, Banks Rd.* ☎ *242/813–7436* 🌐 *www.labougainvillea.com.*

Mate & Jenny's Restaurant & Bar

$ | **PIZZA** | A few miles south of Governor's Harbour, this casual neighborhood restaurant specializes in pizza with a variety of toppings; try one topped with conch. Sandwiches, cocktails, and Bahamian specialties are also served. **Known for:** conch-topped pizza; lively atmosphere; dart games. [$] *Average main: $18* ✉ *South Palmetto Point* ☎ *242/332–1504* 🕓 *Closed Tues. and Aug. No lunch on Sun.*

Pammy's

$ | **BAHAMIAN** | As a family-owned and operated restaurant, everything about Pammy's aims to make their customers feel right at home—from the friendly waitresses to the comfortable atmosphere, and delicious food served in large portions. Pammy's is one of the most popular restaurants among locals and tourists in Governor's Harbour, known for its good food and affordability. **Known for:** grouper burger; chicken wings; pork chops. [$] *Average main: $12* ✉ *Queen's Hwy.* ☎ *242/332–2843* 🕓 *Closed Sun.* 💳 *No credit cards.*

Pascal's Oceanfront Seafood Restaurant

$$$ | **ECLECTIC** | In addition to ocean-view seating in its outdoor dining room, Pascal's also features a swim-up bar, perfect for a leisurely lunch. Relax in the infinity-edge pool while you savor a mango daiquiri and cheeseburger, and take in the magnificent view of the Atlantic. **Known for:** sophisticated atmosphere; fresh local seafood; pool and beachside dining. [$] *Average main: $34* ✉ *Sky Beach Club, Queen's Hwy.* ☎ *242/332–3422* 🌐 *www.pascalsoceanfront.com* 🕓 *Closed Sept. and Oct.*

★ **1648 – An Island Restaurant**

$$$ | **ECLECTIC** | Take in the sunset view as you enjoy a glass of wine and an island-inspired pizza or seafood at 1648–. Located at French Leave Harbour Village, the restaurant boasts a sweeping view of the Bight of Eleuthera and its stunning turquoise water. **Known for:** conch rangoons starter; tropical cocktails; poolside dining. [$] *Average main: $38* ✉ *French Leave Harbour Village, Queen's Hwy.* ☎ *242/332–3777* 🌐 *www.frenchleaveeleuthera.com.*

★ **Tippy's Restaurant & Beachside Bar**

$$ | **ECLECTIC** | Despite its barefoot-casual environment (old window shutters used as tabletops, sand in the floor's crevices), the menu at this open-air beach bistro is a sophisticated mix of Bahamian and European cuisine, with items that change

daily based on the availability of fresh local products. Expect things like lobster salad, specialty pizzas, and fresh fish prepared with some sort of delectable twist. **Known for:** lobster tail; outdoor seating; live local bands on Saturday. [$] *Average main: $28* ✉ *Banks Rd.* ☎ *242/332–3331* 🌐 *www.pineapplefields.com* 🕒 *Closed Mon. and Sept. and Oct.*

Hotels

★ French Leave Resort
$$$$ | RESORT | This Governor's Harbour resort, which welcomed its first guests in August 2013, offers gorgeous waterfront villas, a harbor-view bar and grill, a freshwater pool, and dozens of other luxurious amenities. **Pros:** spacious rooms with modern decor; beautiful harbor and ocean views; luxurious amenities. **Cons:** you'll need a car if you want to explore the island; limited food options; not all villas are oceanfront. [$] *Rooms from: $450* ✉ *Queen's Hwy.* ☎ *242/332–3778* 🌐 *www.frenchleaveeleuthera.com* 🛏 *20 rooms* 🍴 *No meals.*

Hut Pointe Inn
$$ | B&B/INN | Those looking for history and luxury will find much to like about this historic building constructed in 1944 by the first premier of the Bahamas, Sir Roland Symonette. **Pros:** historic building; eco-friendly amenities; quiet and well-maintained property. **Cons:** may be too remote for some; not on beach; 5–10 minutes from the town. [$] *Rooms from: $235* ✉ *Queen's Hwy.* ☎ *760/908–6700* 🌐 *www.hutpointe.com* 🕒 *Closed Sept. and Oct.* 🛏 *7 rooms* 🍴 *No meals.*

La Bougainvillea
$$ | RESORT | This stunning oceanfront boutique hotel opened its doors in 2017, hoping to provide guests with a tranquil island experience, and so far, it has successfully achieved just that. **Pros:** all suites have their own private pools; secluded pink-sand beach; spacious and beautifully decorated suites. **Cons:** no phone or TV in suites; on-site restaurant is expensive; not many facilities. [$] *Rooms from: $275* ✉ *North Palmetto Point, Banks Rd.* ☎ *242/813–7436* 🌐 *www.labougainvillea.com* 🛏 *6 suites* 🍴 *No meals.*

Pineapple Fields Resort
$$ | RENTAL | FAMILY | Across the street from a pink-sand Atlantic beach and Tippy's oceanfront bistro, Pineapple Fields is the perfect base for a disappearing act; hole up in one of 32 condo units, each with front and back verandas, a full kitchen, and a living room with pull-out queen sofa. **Pros:** modern facilities and amenities; large units; secluded beach and Tippy's across the street. **Cons:** some facilities not well-maintained; will need to drive to town; not oceanfront. [$] *Rooms from: $249* ✉ *Banks Rd.* ☎ *242/332–2221* 🌐 *www.pineapplefields.com* 🕒 *Closed mid-Sept.–mid-Oct.* 🛏 *32 rooms* 🍴 *No meals.*

★ Sky Beach Club
$$$ | RESORT | Perched on 22 acres of oceanfront property, this modern resort features three poolside bungalows and large four-bedroom houses. **Pros:** secluded pink-sand beach; top-rated restaurant on-site; spacious villas with modern decor. **Cons:** need a car to get to town; restaurant and pool often gets crowded and noisy; some facilities not well-maintained. [$] *Rooms from: $325* ✉ *Queen's Hwy.* ☎ *242/422–9597* 🌐 *www.skybeachclub.com* 🛏 *7 suites* 🍴 *No meals.*

Unique Village
$ | HOTEL | Just south of Governor's Harbour near North Palmetto Point on marvelous pink Poponi Beach, this resort has large, tropical-style rooms with French doors opening to private balconies. **Pros:** on a gorgeous pink beach; great on-site restaurant that serves three

meals a day; large pool with gazebo and lounge chairs. **Cons:** must go down many wood stairs to access beach; a 10-minute drive to Governor's Harbour; some rooms and amenities are dated. [$] *Rooms from: $110* ✉ *North Palmetto Point, Resort Dr.* ☎ *242/332–1830* 🌐 *www.uniquevillage.com* 🛏 *14 rooms* 🍴 *No meals.*

★ **Villa Allamanda**

$ | **B&B/INN** | Located on one of Governor's Habour's most picturesque hilltops in Cigatoo Estates, surrounded by lush forest, is this laid-back and colorful guesthouse. **Pros:** quiet property; close to the beach; stunning views from every room. **Cons:** limited dining options; not many facilities; car needed to access restaurants and sights. [$] *Rooms from: $194* ✉ *Cigatoo Estates, Jacaranda Dr.* ☎ *242/332–3934* 🌐 *www.villaallamanda.com* 🛏 *8 rooms* 🍴 *No meals.*

Nightlife

Dr. Sea Breeze

MUSIC CLUBS | Dr. Sea Breeze plays calypso at Sky Beach Club in Governor's Harbour and at Rainbow Inn, south of Hatchet Bay. Call ahead for the schedule. ☎ *242/470–0504.*

Globe Princess Theatre

FILM | The Globe Princess hosts a showing of one current film each night at 8:15 pm. Movies change weekly. The concession serves some of the best hamburgers in town and is open for lunch 11–3 weekdays. ✉ *Queen's Hwy.* ☎ *242/332–2735* 🎟 *$5.50* 🕒 *Closed Thurs.*

Ronnie's Hi-D-Way

BARS/PUBS | With a pool table, outdoor basketball court, and large dance floor, Ronnie's is the most popular local hangout in Governor's Harbour. The scene really takes off on Friday and Saturday night, when the bar hosts a DJ. If you drop in for a drink on the weekend, expect to stay a while for dancing to popular reggae and hip-hop tunes. ✉ *Cupid's Cay* ☎ *242/332–2307.*

Shopping

Blue Seahorse Gift Shop

GIFTS/SOUVENIRS | This unique shop is one of the best places to get cool Bahamian souvenirs. They sell handcrafted items, made from shells, sea glass, and pink sand, all from the beaches on the island.½½ ✉ *Queens Hwy.* ✣ *½ mile north of French Leave Resort. Take the first left turn north of the Resort on Queens Hwy.* ☎ *242/470–2358* 🕒 *Closed Sun.*

The Gift Shop at Pineapple Fields

GIFTS/SOUVENIRS | You'll find Bahamian handcrafted art, locally made jewelry, and elegant beachwear in this gift shop, located in the same building as Pineapple Fields' office. ✉ *Pineapple Fields Resort, Banks Rd.* ☎ *242/332–2221* 🌐 *www.pineapplefields.com* 🕒 *Closed Sun. and mid-Sept.–mid-Oct.*

Norma's Gift Shop

GIFTS/SOUVENIRS | A range of unique souvenirs including hand-crafted items, fine china, crystal, and leather goods are sold at this tiny, colorful gift shop. You'll also find clothing (mostly T-shirts and beach sandals), jewelry, and fragrances. ✉ *Haynes Ave.* ✣ *At the corner of Haynes Ave., between Da Perk and First Caribbean Bank* ☎ *242/332–2002* 🕒 *Closed Sun.*

Activities

FISHING

Paul Petty

FISHING | Paul is one of the best in the business for guiding anglers through the flats in Governor's Harbour. With his help, you're sure to hook a bonefish. He is also a knowledgeable reef-fishing and deep-sea-fishing guide. ✉ *Governor's Harbour* ☎ *242/332–2963.*

Rock Sound and South Eleuthera

One of Eleuthera's largest settlements, the village of **Rock Sound** has a small airport serving the island's southern part. Front Street, the main thoroughfare, runs along the seashore, where fishing boats are tied up. If you walk down the street, you'll eventually come to the whitewashed St. Luke's Anglican Church, a contrast to the deep-blue and green houses nearby with their colorful gardens full of poinsettia, hibiscus, and marigolds. If you pass the church on a Sunday, you'll surely hear fervent hymn-singing through the open windows. Rock Sound has the island's largest supermarket shopping center, where locals stock up on groceries and supplies.

The tiny settlement of **Bannerman Town** (population 40) is 25 miles from Rock Sound at the island's southern tip, which is punctuated by an old cliff-top lighthouse. Rent an SUV if you plan to drive out to it; the rutted sand road is often barely passable. The pink-sand beach here is gorgeous, and on a clear day you can see the Bahamas' highest point, Mt. Alvernia (elevation 206 feet), on distant Cat Island. The town lies about 30 miles from the residential Cotton Bay Club, past the quiet little fishing villages of Wemyss Bight (named after Lord Gordon Wemyss, a 17th-century Scottish slave owner) and John Millars (population 15), barely touched over the years.

GETTING HERE AND AROUND

Fly into Rock Sound Airport and rent a car. The airport is just north of town, and The Island School is a 22-mile drive south. If you fly into Governor's Harbour, plan to rent a car at the airport—Rock Sound is about 34 miles south. Taxis are available at both airports, but can be expensive.

Learning in Paradise ◉

The Island School is a pioneering 14-week program for high-school students that's a model of sustainability—students and teachers work together to run a campus where rainwater is captured for use, solar and wind energy are harnessed, food comes from its own small farm, wastewater is filtered and reused to irrigate landscaping, and biofuel is made from cruise ships' restaurant grease to power vehicles and generators. Tours available by appointment. ☎ 242/334–8551

◉ Sights

Cathedral Cave

CAVE | This short but impressive cave is one of South Eleuthera's most unique hidden gems, located behind the ocean hole just south of Rock Sound. A wooden staircase leads down to the relatively small cave formed by karst. Despite the nickname, "spider cave," you won't find many spiders here (even though there are plenty of spider webs). The cave also has high, open ceilings so there isn't need for a flashlight. ⊠ Shermans Hwy., Rock Sound ✛ 1 mile south of Ocean Hole. Entrance is across from the Allen Chapel AME Church (white building).

★ Ocean Hole

BODY OF WATER | A small inland saltwater lake a mile southeast of Rock Sound is connected by tunnels to the sea. Steps have been cut into the coral on the shore so visitors can climb down to the lake's edge. Bring a piece of bread or some fries and watch the fish emerge for their hors d'oeuvres, swimming their way in from the sea. A local diver estimates the hole is about 75 feet deep. He reports that there are a couple of cars at the bottom, too. Local children learn to swim here. ✉ *Queen's Hwy., Rock Sound* ✣ *A Bahamas Heritage sign, across street from church, marks path to Ocean Hole* ☎ *242/332–2142*.

South Eleuthera Mission

HISTORIC SITE | A superb example of a historic Bahamian Colonial building, the South Eleuthera Mission, also called Mission House, sits on the Rock Sound waterfront and is open to visitors during regular business hours. Originally built in the 1850s, the reconstruction to a Methodist Manse was overseen by volunteer Patricia Rose Maclean, a British designer highly experienced in period restoration. The facility now houses a library and Internet café and offers free tours to visitors that want to view the historical house. They also offer after-school programs for kids, a summer youth program and other community-based programs. ✉ *Meridian Hwy., Rock Sound* ☎ *242/334–2948* ⏲ *Closed weekends*.

Beaches

★ Lighthouse Beach

BEACH—SIGHT | You'll need an SUV to cross the rocky terrain to get to this beach, but the drive is well worth the breathtaking views. Lighthouse beach has it all: dramatic cliffs, pink sand, plenty of shade beneath the trees—and you'll likely have it entirely to yourself. Reefs just off the beach make it a great place to spend the day snorkeling. Be aware that there can be a strong current. **Amenities:** none. **Best for:** solitude; snorkeling; walking. ✉ *Southern tip of Eleuthera, Queens Rd., Bannerman Town*.

Whiteland Beach

BEACH—SIGHT | The long, bumpy road is worth driving on just to get to this beautiful secluded beach located on the Atlantic side of the island. Whiteland Beach features an incredible stretch of clear, white sands with beautiful blue waters. The beach is never crowded so it's a great place to relax privately. There are also reef and rock formations close to the shore, which make it a great place for snorkeling. **Amenities:** none. **Best for:** solitude; snorkeling; walking. ✉ *Shermans Hwy., Rock Sound* ✣ *opposite Charles Bay*.

Softball: The Sport of the Island

Fast-pitch softball is a ubiquitous sport in Eleuthera. The Eleuthera Twin City Destroyers were the men's champions of the 2006 Bahamas Softball Federation tournament. On most any weekend afternoon from March to November you can find the team playing at Rock Sound or Palmetto baseball parks on the island, known as the Softball Capital of the Bahamas. Eleuthera pitchers and brothers Edney and Edmond Bethel are both players for the Bahamas National Team, which has been consistently in the top 10 in the world.

Restaurants

★ Frigate's Bar & Grill

$$$ | **BAHAMIAN** | This charming restaurant embodies everything that people love about Eleuthera. The menu offers a range of local favorites, the property is right on the beach (with chairs for lounging after a meal), and the restaurant has an amazing outside deck with a stunning view of Rock Sound's harbor. **Known for:** stunning ocean views; mahi-mahi; grilled grouper. [$] *Average main: $32* ✉ *Meridian Hwy., Rock Sound* ☎ *242/334–2778* 🌐 *www.frigatesbarandgrill.com*.

Harbour Pointe Restaurant

$$ | **CARIBBEAN** | Located at Cape Eleuthera Resort with a breathtaking sunset view, Harbour Pointe offers Caribbean cuisine in a casual setting. The restaurant features indoor and outdoor seating with panoramic views of the pool, marina, and ocean. **Known for:** seafood burgers and sandwiches; beautiful views; chefs will cook what you catch. [$] *Average main: $28* ✉ *Cape Eleuthera Resort and Marina, Rock Sound* ☎ *242/334–8500* 🌐 *www.capeeleuthera.com.*

Northside Restaurant and Bar

$ | **BAHAMIAN** | **FAMILY** | If you want an authentic Bahamian meal, look no further than Northside Restaurant & Bar, a Rock Sound establishment famous for its extremely welcoming owner, Rose, and sweeping Atlantic ocean views. Northside's menu varies based on available fresh seafood, but you can always find Bahamian specialties such as baked macaroni and cheese, plantains, and peas 'n' rice. **Known for:** made-to-order meals; authentic Bahamian cuisine; outdoor dining with ocean views. [$] *Average main: $18* ✉ *Northside Cottages, Rock Sound* ☎ *242/334–2573* 🌐 *www.northsideinneleuthera.com.*

Sammy's Place

$ | **BAHAMIAN** | Owned by Sammy Culmer and managed by his friendly daughter Margarita, Sammy's is a casual restaurant where you can enjoy great service and authentic Eleutheran food. Sammy's serves conch and fish burgers, baked chicken dinner and a variety of club sandwiches and salads. **Known for:** guava duff dessert; conch burger; friendly service. [$] *Average main: $19* ✉ *Albury La., Rock Sound* ☎ *242/334–2121* 💳 *No credit cards.*

🛏 Hotels

★ **Cape Eleuthera Resort and Marina**

$$ | **RESORT** | **FAMILY** | Nestled between the aquamarine and emerald waters of Rock and Exuma sounds, gigantic villas have two bright bedrooms, each with a full bath and a stainless-steel kitchen, while the new beach cottages feature a luxury bathroom and wet bar. **Pros:** handsome resort right on the water; professional and friendly staff; gear rental on-site for water and land excursions (some with fee). **Cons:** isolated from rest of island; need a car to leave resort; on-property restaurant is the only dining option nearby. [$] *Rooms from: $265* ✉ *Cape Eleuthera Dr., Rock Sound* ☎ *242/334–8500* 🌐 *www.capeeleuthera.com* 🛏 *32 suites* 🍴 *No meals.*

Northside Inn Cottages

$ | **RENTAL** | These quaint cottages are nestled into a hillside with an extraordinary view of the Atlantic. **Pros:** beachfront inn; restaurant on-property; friendly staff. **Cons:** steep walk down to the beach; the area is remote; extra fee for air-conditioning. [$] *Rooms from: $140* ✉ *Northshore Dr., Rock Sound* ✥ *Turn off Queen's Hwy. in Rock Sound onto Fish St. Turn left at T-intersection onto Northshore Dr., then right at end of pavement* ☎ *242/334–2573* 🌐 *www.northsideinneleuthera.com* 🛏 *3 cottages* 🍴 *No meals.*

Harbour Island

Harbour Island has often been called the Nantucket of the Caribbean and the most gorgeous of the Out Islands because of its powdery pink-sand beaches (3 miles' worth!) and its pastel-color clapboard houses with dormer windows, set among white picket fences, narrow lanes, cute shops, and tropical flowers.

The frequent parade of the fashionable and famous, and the chic small inns that accommodate them, have earned the island another name: the St. Bart's of the Bahamas. But residents have long called it Briland, their faster way of pronouncing "Harbour Island." These inhabitants include families who go back generations to the island's early settlement, as well as a growing number of celebrities, supermodels, and tycoons who feel that Briland is the perfect haven to bask in small-town charm against a stunning oceanscape. Some of the Bahamas' most handsome small hotels, each strikingly distinct, are tucked within the island's 2 square miles. Several are perched on a bluff above the shore, and you can fall asleep with the windows open and listen to the waves lapping the beach. Take a walking tour of the narrow streets of **Dunmore Town,** named after the 18th-century royal governor of the Bahamas, Lord Dunmore, who built a summer home here and laid out the town, which served as the first capital of the Bahamas. It's the only town on Harbour Island, and you can take in all its attractions during a 20-minute stroll.

GETTING HERE AND AROUND

Access Harbour Island via a 10-minute ferry ride from the North Eleuthera dock. Fares are $5 per person in a boat of two or more, plus an extra dollar to be dropped off at the private Romora Bay Club docks and for nighttime rides.

The best way to get around the island is to rent a golf cart or bike, or hire a taxi, since climbing the island's hills can be strenuous in the midday heat. Staying in Dunmore Town puts you within walking distance to everything you'll need.

Sights

Haunted House of Harbour Island

HISTORIC SITE | According to local tales, this huge mansion was built by newlyweds in 1945. After a huge argument one night, both the wife and husband left the house and were never seen again. The table was set for dinner; the food on the stove and all of their clothing and wedding gifts were left behind. The property has been damaged over the years but is still open for visitors. It's a great place to let your imagination run wild. ⊠ Dunmore Town ⊹ located next to the Aquapazza Restaurant. Follow the pink board signs ☎ 242/333–2621.

Lone Tree

LOCAL INTEREST | If you stroll to the end of Bay Street and follow the curve to the western edge of the island, you'll find the Lone Tree, one of the most photographed icons of Harbour Island. This enormous piece of driftwood is said to have washed up on shore after a bad storm and anchored itself on the shallow sandbar in a picturesque upright position, providing the perfect photo op for countless tourists. ⊠ Bay St. ☎ 242/333–2621 Harbour Island Tourist Board.

Straw Crafts

MARKET | A row of straw-work stands are on Bay Street next to the water, including Jacquline's, Neeka's, Pat's and Dorothy's, where you'll find straw bags, hats, and T-shirts. Food stands sell conch salad, Kalik beer, coconut water, and fruit juices. ⊠ Bay St.

Beaches

★ Pink Sands Beach

BEACH—SIGHT | This is the fairest pink beach of them all: 3 miles of pale pink sand behind some of the most expensive and posh inns in the Bahamas. Its sand is of such a fine consistency that it's almost as soft as talcum powder, and the gentle slope of the shore makes small waves break hundreds of yards offshore; you have to walk out quite a distance to get past your waist. This is the place to see the rich and famous in designer resort wear or ride a horse bareback across the sand and into the sea. **Amenities:** food and drink; toilets; showers. **Best for:** partiers; sunrise; swimming; walking. ⊠ Court Rd., Dunmore Town.

Restaurants

Many Harbour Island hotels and restaurants are closed from September through mid-to-late October.

A stroll through Dunmore Town on Harbour Island is a must for any visitor.

Acquapazza

$$$ | **ITALIAN** | Briland's only Italian restaurant offers a change of pace from the island's standard fare, and a change of scenery, too. It's located at the top of the hill at Romora Bay Resort, with a dockside terrace where you can take in the sunset while sipping one of its exclusively imported Italian wines. **Known for:** Italian wines; hearty portions; seafood pasta. [$] *Average main: $33* ✉ *Romora Bay Resort & Marina, Colebrooke St., Dunmore Town* ☎ *242/333–3240* 🌐 *www.acquapazzabahamas.net.*

Arthur's Bakery

$ | **CAFÉ** | Bread and pastries are baked every morning by *White Shadow* screenwriter and local real-estate agent to the stars Robert Arthur and his Trinidadian wife Anna. The friendly café has a quiet garden nook where you can savor your morning brew with an apple turnover, banana pancakes, or any of the daily breakfast offerings. **Known for:** jalapeño-and-cheese bread; lobster omelet; key lime tart. [$] *Average main: $14* ✉ *Crown St. and Dunmore St., Dunmore Town* 💳 *No credit cards* 🕒 *Closed Sun.*

Bahamas Coffee Roasters

$$ | **DELI** | This charming café in the middle of Dunmore Town imports coffee beans from around the world and roasts them on-island to produce a number of special blends available to enjoy every morning. The vibe is decidedly surfer-chic, with modern artwork on the walls and picnic bench seating. **Known for:** organic chicken sandwich; great coffee; local produce. [$] *Average main: $20* ✉ *Dunmore St., Dunmore Town* ☎ *242/470–8015* 🌐 *www.bahamascoffeeroasters.com* 💳 *No credit cards.*

★ **The Beach Bar at Coral Sands**

$$ | **ECLECTIC** | For lunch with a view, try Coral Sands' oceanfront bar and restaurant, just steps from the pink-sand beach. Executive Chef Ken Gomes creates delicious lunch options that go perfectly with a tropical cocktail or a glass of white wine. **Known for:** shrimp po'boy; gourmet pizzas; spicy fried calamari. [$] *Average main: $30* ✉ *Chapel St., Dunmore Town*

☎ 242/333–2350 🌐 *www.coralsands.com* 🕓 *Closed mid-Aug.–early Nov. No dinner.*

★ The Blue Bar at Pink Sands

$$ | ECLECTIC | The Blue Bar at Pink Sands is a famed, open-air restaurant and bar featuring blue and white decor which complements the pristine pink sand and clear, blue ocean that the restaurant overlooks. You'll have an unbeatable view while sipping one of their signature cocktails and enjoying fish tacos, a grouper ciabatta, or any of the other island-inspired menu options. **Known for:** fish tacos; beachside dining; cracked conch. [$] *Average main: $27* ✉ *Pink Sands Resort, Chapel St., Dunmore Town* ☎ *242/333–2030* 🌐 *www.pinksandsresort.com* 🕓 *No dinner except in summer.*

The Dunmore

$$$$ | CARIBBEAN | Start with a signature cocktail at the handsome mahogany bar before enjoying dinner under the stars on the ocean-view porch at The Dunmore restaurant. Executive Chef Philip Armbrister creates island-inspired dishes that change seasonally—lobster and grouper meals are always on the menu. **Known for:** signature cocktails; charming retro interior; Caribbean bouillabaisse. [$] *Average main: $44* ✉ *The Dunmore, Gaol La., Dunmore Town* ☎ *242/333–2200* 🌐 *www.dunmorebeach.com* 🕓 *Closed mid-Aug.–mid-Nov.*

Dunmore Deli

$ | DELI | The Dunmore Deli satisfies the epicurean demands of Briland's more finicky residents and visitors, while its shaded wooden porch, filled with hanging plants and bougainvillea, makes this the perfect spot for a lazy breakfast or lunch. Treat yourself to the Briland Bread Toast, the amazingly fluffy take on French toast, or pick up one of the inventive deli sandwiches for a picnic on the beach. **Known for:** excellent sandwiches; imported cheeses; fluffy French toast. [$] *Average main: $17* ✉ *King St., Dunmore Town* ☎ *242/333–2644* 🕓 *Closed Sun.*

Heavenly Music

The best live music on Harbour Island is at the Lighthouse Church of God on Chapel Street in Dunmore Town on Sunday mornings. Mick Jagger and Lenny Kravitz have dropped by to hear Pastor Samuel Higgs, drummer and bass player, and guitarist Rocky Sanders, both of whom played Europe's clubs for years before settling down on the island.

★ The Landing

$$$$ | ECLECTIC | You never know which actor or rock star you'll rub elbows with—Richard Gere and Dave Matthews like to dine here—at the Hemingway-esque bar, but none of it matters once you've moved on to the dining room and are under the spell of Swedish chef Vincent Vitlock, whose dishes soar with a Southeast Asian flair. Standouts include the goat cheese ravioli with shrimp, spicy crab capellini, and banana upside-down cake. **Known for:** famous clientele; goat cheese ravioli; outdoor dining. [$] *Average main: $47* ✉ *The Landing, Bay St., Dunmore Town* ☎ *242/333–2707* 🌐 *www.harbourislandlanding.com* 🕓 *Closed Wed. and mid-Aug.–Nov. No lunch.*

Ma Ruby's Restaurant

$$ | BAHAMIAN | Although you can sample local Bahamian fare at this famous eatery, the star of the menu is the cheeseburger, purportedly the inspiration for Jimmy Buffett's "Cheeseburger in Paradise" song. Maybe it's the rustic charm of the breezy patio, or the secret seasonings on the melt-in-your-mouth patty, but this burger served between thick slices of homemade Bahamian bread is definitely otherworldly. **Known for:** cheeseburgers; Ma's coconut tart; island charm. [$] *Average main: $25*

214

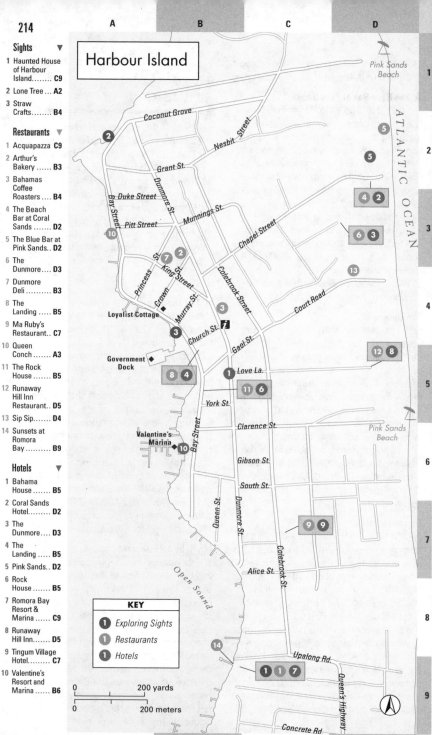

Harbour Island

KEY

① Exploring Sights

① Restaurants

① Hotels

0   200 yards

0   200 meters

Harbour Island is a tranquil place to spend some time.

✉ *Tingum Village Hotel, Colebrooke St., Dunmore Town* ☎ *242/333–2161* 🌐 *www.tingumvillage.com.*

Queen Conch

$ | **BAHAMIAN** | Four blocks from the ferry dock on Bay Street, with a deck overlooking the water, this colorful snack stand—presided over by Lavaughn Percentie—is renowned for its freshly caught conch salad ($12), which is diced in front of you, mixed with fresh vegetables, and ready to eat right at the counter. On weekends, get there early to put in your order, as visitors from the world over place large orders to go. **Known for:** conch specialties; take-out; busy on weekends. [$] *Average main: $12* ✉ *Bay St., Dunmore Town* ☎ *242/333–3811* 💳 *No credit cards* 🕒 *Closed Sun.*

★ The Rock House

$$$$ | **MODERN AMERICAN** | Splendid harbor views and a transporting Mediterranean-loggia vibe create the perfect backdrop for Chef Jennifer Learmonth's California Continental menu, infused with tropical accents. Imaginative dishes include curried Colorado lamb chops and Thai-style stone crab and lobster spring rolls. **Known for:** view overlooking the bay; inventive dishes; extensive wine list. [$] *Average main: $45* ✉ *The Rock House Hotel, Bay St., Dunmore Town* ☎ *242/333–2053* 🌐 *www.rockhousebahamas.com* 🕒 *Closed Aug.–mid-Nov. and Mon.*

Runaway Hill Inn Restaurant

$$$ | **CARIBBEAN** | Enjoy a moonlit dinner on Runaway Hill's beachfront veranda, with views of the pink-sand beach and turquoise waters along with sounds of the ocean waves. The atmosphere feels like a private club with a handsome 1920s interior. **Known for:** stunning ocean views; seafood crepes; yellowfin tuna. [$] *Average main: $40* ✉ *Colebrooke St., Dunmore Town* ☎ *242/333–2150* 🌐 *www.runawayhill.com* 🕒 *Closed Mon. and mid-July–early Nov.*

★ Sip Sip

$$ | **BAHAMIAN** | Locals and travelers alike seek out this popular snow-cone-green house overlooking the beach for a little "sip sip" (Bahamian for gossip) and

delicious inspired food. Chef and owner Julie Lightbourn uses whatever is fresh, local, and in season to create "Bahamian with a twist" dishes; daily specials are listed on the blackboard. **Known for:** lobster quesadilla; spicy conch chilli; lively atmosphere. $ *Average main: $25* ✉ *Court Rd., Dunmore Town* ☎ *242/333–3316* ⊕ *www.sipsirestaurant.com* ⊘ *Closed Tues. and Wed. mid-Aug.–Nov. No dinner.*

Sunsets at Romora Bay

$$ | **BAHAMIAN** | **FAMILY** | This waterfront pavilion at the Romora Bay Club perfectly frames sunsets over Harbour Island, so be sure to get here in time to snag a good seat for the show. Popular with locals, the restaurant serves midpriced Bahamian specialties such as conch fritters for a casual lunch or dinner. **Known for:** sunset's burger; sweet potato gnocchi; live music every day during dinner hours. $ *Average main: $30* ✉ *Romora Bay Resort and Marina, Dunmore St., Dunmore Town* ☎ *242/333–2325* ⊕ *www.romorabay.com* ⊘ *Closed Sept.*

🛏 Hotels

Bahama House

$$$$ | **B&B/INN** | Originally deeded in 1796 and built by Thomas W. Johnson, Briland's first doctor and justice of the peace, this handsome B&B, in a garden filled with bougainvillea, royal poincianas, and hibiscus, thrives thanks to the loving preservation work of genial innkeeper John Hersh. **Pros:** central location in the middle of Dunmore Town; historic house; peaceful garden. **Cons:** not on the beach; limited hotel services; no on-site restaurant. $ *Rooms from: $620* ✉ *Dunmore St., Dunmore Town* ☎ *970/237–5985* ⊕ *www.elevenexperience.com/bahama-house-harbour-island* ⊘ *Closed Aug.–mid-Nov.* 🛏 *11 rooms* ⦿ *Breakfast.*

Coral Sands Hotel

$$$ | **RESORT** | **FAMILY** | An elegant yet energetic flair accents this 8-acre oceanfront resort, right on the beach. **Pros:** direct ocean access; gym and new yoga studio on property; oceanfront restaurant on-site. **Cons:** rooms vary in quality; some rooms can be loud; limited food options. $ *Rooms from: $370* ✉ *Chapel St.* ☎ *242/333–2350, 561/228–1432 within the U.S.* ⊕ *www.coralsands.com* ⊘ *Closed mid-Aug.–early Nov.* 🛏 *38 rooms* ⦿ *Breakfast.*

The Dunmore

$$$$ | **RESORT** | This charming, retro-glam hotel with private cottages evokes a 1940s club in the tropics—with its mahogany bar, casual yet elegant dining room, and faded paperbacks in the clubhouse library, it's a favorite with the New England yachting set. **Pros:** on the beach with ocean-side bar service; spacious bathrooms; private terraces and lawn chairs for every cottage. **Cons:** cottages too close for real privacy; small clubhouse; not all cottages have a view of the ocean. $ *Rooms from: $550* ✉ *Gaol La., Dunmore Town* ☎ *242/333–2200, 877/891–3100* ⊕ *www.dunmorebeach.com* ⊘ *Closed Aug. 15–Nov. 15* 🛏 *18 cottages* ⦿ *No meals.*

The Landing

$$ | **B&B/INN** | Spare white walls and crisp white linens evoke a timeless, understated chic at The Landing, which is acclaimed as much for its singular style as for its superb cuisine. **Pros:** chic and comfortable rooms; glorious outdoor shower; acclaimed dining. **Cons:** basic amenities; limited hotel services; not on the beach. $ *Rooms from: $265* ✉ *Bay St., Dunmore Town* ☎ *242/333–2707* ⊕ *www.harbourislandlanding.com* ⊘ *Closed mid-Aug.–Nov.* 🛏 *13 rooms* ⦿ *No meals.*

★ Pink Sands

$$$$ | **RESORT** | Harbour Island's famed beachfront resort has long been praised by celebrities—Martha Stewart, Nicole Kidman, and Brooke Shields—and honeymooners alike for its 25 secluded acres of beautiful rambling gardens and private cottages. **Pros:** truly private cottages; snorkeling equipment, kayaks, and paddleboards available; discreet and well-trained staff. **Cons:** some cottages are a long walk from the restaurant and beach; cottages don't have kitchens; pool and fitness center are small. [$] *Rooms from: $540* ✉ *Chapel St., Dunmore Town* ☎ *242/333–2030* 🌐 *www.pinksandsresort.com* 🛏 *27 cottages* 🍴 *No meals.*

★ **Rock House**

$$$ | HOTEL | With a drawing room straight out of a villa on the Amalfi Coast, the Rock House is Harbour Island's most luxurious boutique hotel. **Pros:** top-rated restaurant on-site; many rooms have an enclosed terrace or a private cabana; best gym on the island. **Cons:** not on the beach; lack of views from some rooms; not ideal for families with young children. [$] *Rooms from: $315* ✉ *Bay St., Dunmore Town* ☎ *242/333–2053* 🌐 *www.rockhousebahamas.com* 🕒 *Closed Aug.–mid-Nov.* 🛏 *10 rooms* 🍴 *Free Breakfast.*

Romora Bay Resort & Marina

$$$ | RESORT | FAMILY | Three pink Adirondack chairs on the dock welcome you to this colorful and casual resort situated on the bay side of the island. **Pros:** two of the island's best restaurants are on-site; water views from every room; private bay-side beach. **Cons:** sloping steps from dock to cottages are a hassle for luggage; some room amenities are dated; no breakfast at either restaurants. [$] *Rooms from: $390* ✉ *South end of Dunmore St., Dunmore Town* ☎ *242/333–2325* 🌐 *www.romorabay.com* 🛏 *14 rooms* 🍴 *No meals.*

Runaway Hill Inn

$$$$ | B&B/INN | This quiet seaside inn on gorgeous, rolling grounds feels far removed from the rest of the island, which is precisely the point. **Pros:** oceanfront location with direct beach access; great restaurant on-site; intimate character. **Cons:** limited service; not as chic a vibe as nearby resorts; some amenities are dated. [$] *Rooms from: $409* ✉ *Colebrooke St., Dunmore Town* ☎ *242/333–2150, 843/278–1724* 🌐 *www.runawayhill.com* 🕒 *Closed mid-Aug.–early Nov.* 🛏 *12 rooms* 🍴 *No meals.*

Tingum Village Hotel

$ | B&B/INN | FAMILY | Each of the rustic cottages on this property, owned by the Percentie family, is named after a different island of the Bahamas. **Pros:** family-friendly; local flavor; Ma Ruby's restaurant on-site. **Cons:** no-frills interior and furnishings; not on beach or harbor; rustic grounds. [$] *Rooms from: $165* ✉ *Colebrooke St., Dunmore Town* ☎ *242/333–2161* 🛏 *30 rooms* 🍴 *Free Breakfast.*

Valentine's Resort and Marina

$$$$ | RESORT | FAMILY | With the largest marina on Harbour Island, equipped with 51 slips capable of accommodating yachts up to 160 feet, this resort is ideal if you are a self-sufficient traveler or family that doesn't require many amenities but enjoys spacious condo-style rooms and water-focused activities. **Pros:** modern rooms; state-of-the-art marina; large swimming pool. **Cons:** not oceanfront; impersonal condo-style quality; many rooms lack harbor views. [$] *Rooms from: $465* ✉ *Bay St., Dunmore Town* ☎ *242/333–2142* 🌐 *www.valentinesresort.com* 🛏 *41 rooms* 🍴 *No meals.*

🍸 Nightlife

Beyond the Reef

BARS/PUBS | The party starts at this waterfront bar at sunset and extends well into the evening. Drink specials are available all day and you can find great Bahamian food at any one of its neighboring vendors. Live entertainment is provided by the Briland's very own 123 band on weekends. ✉ *Bay St., Dunmore Town* ☎ *242/333–3478.*

Daddy D's

DANCE CLUBS | This is the place to be on the weekends and holidays in Harbour Island. The dance floor takes off around midnight and is a popular spot for young

Did You Know?

The five horses that visitors can ride on Pink Sands Beach are wild Bahamian horses from South Eleuthera, trained by Harbour Island resident Martin Saunders. They roam free on the beach and roll in the surf when they're not carrying riders. One of the horses is infamous for going to the nearby cemetery and turning on the faucet for water.

locals and tourists alike. DJ and owner Devon "Daddy D" Sawyer spins pop music, hip-hop, and reggae tunes late into the night. ⊠ *Dunmore St., Dunmore Town* ☎ *242/359–7006* ⊕ *www.daddyd.com.*

Gusty's Bar

BARS/PUBS | Enjoy a brew on the wrap-around patio of Gusty's, on Harbour Island's northern point. This lively hot spot has sand floors, a few tables, and patrons shooting pool. On weekends, holidays, and in high season, it's an extremely crowded and happening dance spot, especially after 10 pm. ⊠ *Bay St., Dunmore Town* ☎ *242/333–2165.*

🛍 Shopping

ART GALLERIES

Princess Street Gallery

ART GALLERIES | Princess Street Gallery displays original art by local and inter-nationally renowned artists, as well as a diverse selection of illustrated books, home accessories, and locally made crafts. ⊠ *Princess St., Dunmore Town* ☎ *242/333–2788* ⊕ *www.harbourisland-gallery.com* ⊗ *Closed Sun.*

CLOTHING

Blue Rooster

CLOTHING | This is the place to go for festive party dresses, sexy swimwear, fun accessories, and exotic gifts. ⊠ *King St., Dunmore Town* ☎ *242/333–2240* ⊗ *Closed Sun.*

Calico Trading Co

CLOTHING | This high-end boutique offers a variety of designer clothing for men, women, and children. They also sell unique gift items, sandals, and jewelry. ⊠ *Valentines Resort and Marina, Bay St., Dunmore Town* ☎ *242/333–3826.*

Miss Mae's Fine Tings

CLOTHING | Miss Mae's sells an exquisite and discerningly curated collection of fashion-forward clothing, accessories, and gifts from international designers

and artisans. ⊠ *Dunmore St., Dunmore Town* ☎ *242/333–2002.*

Sugar Mill Trading Co.

CLOTHING | Owned by former fashion model India Hicks, the cousin of Prince Charles, this upscale boutique is where you'll find a glamorous selection of resort wear, accessories, and gifts from designers around the world. ⊠ *Bay St., Dunmore Town* ☎ *242/333–3558* ⊗ *Closed Sun.*

GIFTS AND SOUVENIRS

A and A Hidden Treasures

CRAFTS | This family-owned souvenir shop sells authentic homemade Bahamian crafts. You'll find wonderful straw bags, baskets, and hats as well as conch shell necklaces and bracelets. ⊠ *Colebrook St., Dunmore Town* ☎ *242/448–1556.*

Dilly Dally

GIFTS/SOUVENIRS | Here you can find Bahamian-made jewelry, maps, T-shirts, CDs, decorations, and other fun island souvenirs. ⊠ *Dunmore St., Dunmore Town* ☎ *242/333–3109* ⊗ *Closed Sun.*

Pink Sands Gift Shop

GIFTS/SOUVENIRS | This shop offers a trendy selection of swimwear, accesso-ries, casual clothing, and trinkets. ⊠ *Pink Sands Resort, Chapel St., Dunmore Town* ☎ *242/333–2030.*

The Shop at Sip Sip

GIFTS/SOUVENIRS | The Shop at Sip Sip sells its own line of T-shirts and a small but stylish selection of handmade jewelry, custom-designed totes, Baha-mian straw work, and gifts found by owner Julie Lightbourn on her far-flung travels. ⊠ *Court Rd., Dunmore Town* ☎ *242/333–3316.*

🏃 Activities

BIKING

Michael's Cycles

BICYCLING | Bicycles are a popular way to explore Harbour Island; rent one—or golf carts, motorboats, Jet Skis, and kayaks—at Michael's Cycles. The cost is $15 a day per bike. ✉ *Colebrooke St., Dunmore Town* ☎ *242/333–2384, 242/464–0994*.

BOATING AND FISHING

Harbour Island's marine ecosystem provides great opportunities for deep-sea fishing, bonefishing, spearfishing, and spin fishing. The Harbour Island Tourist Office can help organize bone- and bottom-fishing excursions, as can all of the major hotels.

Stuart Cleare

FISHING | Bonefish Stuart is one of Harbour Island's best bonefishing guides. You'll want to call well in advance to arrange a trip with him. Bonefishing trips are $395 for half day and $695 for full day. ☎ *242/333–2072*.

SCUBA DIVING AND SNORKELING

Valentine's Dive Center

SCUBA DIVING | This dive center rents and sells equipment and provides all levels of instruction and certification. They also offer daily snorkeling and dive trips. ✉ *Valentine's Resort and Marina, Bay St., Dunmore Town* ☎ *242/333–2080* 🌐 *www.valentinesdive.com*.

SPAS

The Island Spa

SPA/BEAUTY | For romantic couples massages in the privacy of your own room, book Karen at The Island Spa. She makes in-room visits and offers evening beach massages, body scrubs, and aromatherapy. In addition to massages, The Island Spa can also do bridal hair and makeup, manicures, and pedicures—ideal for a destination wedding. ✉ *Colebrook St., Dunmore Town* ☎ *242/333–3326* 🌐 *www.theharbourislandspa.com* ☞ *Services: aromatherapy, massage, nail treatment, scrubs, wedding hair and makeup.*

Spanish Wells

Off Eleuthera's northern tip lies St. George's Cay, the site of **Spanish Wells.** The Spaniards used this as a safe harbor during the 17th century while they transferred their riches from the New World to the Old. Residents—the few surnames go back generations—live on the island's eastern end in clapboard houses that look as if they've been transported from a New England fishing village. Descendants of the Eleutheran Adventurers continue to sail these waters and bring back to shore fish and lobster (most of the Bahamas' langoustes are caught here), which are prepared and boxed for export in a factory at the dock. So lucrative is the trade in crawfish, the local term for Bahamian lobsters, that the 1,500 inhabitants may be the most prosperous Out Islanders.

GETTING HERE AND AROUND

You can reach Spanish Wells by taking a five-minute ferry ride ($7) from the Gene's Bay dock in North Eleuthera. You can easily explore the area on foot, or rent a golf cart.

🍴 Restaurants

Budda's Snack Shack

$$ | **BAHAMIAN** | Budda's Snack Shack is one of the most unique restaurants in all of Eleuthera, with a kitchen that was once an old school bus. The quirky restaurant is a favorite among locals and tourists for its delicious food and laid-back atmosphere. **Known for:** fun atmosphere; great fried chicken; conch burger. [$] *Average main: $20* ✉ *12th St.* ☎ *242/333–4111* 🌐 *www.buddabahamas.com* 🕒 *Closed Sun.*

The Generation Gap

$$ | **BAHAMIAN** | This casual diner is a hub of activity during lunch hours, particularly because of its chill atmosphere and a menu that features popular lunchtime meals. In addition to American soda

shop favorites like cheeseburgers, subs, and hot dogs, the menu also includes Bahamian fare such as fried grouper sandwiches and conch dishes. **Known for:** johnnycake breakfast sandwich; chocolate lasagna; authentic Bahamian meals. $ *Average main: $25* ⊠ *Main St., 13th and Samuel Guy Sts.* ☎ *242/333–4230* ⊟ *No credit cards* ⊘ *Closed Sun.*

Papa's Scoops

$ | **CAFÉ** | This small and unsuspecting shack is where you'll find the best dessert in Spanish Wells. Soft-serve homemade ice cream in a variety of flavors like cheesecake, blueberry, and coconut keep visitors coming back every night to Papa Scoop's front yard. **Known for:** homemade ice cream; delicious slushies; ice-cream sandwiches. $ *Average main: $5* ⊠ *Main St.* ☎ *242/333–4364* ⊘ *No lunch* ⊟ *No credit cards.*

★ The Shipyard Restaurant & Bar

$$$ | **ECLECTIC** | With its excellent menu, well-prepared food, and stunning views, locals of Spanish Wells have agreed that this restaurant has been one of the best additions to the island in recent years. The Shipyard Restaurant & Bar is located on the eastern tip of Spanish Wells, just where the ocean separates the town from North Eleuthera. **Known for:** gorgeous ocean views; lobster macaroni and cheese; shipyard steak. $ *Average main: $35* ⊠ *Main St.* ☎ *242/333–5010* ⊘ *Closed Tues.*

Wreckers

$$ | **MEDITERRANEAN** | The scenic views over the harbor, great service, and variety of flavorful Bahamian meals makes the Sandbar Beach Bar and Grill a culinary delight. Choose from the menu of local Bahamian dishes or the Mediterranean specialty pasta and pizza. **Known for:** views of the harbor; relaxed atmosphere; delicious flatbread pizza. $ *Average main: $28* ⊠ *Spanish Wells Yacht Haven & Resort, South St.* ☎ *242/333–5222* ⊕ *www.swyachthaven.com.*

🛏 Hotels

Howard Beach House

$$$$ | **RENTAL** | **FAMILY** | Over the last few years, the Howard Beach House has had major renovations to transform the former Spanish Wells Beach Resort into the private, luxury vacation home that it is today. **Pros:** tranquil vacation home; great for families; right on the beach. **Cons:** located in a secluded area; limited amenities; expensive housekeeping fee. $ *Rooms from: $425* ⊠ *North Beach, 13th St. N* ☎ *519/823–6600* ⊕ *www.howardbeachhouse.com* ⊟ *No credit cards* ⊅ *4 rooms* ⦿| *No meals.*

Spanish Wells Yacht Haven & Resort

$$ | **B&B/INN** | In peaceful Spanish Wells is the new and improved Spanish Wells Yacht Haven & Resort, a gorgeous boutique hotel that was rebuilt in 2017. **Pros:** all rooms have a terrace with pool and marina views; great on-site restaurant; upgraded amenities. **Cons:** no beach access; rooms don't have full service kitchens; not many facilities. $ *Rooms from: $265* ⊠ *South St.* ☎ *242/333–4255* ⊕ *www.swyachthaven.com* ⊅ *7 rooms* ⦿| *No meals.*

🏃 Activities

FISHING

Spanish Wells Fishing Charters

FISHING | For over 30 years, Spanish Wells Fishing Charters has been offering guided fishing tours, excursions, and other beach adventures in Spanish Wells. ⊠ *South St.* ☎ *242/359–7894* ⊕ *www.spanishwellsfishing.com.*

Chapter 7

THE EXUMAS

Updated by
Sheri-kae McLeod

⊙ Sights	🍴 Restaurants	🏨 Hotels	🛍 Shopping	🍸 Nightlife
★★★★★	★★★★★	★★★★★	★★☆☆☆	★★☆☆☆

WELCOME TO THE EXUMAS

TOP REASONS TO GO

★ **Party like a local:** Hot spots include Shirley's or any other restaurants at the Fish Fry for cracked conch and fresh seafood, and Chat 'N' Chill on Stocking Island for Sunday pig roasts.

★ **Island-hop:** Spend a couple of days boating through the 365 cays (one for every day of the year, as the locals say), and spot iguanas, swimming pigs, and giant starfish.

★ **Enjoy empty beaches:** Empty stretches of bleach-white sand are yours to explore.

★ **Explore the Land and Sea Park:** Snorkel in the 176-square-mile Exuma Cays Land and Sea Park and see queen conchs, starfish, and thriving coral reefs, as well as the endangered hawksbill and threatened green and loggerhead turtles.

Thirty-five miles southeast of Nassau, Allan's Cay sits at the top of the Exumas chain of 365 islands (most uninhabited) that skip like stones for 120 miles south across the Tropic of Cancer. Flanked by the Great Bahama Bank and Exuma Sound, the islands are at the center of the Bahamas. George Town, the Exumas' capital and hub of activity, is on Great Exuma, the mainland and largest island, near the bottom of the Exumas' chain. Little Exuma is to the south and connected to the mainland by a bridge. Together, these two islands span 50 miles.

1 Great Exuma. George Town hosts the 14-day George Town Cruising Regatta and the Bahamian Music and Heritage Festival. Dazzling white beaches and fish fries offering cold Kaliks crop up along the coasts of the entire island. Visitors come to fish, dive, and snorkel. Luxurious resorts and inns offer solitude or hopping beach parties.

2 Little Exuma. The Tropic of Cancer runs through the chain's second-largest island, which is duly noted on the steps leading to Tropic of Cancer Beach, one of the most spectacular on the island.

3 The Exuma Cays. If you're looking for a true escape, boat over to the cays where celebrities like Johnny Depp own spectacular islands. The renowned Exuma Cays Land and Sea Park toward the chain's north end has gorgeous crystal-clear water and white sand.

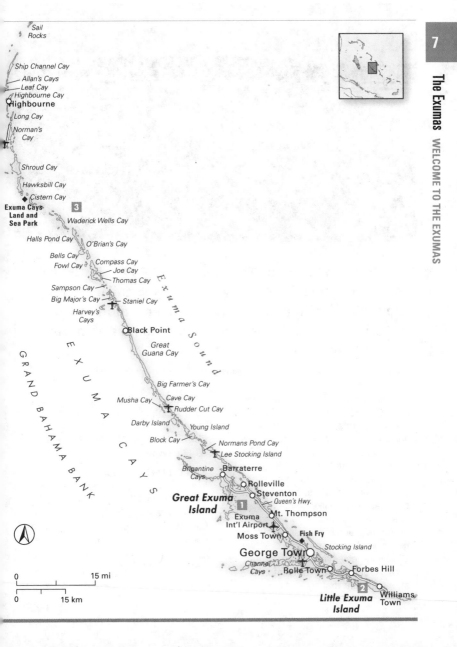

Sail Rocks

Ship Channel Cay

Allan's Cays
Leaf Cay
Highbourne Cay
Highbourne

Long Cay

Norman's Cay

Shroud Cay

Hawksbill Cay

Cistern Cay

Exuma Cays Land and Sea Park [3]

Waderick Wells Cay

Halls Pond Cay

O'Brian's Cay

Bells Cay
Fowl Cay
Compass Cay
Joe Cay
Thomas Cay

Sampson Cay
Big Major's Cay
Staniel Cay

Harvey's Cays

Black Point

Great Guana Cay

Exuma Sound

Big Farmer's Cay

Musha Cay
Cave Cay
Rudder Cut Cay

Darby Island
Young Island

Block Cay

Normans Pond Cay
Lee Stocking Island

Brigantine Cays
Barraterre

Rolleville
Steventon
Queen's Hwy.

Great Exuma Island [1]

Exuma Int'l Airport
Mt. Thompson

Moss Town
Fish Fry

George Town
Stocking Island

Channel Cays
Rolle Town
Forbes Hill

Little Exuma Island [2]
Williams Town

GRAND BAHAMA BANK

EXUMA CAYS

0 — 15 mi

0 — 15 km

EXUMA CAYS LAND AND SEA PARK

Created by the Bahamas National Trust in 1958, the 176-square-mile Exuma Cays Land and Sea Park was the first of its kind in the world—an enormous open aquarium with pristine reefs, an abundance of marine life, and sandy cays.

The park appeals to divers, who appreciate the vast underworld of limestone, reefs, drop-offs, blue holes, caves, and a multitude of exotic marine life including one of the Bahamas' most impressive stands of rare pillar coral. Since the park's waters have essentially never been fished, you can see what the ocean looked like before humans intervened. For landlubbers there are hiking trails and birding sites; stop in the main office for maps. More than 200 bird species have been spotted here. At Shroud Cay, jump into the strong current that creates a natural whirlpool whipping you around a rocky outcropping to a powdery beach. ⊠ *Between Conch Cut and Wax Cay Cut* ☎ *242/601–7438, VHF Channel 9 or 16* ⊕ *www.exumapark.info.*

BEST TIME TO GO

In summer the water is as warm as bathwater and usually just as calm. The park has vastly fewer boats than in the busy winter season, when the channel becomes a blue highway for a parade of sailing and motor vessels. Bring insect repellent in summer and fall.

BEST WAYS TO EXPLORE

By Boat. Boaters can explore the sandy cays and many islets that are little more than sandbars. The water is so clear it's hard to determine depths without a depth finder, so go slow and use your charts. Some routes are only passable at high tide. Get detailed directions before you go into the park, and be sure to stop by the park headquarters on Warderick Wells Cay for more information. Make sure you have a VHF marine radio on the boat or carry a handheld VHF radio so you can call for help or directions.

On Foot. The park headquarters has a map of hiking trails—most are on Warderick Wells Cay—that range from 2-mile walks to two-hour treks. Wear sturdy shoes, because trails are rocky. You'll see red, black, and white mangroves; limestone cliffs; and lots of birds—white-tail tropic birds, green herons, blue herons, black-bellied plovers, royal terns, and ospreys. Take sunscreen and water, and be aware that there's very little shade.

By Kayak. Visitors do sometimes take kayak trips from neighboring cays into the park and camp on the beach. The park has two kayaks that can be used free of charge by boaters moored in the

park. As you paddle, look for sea turtles, which might pop up beside you.

Underwater. You have to go underwater to see the best part of the park—spiny lobsters walking on stilt legs on the sandy floor, seagrass waving in the currents, curious hawksbill turtles (critically endangered), solemn-faced groupers, and the coral reefs that support an astonishing range of sea life. Bring your own equipment.

FUN FACT

The park has one native land mammal—the hutia, a critically endangered nocturnal rodent that looks similar to a gray squirrel.

MAKING A DIFFERENCE

How successful has the Exuma Cays Land and Sea Park been? About 74% of the grouper in the northern Exumas' cays come from the park. Crawfish tagged in the park have been found repopulating areas around Cat Island 70 miles away. The concentration of conch inside the park is 31 times higher than the concentration outside. This conservatively provides several million conchs outside the park for fishermen to harvest each year.

A sign marks where to find blow holes at the park.

The Exumas are known for their gorgeous 365 cays. Get the wind and sea salt in your hair as you cruise through the pristine 120-mile chain. Combine the epic scenery with fresh seafood and friendly locals, and you have one of the best vacation destinations in the Bahamas.

There is not a casino or cruise ship in sight on the Exumas, and those who love the remote beauty of the windswept cays keep coming back.

In 1783 Englishman Denys Rolle sent 150 slaves to Great Exuma to build a cotton plantation. His son Lord John Rolle later gave all of his 5,000 acres to his freed slaves, and they took the Rolle name. On Great Exuma and Little Exuma you'll still find wild cotton, testaments from plantations first established by Loyalists after the Revolutionary War. Today the Exumas are known as the Bahamas' onion capital, although many of the 7,000 residents earn a living by fishing and farming, and, more recently, tourism.

The Exumas attract fishermen after bonefish, the feisty breed that prefers the shallow sandy flats that surround these islands. The healthiest coral reefs and fish populations in the country make for excellent diving and snorkeling.

Some cays are no bigger than a sandbar, but you won't stay on the sand long as Perrier-clear waters beckon. Beaches won't be hard to find on the tiny cays; on Great Exuma, look for "Beach Access" signs on the Queen's Highway.

Planning

When to Go

High season is December through April, when weather is in the 70s (lows can dip into the 60s). Hotels sell out for events such as the George Town Cruising Regatta and the Bahamian Music and Heritage Festival in March, and the National Family Islands Regatta in April.

Room rates are cheaper in summer, but fall (late August through November, the height of hurricane season) offers the best deals. Weather during this time can be rainy and hot. Some inns close for September and October.

Festivals

WINTER
George Town Cruising Regatta
FESTIVALS | The George Town Cruising Regatta in February is 14 days of festivities including sailing, a conch-blowing contest, dance, food and entertainment, and sports competitions. ⊠ *George Town.*

Junkanoo

CULTURAL FESTIVALS | The Exumas' Junkanoo Parade on Boxing Day (December 26) starts at 7 pm in George Town and normally ends around 10 pm at Regatta Park. Dancing, barbecues, and music happen before and after the parade. ⊠ *George Town.*

Staniel Cay Cruising Regatta

FESTIVALS | The Annual New Year's Day Cruising Regatta at the Staniel Cay Yacht Club marks the finale of a two-day celebration. ⊠ *Staniel Cay.*

Bahamian Music and Heritage Festival

CULTURAL FESTIVALS | March's Bahamian Music and Heritage Festival brings local and nationally known musicians to George Town, along with arts and crafts, Bahamas sloop exhibitions, storytelling, singing, poetry reading, and gospel music. ⊠ *George Town.*

National Island Family Regatta

FESTIVALS | One of the oldest and most important traditions in the Bahamas, the National Island Family Regatta brings together sailors and families to enjoy five days of fun in April. ⊠ *George Town.*

SUMMER

Junkanoo Summer Festival

CULTURAL FESTIVALS | The Junkanoo Summer Festival in July and August is held beachside at the Fish Fry in George Town, and features local and visiting bands, kids' sunfish sailing, arts and crafts, and boat-building displays. It typically takes place on a Saturday afternoon. ⊠ *George Town.*

Getting Here and Around

AIR

The airport is 10 miles north of George Town. Taxis wait at the airport for incoming flights; a trip to George Town costs $30 for two people; to Williams Town, $80; to February Point, $30; to Emerald Bay, $30; to Grand Isle, $30.

Each additional person is $3. Staniel Cay Airport accepts charter flights and private planes.

CONTACTS Exuma International Airport (GGT). ☎ *242/345–0607, 242/524–9118 Airport Manager* ⊕ *www.exumaairport. com.*

BOAT AND FERRY

The Bahamas Ferries vessels *Seawind* and *Sealink* travel from Nassau to George Town on Monday and Wednesday, arriving in Exuma the next day (on Tuesday and Thursday). The trip takes 14 hours and costs $74 one way, $135 round-trip.

The mail boat M/V *Grand Master* travels from Nassau to George Town on Tuesday and returns to Nassau on Friday. The trip takes 12 hours and costs $40 each way. M/V *Captain "C"* leaves Nassau on Tuesday for Staniel Cay, Big Farmer's Cay, and Ragged Island, returning to Nassau on Friday. The trip is 14 hours and costs $45. Contact the Dockmaster's Office for more information.

Elvis Ferguson operates a boat taxi from Government Dock to Chat 'N' Chill on the hour throughout the day. If you plan on leaving the island after 6 pm, tell the captain in advance.

CONTACTS Dockmaster's Office. ☎ *242/393–1064.* **Elvis Ferguson.** ⊠ *Government Dock, George Town* ☎ *242/464– 1558* ⊕ *www.elviswatertaxi.com.*

CAR

If you want to explore Great Exuma and Little Exuma, you'll need to rent a car. Most hotels can arrange car rentals.

CONTACTS Airport Car Rentals. ⊠ *George Town Airport, George Town* ☎ *242/345– 0090, 242/225–4267* ⊕ *www.exumacarrental.com.* **Berlies Car Rental.** ⊠ *Exuma International Airport, George Town* ☎ *242/336–3290* ⊕ *www.berliescarrentals.com.* **Thompson's Rentals.** ☎ *242/336– 2442* ⊕ *www.exumacars.com.*

TAXI

Taxis are plentiful on Great Exuma, and most offer island tours. A half-day tour of George Town and Little Exuma is about $150 for two people.

CONTACTS Exuma Travel and Transportation Limited. ☎ 242/345–0232. **Junior Taxi Service.** ✉ Exuma International Airport, George Town ☎ 242/345–0641. **Luther Rolle Taxi Service.** ☎ 242/357–0662.

Hotels

Stay in simple stilt cottages, fabulous rooms with butler service, atmospheric old inns, modern condo rentals, all-inclusives, ecolodges, or bed-and-breakfasts—temporary homes-away-from-home for every taste and price point.

The mainland of Great Exuma has had an energetic growth spurt that includes some of the country's most luxurious hotels, including Sandals Emerald Bay, Grand Isle Resort and Spa, and Hideaway at Palm Bay.

Restaurants

Exuma restaurants are known for terrific Bahamian home cooking—cracked conch, fried chicken served with peas 'n' rice, or macaroni baked with egg and loads of cheese. Try conch salad at the cluster of wooden shacks called the Fish Fry, just north of George Town. Pea soup and dumplings is a specialty here, and many local restaurants serve it as a weekly lunch special. Lots of restaurants on the island close during the hurricane season, especially from August to November. Be sure to check or call before visiting.

Restaurants at larger resorts have upscale dining, including Continental twists on local cuisine as well as imported steaks and gourmet pizzas.

Restaurant prices are based on the median main course price at dinner, excluding gratuity, typically 15%, which is often automatically added to the bill. Hotel prices are for two people in a standard double room in high season, excluding service and 6%–12% tax.

WHAT IT COSTS in Dollars			
$	**$$**	**$$$**	**$$$$**
RESTAURANTS			
under $20	$20–$30	$31–$40	over $40
HOTELS			
under $200	$200–$300	$301–$400	over $400

Tours

BOAT TOURS
★ **Bahamas Revisited**

GUIDED TOURS | Bahamas Revisited offers weeklong sailing excursions into the Exuma Cays aboard a 70-foot schooner. Guests can expect to feed iguanas, swim with pigs, snorkel with sharks, and lounge on sandbars all while giving to a great cause: a portion of each guest's payment funds free education excursions for underprivileged Bahamian youth. ☎ 242/427–6345 ⊕ www.bahamasrevisited.com.

Charter World

BOAT TOURS | This company offers a variety of yacht charters. ☎ 954/603–7830 ⊕ www.charterworld.com.

Four C's Adventures

BOAT TOURS | Various private and group charters are available through Four C's Adventures, including snorkeling, fishing, and sightseeing tours. ☎ 242/357–0325, 242/355–5077 ⊕ www.exumawatertours.com.

Did You Know?

The Tropic of Cancer cuts through Little Exuma. A helpful line marking the spot on the steps leading down to Tropic of Cancer Beach makes a great photo op.

Exuma Cays Adventures

ADVENTURE TOURS | This company offers several tour options, including a trip through the Exuma Cays, a snorkeling excursion to Long Island, and tours of Elizabeth Harbour in a glass-bottom boat. ☎ *242/357–0390, 242/551–8044* ⊕ *www. exumacaysadventures.com.*

Exuma Water Sports

BOAT TOURS | Come here for guided Jet Ski tours through the Exuma Cays, as well as a scenic boat cruise that includes snorkeling at Thunderball Grotto. ☎ *242/357–0770* ⊕ *www.exumawater-sports.com.*

Island Boy Adventures

ADVENTURE TOURS | Island Boy Adventures offers fishing charters, beach tours, snorkeling, and other ocean adventures in Exuma. ☎ *242/357–0459* ⊕ *www. islandboyadventures.com.*

Sun Fun Tours

BOAT TOURS | Operated by Captain Tyrone, Sun Fun Tours offers a range of tour packages through the cays of Exuma. ☎ *242/434–6225, 242/225–9818* ⊕ *www. sunfunexuma.com.*

ISLAND TOURS

Exuma Travel and Transportation Limited

BUS TOURS | This company provides bus tours of Great Exuma and Little Exuma and can accommodate large parties. ☎ *242/345–0234.*

Island Routes

ADVENTURE TOURS | From reading road trips to historical tours and ocean adventures, Island Routes offers the opportunity to experience the best of Exuma. ☎ *305/663–4364, 877/384–4360* ⊕ *www. islandroutes.com.*

Activities

SCUBA DIVING AND SNORKELING

Exuma Cays Land and Sea Park and **Thunderball Grotto** are excellent snorkeling and dive sites.

Dive Exuma

DIVING/SNORKELING | Located in the heart of George Town on the Government Dock, this company offers daily dives, PADI courses, snorkel tours, and private charters. ☎ *242/336–2893, 242/357–0313* ⊕ *www.dive-exuma.com.*

Minns Water Sports

Minns Water Sports in Exuma is your one-stop shop for boat rentals, marine supplies, and snorkeling equipment. ☎ *242/336–3483, 242/336–2604* ⊕ *www. mwsboats.com.*

Staniel Cay Adventures

SCUBA DIVING | Explore the beautiful waters of Staniel Cay with Staniel Cay Adventures. The company provides a boutique scuba diving experience, catering to small groups of up to six people. ☎ *242/524–8062* ⊕ *www.stanielcayadventures.com.*

Visitor Information

CONTACTS Exuma Tourist Office. ✉ *Queen's Hwy., George Town* ✛ *Located in Turnquest Star Plaza* ☎ *242/336–2430* ⊕ *www.bahamas.com.* **Out Islands Promotion Board.** ⊕ *www.myoutisland. com.*

Great Exuma

George Town is the capital and largest town on the mainland, a lovely seaside community with darling pink government buildings overlooking Elizabeth Harbour. The white-pillared, colonial-style Government Administration Building was modeled on Nassau's Government House and houses the commissioner's office, police headquarters, courts, and a jail. Atop a hill across from it is the whitewashed St. Andrew's Anglican Church, originally built around 1802. Behind the church is the small, saltwater Lake Victoria. It was once used for soaking sisal used for making baskets and ropes. The straw market, a half dozen outdoor shops shaded by a huge African fig tree, is a short walk from town. You can bargain with fishermen for some of the day's catch at the Government Dock, where the mail boat comes in.

Small settlements make up the rest of the island. **Rolle Town,** a typical Exuma village devoid of tourist trappings, sits atop a hill overlooking the ocean 5 miles south of George Town. Some of the buildings are over a century old. **Rolleville** overlooks a harbor 20 miles north of George Town. Its old slave quarters have been transformed into livable cottages.

GETTING AROUND

Dining and sightseeing beyond your resort may require you to rent a car, as taxis can get expensive if you're going long distances.

Sights

Fish Fry

RESTAURANT—SIGHT | Fish Fry is the name given to a jumble of beachside restaurants, such as Charlie's and Shirley's, about 2 miles north of George Town. They're favored by locals for made-to-order fish and barbecue. Some shacks are open weekends only, but most are open nightly until at least 11 pm. There's live Rake 'n' Scrape Monday nights and DJs on Friday and Saturday. Eat at picnic tables by the water and watch the fishing boats come into the harbor. This is a popular after-work meeting place on Friday night, and a sports bar attracts locals and expats for American basketball and football games. ⊠ *Queen's Hwy., George Town.*

Rolle Town Tombs

MEMORIAL | Seek out the three Rolle Town Tombs, which date back to Loyalists. The largest tomb bears this poignant inscription: "Within this tomb interred the body of Ann McKay, the wife of Alexander McKay who departed this life the 8th November 1792. Aged twenty-six

years and their infant child." The tombs are off the main road; look for a sign. The settlement has brightly painted buildings, several more than a century old. ⊠ *Deep Creek.*

★ Stocking Island

ISLAND | Slightly more than a mile off George Town's shore lies Stocking Island. The 4-mile-long island has only 10 inhabitants, the upscale Kahari Resort, St Francis Resort, lots of walking trails, two gorgeous white beaches rich in seashells and popular with surfers, and plenty of good snorkeling sites. Jacques Cousteau's team is said to have traveled some 1,700 feet into Mystery Cave, a bluehole grotto 70 feet beneath the island. Stocking Island is the headquarters for the wildly popular George Town Cruising Regatta.

Three Sisters Rocks

VIEWPOINT | From the top of Mt. Thompson, rising from the Three Sisters Beach, there is a pleasing view of the Three Sisters Rocks jutting above the water just offshore. Legend has it that the rocks were formed when three sisters, all unwittingly in love with the same English sailor, waded out into deep water upon his departure, drowned, and turned into stone. If you look carefully next to each "sister," you'll see smaller boulders. These represent the "children" who the fickle sailors left with the three sisters. This sight is also a great snorkeling and diving spot. ⊠ *Queen's Hwy., Mount Thompson ✛ Mt. Thompson is about 12 miles north of George Town, past Moss Town.*

Beaches

★ Coco Plum Beach

BEACH—SIGHT | This stunning white-sand beach in Great Exuma is known for its great shelling and sand dollars during low tide. The beach is dotted with palm trees that provide shaded areas perfect for picnics and relaxing on the sand. Popular

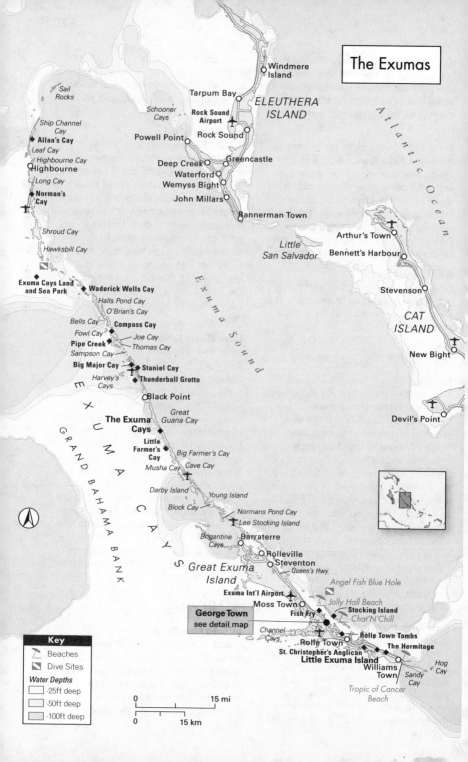

among both kids and adults are the swing sets in the water, which many use for photo ops. Watching the kite surfers that sometimes frequent the beach is another way to pass the time. **Amenities:** none. **Best For:** swimming; solitude. ⊠ *Queens Hwy.* ✛ *Near Blow Hole Cay, in between Steventon and Rolleville.*

Jolly Hall Beach

BEACH—SIGHT | A curve of sparkling white sand shaded by casuarina trees, this long beach is located just north of Palm Bay Beach Club. It's quiet and the shallow azure water makes it a great spot for families or romantics. When it's time for lunch, walk over to Palm Bay, Exuma Beach Resort, or Augusta Bay, three small nearby inns. Watch your bags when high tide comes in; much of the beach is swallowed by the sea. That's the signal for a cold Kalik and grouper sandwich. **Amenities:** none. **Best for:** solitude; sunrise; swimming; snorkeling. ⊠ *Queen's Hwy., George Town.*

🍴 Restaurants

★ Big D's Conch Shack

$$ | BAHAMIAN | For the freshest—and according to locals, best—conch salad and the coldest beer, look for the splatter-painted seaside shack a stone's throw from Grand Isle Resort. Big D catches the conch right outside the restaurant and the salads are often prepared in front of customers. **Known for:** conch salad; fresh fish; ocean view. $ *Average main: $20* ⊠ *Queen's Hwy., Steventon* ☎ *242/358–0059* ⊗ *Closed Mon. Closed Aug. 1 to early Oct.*

★ Chat 'N' Chill

$$ | BAHAMIAN | Yacht folks, locals, and visitors alike rub shoulders at Kenneth Bowe's funky open-air beach bar on the point at Stocking Island. All of the food is grilled over an open fire; awesome conch burgers with secret spices, freshly made conch salad, pulled pork, and ribs attract diners from all over Great Exuma.

Peacocks 👁

During your walks, you might glimpse peacocks on Great Exuma. Originally, a peacock and a peahen were brought to the island as pets by a man named Shorty Johnson, but when he left to work in Nassau he abandoned the birds, which gradually proliferated into a colony. The birds used to roam the streets, but development has forced them into the bush, so they are rarer sights these days.

Known for: conch burger; ribs; BBQ pork (Sunday only). $ *Average main: $20* ⊠ *1 Stocking Island* ☎ *305/504–5100* ⊕ *www. chatnchill.com.*

Driftwood Café

$ | DELI | Located in central George Town just across from the Club Peace and Plenty, this café is a pleasant spot for a cup of coffee and hot breakfast sandwich in the morning. Driftwood Café also offers lunch, with specialties such as pizza, subs, and salads served with fresh lemonade or iced tea. **Known for:** basil pesto chicken salad; pancakes and waffles; iced tea. $ *Average main: $10* ⊠ *Queen's Hwy., George Town* ☎ *242/336–3800* ⊟ *No credit cards* ⊗ *Closed Sun.*

Eddie's Edgewater

$$ | BAHAMIAN | In the heart of George Town is Eddie's Edgewater, an authentic Bahamian restaurant serving three meals per day. The dining terrace offers a stunning view of Lake Victoria, while the indoor dining room and large bar at the front is a popular hangout spot on Monday when there's live music, lots of drinking, and dancing. **Known for:** Monday night Rake 'n' Scrape; best grouper fingers according to locals; call ahead for lunch. $ *Average main: $20* ⊠ *Queens*

The Straw Market in George Town features handmade crafts.

Hwy., George Town ☎ *242/336–2050* ⏲ *Closed Sun.*

★ **La Fourchette**

$$ | **FRENCH FUSION** | Enjoy favorites from French and Bahamian cuisine at La Fourchette, which offers an intimate dining experience and great food in a beautiful setting. The view of pastel buildings and the pristine beach will amaze you, especially during dinner time when the sun sets. **Known for:** chocolate crepe dessert; grilled lobster; romantic atmosphere. [$] *Average main: $30* ✉ *Queens Hwy., Rokers Point Settlement* ☎ *242/524–8622* 🌐 *www.lafourchettebahamas.com* ⏲ *Closed Sept.–mid-Oct.* 💳 *No credit cards.*

★ **The Palapa Grill at Grand Isle Resort**

$$$ | **EUROPEAN** | Their fusion of Caribbean and Bahamian spices, fresh seafood, and the tropical outdoor setting are not to be missed at The Palapa Grill. This poolside restaurant serves three meals a day and offers a stunning view of the ocean. **Known for:** unique location; special house drinks and wines; sweet potato fries. [$] *Average main: $37* ✉ *Grand Isle Resort, Queen's Hwy., Rokers Point Settlement* ☎ *242/358–5000* 🌐 *www.grandisleresort.com.*

Plus39 Peace and Plenty

$$ | **ITALIAN** | The restaurant offers a unique dining experience, combining delicious Italian cuisine (Chef Mattia is a native of Italy) with local Bahamian food served right on Elizabeth Harbor. They host a Bahamian BBQ night, but the Italian meals here are a must-try. **Known for:** live music and local bands; Thursday night BBQ; extensive wine list. [$] *Average main: $29* ✉ *Peace & Plenty Hotel and Beach Club, Queen's Hwy., George Town* ☎ *242/336–2551* 🌐 *www.peaceandplenty.com* ⏲ *Closed Sept.*

Prime Island Meats and Deli

$ | **DELI** | Stop by this deli to stock up on deli meats, cheeses, and gourmet meats like steak, filet mignon, pork chops, and more for your stay. Owners Ron and Susan Kemp also sell delicious chicken salad, crab salad, potato salad, and more. **Known for:** rotisserie chicken; broccoli salad; widest selection of meats in Great Exuma. $ *Average main: $10* ⊠ *Queen's Hwy., Hoopers Bay, George Town* ☎ *242/336–3627* ⊘ *Closed Sun.*

Shirley's at the Fish Fry

$$ | **BAHAMIAN** | At the buzzing Fish Fry hot spot in Great Exuma, Shirley's is the most popular restaurant of them all, with its chill atmosphere and delicious food. The colorful, quaint little shack is just a stone's throw away from the beach so there's a great view from the dining deck outdoors. **Known for:** great local vibe; ocean view from deck; fresh seafood. $ *Average main: $30* ⊠ *Queens Hwy., George Town* ☎ *242/422–3642* ⊘ *Closed Thurs. Closed Sept. and Oct.* ═ *No credit cards.*

⋆ Shoreline Restaurant and Bar

$$ | **BAHAMIAN** | Take in the Great Exuma shoreline while sipping on a cold Kalik or mango daiquiri at this casual oceanfront restaurant. The menu features a range of Bahamian favorites, like cracked conch, fish tacos, and grouper fingers, and the staff is extremely friendly. **Known for:** cold beers; great beach; classic Bahamian meals. $ *Average main: $22* ⊠ *105 Kingsway Dr., Rolleville* ☎ *242/345–6201* ⊘ *Closed Sun. and mid-Aug.–late Sept.*

Splash Bar & Grill

$$ | **BAHAMIAN** | The Splash Bar and Grill located at Hideaways at Palm Bay is a fun eatery with a stunning view of the harbor and Stocking Island, which you can see looking out from the wraparound windows. There's also an outdoor dining area if you prefer feeling the ocean breeze and warm weather while you eat. **Known for:** stuffed burgers; bar with swings; beach access. $ *Average main: $20* ⊠ *Queen's Hwy., George Town* ☎ *242/336–3587* ⊕ *www.hideawayspalmbay.com* ⊘ *Closed mid-Aug.–Nov. 1.*

The Golden Ticket

Sandals restaurants are only open to guests—unless you buy a $200 day pass (from 10 am to 6 pm) or evening pass, at the same cost, (from 6 pm to 2 am) that gives you access to all the restaurants and bars. An all-day pass, valid for 24 hours, costs $350.

🛏 Hotels

⋆ Augusta Bay Bahamas

$ | **RESORT** | The perfect balance of luxury and casual chic, without the mega-resort feel, this 16-room resort on 300 feet of narrow beach is a mile north of George Town. **Pros:** luxurious rooms; great water views; friendly service. **Cons:** beach almost disappears at high tide; need a car to drive to town and shops; many services come at an extra cost. $ *Rooms from: $175* ⊠ *Queen's Hwy., George Town* ☎ *242/336–2251* ⊕ *www.august-abaybahamas.com* ⇱ *16 rooms* ⁙ *Free Breakfast.*

Exuma Palms Hotel

$ | **HOTEL** | Located on the beachfront of Three Sisters Beach, this hotel offers private beach access and equally private rooms with modern furniture and amenities. **Pros:** rooms are modern and spacious; private beach; quiet and clean property. **Cons:** no pool; many amenities show sign of wear; you need a car to get into town. $ *Rooms from: $150* ⊠ *Farmer's Hill, Queens Hwy.* ☎ *242/358–4040* ⇱ *12 rooms* ⁙ *Free Breakfast.*

February Point Resort Estates

$$$$ | **RESORT** | **FAMILY** | This gated residential community and resort is made up of 40 villas and privately owned homes—27 of the villas are available as guest accommodations. **Pros:** elegant accommodations; waterfront restaurant on-property; villas are completely private. **Cons:** more like a gated community than a resort; ongoing construction can be noisy; no entertainment within the community. $ *Rooms from: $425* ✉ *Queen's Hwy., George Town* ☎ *242/336–2695* ⊕ *www.februarypoint.com* ↷ *27 villas* ⍿◉⍿ *No meals.*

★ Grand Isle Resort and Spa

$$ | **RESORT** | **FAMILY** | This luxurious 79-villa complex boasts one of the island's few spas, an infinity pool overlooking the ocean, and a poolside patio restaurant. **Pros:** the ultimate in luxury accommodations; friendly staff; on-site spa and restaurant. **Cons:** 20-minute drive from George Town and not much to do near the resort; lacks local flavor; golf-cart parking is at an extra fee. $ *Rooms from: $300* ✉ *Off Queens Hwy., Rokers Point Settlement* ☎ *242/358–5000* ⊕ *www.grandisleresort.com* ↷ *79 villas* ⍿◉⍿ *No meals.*

Hideaways at Palm Bay

$$ | **RESORT** | **FAMILY** | Formerly called Palm Bay, one of George Town's most modern accommodations, is all about light and color. **Pros:** roomy accommodations; friendly young staff; great restaurant and bar on-site. **Cons:** beach all but disappears at high tide; accommodations are close together; free Wi-Fi is unreliable. $ *Rooms from: $206* ✉ *Queen's Hwy.* ✛ *1 mile from George Town* ☎ *888/396–0606, 242/336–2787* ⊕ *www.hideawayspalmbay.com* ↷ *40 rooms* ⍿◉⍿ *Free Breakfast.*

★ Kahari

$$$$ | **HOTEL** | The refurbished Kahari Resort on Stocking Island, just off the coast of Great Exuma offers privacy, exclusivity, and tranquility to its guests. **Pros:** on the beach; secluded rooms with private outdoor showers; lots of island activities can be arranged. **Cons:** can only be accessed via boat from airport; location is very isolated; many of the services cost extra. $ *Rooms from:*

$465 ✉ *Stocking Island, George Town* ☎ *888/203–4843* ⊕ *www.kahariresort.com* ◷ *Closed Sept.–Nov.* ↷ *12 rooms* ⍿◉⍿ *No meals.*

Peace and Plenty Resort and Beach Club

$ | **HOTEL** | The first Exumas hotel and granddaddy of the island's omnipresent Peace and Plenty empire, this pink, two-story lodge is in the heart of the action in George Town. **Pros:** in the middle of George Town action; friendly staff; ocean-view balconies in some rooms. **Cons:** no beach; have to take a water taxi to Stocking Island; property can be noisy due to ongoing renovations. $ *Rooms from: $180* ✉ *Queen's Hwy., George Town* ☎ *242/336–2551* ⊕ *www.peaceandplenty.com* ◷ *Closed Sept.* ↷ *35 rooms* ⍿◉⍿ *No meals.*

Regatta Point

$ | **HOTEL** | Soft pink with hunter-green shutters, this handsome two-story guesthouse overlooks Kidd Cove from its own petite island. **Pros:** private island feel; has its own beach; fantastic harbor views. **Cons:** water at the beach doesn't look clean; no restaurant; service on property can be poor. $ *Rooms from: $198* ✉ *Kidd Cove, George Town* ☎ *242/336–2206, 800/561–7954* ⊕ *www.regattapointbahamas.com* ↷ *6 suites* ⍿◉⍿ *No meals.*

★ Sandals Emerald Bay

$$$$ | **RESORT** | The former luxurious Four Seasons is now the even more luxurious Sandals Emerald Bay, an all-inclusive resort of pink and aqua buildings facing a 1-mile-long stretch of powdery white sand. **Pros:** spa and golf on-property; magnificent beach and swimming pools; great water sports. **Cons:** the resort is isolated; lacks Bahamian flavor; rooms near entertainment areas can be noisy. $ *Rooms from: $750* ✉ *Queen's Hwy., Rokers Point Settlement* ☎ *242/336–6800, 800/726–3157* ⊕ *www.sandals.com* ↷ *245 suites* ⍿◉⍿ *All-inclusive.*

Sandals Emerald Bay on Great Exuma has one of the island's best beaches.

★ St Francis Resort

$$ | **HOTEL** | The idyllic St Francis Resort on Stocking Island is the perfect tropical getaway for those looking for a beautiful and quiet property surrounded by lush forests, blue holes, and gorgeous beaches. **Pros:** two beaches nearby; great restaurant on-site; location is perfect for a peaceful vacation. **Cons:** no TVs in the rooms; dated decor; property is very remote. $ *Rooms from: $260* ✉ *Stocking Island, George Town* ☎ *242/557–9629* ⊕ *www.stfrancisresort.com* ⊘ *Closed late Aug.–Nov.* ⊷ *8 rooms* ⦿ *Free Breakfast.*

ⓨ Nightlife

Club Celebrity Sporting Lounge

DANCE CLUBS | Local celebrities frequent the aptly named Club Celebrity Sporting Lounge. Great music and Bahamian food and beverages are available here until the wee hours of the morning. ✉ *Rokers Point Settlement* ☎ *242/357–0245.*

Eddie's Edgewater

BARS/PUBS | On Monday, head to Eddie's Edgewater for rousing Rake 'n' Scrape music. The front porch is a popular spot, where locals hang out all week long. ✉ *Queens Hwy., George Town* ☎ *242/336–2050.*

Fish Fry

BARS/PUBS | There's always something going on at the Fish Fry, a cluster of shacks 2 miles north of George Town. A DJ is usually there on Friday and Sunday. ✉ *Queen's Hwy., George Town.*

Two Turtles Inn

BARS/PUBS | Two Turtles Inn is the other hot spot on Friday, when everyone comes to town to celebrate the end of the work week. 2T, as it's known, puts on a barbecue with live music. A week is too long to wait, so the celebration is repeated on Tuesday nights. ✉ *George Town* ☎ *242/336–0009.*

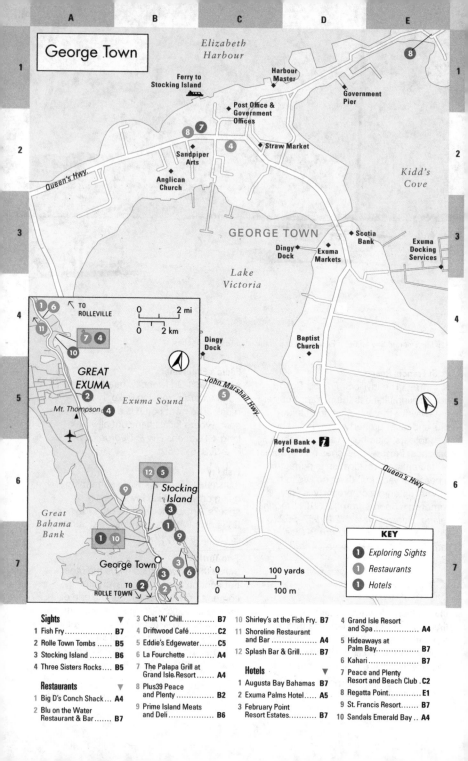

George Town

Elizabeth Harbour

Kidd's Cove

GEORGE TOWN

Lake Victoria

Exuma Sound

Stocking Island

Great Bahama Bank

George Town

Great Exuma

Mt. Thompson

TO ROLLEVILLE

TO ROLLE TOWN

Ferry to Stocking Island

Harbour Master

Government Pier

Post Office & Government Offices

Straw Market

Sandpiper Arts

Anglican Church

Scotia Bank

Dingy Dock

Exuma Markets

Exuma Docking Services

Dingy Dock

Baptist Church

Royal Bank of Canada

John Marshall Hwy.

Queen's Hwy.

0   2 mi
0   2 km

0   100 yards
0   100 m

KEY

1 Exploring Sights
1 Restaurants
1 Hotels

Sights ▼
1 Fish Fry **B7**
2 Rolle Town Tombs **B5**
3 Stocking Island **B6**
4 Three Sisters Rocks **B5**

Restaurants ▼
1 Big D's Conch Shack ... **A4**
2 Blu on the Water
   Restaurant & Bar **B7**
3 Chat 'N' Chill **B7**
4 Driftwood Café **C2**
5 Eddie's Edgewater **C5**
6 La Fourchette **A4**
7 The Palapa Grill at
   Grand Isle Resort **A4**
8 Plus39 Peace
   and Plenty **B2**
9 Prime Island Meats
   and Deli **B6**
10 Shirley's at the Fish Fry. **B7**
11 Shoreline Restaurant
   and Bar **A4**
12 Splash Bar & Grill **B7**

Hotels ▼
1 Augusta Bay Bahamas **B7**
2 Exuma Palms Hotel **A5**
3 February Point
   Resort Estates **B7**

4 Grand Isle Resort
   and Spa **A4**
5 Hideaways at
   Palm Bay **B7**
6 Kahari **B7**
7 Peace and Plenty
   Resort and Beach Club . **C2**
8 Regatta Point **E1**
9 St. Francis Resort **B7**
10 Sandals Emerald Bay .. **A4**

🛍 Shopping

Exuma Markets

GIFTS/SOUVENIRS | At this grocery store located in the center of George Town, yachties tie up at the skiff docks in the rear, on Lake Victoria. Boaters can also send emergency emails and faxes from this location. ✉ *Across from Scotia Bank, Queen's Hwy., George Town* ☎ *242/336–2033.*

★ Marilyn's Gift Shop

GIFTS/SOUVENIRS | This quaint and clean shop in George Town is fully stocked with souvenirs. Clothing, Bahamian hand-made crafts, jewelry, and much more are sold here. A second location is at the Exuma International Airport. ✉ *Queens Hwy., George Town* ✛ *Between Two Turtles Inn and George Town Library* ☎ *242/345–0321.*

Sandpiper Arts & Crafts

GIFTS/SOUVENIRS | Here you can find upscale souvenirs, from high-quality cards and books to batik clothing and art. ✉ *Queen's Hwy., George Town* ☎ *242/336–2084* ☉ *Closed Sun.*

Straw Market

GIFTS/SOUVENIRS | The Straw Market offers a wide range of Bahamian straw bags, hats, and beachwear at a half dozen open-air shops under a huge African fig tree. Prices are negotiable. ✉ *Queen's Hwy., George Town* ☉ *Closed Sun.*

🤸 Activities

ADVENTURE TOURS

Island Boy Adventures

BEACHES | Floating down the lazy river at Moriah Harbor Park, boating through the Exuma Cays to swim with the pigs, and diving for lobster are just a few of the activities offered by experienced Captains Evvie and Tonio. If you're not sure what to choose, let Island Boy Adventures help you plan your day—you won't be disap-pointed. ✉ *George Town* ☎ *242/357–0459* ⊕ *www.islandboyadventures.com.*

Capturing Waves

Here are a few tips for capturing the water's incredible shades of blue: shoot early—before 9 am—on a sunny day, or late in the afternoon. Make sure the sun is behind you. Use a tripod, or hold the camera still. Find a contrasting color—a bright red umbrella or a yellow fishing boat.

BOATING

Because of its wealth of safe harbors and regatta events, the Exumas are a favorite spot for yachtsmen. Renting a boat allows you to explore the cays near George Town and beyond, and a number of area hotels allow guests to tie up rental boats at their docks. For those who want to take a water jaunt through Stocking Island's hurricane holes, sail-boats are ideal.

FISHING

In the shallow flats off Exuma's wind-ward coast the elusive bonefish, the "ghosts of the sea," roam. Patient fish-ermen put featherweight, thumbnail-size flies on the lines, calculate the tides and currents, and cast out about 50 feet in hope of catching one. For sure success, avid fishermen pay guides about $300 a day to help them outsmart the skinny gray fish that streak through crystal water. Most hotels can arrange for expert local guides, and a list is also available from the Exuma Tourist Office. The season is year-round and highly prized among fly fishermen.

Exuma Bonefish Guides Association

FISHING | These guides are all highly qual-ified to help you hook a bonefish. A full day on the flats costs $490.

Fish Rowe Charters

FISHING | This charter company has a 40-foot Hatteras that holds up to four fishermen. Deep-water charters run $900 for a half day, $1,350 for ¾ day, and $1,800 for a full day. ☎ 242/357–0870 ⊕ www.fishrowecharters.com.

Steve Ferguson

FISHING | Stevie is an experienced guide who will help you hook feisty bonefish. ☎ 242/422–7033, 242/345–0153 ⊕ www. bonefishstevie.com.

GOLF

Sandals Emerald Reef Golf Club

GOLF | Golf legend Greg Norman designed the 18-hole, par-72 championship course, featuring six ocean-side holes, at Sandals Emerald Bay, the island's only golf course. There are preferred tee times for hotel guests. ⊠ Sandals, Queen's Hwy., Rokers Point Settlement ☎ 242/357–6800 ⊕ www.sandals.com ⊠ $125 for nonguests. Golf cart rental for guests is $65 ⅃ 18 holes, 7000 yards, par 72.

SCUBA DIVING

The popular **Angel Fish Blue Hole,** just minutes from George Town, is filled with angelfish, spotted rays, snapper, and the occasional reef shark. However, while it is full of mesmerizing schools of colorful fish, it is for experienced divers only.

Dive Exuma

SCUBA DIVING | This outfitter provides dive instruction, certification courses, scuba trips, and snorkel tours. One-tank dives are $90; two-tank dives are $145; and a private snorkel charter for half day is $550. ⊠ Government Dock, George Town ☎ 242/357–0313, 242/336–2893 ⊕ www. dive-exuma.com.

SNORKELING

Minn's Water Sport

DIVING/SNORKELING | You can rent or purchase snorkelling gear at Minn's. They also offer daily boat rentals. ⊠ Queen's Hwy., George Town ☎ 242/336–3483 ⊕ www.mwsboats.com.

SPAS

Red Lane Spa

SPA/BEAUTY | Located on the Sandals Emerald Bay property, this elegant spa has 16 treatment rooms, a steam room, and a fitness center. Couples massages and "sun lover" relief are among the treatments offered. The spa is open to the public, but you'll need to call ahead to make your appointment. ⊠ Sandals Emerald Bay, Queen's Hwy., Rokers Point Settlement ☎ 242/336–6800 ⊕ www. sandals.com ☞ Steam room. Gym with: cardiovascular machines, free weights, weight-training equipment. Services: body wraps, facials, massage, scrubs, nail treatment. Classes and programs: Pilates, yoga.

SeaStar Spa

SPA/BEAUTY | Seawater therapy, or the art of marine healing, is the philosophy at SeaStar Spa, located at Grand Isle Resort. Relax in one of three treatment rooms, including one designed especially for couples. The spa is open every day and offers a number of massages, scrubs, and wraps utilizing natural ingredients such as ginger, lime, coconut, and island spices. SeaStar also has a special "children's spa" menu, which includes shorter massages and pedicures as well as hair braiding. ⊠ Grand Isle Resort, Rokers Point Settlement ☎ 242/358–5000 ⊕ www.grandisleresort.com ☞ Services: aromatherapy, massage, nail treatment, scrubs, waxing, facials, children's spa.

TENNIS

February Point

TENNIS | Nonguests can use the two Laykold cushion–surfaced courts and adjacent fitness center at February Point for $15 a day. ⊠ February Point Resort, Queen's Hwy., George Town ☎ 242/336–2661 ⊕ www.februarypoint.com.

You'll swim among multicolored tropical fish at Staniel Cay.

Little Exuma

Scenes from two *Pirates of the Caribbean* movies were filmed on the southern end of Little Exuma—only 12 square miles—and on one of the little cays just offshore. But that's just one of the many reasons people are drawn to this lovely island, which is connected to Great Exuma to the north by a narrow bridge. Rolling green hills, purple morning glories spilling over fences, small settlements with only a dozen houses, and glistening white beaches make this a romantic afternoon escape. Near **Williams Town** is an eerie salt lake, still and ghostly, where salt was once scooped up and shipped away. You can hike old footpaths and look for ruins of old plantation buildings built in the 1700s near the Hermitage, but you'll have to look beneath the bushes and vines to find them. Little Exuma's best beach is Tropic of Cancer Beach (also known as Pelican's Bay Beach); it is a thrill to stand on the line that marks the spot. You're officially in the tropics now.

GETTING HERE AND AROUND

Little Exuma is hot with little shade. It's possible to walk or bike, but a car or scooter is the best way to get around the island.

VISITOR INFORMATION

People-to-People Program

This group hosts a tea where visitors can learn about bush medicine and other aspects of local life, and get to know Exuma islanders. ☎ *242/336–2430* ⊕ *www.bahamas.com/our-people-people-experience.*

◉ Sights

Hermitage

ARCHAEOLOGICAL SITE | The Hermitage estate ruins are testaments to the cotton plantation days. The small settlement was built by the Ferguson family from the Carolinas who settled here after the American Revolutionary War. Visitors can see the foundations of the main house and tombs that date back to the 1700s. The tombs hold George Butler

(1759–1822), Henderson Ferguson (1772–1825), and Constance McDonald (1755–59). A grave is believed to be that of an unnamed slave. ✉ *Williams Town.*

St. Christopher's Anglican
RELIGIOUS SITE | This is the island's smallest church, built in 1939 when the parish priest, Father Marshall, heard that a schooner loaded with timber from the Abacos had wrecked off Long Island. He visited the local Fitz-Gerald family and suggested they use the timber to build a church, which they did. Visitors can see the church and pews, all built of salvaged wood. ✉ *Queen's Hwy., Ferry.*

Beaches

★ **Tropic of Cancer Beach** (*Pelican's Bay Beach*)
BEACH—SIGHT | This is the beach most visitors come to the Exumas for, although don't be surprised if you're the only one here at noon on a Saturday. It's right on the Tropic of Cancer; a helpful line marking the spot on the steps leading down to the sand makes a great photo op. The beach is a white-sand crescent in a protected cove, where the water is usually as calm as a pond. A shady wooden cabana makes a comfortable place to admire the beach and water. *Pirates of the Caribbean* 2 and 3 were filmed on nearby Sandy Cay. Have lunch at the cast's favorite place, the open-air Santana's in Williams Town, a 10-minute drive from the beach. **Amenities:** none. **Best for:** solitude; snorkeling; swimming; walking. ✉ *Williams Town.*

Restaurants

★ **Santana's Bar and Grill**
$$ | **BAHAMIAN** | Santana's claim to fame, besides the beautiful ocean view and the delicious food, is that it was a favorite dining and hangout spot for the cast and crew during the filming of *Pirates of the Caribbean.* The menu features a range of Bahamian and American dishes, and Mom's bakery next door is famous for her fresh bread and mouthwatering rum cakes. **Known for:** shark feeding at the beach; fried lobster; mouthwatering rum cakes. [$] *Average main: $25* ✉ *Queen's Hwy., Williams Town* ☎ *242/345–4102* 🕒 *Closed Sun.*

★ **Tropic Breeze Beach Bar & Grill**
$$ | **CARIBBEAN** | Tropic Breeze Beach Bar and Grill is one of the most tranquil oceanfront restaurants in Great Exuma, with an outdoor dining area that wraps around the restaurant so you can enjoy the tropical sea breeze and views of the Caribbean sea. Chef Khriston, a Le Cordon Bleu Graduate, prepares the best and most popular Caribbean dishes—be sure to try the Jerk Wings with a cold beer. **Known for:** jerk wings; surf and turf burger; stunning ocean which is perfect for swimming. [$] *Average main: $27* ✉ *Queens Hwy., Williams Town* ☎ *242/345–4100* 🕒 *Closed Sun. and Mon. Closed Aug.–mid-Oct.*

The Exuma Cays

A band of cays—with names like **Rudder Cut, Big Farmer's, Great Guana,** and **Leaf**—stretches northwest from Great Exuma. It will take you a full day to boat through all 365 cays, most uninhabited, some owned by celebrities. Along the way you'll find giant starfish, wild iguanas, swimming pigs, dolphins, sharks, and picture-perfect sandbars. The Land and Sea Park, toward the northern end of the chain, is world-renowned.

GETTING HERE AND AROUND

Most people visit the cays with their own boats; you'll need one to island-hop, although you can fly into Staniel Cay. The channels are confusing for inexperienced boaters, especially at low tide, and high tide can hide reefs and sandbars just underneath the surface. If this sounds intimidating, look into booking a boat tour. Once on a cay, most are small

The famous swimming pigs of Big Major Cay will be happy to meet you at your boat.

enough to walk. Golf carts are popular on Staniel Cay.

Sights

Allan's Cay
ISLAND | Allan's Cay is at the Exumas' northernmost tip and home to the rare Bahamian iguana. Bring along some grapes and a stick to put them on, and these little guys will quickly become your new best friends.

Big Major Cay
ISLAND | FAMILY | Just north of Staniel Cay, Big Major's Cay is home to the famous swimming pigs (it's also called Pig Beach). These guys aren't shy; as you pull up to the island they'll dive in and swim out to greet you. Don't forget to bring some scraps; Staniel Cay restaurant gives guests bags before they depart.

Compass Cay
ISLAND | Explore the many paths on the island, which is 1½ miles long and 1 mile wide, or sit on the dock and watch the sharks swim below—don't worry, they're harmless nurse sharks. There are five houses for rent on the island, all come with a 13-foot Boston Whaler. There's also a small convenience store stocked with snacks and beverages. ✉ *Compass Cay* ⊕ *www.compasscaymarina.com.*

★ Exuma Cays Land and Sea Park
NATIONAL/STATE PARK | Created by the Bahamas National Trust in 1958, the 176-square-mile Exuma Cays Land and Sea Park was the first of its kind in the world—an enormous open aquarium with pristine reefs, an abundance of marine life, and sandy cays. For landlubbers there are hiking trails and birding sites. At Shroud Cay, jump into the strong current that creates a natural whirlpool whipping you around a rocky outcropping to a powdery beach. On top of the hill overlooking the beach is Camp Driftwood, made famous by a hermit who dug steps to the top, leaving behind pieces of driftwood. ✉ *Park Headquarters* ☎ *242/601–7438* ⊕ *www.eclsp.com* ☞ *VHF Channel 9 or 16.*

Staniel Cay Yacht Club is popular for fishing.

Little Farmer's Cay

ISLAND | If you're looking for a little civilization, stop off at Little Farmer's Cay, the first inhabited cay in the chain, about 40 minutes (18 miles) from Great Exuma. The island has a restaurant and a small grocery store where locals gather to play dominoes. But don't expect too big of a party; just 70 people live on the island. A walk up the hill will reward you with fantastic island views.

Norman's Cay

ISLAND | North of the Exuma Cays Land and Sea Park is Norman's Cay, an island with 10 miles of rarely trod white beaches, which attracts the occasional yachter. It was once the private domain of Colombian drug smuggler Carlos Lehder. It's now owned by the Bahamian government. Stop by Norman's Cay Beach Club at MacDuff's for lunch or an early dinner and that it's-five-o'clock-somewhere beach cocktail. ⊠ *Norman's Cay*.

Pipe Creek

SCENIC DRIVE | Boaters will want to explore the waterways known as Pipe Creek, a winding passage through the tiny islands between Staniel and Compass cays. There are great spots for shelling, snorkeling, diving, and bonefishing. Staniel Cay is a good place for lunch or dinner.

★ Staniel Cay

ISLAND | This is the hub of activity in the cays, and a favorite destination of yachters thanks to the Staniel Cay Yacht Club. Shack up in one of the cotton candy–color cottages and visit the club's restaurant for lunch, dinner, and nightlife. The island has an airstrip, one hotel, and paved roads, and everything is within walking distance. ⊠ *Staniel Cay*.

Thunderball Grotto

CAVE | Just across the water from the Staniel Cay Yacht Club is one of the Bahamas' most unforgettable attractions: Thunderball Grotto, a lovely marine cave that snorkelers (at low tide) and experienced scuba divers can explore. In the central cavern, shimmering shafts of sunlight pour through holes in the soaring ceiling and illuminate the glass-clear water. You'll see right away why this cave was chosen as an exotic setting for such movies as 007's *Thunderball* and *Never Say Never Again,* and the mermaid tale *Splash.* ✉ *Staniel Cay.*

🍴 Restaurants

★ Hill House Restaurant
$$$$ | **BAHAMIAN** | Housed in a charming British-style villa at the heart center of Fowl Cay Resort, this upscale restaurant serves fresh Bahamian-inspired modern cuisine. Located at one of the highest points on Fowl Cay, enjoy spectacular 360° views of the surrounding islands and sea while seated on the outdoor patio with a pool. **Known for:** fresh seafood; delectable hors d'oeuvres and innovative cuisine; lively cocktail hour. [$] *Average main: $50* ✉ *Fowl Cay Resort, Big Major's Cay* ☎ *242/355–2046 reservations* 🌐 *www.fowlcay.com* 🕒 *Closed Sept.*

MacDuff's Restaurant
$$ | **BAHAMIAN** | MacDuff's Restaurant offers a pleasant and mellow fine dining experience, with delicious food and world-class service. The rustic-chic decor and exposed wood beams are designed to remind customers of the paradise that surrounds them, as does the outdoor dining area with a view of the ocean. **Known for:** great cocktails; ocean view; conch burgers. [$] *Average main: $25* ✉ *Norman's Cay* ☎ *242/357–8846* 🕒 *Closed Tues.*

Sea Level at Staniel Cay Yacht Club
$$$ | **BAHAMIAN** | The view of the Exuma ocean is the perfect backdrop for a delicious meal in the dining room at this waterfront restaurant. Bahamian specialties such as cracked conch, fresh grouper, snapper, and grilled lobster with homemade bread are on the menu. **Known for:** ocean view; local fare; traditional Bahamian cuisine. [$] *Average main: $35* ✉ *Staniel Cay* ☎ *242/355–2024* 🌐 *www.stanielcay.com* 🕒 *Closed Oct.*

🛏 Hotels

Compass Cay
$$$$ | **RENTAL** | Five spacious houses on the island, which is 1.5 miles long and 1 mile wide, are so far apart and separated by lush palm and hardwood hammocks that you feel you have the island to yourself. **Pros:** remote tranquility; boat included; all houses are fully equipped with amenities. **Cons:** expensive to get to; too remote; not many activities. [$] *Rooms from: $2400* ✉ *Compass Cay* ☎ *772/532–4793* 🌐 *www.compasscay-marina.com* 🛏 *5 villas* 🍴 *No meals.*

★ Fowl Cay Resort
$$$$ | **RESORT** | Simply speaking, the all-inclusive Fowl Cay Resort is a Caribbean paradise; set in the breathtaking turquoise waters of the central Exumas chain of little islands and cays in the Bahamas, it was originally used to keep chickens by the locals (hence the name). **Pros:** spacious and tasteful villas; each villa has its own personal boat and gold cart; three private beaches nearby. **Cons:** Internet can be spotty on island; some rooms show minor wear and tear; resort pool is small. [$] *Rooms from: $1792* ✉ *Fowl Cay* ✈ *7-min boat ride from Staniel Cay airstrip* ☎ *877/845–5275, 242/355–2046* 🌐 *www.fowlcay.com* 🕒 *Closed Sept.* 🛏 *6 villas* 🍴 *All-inclusive.*

MacDuff's Cottages & Restaurant
$$$$ | **RENTAL** | Surrounded by tranquil seas, lush landscapes, and remote island living, this private retreat, with six oceanfront cottages and a restaurant, offers the beauty of a tropical paradise and the remoteness of a private escape. **Pros:** Out Island tranquility; spacious cottages; good restaurant on-site. **Cons:** expensive to get there; no Wi-Fi available; not many activities. [$] *Rooms from: $1000* ✉ *Norman's Cay* ☎ *242/357–8846* 🌐 *www.macduffscottages.com* 🛏 *6 cottages* 🍴 *All-inclusive.*

★ **Staniel Cay Yacht Club**
$$ | RENTAL | The Staniel Cay Yacht Club is nothing short of legendary, once drawing such luminaries as Malcolm Forbes and Robert Mitchum to its property. **Pros:** great restaurant; authentic Bahamian experience; great for families; children's activities can be arranged. **Cons:** expensive to get to without a private boat or plane; no TVs in many of the rooms; most services cost extra. [$] *Rooms from: $205* ✉ *Staniel Cay* ☎ *242/355–2024, 954/467–6658* 🌐 *www.stanielcay.com* 🕓 *Closed last two weeks of Oct.* 🛏 *14 cottages* 🍴 *No meals.*

🍸 Nightlife

Staniel Cay Yacht Club
BARS/PUBS | Staniel Cay Yacht Club has a relatively busy bar, hopping with yachters from all over the world. ✉ *Staniel Cay* ☎ *242/355–2024.*

🏃 Activities

BOATING AND FISHING

Staniel Cay Yacht Club
BOATING | Rent a 13- or 17-foot Whaler and arrange for a fishing guide at Staniel Cay Yacht Club, a prime destination for serious bonefishers. Regular excursions can also be arranged for any resort guest. ✉ *Staniel Cay* ☎ *242/355–2024* 🌐 *www.stanielcay.com.*

THE SOUTHERN OUT ISLANDS

8

Updated by
Noelle Nicolls

👁 **Sights**
★★★★★

🍴 **Restaurants**
★★★★☆

🛏 **Hotels**
★★★☆☆

🛍 **Shopping**
★☆☆☆☆

🍸 **Nightlife**
★★☆☆☆

WELCOME TO
THE SOUTHERN OUT ISLANDS

TOP REASONS TO GO

★ **Stage a disappearing act:** Discover your inner castaway on islands way off the trampled tourist track. Pink or white sand, calm azure coves, or rolling ocean waves—you'll have your pick.

★ **Tell your own tall fishing tale:** Whether deep-sea fishing past the Wall off southern Inagua or bonefishing in the crystal-clear shallows on Cat Island's east coast, your fish-capades will be ones to remember.

★ **Explore historic lighthouses:** Surrounded by treacherous shoals and reefs, the Southern Out Islands have the country's most famous 19th-century lighthouses, most of which you can climb for stunning views.

★ **Feast on the reefs and walls:** Spectacular diving and snorkeling, and even specialty shark dives, are on the menu for nature lovers when visiting these secluded southern isles with their calmer, clearer waters undisturbed by cold fronts.

1 Cat Island. Stunning pink and white beaches, the highest hilltop in the country (the 206-foot Mt. Alvernia), 200-year-old deserted stone cottages, and superb diving and fishing attract loyal visitors. A few small resorts offer low-key luxury.

2 San Salvador. Located on one of the largest reefs in the world, the tiny island's crystal-clear waters are a scuba diver's dream.

3 Long Island. Ringed with stunning beaches that reach to the west out into the Bahamas Banks and string along the easterly reef-strewn Atlantic deep blue coast, this island is off the beaten path, yet offers comfortable resorts and inns, as well as the world's deepest blue hole.

4 Crooked and Acklins islands. Fishing and more fishing are the reasons to come here, except when you take the day off to dive and snorkel. The Wall, a famed dive site about 50 yards off Crooked Island's coast, drops from 45 feet to thousands.

5 Inagua. The biggest attraction here is the island's 60,000 pink flamingos. Anglers come to fish tarpon and bonefish with famed fishing guide Ezzard Cartwright, and to explore the Spanish galleons that sank off the coast.

Arthur's Town

Cat Island
1

N

Port Howe

Exuma Sound

Great Exuma Island

Co

Ragged Island Range

New Bight
▲ Mt. Alvernia

San Salvador 2
Cockburn Town ○

Conception Cay

Rum Cay
○ Stella Maris   Port Nelson

Long Island 3
Deadman's Cay ○
○ Clarence Town

Atlantic

Samana Cay

Ocean

Crooked Island Passage

○ Colonel Hill
Crooked Island 4 ○ Richmond
Long Cay
Plana Cay

Mayaguana Passage

Mayaguana Island

○ Spring Point
Acklins Island

Little Inagua Island

Great Inagua Island 5
Lake Windsor

Matthew Town ○

0 ———— 30 mi
0 ———— 30 km

INAGUA NATIONAL PARK

Nothing quite prepares you for your first glimpse of the West Indian flamingos that nest in Inagua National Park: brilliant crimson-pink, up to 5 feet tall, with black-tipped wings. A dozen flamingos suddenly fly across a pond, intermixed with fantastic pink roseate spoonbills.

It's a moving experience, and yet because of the island's remote location, as few as 100 people witness it every year. By 1952, Inagua's flamingos had dwindled to about 5,000. The birds were hunted for their meat, especially the tongue, and for their feathers. The government established the 287-square-mile park in 1963, and today 60,000 flamingos nest here, the world's largest breeding colony of West Indian flamingos. The birds like the many salt ponds on Inagua that supply their favorite meal—brine shrimp.

You must contact the **Bahamas National Trust**'s Nassau office (☎ *242/393–1317* ⊕ *www.bnt.bs*) or **Wardens Henry**

Nixon and Randolph "Casper "Burrows (☎ *242/464–7618*, ☎ *242/395–0856*, or the office ☎ *242/339–2128*) to make reservations for your visit. All visits to the park are by special arrangement. *10 miles west of Matthew Town.*

BEST TIME TO GO

Flamingos are on the island year-round, but for the greatest concentration, visit during nesting season from late February through June. Around early March their courtship displays are an elaborate mass dance, and the chorus fills the air for miles around. They parade shoulder-to-shoulder, performing wing salutes, head wagging, and contorted preening with expanded wings.

The courtship displays end around April and then the pairs build small volcano-like nest mounds from a few inches to 2 feet tall. Early morning and late afternoon are the best times to come. If you visit right after their hatching, the flocks of fuzzy, gray baby flamingos—they can't fly until they're older—are entertaining and the 50 shades of gray and pink are a photographer's delight.

BEST WAYS TO EXPLORE

With a guide. Senior Park Warden Henry Nixon or Deputy Randolph "Casper" Burrows leads all tours into the park and to Union Creek Reserve. They'll drive you past small flocks of flamingos in the salt ponds and answer questions. Nixon is difficult to reach by phone, but your best chance is in the early evening.

By kayak. You can't kayak in the park's salt ponds because they're too shallow, but you can in Lake Windsor, also called Lake Rosa (or locally known as *The Pond*), a huge inland lake with its eastern half in the park. Because of badly washed-out dirt roads, you'll need a good 4x4 SUV or truck to reach the lake.

On foot. The best way to see flamingos up close is by parking the car and walking, or sitting quietly for a while in a thicket of mangroves. Flamingos are skittish and easily spooked. Although the ponds and mangroves look a lot like the Florida Everglades, there are no alligators or poisonous snakes here. Make sure you have insect repellent on before you take off; the mosquitoes are in abundance.

FLAMINGO FACTS

Flamingos are the national bird, and protected from hunters by law.

Females lay one egg a year, and both parents take turns sitting on it for 28 days. Both parents also produce milk in the crop at the base of the neck for the chick for three months. The parents' feathers turn white while they feed the chick because they lose carotene.

Flamingos are monogamous and usually mate for life, but are extremely social birds that like to live in groups.

Their "knees," which seem to bend backward, are actually ankles (the knees are tucked under their feathers). What looks like the leg is actually the foot extending from the ankle.

Standing on one leg is the most comfortable position for a flamingo.

Brine shrimp, the flamingo's main source of food, give the mature bird its brilliant deep pink.

RAKE 'N' SCRAPE

Rake 'n' Scrape music's contagious cadence, created by instruments made mostly from recycled objects, brings on a particularly strong urge to get up and shake it.

Most closely linked in sound, rhythm, and composition to zydeco music out of New Orleans, Rake 'n' Scrape is folk music at its best. It's unclear just where Rake 'n' Scrape originated, but most believe it has roots in Africa, made the voyage to the Bahamas with slaves, and was adapted over the years. Today's Rake 'n' Scrape was cultivated on remote Cat Island. Lacking money for and access to modern instruments, the resourceful locals made use of whatever supplies were available. Years later, many of these musicians could have their pick of shiny, finely tuned instruments, but sticking with what they know makes beautiful music.

HAVE A LISTEN

International recording artist and Cat Islander **Tony McKay,** who went by the stage name *Exuma*, incorporated Rake 'n' Scrape into his compositions. He paid homage to the style with the song "Goin' to Cat Island."

George Symonette's "Don't Touch Me Tomato" had a resurgence in a recent television commercial for Cable Bahamas. Symonette is associated with Goombay, a music style popular in Nassau in the 1950s. Goombay soon died out, giving way to closely related Rake 'n' Scrape.

Comprised of six Harbour Islanders, **The Brilanders** have toured with Jimmy Buffet. Their hit song "Backyard Party" is a sound track standard at just about any Bahamian party.

INSTRUMENTS

An authentic Rake 'n' Scrape band uses recycled objects to make music. An ordinary saw held in a musician's lap, then bent and scraped, becomes an instrument. A piece of wood, some fishing line, and a tin washtub is a good stand-in for the brass section. Plastic juice bottles are filled with pigeon peas, painted in bright colors, and turned into maracas. Add a goatskin drum, and you have all you need for a Rake 'n' Scrape ensemble, although many bands now add a concertina, guitar, or saxophone.

MAJOR PLAYERS

Authentic Rake 'n' Scrape is a dying art. The handful of groups scattered throughout the Bahamas are comprised of older men, as younger Bahamians prefer more modern sounds. Today **Ophie and Da Websites, The Brilanders, Thomas Cartwright,** and **Bo Hogg** are among the few groups still performing old-style Rake 'n' Scrape. Other modern Bahamian musicians, such as **K.B., Phil Stubbs, D Mac and Rhythm and Youth** work

the sound and rhythm into their own signature styles, along with the late **Ronnie Butler**.

The popular four-day **Rake 'n' Scrape Festival** each June on Cat Island hosts dozens of bands from all over the Bahamas and the Caribbean.

On Harbour Island, **Gusty's** and **Vic-Hum Club** usually work at least one night of Rake 'n' Scrape into the weekly live music schedule. **The Brilanders** often play at **Seagrapes**.

DANCE LIKE A LOCAL

The Rake 'n' Scrape rhythm is so captivating that even the most rhythmically challenged will be hard-pressed to stand still. As the first beats are played, look around and see what the old folk do. It's not unusual to see a man stick his leg out (whether he's sitting or standing), lift his pants leg a bit, and let his footwork get fancy, doing a dance called "stomping the roach."

At festivals, schoolchildren usually dance the quadrille or heel-toe polka. If you ask a Bahamian to show you how to "mash de roach" or dance "the conch style," they may jump up and put on a show.

Wild and windswept, the southern Bahamian islands are idyllic Edens for those adventurers who want to battle a tarpon, dive a "wall" that drops thousands of feet, photograph the world's largest group of West Indian flamingos, or just sprawl on a sun-splashed beach with no sign of life—except maybe for a Bahama parrot pelting seeds from a guinep tree.

The quiet, simpler way of life on the Southern Out Islands is startlingly different from Nassau's fast-paced glitz and glamour, and even more secluded than the northern Out Islands. You won't find huge resorts, casinos, or fast-food restaurants here, not to mention stoplights. Instead, you'll be rewarded with a serene vacation that will make your blood pressure drop faster than a fisherman's hook and sinker.

Sportsmen are drawn to the Southern Islands to outsmart the swift bonefish, and fish for marlin, black and bluefin tuna, wahoo, and swordfish. Yachties roam these islands on their way to the Caribbean, and vacationers rent Hobie Cats and kayaks. On all these islands, divers and snorkelers come to see healthy reefs, abundant underwater wildlife, and even sharks. Romantics and honeymooners head south for the glorious sunsets viewed from the verandas of beachside cottages, and for the lovely pink beaches. Bird-watchers arrive with binoculars in hand to see the green-and-red Bahama parrots, Bahama pintails, tricolor and crested night herons, and, of course, flamingos. They can also try to spot the Bahama woodstar hummingbird, which is very similar to one of the world's newest discovered species, the Inaguan lyretail hummingbird.

Hurricanes Joaquin in 2015, Matthew in 2016, and Irma in 2017, damaged portions of the Southern Islands—yet only seemed to prove how resilient these hardy and community-minded folk are. Friends, families, and companies from neighboring islands and the United States and Canada poured in generous donations. While never fully complete, repairs to infrastructure and in the tourism sector were relatively quick.

The neighborliness and hospitality of the residents is well-known, and visitors are often taken aback by their instant inclusion in the community. You can't walk 100 feet without someone offering a welcome ride on a hot day or a taxi driver offering you fresh fruit from his car trunk. Ask an islander where a certain restaurant is and they will walk with you until you see it. On Inagua, express any disappointment such as not seeing a flamingo up close, and the person standing behind you at the store will get on their cell phone. (There's a big flock now at the Town Pond.) The scenery is gorgeous, but this genuine rapport is what brings regulars back time and again to these tiny communities.

Planning

When to Go

Few visitors make it to these Southern Islands, but those who do come at different times. Europeans tend to arrive in summer and stay for a month or longer. Sailors come through on their way to the Caribbean in fall and return to the Bahamas in spring or summer on trips back to North America. Fishermen arrive all year and divers prefer the calm seas in summer. Those looking for a winter warm-up visit from December to April, when temperatures are in the 70s. These months have the lowest rainfall of the year, but the ocean is chilly and, during cold fronts, is choppy for divers and boaters. Christmas, New Year's, and Easter are usually booked, so reserve rooms months in advance.

Many inns and resorts are closed in September and October for annual repairs, owners' vacations, and hurricane season, which technically runs from June through November. Mosquito repellent is usually needed year-round (except when string winds blow), but is imperative in summer and fall, especially after a period of rain when both mosquitoes and no-see-ums come out in full force, especially at sunset. Note that they remain in the sand on your feet and towels even after you leave the beach, so make sure to rinse or leave your towel outside your room.

The Southern Islands are generally a couple degrees warmer than Nassau, but farther south are more consistent trade winds in summer. You may need a windbreaker in winter, particularly on a boat. If possible, time your visit for Junkanoo on New Year's morning, sailing regattas in June and July, and special events such as the Cat Island's Rake 'n' Scrape Festival in early June.

Festivals

WINTER
Junkanoo
CULTURAL FESTIVALS | Inagua puts on a spirited junkanoo parade on Boxing Day, December 26, and New Year's Day. Parades start at 4:30 am; you have to make the decision to stay up all night or get up early. There's food at the fish fry at Kiwanis Park in the center of town, where the parades end. ⊠ *Matthew Town.*

SUMMER
Cat Island Rake 'n' Scrape Festival
MUSIC FESTIVALS | The annual Cat Island Rake 'n' Scrape Festival celebrating the indigenous music is held in early June on the Bahamian Labour Day weekend. Each day the festivities begin with breakfast and lunch in the park with games of dominoes and checkers. At 7 pm the site is cleared for the Battle of the Rake 'n' Scrape Bands. You can also enjoy a gospel concert, cultural dance troupes, a children's corner with games, arts and crafts, and a fishermen and farmers' market. Nearby restaurants expand their menus for the after-parties. Between 1,000 and 2,000 people attend and fill local hotels, inns, and guesthouses, so book early. Two mail boats, Bahamasair, and private charters serve the festival, which takes place in the town square near Arthur's Town Airport. ⊠ *Arthur's Town Square, North Cat Island, Arthur's Town* ⛴ *$20.*

Cat Island Regatta
CULTURAL FESTIVALS | Growing in popularity (thanks to its Kalik Beer sponsorship), the annual Cat Island Regatta, held on the

beach in New Bight over the Emancipation holiday weekend in early August, has parties, live music, games, dancing, and lots of island cooking. Some 30–40 island sloops compete in various classes over three days. Expect some Rake 'n' Scrape and party music from national and local live entertainers. Games can include dominoes, water relay races, ugliest man, water balloon toss, hula hoop relays, coconut races, and more. Book flights and lodging well in advance. ⊠ New Bight ⊕ www.bahamas.com/event/cat-island-regatta ☜ Free.

Inagua Heritage & Salty Festival

CULTURAL FESTIVALS | More oriented to locals and their families, and sponsored by the Morton Salt Company, this home-coming-type heritage festival takes place over the Emancipation holiday weekend in early August. Most activities are in Matthew Town's marketplace with a Sunday Beach Bash on Farquharson Beach, 8 miles north of the town. Visitors are most welcome and encouraged to join in. Celebrations include an ecumenical church service, gospel choirs, a Junkanoo rush-out, fireworks, live bands, games, and cultural activities including the plaiting of the maypole and climbing the greasy pole. Along with festival staples such as barbecued meats and fresh seafood, it's a great chance to savor some of the island's more unusual delicacies such as spiced souses and baked breads and tarts. ⊠ Matthew Town ⊕ www.bahamas.com/islands/inagua ☜ Free.

Long Island Sailing Regatta

FESTIVALS | The annual Long Island Sailing Regatta, featuring Bahamian-made boats, is a three-day event the first weekend of June. Held in Salt Pond, the regatta is the island's biggest event and the Bahamas' second-largest regatta, attracting competitors from all over the islands. Booths featuring handmade crafts and Bahamian food and drink dot the site, and local bands provide lively entertainment beginning at sundown. Salt Pond is 10 miles

south of Simms. ⊠ Salt Pond ⊕ www.bahamas.com/event/long-island-regatta.

FALL
Discovery Day Festival

CULTURAL FESTIVALS | Though October 12 is now known as National Heroes Day across The Bahamas, it was not too long ago commemorated as "Discovery Day." However, the island of San Salvador continues to recognize the day Christopher Columbus arrived in the new world for he landed right on one of their beaches. The Discovery Day Homecoming Festival is a week-long event that takes places at various venues across the island, including Graham's Harbour on the far north of the island and Long Bay, where memorials mark the spot that Columbus landed. Festival days depend on when the public holiday falls, but always include food, drink, craft, a mix of live bands, DJs, and fun games such as sack race, coconut barking, pineapple eating, beer drinking, and a staged cultural dancing show. An evening ecumenical service and gospel concert usually kicks things off while a Beach Bash closes the festivities out. ⊠ Graham's Harbour on San Salvador's far north beach, and Long Bay Beach, south of Cockburn Town ⊕ www.bahamas.com/islands/san-salvador ☜ Free except for main concert area.

Getting Here and Around

AIR

All of the Southern Out Islands have at least one airport, and several have multiple airports. Flights are primarily from the Nassau hub using local airlines and charter companies. San Salvador has scheduled flights from Montreal in Canada, Fort Lauderdale in Florida, and from Paris in France. See individual island sections for more details.

BOAT AND FERRY

Mail boats link all of these islands to Nassau, and, only for a popular festival, Bahamas Ferries may add a special service to supply the extra demand. *See individual island sections for more details.* If you plan to use the mail boat for transportation, check schedules by calling the Dockmaster's Office in Nassau. They change frequently.

CONTACTS Association of Bahamas Marinas. ☎ *844/556–5290 toll-free, 954/462–4591 Florida* ⊕ *www.bahamasmarinas. com.* **Mailboat Port/Dockmaster's Office in Nassau.** ✉ *Potter's Cay, Nassau* ☎ *242/393–1064 Dockmaster's office, 242/394–1237.*

CAR AND TAXI

You can rent a car on all of the islands. Taxi service is also available. Regardless, transportation tends to be expensive because of the isolation and cost of fuel.

Hotels

The inns in the Southern Out Islands are small and intimate, and usually cater to a specific crowd such as anglers, divers, or those who just want a quiet beach experience. Club Med Columbus Isle, an upscale resort on San Salvador, is an exception, with 236 rooms and a wide range of activities. Fernandez Bay Village in southern Cat Island is also more a full service resort with seven cottages, five villas, and a long menu of activities and dining.

Most inns are on the beach, and many have one- and two-bedroom cottages with private verandas, offering three meals a day or self-catering along with free kayaks, paddleboards, and bikes. They'll either pick you up at the airport, ask you to get a taxi or arrange a car rental. Fishing guides, charters, dive trips, and sightseeing tours are just a call away, but you should book them in advance. If the hotel doesn't close in off-season, some of the best deals are available in September through early December. U.S. holidays and local holidays or festivals can quickly fill the islands' rooms. Club

Med Columbus Isle offers early-bird booking bonuses and runs pricing promotions year-round.

Restaurants

Out Island restaurants are often family-run and focus on home-style dishes. If you want to dine at a restaurant or another inn, it's crucial to call ahead. Dinner choices largely depend on what's planned or what fishermen and mail boats bring in; be prepared for limited choices. If you are renting, bring lots of food and snacks.

Anticipate tasty Bahamian fresh fish, lobster, conch, fresh-baked bread, and coconut tarts, along with a smattering of American and international dishes. Fish, lobster, and conch—which is served stewed, as a salad, or cracked (battered and deep fried)—is served at almost every restaurant for lunch and dinner. Chicken served many ways is a Bahamian staple and the skills of Bahamian cooks to prepare tasty chicken are legendary. These islands have breezy roadside conch stands—typically near a settlement or a beach or with sea views—that deserve a special trip from your hotel. On Friday and Saturday nights many restaurants and bars crank up the music and visitors and locals will drink and dance 'til late.

Restaurant prices are based on the median main course price at dinner, excluding gratuity, typically 15%, which is often automatically added to the bill as well as 12% VAT. Hotel prices are for two people in a standard double room in high season, excluding service and the 12% VAT. Some resorts can charge a 6% resort levy that goes to the Bahama Out Island Promotion Board. These BOIPB hotels typically offer a higher standard of service.

8

The Southern Out Islands PLANNING

WHAT IT COSTS in Dollars

	$	$$	$$$	$$$$
RESTAURANTS				
	under $20	$20–$30	$31–$40	over $40
HOTELS				
	under $200	$200–$300	$301–$400	over $400

Visitor Information

CONTACTS Association of Bahamas Marinas. ☎ 844/556–5290 toll-free, 954/462–4591 Florida ⊕ www.bahamasmarinas.com. **The Bahamas Ministry of Tourism.** ☎ 242/302–2000 in Nassau ⊕ www.bahamas.com. **Bahamas Out Islands Promotion Board.** ☎ 242/322–1140 in Nassau ⊕ www.myoutislands.com.

Cat Island

Cat Island is made up of exquisite pink-sand beaches and sparkling white-sand-ringed coves, as calm and clear as a spa pool. Largely undeveloped, the island has the tallest hill in the Bahamas, a dizzying 206 feet high, with a historic tiny stone abbey on top. The two-lane Queen's Highway runs the 48-mile length of the island from north to south, mostly along the western gorgeous sandy coastline, through quaint seaside settlements and past hundreds of abandoned stone cottages. Some are 200-year-old slave houses, crumbling testaments to cotton and sisal plantation days, while others, too old to have modern utilities, were abandoned. Trees and vines twist through spaces that used to be windows and roofs and the deep-blue ocean can be seen through missing walls. In 1938 the island had 5,000 residents and today only about 1,500. Many of the inhabitants left the cottages long ago out of necessity, to find work in Nassau and Florida, but the houses remain because they still mark family land.

Cat Island was named after a frequent visitor, the notorious pirate Arthur Catt, a contemporary of Edward "Blackbeard" Teach. Another famous islander is Sir Sidney Poitier, who grew up here before leaving to become a groundbreaking Academy Award–winning movie actor and director.

GETTING HERE AND AROUND
AIR
Cat Island has two airports: Arthur's Town (ATC) in the north and the New Bight (TBI) mid-island. Two airlines fly in from Nassau to both airports: Southern Air four days a week, and SkyBahamas daily. (SkyBahamas has a connecting flight from Fort Lauderdale to Nassau in the early morning four days a week, providing convenient connections from Florida.) To reach these Southern Islands from Nassau, Stella Maris Air Service has a great reputation and, from Fort Lauderdale or Miami, you can arrange a charter through Eastern Air Express, Monarch Air Group, or Triton Airways to fly you direct, avoiding Nassau. For the best price, call around for a plane with the right number of seats. If you are going to Fernandez Bay Village or Hawk's Nest Resort, fly into the Bight. If you are going to Pigeon Cay, Orange Creek Inn, Shanna's Cove, or Tailwinds, fly to Arthur's Town. For a full list of scheduled and charter airlines see ⊕ www.bahamas.com/islands/cat/getting-here. For contact information of individual airlines, see also Air Travel in Travel Smart.

AIRPORT CONTACTS New Bight Airport. ☎ 242/342–2016.

BOAT
Mail boats that bring supplies to the island each week make for an adventurous way to get around. You'll ride with groceries, large and small appliances, automobiles, and sometimes even livestock. All boats depart from Potter's Cay in Nassau. The M/V New G and the M/V KCT sails to north and south Cat Island. Contact the Dockmaster's Office for schedules and fares as they change frequently.

Great Itineraries

Note: If you don't have a boat, island-hopping is difficult in these parts, because to fly between these islands you either have to transfer back to Nassau or charter your own plane. Most visitors choose one island as a base, but if you have 10 days or more you can easily spend time on two islands.

If You Have 5 Days

Fly into **The Bight** on Cat Island, check into **Rollezz Villas Beach Resort** or another inn and catch what's left of the day on the gorgeous Old Bight beach, enjoying the shaded cabanas and paddleboards made available to guests. Dine in at the open-air restaurant on the property. On Day 2 jump in your rent-a-car and head north to explore Cat Island and visit **Arthur's Town.** Go on a prearranged afternoon **snorkel or dive excursion** at **Shannas Cove,** staying to enjoy their beach. From the clubhouse's high balcony, enjoy the views at dusk with a Goombay Smash and their excellent cuisine. Stop off at **The Hot Spot** for a Bahama Mama nightcap on your way home. Book Day 3 with a morning fishing charter at **Hawk's Nest Resort & Marina** to catch some game fish off the ocean wall. Drive back, touring **Old Bight** with its ancient plantation ruins and **New Bight** for some souvenir shopping. Then climb the Bahamas' highest "mountain," the 206 foot **Mt. Alvernia,** to see the **Hermitage,** the ruins of a famous little abbey. Enjoy the evening at the Fish Fry on **New Bight Beach** with some island music, fresh conch, fish or lobster, washed down with sky juice. Day 4 is for relaxing around Rollezz Villas and getting to know the local owners and managers, who live on-site. Walk the white-sand beach, sink in the soft powder, snorkel or paddle a kayak into the shallows to the south where you can turtle spot in the mangrove creeks. Day 5, take an early morning flight.

If You Have 10 Days

Day 6. Arrive at **Stella Maris Airport** and check in to the famed resort there. Head down to the **Moonshine Bar & Grill** on the ocean, capture views from the boardwalk, and take a dip in the man-made, wave-washed ocean hole. Enjoy dinner at the resort. On Day 7, book a morning **snorkel or dive** at the resort's dive shop, with fabulous reef, wreck, shark, night, and wall dives. In the afternoon, join the resort's excursion to a beach on the western side for some **snorkeling or kayaking.** Arrange for dinner at **Chez Pierre's** in Miller's Bay, a small inn celebrated for its cuisine. Day 8, pack an ice chest, bring your swimsuits, and hire a car. Make it your goal to see and swim at **Dean's Blue Hole,** a stunning ocean hole surrounded by cliffs and a beach and the location of the world's free-diving championships. First, head south to Dean's. Then if you have time, head farther south to see **Galloway's Landing Beach.** Heading back, enjoy lunch at **Flying Fish Marina's Outer Edge Grill,** see Hamilton's Cave near Deadman's Cay, and stop at **Max's Conch Bar & Grill.** On Day 9, book a **Bonafide Bonefishing** tour for the morning, then take Stella Maris's excursion to **Cape Eleuthera** to enjoy the stunning beach. (If you have a four-wheel drive, you can even negotiate the rocky road to **Columbus Monument** and see some breathtaking hilltop views.) At Cape Eleuthera, enjoy gorgeous sunsets, cocktails, and a delightful dinner. Day 10, shop for souvenirs at a resort's boutique and go for a final swim in the pool.

Mailboat Port/Dockmaster's Office in Nassau. ✉ *Potter's Cay, Nassau* ☎ *242/393–1064 Dockmaster's office, 242/394–1237.*

CAR

The New Bight Service Station and Gilbert's New Bight Market rent cars on the southern end of Cat Island and will pick you up from the New Bight Airport. Robon Enterprises rents cars for the north (for those flying into Arthur's Town). It's important to rent a car from an agency that services the end of the island where you are staying because companies will not deliver cars to renters at the opposite end of the island. However, all inns and resorts can arrange rental cars for you upon arrival, and many people arrange their cars through their lodging. Rates depend on the number of days you're renting but are expensive, averaging $85 per day plus gas (which is also very expensive).

The best way to enjoy the overall Cat Island experience is to rent a car. Various settlements are not within walking distance. The two-lane, potholed Queen's Highway runs the 48-mile length of the island from north to south. You can also tour the island with a guide from Cat Island Experience.

CAR RENTAL CONTACTS Alvernia Food's & Car Rental. ✉ *Smith's Bay* ☎ *242/342–2042* ⊕ *alvernia-foods-car-rental.business. site.* **Gilbert's Car Rentals and Market.** ✉ *Across from Gilbert's Inn, New Bight* ☎ *242/342–3011.* **New Bight Car Rentals.** ☎ *242/342–3014.* **Robon Enterprises Car Rental.** ✉ *In Bennett's Harbour, near Arthur's Town Airport, Arthur's Town* ☎ *242/354–6120, 242/359–9643.*

TAXI

Taxis wait for incoming flights at the New Bight and Arthur's Town airports, but be warned that fares can be expensive, starting at about $20 for the 10-minute trip from the New Bight Airport to the community of New Bight. Most inns and resorts will make arrangements for airport transfers, often complimentary.

Arthur's Town and Bennett's Harbour

Arthur's Town's claim to fame is that it was the boyhood home of actor Sidney Poitier, who wrote about growing up here in his autobiography. His parents and relatives were farmers. The presence of Young Marine Explorers, a local marine conservation nonprofit, has mobilized the local community around many environmental conservation initiatives, including coral reef restoration projects.

When you drive south from Arthur's Town, which is nearly at the island's northernmost tip, you'll wind along a road that passes through small villages and past bays where fishing boats are tied up. Fifteen miles south of Arthur's Town is Bennett's Harbour, one of the island's oldest settlements. Fresh-baked breads and fruit are sometimes sold at makeshift stands at the government dock, and there is good bonefishing in the creek.

🍴 Restaurants

★ **Shannas Cove Restaurant**
$$$$ | EUROPEAN | This resort restaurant boasts a beautiful towering view above the sea and the north point of the island and offers three meals a day on the breezy veranda or in the cool interior. Owners Frank and Gabi, and chef Simon, take their European cuisine seriously and they please and surprise hotel guests and those from other resorts who drive far to dine here. **Known for:** homemade breads; extensive menu; reservations necessary. $ *Average main: $48* ✉ *Shanna's Cove, north of Orange Creek, Bennett's Harbour* ☎ *242/354–4249* ⊕ *www. shannas-cove.com* ▤ *No credit cards* ☺ *Closed Sept.*

Yardie's Restaurant, Bar & Conch Stand
$ | **JAMAICAN** | Yardie's owners, Odette and Derrick Rolle, serve up large-size genuine Jamaican and Bahamian dishes such as jerk chicken, steamed pork chops, curried mutton, barbecue ribs, and their famous fresh conch salad. If you really want an island meal, try the breakfast grits with tuna or corned beef. [$] *Average main: $15* ✉ *North Cat Island, Bennett's Harbour* ☎ *242/354–6076* 💳 *No credit cards.*

Hotels

Pigeon Cay Beach Club
$ | **RESORT** | In a wide bay a half mile off the main road just south of Alligator Point, this family-owned-and-operated resort has seven deluxe cottages and a "big house" with several rooms that are colorfully decorated and perched steps away from a secluded 3-mile stretch of pristine sugary white beach. **Pros:** fully equipped kitchens in rooms; bicycles, kayaks, and snorkel gear available; cars available for a small fee. **Cons:** no TV; surcharge for airport transfers; meals are served only a few times a week. [$] *Rooms from: $180* ✉ *Rokers* ✣ *3 miles south of Bennett's Harbour* ☎ *242/354–5084* 🌐 *www.pigeoncaybahamas.com* 🛏 *11 rooms, some in big house or cottages* 🍴 *No meals.*

Shannas Cove Resort
$$ | **RESORT** | This quiet and secluded owner-run beach resort is perched high on the hill on the northern tip of Cat Island, granting sweeping views of the beautiful beach at Shanna's Cove and the north of the island. **Pros:** stunning private beach; excellent on-site restaurant; nicely designed, roomy cottages with air-conditioning. **Cons:** no TVs; isolated from the rest of the island; no children under 18. [$] *Rooms from: $220* ✉ *North of Orange Creek, Arthur's Town* ☎ *242/354–4249* 🌐 *www.shannas-cove.com* 🕒 *Closed Sept.* 🛏 *5 villas* 🍴 *No meals.*

Nightlife

The Hot Spot Restaurant & Karaoke Bar
BARS/PUBS | Owners Ted and Melony (the latter is also the fabulous cook here) entertain locals and visitors with great indigenous food and karaoke. Noted for the Bahamian touches, like coconut sky juice, the 46-ounce Como Hill cocktail, and other drinks served in pea cans. Some claim Melony's food, served on palms and sea grape leaves, is the best they've had. Spurred on by tuneful locals and visitors pumping out a great selection of music, this place can rock until 3 am. If the music's too loud you can dine and drink on the deck. This is the north's best nightlife spot. ✉ *North Cat Island, Arthur's Town* ☎ *242/464–6505* 🎟 *Free.*

Activities

SCUBA DIVING

Coral Reefs teeming with fish and mysterious shipwrecks make great diving off the north end of the island, where visibility ranges from 165 to 200 feet thanks to a natural filtering system of limestone and rich fauna.

Diving with Shannas Cove Resort
SCUBA DIVING | This is not a certified dive shop, but Frank, one of the owners of Shannas Cove, is a master diver and takes only up to four divers at a time—making it very safe for beginners and pros alike. Shannas offers north Cat Island's amazing range of dives: from wrecks to walls, and reefs with amazing visibility, all from the 22-foot catamaran. Diving spots can be reached within 5 to 30 minutes. Well-maintained equipment is available for rent. ✉ *Shannas Cove Resort, North of Orange Creek, Arthur's Town* ☎ *242/354–4249, 242/359–9668 cell* 🌐 *www.shannas-cove.com* 🕒 *Closed Sept.*

Old Bight and New Bight

In this small residential village, just over 8 miles south of the New Bight Airport, beaches, historic ruins, and gas stations are what necessitate at least one stop from visitors. Five miles of undisturbed pink speckled beach can be found on the southwestern coast of Cat Island. Although there is access to basic amenities on **Old Bight Beach** at the boutique **Rollezz Villas Beach Resort,** the light touch development from the southern end of **Joe Sound Creek** across the crescent-shaped beach ensures absolute solitude for most beachgoers. Top up at **Favor's Service Center** (☎ 242/342–4107), a gas station, car rental, beauty salon, and plant nursery, or **Pilot Harbour Service Station**.

Yachts anchor off the coast of Regatta Beach, and boaters dingy in to the Custom House amid a cluster of government buildings in this quaint community, the largest town on the island. Houses face the Queen's Highway, which twists through green hills. Yachties and visitors stock up at the small grocery store and a bakery. The island's most iconic sight is **Mt. Alvernia,** which is crowned with a historic little abbey. There's also a colorful **Fish Fry,** a collection of fish shacks on Regatta Beach that's a lively hangout at nights and on weekends, lovely old churches, and eerie abandoned stone cottages, many of which are plantation ruins. The town sits along a thin, Australian pine-lined white beach on the west coast, and has peaceful saltwater estuaries that are nesting areas for great blue herons, egrets, and pelicans.

◉ Sights

★ The Hermitage

MOUNTAIN—SIGHT | At the top of 206-foot Mt. Alvernia, the highest point in the Bahamas, the Hermitage is the final resting place of Father Jerome, an architect who traveled the world and eventually settled in the Bahamas. An Anglican who converted to Roman Catholicism, he built many structures including this hermitage on Mt. Alvernia, churches in Long Island, and a monastery in Nassau. He retired to Cat Island to live out his last dozen years as a hermit, and his final act of religious dedication was carving steps to the top of Mt. Alvernia. Along the way he also carved the Stations of the Cross. At the summit, he built an abbey with a small chapel, a conical bell tower, and living quarters comprising three closet-size rooms. He died in 1956 at the age of 80.

The pilgrimage to the Hermitage begins next to the commissioner's office at New Bight at a dirt path that leads to the foot of Mt. Alvernia. A caretaker clears the weeds around the tomb—islanders regard it as a shrine—and lights a candle in Father Jerome's memory. ⊠ *New Bight.*

⊕ Beaches

Fernandez Bay Beach

BEACH—SIGHT | Imagine the perfect calm cove in the tropics—a 1-mile stretch of glistening, pristine white sand, inviting shade under coconut palms and sea grape trees, quaint resort cottages and verandas facing the spectacular sand, and calm azure water. Fernandez Bay Village has an elevated restaurant and bar overlooking the water. Kayaks and paddleboards are available to guests. The beach is uncrowded and known for its calm waters and offshore snorkeling. **Amenities:** food and drink; water sports. **Best for:** solitude; snorkeling; sunset; swimming; walking. ⊠ *Just north of New Bight Airport near an off-road beach community* ☎ 242/824–3043.

Ocean Beach

BEACH—SIGHT | On the eastern Atlantic side, 4 miles from Queen's Highway at Smith's Bay is Ocean Beach, 1.8 miles of pink sand and cool breezes. This is a stunning beach that sits below a towering sand dune. There's no shade here and you should bring whatever water-sports equipment you want. When conditions are right it's good for surfing and, when calm, paddleboarding, kayaking, and snorkeling on the nearby reefs. Bring water and snacks. Only reasonably accessed with a four-wheel-drive vehicle due to the rugged off road that leads to this beach. **Amenities:** none. **Best for:** snorkeling. ⊠ *4 miles east of Smith's Bay.*

Old Bight Beach
BEACH—SIGHT | Fall asleep on this beach and be completely undisturbed. Walk the five-mile stretch and find only your footprints. The peace and solitude you find at Old Bight Beach is due to the light-touch development along this southwestern part of Cat Island's coast. If you need access to the basic comforts, a small boutique resort is seamlessly blended into the natural surroundings on the southern end of the beach. **Amenities:** food and drink; nonmotorized water sports. **Best for:** solitude; sunset; swimming; walking. ⊠ *Just south of New Bight Airport near Favor's Service Centre, Old Bight Beach* ☎ *242/557–0005.*

🍴 Restaurants

Bridge Inn Restaurant
$$ | BAHAMIAN | Owned by the large, gregarious Russell family, who have passed on the family's culinary traditions from generation to generation, you will find locals at this lunch spot enjoying delicious Cat Island specialties, including grits and crab cakes, cracked conch, pan-seared whole snapper, barbecued ribs, conch salad, conch chowder, and lobster with peas 'n' rice. Everything is made by a member of the Russell family. **Known for:** ask for chef's suggestions; call ahead to place order; family run. $ *Average main: $20* ⊠ *1 block off Queen's Hwy., look for the sign* ☎ *242/342–3013.*

🛏 Hotels

★ Fernandez Bay Village
$$ | RESORT | This owner-run resort is one of the Bahamas' most famous and successful, and one of the best kick-back retreats anywhere. **Pros:** private spacious accommodations; crescent-shape white-sand beach in shade; lots of water sports there and activities off-site. **Cons:** no TV; Wi-Fi in the main clubhouse only; insect repellent needed outside in the evening. $ *Rooms from: $283* ⊠ *1 mile north of New Bight Airport* ☎ *242/824–3043, 954/302–7422 toll-free* ⊕ *www.fernandezbayvillage.com* ⤴ *17 rooms* ⦿ *No meals.*

★ Rollezz Villas Beach Resort
$$ | HOTEL | FAMILY | This family-run boutique hotel is jam-packed with island charm thanks to the creativity and talent of the owners who handmade the decor and furniture with local fabrics, native straw plait, and other natural material. **Pros:** secluded beachfront villas; 12-mile stretch of stunning beach; kayaks, paddleboard, pedal boat. **Cons:** insect repellent needed outside in the evening; limited supplies in hotel boutique; limited entertainment. $ *Rooms from: $259* ⊠ *Joe Sound Creek* ☎ *242/557–0005, 305/280–5719* ⊕ *rollezz.com* ⤴ *8 rooms* ⦿ *No meals.*

🍸 Nightlife

Regatta Beach Fish Fry
GATHERING PLACES | For an authentic Bahamian experience, don't miss the Regatta Beach Fish Fry on Regatta Beach, just south of the government buildings in the town center. On weekends, at least two fish shacks open late in the afternoon and stay lively on into the night. It's a great place for sunset watching and mingling with locals. ⊠ *Regatta Beach.*

Cat Island

Man-O-War Point
Grape Point
Flamingo Point

Orange Creek
Arthur's Town
Northeast Point
Bonamy Town
Dumfries

Willson Bay

Bennett's Harbour

Alligator Point
The Bluff

Stevenson

Hearts Bay Hill

Atlantic Ocean

Exuma Sound

Queen's HWY

Ocean Beach

Smith Town

Fernandez Bay Beach

Sandy Point

New Bight
The Bight
Mt. Alvernia
The Hermitage

Pigeon Bay

Old Bight
Old Bight Beach
Gambier Lake
Greenwood Beach

McQueens

Hawks Nest Point

Baintown
Port Howe

Hawk's Nest Airstrip
Cutlass Bay
Columbus Point

Castle Point
The Cave
Vlady's Reef

Devil's Point

Key
Beaches
Dive Sites
Water Depths
-25ft deep
-50ft deep
-100ft deep

0   10 mi
0   10 km

TO TARTAR BANK

The Hermitage on Mt. Alvernia is Cat Island's most iconic sight.

Shopping

Pam's Boutique

CLOTHING | This little shop at Fernandez Bay Village has reasonably priced resort wear including sarongs, Havaiana flip-flops, logo hats, and T-shirts. They also sell jewelry, bags, coffee cups, postcards, local art, and books. This is one of your few chances to get a Cat Island T-shirt. ⊠ *Fernandez Bay Village* ☎ *242/824–3043, 954/302–7422.*

Activities

FISHING

Cat Island Fishing

FISHING | On Cat Island you have myriad ways to fish: deep-sea, bone-, fly-, and bottom-fishing. Several expert guides can do all but each has his own specialty. Mark Keasler is great for bonefishing, Nathaniel Top Cat is great for deep-sea trolling, and Carl Pinder is great for reef fishing. Call Rollezz Villas, Fernandez Bay or the local tourist office to let them find out who is available for which type of fishing. They also do snorkeling tours and beach picnics. ⊠ *New Bight* ☎ *242/338–8668.*

TOURS

The Cat Island Experience

GUIDED TOURS | C&O Tours, comprising Pastor Chris, son Danny, and wife Olive King, have eight-seater air-conditioned vans for guided tours of Cat Island. They have customizable tours, both for the north and the south, which include much of the same sites. The tour in the south includes beaches, Mt. Alvernia, the minimonastery on the Bahamas' highest point at 206 feet, a step-down well, bat caves, cotton plantations and ruins, the old cotton railroad, an old lighthouse, churches, and also the modern structures and utilities. Chris and family can answer your many questions and give good, historical background. It's one of the most rewarding activities, giving you a lasting connection to the island. ⊠ *New Bight* ☎ *242/464–6181 Chris King Owner, 242/474–8462 Danson King Manager* 🖃 *$200 for half day, $350 for full day.*

Port Howe

At the conch shell–lined traffic roundabout at the southernmost end of the Queen's Highway, head east out toward Port Howe, believed by many to be Cat Island's oldest settlement. Nearby lie the ruins of the **Deveaux Mansion,** a stark two-story, whitewashed building overrun with vegetation. Once it was a grand house on a cotton plantation, owned by Captain Andrew Deveaux of the British Navy, who was given thousands of acres of Cat Island property as a reward for his daring raid that recaptured Nassau from the Spaniards in 1783. Just beyond the mansion ruin is the entrance road to the Greenwood Beach Resort, which sits on an 8-mile stretch of unblemished, velvet pink-sand beach, but its fate as an operational hotel was up in the air at the time of this writing.

Beaches

Greenwood Beach

BEACH—SIGHT | An 8-mile stretch of pink sand on the Atlantic Ocean makes this one of the most spectacular beaches on Cat Island. Hypnotized by the beauty, most visitors walk the entire beach, some even farther to an adjoining sandy cove accessible only by foot. After such a long walk, a dip in the shallows of the turquoise ocean is pure bliss. The beach is on the remote southeastern end of the island and is home to just one hotel, Greenwood Beach Resort, which is a good place for a bite and a drink. **Amenities:** none. **Best for:** solitude; snorkeling; swimming; walking. ✉ *Greenwood Beach Resort, 3 miles northeast of Port Howe along a bumpy road* 🌐 *www.greenwoodbeachresort.com.*

Devil's Point

The small village of Devil's Point, with its bright-walled, thatch-roof houses, lies at the southern tip of the Queen's Highway 9 miles southwest of Old Bight. Beachcombers will find great shelling on the pristine beach; keep an eye out for dolphins, which are common in these waters. From Devil's Point, drive north through the arid southwest corner of the island to **McQueens,** then west to the area's biggest resort, Hawk's Nest Resort, which has an airstrip, marina, restaurant, and bar. This resort is well-known to serious anglers and divers, who often fly in to the resort's private airstrip and stay a week to do little else but fish or dive. The southwest end of the island teems with great diving walls, reefs, and wrecks with an abundance of marine life and coral heads.

Restaurants

Hawk's Nest Dining & Clubhouse

$$ | **BAHAMIAN** | High-beamed ceilings, tiled floors, blue-and-lime-green walls, and blue ceramic-topped tables create a cheerful vibe to go with the Bahamian comfort-food menu. If you have your heart set on a menu item, be sure to call your order in by 3 pm. **Known for:** fresh-squeezed juices; poolside dining; TVs showing sports and news. [$] *Average main: $30* ✉ *Hawk's Nest Resort* ✢ *7½ miles by road northwest of Devil's Point* ☎ *242/342–7050, 954/376–3865* 🌐 *www.hawks-nest.com* 🕒 *Closed mid-Sept.–Oct.*

Hotels

Hawk's Nest Resort and Marina

$ | **RESORT** | Catering to private pilots, yachters, and serious fishermen, this small laid-back resort at Cat Island's southwestern tip has its own 3,100-foot runway and a 28-slip full-service marina with a dive shop for guests. **Pros:** three

Fernandez Bay Beach is a perfect, calm cove for swimming.

meals served a day; fully stocked honor bar; PADI certified with great dive spots and shallow walls. **Cons:** long drive from other places on the island; good swimming beach a few yards from main clubhouse; afternoon shark feed can interrupt swimming at the dock. $ Rooms from: $175 ✉ Devil's Point ✈ From Devil's Point village, go 4 miles north and 3½ miles west along white road ☎ 242/342–7050 resort, 954/376–3865 in U.S. and Canada ⊕ www.hawks-nest.com ☉ Clubhouse and hotel closed Sept. and Oct. ⇥ 10 rooms ℟ No meals.

🏃 Activities

FISHING

Hawk's Nest Marina

FISHING | Blue-water angling boat owners make a point of using Hawk's Nest Marina to access the dynamite offshore fishing. Look for wahoo, yellowfin tuna, dolphin, and white and blue marlin along the Exuma Sound drop-offs, Devil's Point, Tartar Bank, and Columbus Point. March through July is prime time, with multiple annual fishing tournaments on the books. Winter fishing from December through February is also good for wahoo. You can arrange bonefishing through the marina with a top guide. ✉ Hawks Nest Resort and Marina ☎ 242/342–7050, 954/376–3865 ⊕ www.hawks-nest.com.

SCUBA DIVING

Cat Island's south coast offers some of the country's best diving. The walls start from very shallow depths, allowing long dive times and great photography. Some of the area's best dive sites, which are most easily reached from Hawk's Nest Marina, are: **Hole in The Wall** (12 miles, 50–100 feet); spectacular break in the wall and entrance to a small channel with lobster or spotted drums; impressive archway, black coral, stingray, sharks, dog snapper, barracudas, and groupers; all kinds of soft and hard coral. **The Oz** (7 miles, 55–100 feet): tunnels and canyons overgrown with soft corals, turtles, reef sharks, reef fish of any color, hogfish, Nassau and other grouper, and oceanic triggerfish. Spectacular when leading to the wall. **Tartar Bank** (6 miles, 40–60 feet): has strong currents, for pro divers only; offshore pinnacle, reef sharks, white-tip sharks, big turtles, and more. **Fish Bowls** (20–30 feet): from micro to macro, a photographer's paradise includes schools of goat fish, Atlantic spadefish, yellowtail, and mutton snapper. White-spotted eels are numerous, along with nurse sharks and lobster. See a spider crab refuge and cleaning station as you follow the reef's ledge. Dives at Hawk's Nest must be booked a month in advance.

Hawk's Nest Marina Dive Shop

SCUBA DIVING | Hawk's Nest at one time was the only PADI-certified dive operation on Cat Island. Today, certified diver Randy Holder conducts guided diving adventures (for guests only), rents diving and snorkeling gear, and has equipment and sundries for sale. The running time to dive sites off the southern tip of the island is 15 to 30 minutes in the shop's 43-foot custom dive boat, outfitted with VHF and GPS. Call ahead for bookings. Dives must be booked one month in advance; $250 minimum to take the dive boat out. Ask for package rates. ⊠ *Devil's Point* ✛ *From Devil's Point, go 4 miles north and 3½ miles along white road* ☎ *242/342–7050, 954/376–3865* ⊕ *www. hawks-nest.com.*

San Salvador

On October 12, 1492, Christopher Columbus disrupted the lives of the peaceful Lucayan Indians when he landed on the island of Guanahani, which he renamed San Salvador. Apparently he knelt on the beach and claimed the land for Spain. (Skeptics of this story point to a study published in a 1986 *National Geographic* article in which Samana Cay, 60 miles southeast, is identified as the exact point of the weary explorer's landing.) Three monuments on the island commemorate Columbus's arrival, and the 500th anniversary of the event was officially celebrated here.

The island is 14 miles long—a little longer than Manhattan Island—and about 6 miles wide, with a lake-filled interior. Some of the most dazzling deserted beaches in the country are here. Most visitors come for Club Med's unique blend of fun and activities; others for the peaceful isolation and the diving. There are more than 50 dive sites and world-renowned offshore fishing and good bonefishing. The friendly locals have a lot to be proud of for their special island and their warmth shows it.

GETTING HERE AND AROUND

AIR

The island has one airport, in Cockburn Town (ZSA), which is modern, comfortable, and has a long runway. A new fuel depot and FBO by Odyssey Aviation means even more long-haul flights will commence and private aircraft can easily refuel here. Air Caraïbes, the French airline, flies from Paris on Thursday, Air Canada from Montreal on Tuesday, and American Eagle once a week from Miami. From Nassau, Bahamasair has daily flights. A host of charter companies fly in from Florida and Nassau. Club Med's website has packages that include air charters, and Riding Rock Resort and Marina can arrange them as well.

CONTACTS San Salvador Cockburn Town Airport. ☎ *242/331–2131.*

BOAT

Mail boats that bring supplies to the island each week make an adventurous mode of transportation. M/V *New G* and M/V *Lady Francis* sails from Nassau on Tuesday at 1 pm with stops in Deadman's Cay, Long Island, and Rum Cay and arrives the next morning. You'll ride with groceries, large and small appliances, automobiles, and sometimes even livestock. All boats depart from Potter's Cay in Nassau. Schedules change frequently

San Salvador has several popular diving sites.

so best to call the Dockmaster's Office in Nassau to get the latest information.

CONTACTS Mailboat Port/Dockmaster's Office in Nassau. ⊠ *Potter's Cay, Nassau* ☎ *242/393–1064 Dockmaster's office, 242/394–1237.* **M/V Lady Francis Mailboat Contact.** ⊠ *Potter's Cay, Nassau* ☎ *242/467–2156.* **M/V New G Mailboat Contact.** ⊠ *Potter's Cay, Nassau* ☎ *242/341–3466.*

BIKE

For a short visit to Columbus Cross or the lighthouse, a bike is a sufficient mode of transportation. Bike rentals are available at Club Med and Riding Rock Resort.

CAR

If you want to see the entire island, rent a car. Queen's Highway forms an oval that skirts the island's coastline, and road conditions are excellent. Car rentals are about $85 a day.

CONTACTS D&W Car Rental. ☎ *242/331–2484, 242/331–2488, 242/331–2184.*

SCOOTER

Scooters are a fun, breezy, and convenient way to get around the entire island.

CONTACTS K's Scooter Rentals. ⊠ *Cockburn Town Airport* ☎ *242/331–2125, 242/331–2651, 242/452–0594.*

TAXI

Club Med meets all guests at the airport. Riding Rock, five minutes away, provides complimentary transportation for guests. If you want to take your own taxi, it's approximately $10 to either resort.

CONTACTS Clifford "Snake Eyes" Fernander. ☎ *242/331–2676, 242/427–8198 cell.*

Fernandez Bay to Riding Rock Point

In 1492 the inspiring sight that greeted Christopher Columbus by moonlight at 2 am was a terrain of gleaming beaches and far-reaching forest. The peripatetic traveler and his crews steered the *Niña*, *Pinta*, and *Santa María* warily among the

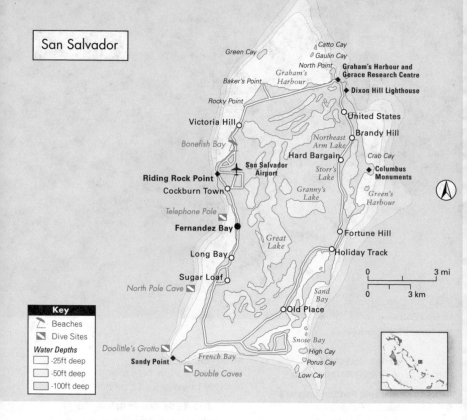

San Salvador

Catto Cay
Green Cay
Gaulin Cay
North Point
Graham's Harbour and
Gerace Research Centre
Baker's Point
Graham's
Harbour
◆ Dixon Hill Lighthouse
Rocky Point
◊ United States
Victoria Hill ◊
◊ Brandy Hill
Bonefish Bay
Northeast
Arm Lake
Hard Bargain ◊
Crab Cay
◆ Columbus
Monuments
San Salvador
Airport
Storr's
Lake
Riding Rock Point ◆
Cockburn Town ◊
Granny's
Lake
Green's
Harbour
Telephone Pole
Fernandez Bay ●
Great
Lake
◊ Fortune Hill
Long Bay ◊
◊ Holiday Track
Sugar Loaf ◊
North Pole Cave
Sand
Bay
0   3 mi
0   3 km
◊ Old Place
Snow Bay
Doolittle's Grotto
French Bay
Sandy Point ◆
High Cay
Porus Cay
Low Cay
Double Caves

Key
Beaches
Dive Sites
Water Depths
-25ft deep
-50ft deep
-100ft deep

coral reefs and anchored, so it is recorded, in **Fernandez Bay.** A cross erected in 1956 by Columbus scholar Ruth C. Durlacher Wolper Malvin stands at his approximate landing spot. An underwater monument marks the place where the *Santa María* anchored. Nearby, another monument commemorates the Olympic flame's passage on its journey from Greece to Mexico City in 1968.

Fernandez Bay is just south of what is now the main community of **Cockburn Town,** midisland on the western shore. This is where the airport is, and where the weekly mail boat docks. This small village's narrow streets contain two churches, a commissioner's office, a police station, a courthouse, a library, a clinic, a drugstore, and a telephone station.

From Cockburn Town to Club Med, you'll pass **Riding Rock Point.** All fish excursions leave from the marina. Riding Rock Resort makes a good spot to stop for a drink, meet locals and divers, and buy a local T-shirt.

🏖 Beaches

★ Bonefish Bay
BEACH—SIGHT | The 3-mile beach in front of Club Med has bright white sand as fine as talcum powder, and water that is such a bright neon shade of turquoise, it appears to be glowing. There are activities such as waterskiing, snorkeling, sailing, kayaking, and paddleboarding in front of Club Med, but the beach is long enough that you'll be able to find an isolated spot. To join in all the fun activities and partying, buy a day pass at the front desk. **Amenities:** food and drink; showers;

toilets; water sports. **Best for:** partiers; snorkeling; swimming; windsurfing. ✉ *Club Med—Columbus Isle, Cockburn Town.*

🍴 Restaurants

Christopher's at Club Med
$$$$ | **ECLECTIC** | Christopher's open-air restaurant has buffets during breakfast, lunch, and dinner, with the latter changing themes nightly: Caribbean Night has local fare such as conch and fresh fish, and other themes include French, Mexican, and Mediterranean. Carving stations and European pastries and breads are impossible to skip, and simple pastas and pizzas are mainstays for the finicky eater. **Known for:** themed dinner buffets; dinner pass includes open bar; nightly entertainment. [$] *Average main: $64* ✉ *Club Med—Columbus Isle, Cockburn Town* ✥ *3 miles north of Riding Rock Point* ☎ *242/331–2000, 855/261–2290* 🌐 *www.clubmed.com.*

★ **Guanahani Beach Club Restaurant**
$$$$ | **ITALIAN** | At this resort restaurant, fresh fruit smoothies, panini on crusty French bread, fresh salads, and various authentic four-course Italian dinners are all made to order by owner-chef Elena Sparta. Try the mille-feuille of smoked salmon and tomatoes; fettuccine with crab; shrimp with lime, basil, and herbs; lemon and rosemary risotto; or duck breast in Cointreau and orange sauce. **Known for:** nonguests should call ahead; outdoor patio over Snow Bay; cozy interior lounge. [$] *Average main: $70* ✉ *Snow Bay, Sunrise Rd., Cockburn Town* ☎ *242/452–0438* 🌐 *www.guanahanibeachclub.com* 💳 *No credit cards* ⏲ *Often closed June–Oct.*

Paradis Restaurant and Bar
$ | **BAHAMIAN** | A typical Bahamian enclosed restaurant, Paradis has a daily changing menu written on a chalkboard. Home-cooked Bahamian and American food such as burgers, conch, ribs, and the fresh catch of the day are tastily prepared. **Known for:** popular with locals; free Wi-Fi; fresh seafood. [$] *Average main: $15* ✉ *Cockburn Town* ✥ *Just north of airport near Club Med* ☎ *242/331–2400.*

Riding Rock Seafront Restaurant
$$$$ | **CARIBBEAN** | This 100-seat restaurant offers seating indoors, by the pool, and on the back patio overlooking the ocean. During slower seasons or depending on resort guests, the restaurant is not always open, and each meal is set between certain hours—make sure to call ahead. **Known for:** tasty conch chowder; fresh catches grilled with lemon and butter; fresh-baked bread at breakfast. [$] *Average main: $45* ✉ *Riding Rock Resort and Marina, Cockburn Town* ☎ *242/331–2631, 800/272–1492,* 🌐 *www.ridingrock.com* ⏲ *Sometimes closed during slow season.*

🛏 Hotels

Club Med–Columbus Isle
$$$$ | **RESORT** | **FAMILY** | This 89-acre oceanfront village is one of Club Med's most luxurious resorts, with state-of-the-art dive facilities and every water sport and activity imaginable. **Pros:** gorgeous beachfront location; revolving dinner themes; full-service dive shop. **Cons:** no children under age two; long walk to outlying rooms; fee for in-room Wi-Fi. [$] *Rooms from: $1299* ✉ *Cockburn Town* ✥ *½ mile by road from airport terminal* ☎ *888/932–2582, 242/331–2000* 🌐 *www.clubmed.com* 🛏 *256 rooms in 2-story bungalows* 🍴 *All-inclusive.*

★ **Guanahani Beach Club**
$$$ | **RESORT** | This cozy, small, owner-operated resort is elegant and sophisticated, offering both quiet solitude on a stunning private beach and serious adventure for sports enthusiasts. **Pros:** excellent on-site restaurant; simple and chic villas; private beach adorned with loungers and hammocks. **Cons:** no children under 16; credit cards not accepted;

Isolated French Bay is on the southern end of San Salvador.

far from other island amenities so you will probably want a rental car. [$] *Rooms from: $365* ✉ *Snow Bay, Sunrise Rd., Cockburn Town* ☎ *242/452–0438* 🌐 *www.guanahanibeachclub.com* ⏲ *Closed mid-June–late Oct.* 🛏 *3 villas* 🍴 *Some meals.*

Riding Rock Resort and Marina

$ | **HOTEL** | Good for serious divers, this modest motel-style resort is a long-standing property on San Salvador and has a restaurant on-site serving breakfast, lunch, and dinner when enough guests warrant. **Pros:** budget-friendly alternative to other resorts; friendly, accommodating staff; rooms are standard but clean. **Cons:** limited entertainment based on occupancy; diving is not daily and dependent on resort guests; rocky beachfront. [$] *Rooms from: $190* ✉ *Cockburn Town* ✥ *½ mile southwest of airport terminal* ☎ *800/272–1492, 242/331–2631* 🌐 *www.ridingrock.com* 🛏 *24 rooms* 🍴 *No meals.*

The Sands Residence Hotel

$ | **HOTEL** | **FAMILY** | The Sands Residence Hotel is a beachfront property with unobstructed views of San Salvador's endless ocean horizon. **Pros:** directly on the beach; spacious rooms; en suite kitchens; free snorkeling. **Cons:** limited entertainment. [$] *Rooms from: 130* ✉ *Queen's Hwy., Cockburn Town* ☎ *242/331–2254 front desk, 242/452–8014 cell* 🌐 *www.sandshotelsansalvadorbahamas.com* 🛏 *20 cottages and rooms.*

🍸 Nightlife

Club Med–Columbus Isle

DANCE CLUBS | Evening passes to Club Med cost $90 and include themed dinners, nightly entertainment, and all you can drink from 7 pm to 1 am. The predinner cocktail parties and beachside tiki hut parties are lively affairs with skilled DJs and rapid-fire, charming bartenders. This place is big enough to slink away to a romantic spot on your own. Entertainment gets going after dinner with staff shows in the open-air theater. ✉ *Club Med, Cockburn Town* ☎ *888/932–2582, 242/331–2000.*

🛍 Shopping

Club Med – Columbus Isle

CLOTHING | Club Med has a boutique that's clearly the best souvenir, swimsuit, and resort-wear shop on the island. It's an independent French franchise chain that has excellent shopping. Browse 45 Club (Club Med's logo brand), Hip Way, Fila, Carrera, Le Mar, gorgeous Colombian swimwear, Havaiana flip-flops, sunglasses, hats, and souvenirs. Great gifts to return home with are the Bahamian-made John Waltlings Fine Rums and Red Turtle Vodka. ⊠ *Club Med, Cockburn Town* ☎ *242/331–2000.*

Simply Bahamian

JEWELRY/ACCESSORIES | A small local crafts and liquor store across the street from the airport sells locally made purses and sarongs featuring Andros batik. ⊠ *Cockburn Town.*

🏃 Activities

SCUBA DIVING

San Salvador is famous for its vibrant wall dives and abundant marine life, including hammerhead sharks, sea turtles, Eagle rays, and more. The **Telephone Pole** is a stimulating wall dive where you can watch stingrays, grouper, snapper, and turtles in action.

Riding Rock Resort & Marina

SCUBA DIVING | The dive operation here (both SSI and PADI recognized) uses mostly buoyed sites to avoid damaging the marine environment by dropping anchor. The 42- and 46-foot dive boats are spacious and comfortable. Resort and certification courses are offered, and all new computerized dive gear is available for rent. Complete dive packages, including meals and accommodations, are available through Riding Rock Resort and Marina. However, dive trips are not offered daily so book well in advance. ⊠ *Riding Rock Resort and Marina, Cockburn Town* ☎ *800/272–1492, 242/331–2631* ⊕ *www.ridingrock.com.*

★ Seafari Dive Center at Club Med Columbus Isle

SCUBA DIVING | The diving operation at Club Med is now run separately by Seafari International, and all dive trips and certifications (PADI and CMAS) are open to Club Med guests and other visitors to the island. This professional dive center consistently offers three dives a day except Thursday, in addition to a weekly night dive, to more than 35 dive sites with permanent moorings. Divers go out on one of two catamarans, 54 and 52 feet. A hyperbaric chamber is on-site, and the staff consists of 11 dive instructors and 4 dive masters. All necessary equipment is available for rent including udive computers, and Nitrox. ⊠ *Club Med, Cockburn Town* ☎ *242/331–2000, 242/331–2195* ⊕ *www.clubmed.us.*

SPORTS CENTERS

Club Med – Columbus Isle

WATER SPORTS | If you are not a guest at Club Med, you can buy a day pass for $150, which gives you access to water sports (including daily guided snorkeling trips, Hobie Cat sailing, paddleboards, kayaks, and windsurfing) and regular sports activities (including group power walks and jogging, beach volleyball, tennis, various aerobics classes, yoga, and tai chi). The day pass includes lunch, dinner, and all you can drink and is good from 10 am to 1 am. A $80 day pass inclusive of all the above except for dinner gets you access from 10 am to 6 pm. ⊠ *Club Med, Cockburn Town* ☎ *242/331–2000* ⊕ *www.clubmed.us.*

Guanahani Surf & Sail Center

WINDSURFING | San Salvador is one of the last "uncrowded kitesurfing paradises," with ideal wind conditions and year-round warm waters. Licensed by IKO (International Kiteboarding Organization), the Guanahani Surf & Sail Center offers in-depth kiteboarding instruction for every level. Led by qualified trainers with Cabrinha kites and boards, courses last anywhere from 3 to 10 hours, and are best done over the course of a few days. The flat, calm, shallow waters in Snow Bay offer the perfect practice and play area. ⊠ *Snow Bay, Sunrise Rd., Cockburn Town* ☎ *242/452–0438* ⊕ *www.guanahanibeachclub.com.*

TOURS

Fernander Tours

In addition to being a taxi driver and island tour guide extraordinaire, Mr. Clifford Fernander is friendly and full of information for the inquisitive tourist. He and son Bruno Fernander offer tours for all visitors. The 2½- to 3-hour tour includes a drive through all the settlements and stops at the best known historic monuments and even some few get to see. Afterward, you'll feel San Salvador is like a second home. ⊠ *Cockburn Town* ☎ *242/331–2676, 242/427–8198.*

Lagoon Tours

Cruise through secluded Pigeon Creek on the island's beautiful southeast corner in a flat-bottom boat that maxes at five people to view baby sharks, sea turtles, and starfish, and top off the trip shell hunting on High Cay. Lagoon Tours caters to all interests from nature walks and historical tours to bird-watching and excursions through the quiet waters of the lagoons. This family-run company is very proud of San Salvador Island and they are happy to show you their favorite off-the-beaten-path spots, with a smile and a cooler full of refreshments. They also conduct kayaking, nature, and bird-watching tours. ⊠ *Cockburn Town* ☎ *242/452–0101 cell, 242/331–2459.*

Nat Walker's Island Adventures

As the island's former Warden for the Bahamas National Trust, Nat Walker has a unique understanding of the island's nature and history, and he will customize island tours to include visits to monuments, private beach picnics, islander restaurants, shopping, and the like. You can choose to see the archaeological site where its earliest inhabitants, the Lucayan Indians, lived; five monuments at Landfall Park commemorating Columbus's arrival in the Americas; a hand-operated Dixon Hill Lighthouse (one of three in the Bahamas); Watling's Estate 18th-century plantation ruins; and the Gerace Research Centre. Nathaniel also has 25-seat buses and rental cars and arranges private beach picnics, as well as snorkeling and reef tours. ☎ *242/331–2111, 242/464–9038.*

Elsewhere on San Salvador

Sometimes you just don't want to stay put at the resort. San Salvador's off-the-beaten-path places require some work to get to, but make for interesting sightseeing. The Gerace Research Centre and the lighthouse are not difficult to reach, but the "other" Columbus monument requires a little more work and an adventurous spirit.

◉ Sights

Columbus Monuments

BEACH—SIGHT | Christopher Columbus has more than one monument on San Salvador Island commemorating his first landfall in the New World on October 12, 1492. The simple white cross erected in 1956 at Landfall Park in Long Bay is the easiest to find, on Queen's Highway just outside Cockburn Town. (Also on the site is the Mexican Monument, which housed the Olympic flame in 1968 on its journey from Greece to Mexico City. The flame has not been lit since, but this location is popular for weekend family picnics and local gatherings.) The older and more difficult to find is the Chicago Herald Monument erected in 1891 to celebrate the 400th anniversary of the explorer's landing. No roads lead to this monument—a sphere hewn from limestone—so you'll have to trek through East Beach on Crab Cay by foot, which is fun for the more adventurous. ⊠ *Queen's Hwy., Cockburn Town* ⊕ *www.bahamas. com/islands/san-salvador.*

Dixon Hill Lighthouse

LIGHTHOUSE | A couple of miles south of Graham's Harbour stands Dixon Hill Lighthouse. Built around 1856, it's the last hand-operated lighthouse in the Bahamas. The lighthouse keeper must wind the apparatus that projects the light, which beams out to sea every 15 seconds to a maximum distance of 19 miles, depending on visibility. A climb to the top of the 160-foot landmark provides a fabulous view of the island, which includes a series of inland lakes. The keeper is present 24 hours a day. Knock on his door and he'll take you up to the top and explain the machinery. Drop a dollar in the box when you sign the guest book on the way out. ⊠ *Cockburn Town* ⊹ *Northeast sector of the island.*

Graham's Harbour and Gerace Research Centre

COLLEGE | Columbus describes Graham's Harbour in his diaries as large enough "to hold all the ships of Christendom." A former U.S. Navy base near the harbor houses the Gerace Research Centre, previously known as the Bahamian Field Station. The GRC is a center for academic research in archaeology, biology, geology, and marine sciences, backed by the University of the Bahamas and affiliated with many U.S. universities. It provides accommodations, meals, and air transportation arrangements for students and researchers from all over the world who come to study in this unique environment. ☎ *242/331–2520* ⊕ *www. geraceresearchcentre.com.*

Sandy Point

ARCHAEOLOGICAL SITE | Sandy Point anchors the island's southwestern end, overlooking French Bay. Here, on a hill, you'll find the ruins of **Watling's Castle,** named after the 17th-century pirate. The ruins are more likely the remains of a Loyalist plantation house than a castle

Historic Lighthouses ◉

Since the 19th century, sailors' lives have depended on the lighthouse beacons that rotate over the Southern Islands and the treacherous reefs that surround them. But for landlubbers, these lighthouses also offer bird's-eye vantage points. Visit the 115-foot Bird Rock Lighthouse on Crooked Island, the Castle Island Lighthouse on Acklins Island, the Inagua Lighthouse, and San Salvador's Dixon Hill Lighthouse.

from buccaneering days. A 5- to 10-minute walk from Queen's Highway will take you to see what's left of the ruins, which are now engulfed in vegetation.

🏃 Activities

SCUBA DIVING

For more information about these and other sites and for dive operators on the island, contact the Riding Rock Resort and Marina or Seafari at Club Med.

The wall dives in San Salvador are known to be spectacular with clear underwater visibility at depths of 100 feet and below. **North Pole Cave** has a wall that drops sharply from 40 feet to more than 150 feet; coral growth is extensive, and you might see a hammerhead or two. **Doctor John's** has a steep drop-off starting at about 35 feet with a system of tunnels and crevices that divers can explore. **Runway 10** is a vertical wall with sloping declines and sharp drops in three main sections between 40 and 200 feet. On this dive you will see sponges in abundance, including barrel sponges, brittle star, and elephant ear sponges.

Long Island

Long Island lives up to its name—80 gorgeous miles are available for you to explore. The Queen's Highway traverses its length, through the Tropic of Cancer and many diverse settlements and farming communities. The island is 4 miles at its widest, so at hilly vantage points you can view both the white cliffs and the raging Atlantic on the east side, and the gentle surf on the Caribbean side.

Long Island was the third island discovered by Christopher Columbus, and a monument to him stands on the north end. Loyalist families came to the island in support of the Crown, and to this day there are Crown properties all over the island, deeded by the king of England. Fleeing the Revolution, their attempt at re-creating life in America was short-lived. The soil and lack of rainfall did not support their crops, cotton being their mainstay. Today you can see wild cotton growing in patches up and down the island, along with the ruins of the plantations.

Fishing and tourism support the 3,000 residents of Long Island. Farms growing bananas, mangoes, papaya, and limes also dot the landscape. Boat-building is a natural art here, and in the south you can always see a boat in progress as you travel the Queen's Highway.

Progress has come to the island slowly. There is now high-speed Internet and cell-phone service, but shops and modern forms of entertainment are still limited. People who come to Long Island don't seem to mind; they're here for the beauty, tranquility, and the friendly people. Deep-sea fishing and diving are readily available, and bonefishing flats attract sportfishermen from all over the world. The beaches provide breathtaking views, shelling, exploring, and magnificent pieces of sea glass. The laid-back lifestyle is reminiscent of a slower, gentler time.

GETTING HERE AND AROUND

AIR

Long Island has two airports: Deadman's Cay (LGI) in the middle south and Stella Maris Airport (SML) in the far north. Bahamasair and Southern Air airlines provide daily service from Nassau to Stella Maris and Deadman's Cay airports. Stella Maris Resort has its own excellent air charter service to and from Nassau and between many Southern Islands including the Exumas. Other charter services are available from Nassau and Fort Lauderdale. Hawkline Aviation is an FBO at Stella Maris, a good fuel stop for private pilots going farther afield.

Guests staying at Cape Santa Maria or Stella Maris Resort should fly into Stella Maris Airport. Chez Pierre Bahamas' guests can fly into either airport, although the Stella Maris Airport is a bit closer. All others should fly into Deadman's Cay Airport midisland. Flying into the wrong airport will cost you not only an hour's drive, but also $100 or more in taxi fares. Listen carefully to the arrival announcement when you approach Long Island; most commercial airlines stop at both airports.

CONTACTS Deadman's Cay Airport.
☎ *242/337–1777, 242/337–7077 Bahamasair Office.* **Stella Maris Airport.**
☎ *242/338–2006.*

BOAT

Mail boats that bring supplies to the island each week make an adventurous mode of transportation. You'll ride with groceries, large and small appliances, automobiles, and sometimes even livestock. All boats depart from Potter's Cay in Nassau. Schedules change frequently. M/V *Mia Dean* travels to Clarence Town weekly in south Long Island and returns Thursday (18 hours; $60 one way). The *Island Link,* a faster RORO boat, stops in Salt Pond and Simms weekly. Bahamas Ferries, also a RORO that takes vehicles, and with its faster, more comfortable passenger lounge, leaves Nassau

Monday and gets into Simms, north Long Island, having stopped in George Town, Exumas.

Mailboat Port/Dockmaster's Office in Nassau. ✉ *Potter's Cay, Nassau* ☎ *242/393–1064 Dockmaster's office, 242/394–1237.*

CAR

A car is absolutely necessary to explore the island or visit any place outside your resort. The Queen's Highway curls like a ribbon from north to south, ending abruptly at the ocean in the north and at a stop sign in the south. It's narrow, with no marked center line, which makes bikes and scooters dangerous modes of transportation. The highway is easily traversed, but some off-roads require four-wheel drive, such as the road to the Columbus Monument, which is rocky and treacherous. The roads to Adderley's Plantation and Chez Pierre's are rough, but a passable adventure.

Most hotels will arrange car rentals, and can have your car waiting on-site or at the airport. Rentals range from $60 to $85. Some include gas; all have a limited number of vehicles. It's best to go for an a SUV or compact SUV with all-wheel drive if you have a choice.

Keep your gas tank full; although there are service stations along the highway, hours can be irregular and some take only cash. Some gas stations are closed on Sunday, so if that's your departure day, be sure to fill up the night before so the tank will be full when you return the car. Gas is expensive in the Outer Islands.

CONTACTS Mr. T's Car Rental. ✉ *Mid–Long Island, Deadman's Cay* ☎ *242/337–1054, 242/357–1678.* **Omar's Rental Cars.** ✉ *Cape Santa Maria Resort* ☎ *242/357–1043.*

TAXI

Taxis meet incoming flights at both airports. From the Stella Maris Airport, the fare to Stella Maris Resort is $10 per couple; to Cape Santa Maria, the fare is $30 per couple, and $150 to Clarence Town. From Deadman's Cay Airport, the fare to Cape Santa Maria is $110 per couple; to Stell Marris the fare is $90 and $60 to Clarence Town. Winter Haven provides free transportation from the Deadman's Cay Airport. A full-day tour of the island by taxi would cost about $350, and a half-day tour would be about $120. However, all taxis are privately owned, so rates can be negotiated. It is generally cheaper to rent a car for the duration of your trip than it is to pay taxi fares every time you want to go somewhere.

CONTACTS Omar Daley. ✉ *North Long Island, Stella Maris* ☎ *242/357–1043, 242/338–2031.*

TOURS
Bahamas Discovery Quest

Discover the beauty of Long Island in a variety of adventures on land and sea: deep-sea, deep-drop, and reef fishing; snorkeling; sponging; crabbing for land crabs at night; sea life ecotours; hiking; beaching; shelling; and historical tours with Long Islander, Charles Knowles, who will take you off the beaten path to meet farmers and taste island dishes you wouldn't easily find on your own. ✉ *Deadman's Cay* ☎ *242/472–2605, 242/337–6024* ⊕ *www.bahamasdiscoveryquest.com.*

Omar's Long Island Guided Tours

Now based at Cape Santa Maria Resort in the far north, Omar is more than just a tour guide. Raised on Long Island, he's fun and friendly and full of knowledge about the land and the people, and he will cater tours to your interests—from showing you the best spots to jump into Dean's Blue Hole, to introductions to local straw and seashell artisans. However, that's just the start of his long list of services: he's also a dive master and boat captain who will feed sharks and lead you through wrecks, a taxi driver who can transport you to and from the airport to your hotel, and the owner of Omar's Rental Cars if you want to explore the island on your own. ✉ *Cape Santa Maria Resort* ☎ *242/357–1043 cell.*

Pontoon Boat Tour by Boneafied Bonefishing

EXCURSIONS | FAMILY | Boneafied Bonefishing's best-known tour is apparent from its name. However, the tour company provides one of the most unique ways to visit Columbus Monument and Blue Sound (also known as Columbus Cove) in North Long Island: a pontoon boat tour through mangrove creeks, across a turtle habitat, and onto the Blue Sound Beach. This boat excursion offers more than a hike to the hilltop monument that marks the arrival of Christopher Columbus. It delivers a beach day in one of the most picturesque inlets in The Bahamas, with shifting sand bars and a lazy river in the shallow channel near the beach. Rather than approaching from the ocean side, as most do, the company's pontoon boat provides a comfortable and stylish cruise from Newton Cay into the Blue Sound, onto a beach below the monument. ✉ *Near Stella Maris Resort, Queen's Highway, Stella Maris* ☎ *242/338–2025, 242/357–1417.*

VISITOR INFORMATION
CONTACTS Long Island Ministry of Tourism. ✉ *Salt Pond, mid–Long Island* ☎ *242/338–8668.*

North Long Island: Cape Santa Maria to Gray's

In the far north you will find two large resort communities: **Cape Santa Maria** and **Stella Maris.** Scattered between are the small settlements of **Seymour's, Glinton's,** and **Burnt Ground.** Columbus originally named the island's northern tip Cape Santa Maria after the largest of his three ships. The beach here is gorgeous, full of private homes and resort villas, and a restaurant, bar, and gift shop that are open to the public. North of the Cape Santa Maria Resort are the **Columbus Monument,**

commemorating Columbus's landing on Long Island, and **Columbus Cove,** where he made landfall. Twelve miles south of the Cape, Stella Maris, which means Star of the Sea, is home to the so-named resort. The Stella Maris Airport sits on the property, along with private homes, restaurants, and bars, the magnificent **Love Beaches,** a full-service marina, and a tackle and gift shop—all open to the public. Just north of Stella Maris, off Queen's Highway, are the ruins of the 19th-century **Adderley's Plantation.**

Traveling south about 8 miles, you'll come to **Simms,** one of Long Island's oldest settlements. The Tropic of Cancer cuts through the island close to here, dividing the subtropics from the tropics.

Farther south are the idyllic communities of **Thompson Bay** and **Salt Pond,** both providing safe harbors for those who visit by sailboat. Salt Pond, a hilly bustling settlement so named for its many salt ponds, hosts the annual Long Island Regatta. Continuing south, you will pass the settlements of **the Bight** and **Gray's** before reaching **Deadman's Cay.**

◉ Sights

Adderley's Plantation

HISTORIC SITE | Just north of the Stella Maris Airport, west of the main road, are the ruins of 19th-century Adderley's Plantation, a cotton plantation that once occupied all of Stella Maris. Clearly marked, the road is marginally passable by car. It is about a 1-mile drive and then a fairly long walk. The walking path is marked by conch shells, and leads to the cotton plantation ruins. Seven buildings are practically intact up to roof level, but it is overgrown with vegetation. For historians, it is well worth the time. ✉ *North of Stella Maris Airport, Stella Maris.*

Columbus Monument

HISTORIC SITE | Two miles north of Cape Santa Maria is the Columbus Monument, commemorating Columbus's landing on

Long Island. The road to the monument is off the Queen's Highway, and while the sign is often not visible, any Long Islander will gladly give you directions. The 3-mile treacherous road is too rough for vehicles without four-wheel drive, and most rental car companies won't let you drive it without an SUV, yet it is an extremely long hike. At the end of the road is a steep hill, called Columbus Point, and a climb to the summit affords a spectacular vista. This is the highest point on Long Island, and the second highest in the Bahamas. Farther north on Queen's Highway is Columbus Harbour, on Newton's Cay. Columbus made landfall in this cove, protected by limestone outcroppings. The more adventurous can follow the beach to the left, where a rough walking path leads to three other coves; each one a delight. Two coves up you will find sea glass scattered on the beach like sparkling jewels, and by climbing through limestone formations, you will discover another cove perfect for snorkeling. ✉ *North of Cape Santa Maria Resort.*

Beaches

Cape Santa Maria Beach

BEACH—SIGHT | Known as one of the Bahamas' top beaches, and located on the leeward side of the island at Cape Santa Maria Resort, the water colors here range from pale blue to aqua to shades of turquoise. The 4-mile stretch of soft white sand beckons you to stroll, build sand castles, sun worship, or wade into the calm shallow waters. In the early morning, you're likely to see a ray swimming along the shore. The resort has a beachside restaurant and lounge chairs for guests, in addition to kayak and paddleboard rentals, but there's also plenty of sand to find a secluded stretch all your own. **Amenities:** food and drink; water sports. **Best for:** solitude; snorkeling; sunset; swimming; walking. ✉ *Cape Santa Maria Resort.*

Restaurants

After a period of rain, the mosquitoes and no-see-ums come out, so bring mosquito repellent with you when dining outdoors.

Beach House Restaurant at Cape Santa Maria

$$ | **SEAFOOD** | **FAMILY** | Upstairs in the Cape Santa Maria Beach House, guests enjoy sweeping vistas of the turquoise bay during the day, and bobbing boat lights in the evening along with the gentle sounds of the sea. Breakfast can be light with yogurt parfait and a seasonal fruit medley, or a splurge with banana bread French toast topped with caramelized plantains or Bahamian-style eggs Benedict. **Known for:** nightly happy hour with free conch fritters; oceanfront bar; banana bread French toast. [$] *Average main: $30* ✉ *Cape Santa Maria Resort* ☎ *242/338–5273, 800/663–7090* 🌐 *www.capesantamaria.com* 🕓 *Closed Sept. and Oct.* ☞ *Meal plans available.*

★ **Chez Pierre Bahamas**

$$ | **ECLECTIC** | At this airy oceanfront restaurant a few steps from the beach, Chef Pierre has been serving sumptuous cuisine since 2002. This curmudgeonly chef serves the best food on the island, hands down. **Known for:** pasta and seafood dishes; delicious pizza; chef expects guests to be on time. [$] *Average main: $28* ✉ *Miller's Bay* ☎ *242/338–8809, 242/357–1374* 🌐 *www.chezpierrebahamas.com.*

Moonshine Bar & Grill

$ | **BAHAMIAN** | **FAMILY** | The views surrounding Stella Maris Resort Club's new poolside bar are as beautiful as the frozen fresh-fruit daiquiris they serve. Once a week, the delightful Bodo, legendary local guitarist and Rake 'n' Scrape musician, plucks your heartstrings with Bahamian and calypso songs. **Known for:** the Moonshine panini; weekly live music; coastal bluff views. [$] *Average main: $15* ✉ *Stella Maris Resort Club, Stella Maris*

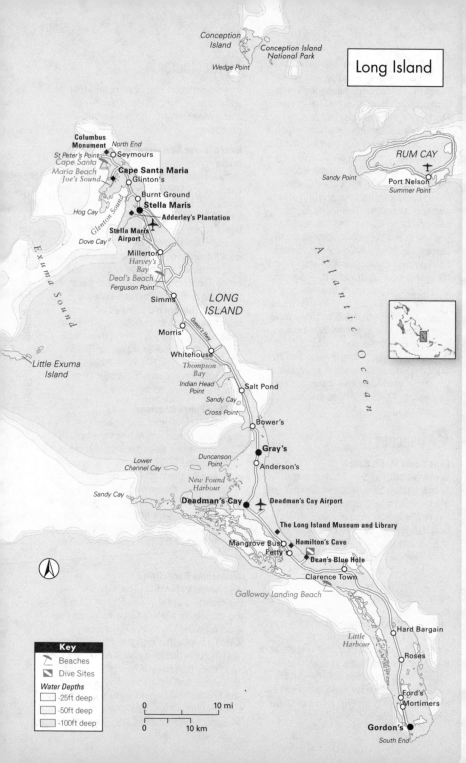

☎ 242/338–2050 🌐 *www.stellamarisresort.com.*

Stella Maris Resort Club Restaurant & Bar
$$ | **SEAFOOD** | Charming and experienced chef Bruno and his capable team do a superb job pleasing upmarket American and European palates. Dine in the cool inside or on the stone terrace. **Known for:** room-service pizza; delicious liqueur coffees; fresh fish. [$] *Average main: $30* ✉ *Stella Maris Resort Club, Stella Maris* ☎ *242/338–2050* ⏲ *Closed Sept.*

Hotels

C Shells Guest Quarters
$ | **B&B/INN** | **FAMILY** | These quaint, self-catering full-kitchen suites sit just steps away from a quiet private beach on Salt Pond, with a large grassy garden space—perfect for family picnics, naps in the hammock, and a vacation without the bustle of a busy resort. **Pros:** friendly, accommodating owners; cable TV, Wi-Fi, and DVD library; affordable. **Cons:** no maid service; no on-site restaurant; rental car is essential to explore the island. [$] *Rooms from: $110* ✉ *Salt Pond* ☎ *242/338–0103, 954/889–5075* 🌐 *www.cshellsguestquarters.com* 🛏 *4 suites* 🍴 *No meals.*

★ Cape Santa Maria Beach Resort and Villas
$$ | **RESORT** | **FAMILY** | This stunning resort consists of spacious, new beachfront villas that sleep up to eight and beachfront one-bed and two-bed bungalows that each have a screened-in veranda—all overlooking serene turquoise waters on a gorgeous 4-mile-long white-sand beach. **Pros:** only 15 minutes from Stella Maris Airport; friendly staff arranges excursions; great swimming beach. **Cons:** secluded location means you'll need a rental car to explore; no TVs in rooms and no Wi-Fi in bungalows; seven-night stay required during Christmas holiday season. [$] *Rooms from: $239* ✉ *Galliot Cay, off Seymour's* ☎ *242/338–5273, 800/926–9704 toll-free in U.S. and Canada, 250/598–3366 free outside U.S. and Canada* 🌐 *www.capesantamaria.com* ⏲ *Closed Sept. and Oct.* 🛏 *20 bungalows, 18 luxury villas* 🍴 *No meals* ☞ *Kids 12 and under stay free.*

Chez Pierre Bahamas
$ | **B&B/INN** | Lining lovely Miller's Bay beach, this rustic, remote resort has six simple cabins on stilts right on the beach, making it a real "get-away-from-it-all" place (guests should be self-sufficient and adventurous). **Pros:** screened-in porches; large private beach; excellent on-site restaurant serves three meals a day. **Cons:** must rent a car to explore the island; no air-conditioning; bathroom water is slightly salty. [$] *Rooms from: $175* ✉ *Miller's Bay* ☎ *242/338–8809, 242/357–1374 cell* 🌐 *www.chezpierrebahamas.com* 🛏 *6 cottages* 🍴 *Some meals.*

Grotto Bay Bahamas
$ | **B&B/INN** | In the settlement of Salt Pond is this small private hideaway, a labor of love for owners Kris and Jean who offer two lovely guest rooms with sweeping decks facing the ocean on the lower level of their home, along with a newer beach house that sleeps five guests. **Pros:** centrally located for exploring north and south; personalized service; beautiful lush landscaping. **Cons:** no in-house restaurant, bar, or meals; you need to rent a car to explore the island; owners live right above the guest rooms. [$] *Rooms from: $145* ✉ *Salt Pond* ☎ *242/338–0011, 954/840–7724* 🌐 *www.grottobaybahamas.com* 💳 *No credit cards* 🛏 *2 rooms, 1 beach house* 🍴 *No meals.*

★ Stella Maris Resort Club
$$ | **RESORT** | **FAMILY** | Stella Maris is more than a resort, it is a long-standing family-fun community that sits atop a hilly ridge offering many accommodations choices (including private homes), complemented by multiple pools, breathtaking views of the Atlantic, fun

Cape Santa Maria Beach Resort is the best on the island.

bars and restaurants, and activities for every interest—it's also in walking distance from Stella Maris Airport. **Pros:** all accommodations have an ocean view or balcony; free activities like island tours and sailing; parties and events hosted by resort for guests. **Cons:** long walks between rooms, clubhouse, beach bar; rooms somewhat dated but clean and comfortable; not beachfront but free bus to other beaches. [$] *Rooms from: $250* ✉ *Stella Maris* ☎ *800/426–0466, 242/338–2050 resort* 🌐 *www.stellamaris-resort.com* 🛏 *16 rooms, 4 cottages, 6 houses* 🍴 *No meals.*

Nightlife

Stella Maris Resort

BARS/PUBS | This resort often has live music on the weekends, including Rake 'n' Scrape. Every Thursday night is their Rum Punch Party, which includes rum punch, conch fritters, and dinner. Cost is $55 for nonguests. The clubhouse bar has a pool table and foosball, plus a huge rum collection. The restaurant has an excellent selection of wines. Ask about the frequent (in winter) Cave Party where folks gather round and dine on barbecued treats in a cave. Call ahead to make reservations. ✉ *Stella Maris Resort Club, Stella Maris* ☎ *242/338–2050.*

Shopping

Bonafide Bonefishing Fly Shop

SPORTING GOODS | This fly-and-tackle shop and souvenir boutique, usually open Monday, Wednesday, Friday, and Saturday 9 am to 5 pm, is located in Stella Maris on Queens Highway. In addition to fishing gear, they sell cold drinks and snacks, souvenirs, gifts, apparel, and jewelry. James "Docky" Smith is the fishing guru behind Bonafide Bonefishing. A Long Islander, he is a popular and knowledgeable bonefishing guide who "knows the flats." ✉ *Queens Hwy., Stella Maris* ☎ *242/338–2035, 242/357–1417, 242/338–2025* 🌐 *www.bonafidebonefishing.com.*

Cape Santa Maria Resort
GIFTS/SOUVENIRS | There is a small gift shop in the lobby with clothes, swimsuits, island straw works, island books, souvenirs, cold drinks, and sundries. ⊠ *Cape Santa Maria Resort's Beach House lobby* ☎ *242/338–5273, 800/926–9704* ⊕ *www.capesantamaria.com*.

Hillside Food Supply
CONVENIENCE/GENERAL STORES | Hillside is probably the largest store on Long Island and the ideal place to stock up if you're self-catering or want snacks in between mealtimes. Here you can find lots of fresh produce and dairy items (that you can't import into the Bahamas), dry foods, toiletries, and supplies. In the back of the store you will find just about anything, from snorkeling gear and ice chests to towels and assorted housewares. Hillside can also tell where and how to get fresh lobster, snapper, grouper, and more. There are seafood vendors living nearby. ⊠ *Salt Pond, mid–Long Island* ☎ *242/338–0022*.

Midway Mini Mart
CONVENIENCE/GENERAL STORES | Well-stocked convenience store. ⊠ *The Bight* ☎ *242/337–7230*.

Tingum's Boutique
GIFTS/SOUVENIRS | *Tingums* is Bahamian for "I don't know what to call it." This cute gift shop sells clothing, jewelry, gifts, souvenirs, books, and toiletries. ⊠ *Stella Maris Resort Club, Stella Maris* ☎ *242/338–2050*.

🏃 Activities

DIVING AND SNORKELING
Conception Island Wall is an excellent wall dive, with hard and soft coral, plus interesting sponge formations. The M/V *Comberbach*, a 103-foot British freighter built in 1948, sank off Cape Santa Maria in 1984, and was scuttled by the Stella Maris Resort in 1986 to create an artificial reef and excellent dive site. Take a guided diving excursion to **Shark's Reef** and watch a scuba master safely feed dozens of sharks.

Cape Santa Maria Resort
BICYCLING | This resort uses expert divers and guides for myriad diving and snorkeling trips to various reefs, walls, and wrecks around Long Island as well as trips to Conception Island; dive and snorkel equipment is available for rent. In addition, visitors can rent stand-up paddleboards and Hobie Cat sailboats to explore the coast of Cape Santa Maria Beach and its surrounding bays. ⊠ *Cape Santa Maria Resort* ☎ *242/338–5273, 800/926–9704* ⊕ *www.capesantamaria.com*.

Stella Maris Resort
SCUBA DIVING | This resort offers diving and snorkeling trips. In addition to daytime dives to some of Long Island's most interesting sites, including Dean's Blue Hole, you can do an overnight dive cruise. They also offer PADI Resort Dive and Open Water Certification courses and Advanced Open Water upon request. Equipment is available for rental. ☎ *242/338–2050*.

FISHING
Bonafide Bonefishing
FISHING | James "Docky" Smith is highly regarded as one of the best bonefishing guides in the Bahamas. He does full- and half-day bonefishing excursions, as well as reef-fishing trips. He is also an expert fly-casting instructor. Book well in advance. His operation is based out of the Bonafide tackle shop in Stella Maris, open three days a week, which rents conventional and fly-fishing gear, prepares snacks and box lunches, and sells a range of tackle, clothing, and flies. Full days of bonefishing are $550 (maximum two anglers); reef, bottom, or deep-sea fishing are $1,200 (maximum six anglers). Call ahead. ⊠ *Queen's Hwy., Stella Maris* ✛ *Near Stella Maris Resort* ☎ *242/338–2025, 242/357–1417*.

Stella Maris Resort

FISHING | Stella Maris Resort arranges deep-sea fishing, bonefishing, and reef-fishing trips with well-trained guides. The small fleet includes a 32-foot single engine inboard that can accommodate up to six fishermen and a 38-foot twin engine that can take up to eight for their deep-sea and reef-fishing trips and a 16-foot Hells Bay or 17-foot Maverick with poling platforms for a half or full day of bonefishing the flats. Rods and bait is available for rent and purchase. ☎ *242/338–2050.*

South Long Island: Deadman's Cay to Gordon's

The most populated area on the island is **Deadman's Cay.** This umbrella central settlement covers all the communities stretching from **Gray's** to the north to **Scrub Hill,** and is the social, economic, and educational center of the island. The Deadman's Cay Airport is in Lower Deadman's Cay and the infamous Max's Conch Bar is only a short distance to the south. Shops, restaurants, and bars dot this area, along with amazing views of the Bahamas Banks.

Past Scrub Hill is **Dean's Blue Hole,** the deepest blue hole in the world. Free-diving contests, without use of any breathing apparatus, are held here each year, and divers come from all over the world to challenge the record. Fantastic snorkeling can be had around the blue hole's edges.

Clarence Town is the capital of Long Island and home to the Flying Fish Marina in one of the prettiest and safest harbors in the Out Islands. Situated at the top of the highest hills in town are the twin-towered Moorish style churches of **St. Paul's** and **St. Peter's,** designed by Father Jerome. Clarence Town is the last large settlement on the south end of the island.

South of Clarence Town you will find **Galloway Landing,** a long stretch of amazing beaches and saltwater canals dug into the limestone hills by the now defunct Diamond Salt Mine. From here to **Gordon's** is the most undeveloped stretch of the island. Plantation ruins are at **Dunmone's,** secluded beaches at **Ford's,** and the incredible pink flamingos at Gordon's along with the biggest assortment of sea glass.

◉ Sights

Some of the biggest changes on Long Island have taken place at **Flying Fish Marina** (⊕ *www.flyingfishmarina.com*) in Clarence Town. The full-service, 20-slip marina offers fuel, a new store, and a new, upscale restaurant.

★ Dean's Blue Hole

BEACH—SIGHT | Known as the second deepest blue hole in the world with a depth of 663 feet, Dean's Blue Hole is the most amazing sight on the island and one of the most popular photo sites in the land. A blue hole is a term for a water-filled sinkhole with an entrance below the water level. Free divers from around the world gather here annually to take the plunge. In 2010 William Trubridge broke the world record for free immersion diving to 407 feet without fins. Dean's Blue Hole is surrounded by a pretty cliff and a superb beach. The shallows at the edge of the hole are perfect for snorkeling and swimming, and the more adventurous visitors can jump into the water from the cliffs above. To find the blue hole, watch for the well-marked sign on your left (going east on Queen's Highway) after passing through Scrub Hill. ⊠ *Just south of Scrub Hill on east coast, north of Clarence Town, Clarence Town.*

Hamilton's Cave

CAVE | The largest cave system in the Bahamas, Hamilton's Cave features stalactites and stalagmites, and passages

A gray shark circles a boat off Long Island.

over 45 feet wide and 9 feet high. The Lucayan Indians were thought to have lived here about AD 500 and many Lucayan artifacts were discovered in 1936. Hamilton's Cave sits on the private property of Leonard Cartwright, who will take you on a guided tour, complete with flashlights, as you explore inside the dark depths of his childhood playground. For added excitement, plan to go closer to dusk when the resident bats are most active! ⊠ *Queen's Hwy., Deadman's Cay* ☎ *242/337-0235, 242/472-1796* 🖃 *$10.*

The Long Island Museum and Library

HOUSE | The Long Island Museum and Library is housed in a beautiful little pink cottage with island trees in front. Learn the history of Long Island and see artifacts collected by local Long Islanders in hopes of preserving their cultural heritage. It's a fascinating collection and exhibit, professionally designed by the Bahamas, Antiquities, Monuments and Museum Corporation. Island wares, homemade jellies, and other island goods are for sale, in addition to books on Long Island and a popular Bahamian calendar painted in watercolors by local artist Nick Maillis. ⊠ *Buckley's, near Scotia Bank, Queen's Hwy.* ☎ *242/337-0500* ⊕ *www. ammcbahamas.com* 🖃 *$3* ☺ *Closed Sun.*

St. Paul's & St. Peter's Churches

RELIGIOUS SITE | The twin, towered Moorish churches of St. Paul's (Anglican) and St. Peter's (Catholic) are two of the island's most celebrated landmarks. Father Jerome, often referred to as the hermit of Cat Island, built St. Paul's when he was Anglican; later, after converting to Catholicism, he built St. Peter's. The architecture of the two churches is similar to the Spanish missions in California. The churches are open sporadically, but tours are available through the Ministry of Tourism. ⊠ *Atop of Clarence Town Hill, Clarence Town.*

Beaches

Galloway Landing Beach

BEACH—SIGHT | This remarkable beach on the southeast coast of the island, south of Clarence Town, is relatively unknown and visited mostly by the locals. Swim and sun at the first beach, or walk a short distance south to an even more wonderful and secluded stretch of sand. Here, canals carved into the limestone hills by the now defunct Diamond Salt Mine are filled with the palest blue ocean water and are home to small marine life. It's a wonderful area to kayak, snorkel and swim, and collect sea glass. A bit farther south, a narrow bridge leads to beyond-stunning lagoons and ocean flats. **Amenities:** none. **Best for:** solitude; snorkeling; swimming; walking. ✉ *Clarence Town* ✣ *2.4 miles southwest of Clarence Town.*

Restaurants

Forest Take-Away

$ | **BAHAMIAN** | This family-owned and -operated takeout restaurant is a favorite with the locals for tasty, island food and value. It offers barbecued ribs, cracked conch, conch burgers, fish fingers, chicken snacks and dinners, and the ever-popular Forest Burger, a hamburger with boneless ribs and sautéed onions. **Known for:** cold beer while you wait; shaded picnic table seating; local favorite. [$] *Average main: $12* ✉ *Just off Queen's Hwy., Deadman's Cay* ☎ *242/337–1246* 💳 *No credit cards* 🕓 *Closed Sun. and Mon.*

Max's Conch Bar and Grill

$ | **BAHAMIAN** | This island treasure and possibly the area's most-recommended dining spot, is praised up and down by locals and visitors alike. Quintessentially Bahamian, you can sit all day on a stool at the colorful roadside hexagonal gazebo or at a table in the garden patio amid chickens and a goat, enjoying beers and nibbling on excellent conch salad prepared right in front of you. **Known for:** warm hospitality; conch fritters; traditional Bahamian recipes. [$] *Average main: $15* ✉ *Deadman's Cay* ☎ *242/337–0056* 🕓 *Closed Sun.*

Outer Edge Grill at Flying Fish Marina

$$ | **BAHAMIAN** | Outer Edge Grill is what local Long Islanders call a "poop deck," meaning a restaurant on the water. Open daily for lunch and dinner, Outer Edge serves up Bahamian favorites like conch fritters and fish fingers, along with sweet potato french fries, mozzarella sticks, and homemade desserts. **Known for:** open Sunday; Bahamian favorites; homemade desserts. [$] *Average main: $20* ✉ *Clarence Town Harbour, Flying Fish Marina, just down from Winter Haven Inn, Clarence Town* ☎ *242/337–3445 restaurant, 954/654–7084 in U.S. and Canada, 242/337–3430 marina resort* 🌐 *www.flyingfishmarina.com.*

Rowdy Boys Bar and Grill at Winter Haven Inn

$$ | **BAHAMIAN** | Don't let the name scare you—it's named after the Knowles family's well-known construction company and the owners' two sons. Breakfast, lunch, and dinner can be served in the cool inside or out, and feature authentic Bahamian and American fare. **Known for:** Friday pig roast; open Sunday; whirlpool and tiki bar. [$] *Average main: $24* ✉ *Winter Haven Inn, Clarence Town* ☎ *242/337–3062* 🌐 *www.winterhavenbahamas.com.*

Seaside Village at Jerry Wells

$ | **BAHAMIAN** | Located at the end of Jerry Wells Road, this charming, authentic conch shack stuck out on a dock in the water is truly local, offering friendly service, fun music, and good food. Sling back in the hammock, catch some tunes and breeze as you (if you're lucky) watch the almost-tame osprey, "Iron," snack on fish morsels. **Known for:** fresh-caught conch; grouper cooked to order; best conch salad. [$] *Average main: $15* ✉ *Jerry Wells Rd., on west coast just south of Deadman's Cay Airport, Deadman's Cay* ☎ *242/337–0119* 💳 *No credit cards.*

🛏 Hotels

Gems at Paradise

$ | **HOTEL** | Situated on 16 acres of pink-sand beachfront property, overlooking the low-lying Clem Cay and the Atlantic Ocean as far as the eye can see, this resort occupies a rare and superb site. **Pros:** gorgeous location and views; easy access to fishing and water sports; car rentals available on-site. **Cons:** many rooms have stairs; no on-site restaurant; car rental is essential. $ *Rooms from: $152* ✉ *Clarence Town* ☎ *242/337–3016* ⊕ *www.gemsatparadise.com* ⇨ *8 rooms, 2 condos* ⦿ *All meals.*

Greenwich Creek Lodge

$ | **B&B/INN** | One of Long Island's newest places is the tranquil Greenwich Creek Lodge on the west waters of Cartwright's—a simple two-story 11-room boutique inn with elevated views of the salt flats and the Exuma Sound, and each room opening onto a wraparound porch or balcony. **Pros:** on the water with boat access; serves three meals a day and has a bar; free Wi-Fi and TV/DVD available; swimming pool and small gym. **Cons:** beach 2 miles away; no TVs in rooms; no private balcony space. $ *Rooms from: $145* ✉ *Off Queen's Hwy., in Cartwright's, 3 miles south of Deadman's Cay Airport, Deadman's Cay* ☎ *242/337–6278 resort, 242/359–0980 cell* ⊕ *greenwichcreeklodge.com* ⇨ *11 rooms* ⦿ *Some meals.*

Harbor Breeze Villas

$ | **RENTAL** | Long Island's newest luxury villas are nestled among garden pathways atop a hillside, each with private balconies affording views of Clarence Town Harbour and the Atlantic Ocean. **Pros:** owner rents cars and will stock your villa with groceries ahead of your arrival; complimentary transfers to Arthur's Town Airport; laundry facilities on-site. **Cons:** no on-site restaurant or bar; not on beach; office can be hard to reach by phone. $ *Rooms from: $135* ✉ *Lochabar, just south of Clarence Town, Clarence Town* ☎ *242/337–3088* ⊕ *www.harborbreezevillas.com* ⇨ *15 villas* ⦿ *No meals.*

Winter Haven Inn

$ | **HOTEL** | In the heart of Clarence Town, this small, colorful inn has two-story houses with rooms overlooking the indigo waters of the Atlantic. **Pros:** complimentary airport transfers and Wi-Fi; good on-site restaurant serves three meals a day; family-owned. **Cons:** no kitchen facilities in-room; you must rent a car for exploring; rough, rocky beach not good for swimming. $ *Rooms from: $190* ✉ *Clarence Town* ☎ *242/337–3062, 866/348–5935* ⊕ *www.winterhavenbahamas.com* ⇨ *15 rooms* ⦿ *No meals.*

🍸 Nightlife

Lloyd's Sporting Lounge & Entertainment Center

DANCE CLUBS | The long name is Lloyd's Sporting Lounge & Entertainment Center and, for Long Island, it has quite a bit. This new, comfortable, and smartly designed sports bar and lounge has big-screen TVs for sports, and five pool tables. In a separate room they also have a dance/disco to the live tunes of the D Changes Band and DJs every Friday and Saturday night. Lloyd's hosts frequent pool tournaments and people flock to enjoy happy hour from 5 to 7 pm weekdays when beer buckets are four for $12. Other times, beers and rum and Cokes are a reasonable $6.72. Their food is also good and affordable: Long Island mutton, chicken, steaks, seafood, and various fettuccine main courses average $11 for chicken to $32 for T-bone steak. Lloyd's is well-thought-out and rather luxurious for the Out Islands—very enjoyable especially for big-group entertainment and dining, to catch sports on TV, or to dance to some live music. ✉ *Queen's Hwy., opposite Turtle Cove Rd. that leads to Dean's Blue Hole, Clarence Town* ☎ *242/337–5762.*

🛍 Shopping

It's All Under the Sun

CONVENIENCE/GENERAL STORES | As the name suggests, this "department store" has everything from a café with used books and Wi-Fi to office supplies, toys, baby stuff, souvenirs, beach bags, hats, and snorkeling and fishing gear. Owner Cathy Darville also sells fruit smoothies, deli sandwiches, and homemade ice cream. ⊠ *Off Queen's Hwy. in Mangrove Bush, near Cartwright's settlement* ☎ *242/337–0199* ⊗ *Closed Sun.*

🏃 Activities

FISHING

Deadman's Cay Bonefish Adventures

FISHING | Since 2002, Samuel Knowles Bonefish Adventures has drawn a loyal following of saltwater anglers from around the globe, earning a reputation as one of the most popular bonefishing programs in the islands. The main attraction is their expert guides, who are Long Islanders, fourth- and fifth-generation bonefishermen, and champions of four of the five Bahamas bonefishing tournaments. Their location at the center of Long Island's pristine shoreline, with unique landlocked flats, creates an unforgettable fishing adventure for all ages and experience levels. They offer stay/fish/dine packages at Smith-Wells Bonefish Lodge: $2,395 for seven nights/six days fishing. ⊠ *Deadman's Cay* ☎ *242/337–0246, 242/357–1178* ⊕ *www.smith-wells.com.*

Long Island Bonefishing Lodge

FISHING | This modern lodge offers all-inclusive stay/fish/dine packages for fly-fishermen. Packages include three meals and fishing from 8 am to 4 pm. LIBL specializes in and encourages DIY fishing where, although your guide is present, you're mostly in your own privacy, and he can boat you to other flats to find success. Most of Long Island's vast flats are wade-able shallows. The main clubhouse has gorgeous flats views. The two duplexes are modern and comfortable, and sleep a total of eight. ⊠ *Deadman's Cay* ☎ *242/472–2609* ⊕ *www.longislandbonefishinglodge.com* 🛏 *$1750 per person double occupancy. All-inclusive stay/fish/dine package Oct.– May. Visit must start or end on Sun.*

Winter Haven Inn

FISHING | Winter Haven Inn organizes fishing and boating adventures through various local guides. ⊠ *Clarence Town* ☎ *242/337–3062* ⊕ *www.winterhavenbahamas.com.*

Crooked and Acklins Islands

Crooked Island is 30 miles long and surrounded by 45 miles of barrier reefs that are ideal for diving and fishing. They slope from 4 feet to 50 feet, then plunge to 3,600 feet in the **Crooked Island Passage,** once one of the most important sea roads for ships following the southerly route from the West Indies to the Old World. If you drive up to **the Cove** settlement, you get an uninterrupted view of the region all the way to the narrow passage at **Lovely Bay** between Crooked Island and Acklins Island. Two lighthouses alert mariners that they are nearing the islands.

The tepid controversy continues today over whether Columbus actually set foot on Crooked Island and its southern neighbor, Acklins Island. What's known for sure is that Columbus sailed close enough to Crooked Island to get a whiff of its island herbs. Soon after, the two islands became known as the "Fragrant Islands." Today Crooked and Acklins islands are known as remote and unspoiled destinations for fishermen, divers, and sailors who value solitude. Here phone service can be intermittent, Internet access can be hard to find, and some residents depend on generators for electricity. Even credit-card use is a relatively new development. The first known settlers didn't arrive until the late 18th century, when Loyalists brought slaves from the United States to work on cotton plantations. About 400 people, mostly fishermen and farmers, live on each island today. Two plantation-era sites, preserved by the Bahamas National Trust, are on Crooked Island's northern end, which overlooks Crooked Island Passage that separates the cay from Long Island. Spanish guns have been discovered at one ruin, **Marine Farm,** which may have been used as a fortification. An old structure, **Hope Great House,** has orchards and gardens.

GETTING HERE AND AROUND
AIR
Crooked and Acklins have one airport each: Colonel Hill Airport (CRI) on Crooked Island and Spring Point Airport (AXP) on Acklins Island. Neither is open unless there's a flight expected. Bahamasair flies from Nassau to Crooked and Acklins islands twice a week. The flights are quite early in the morning, making it hard to fly in from overseas without staying one night in Nassau. Many Crooked Island visitors have found a solution to that: fly in on a private aircraft direct from the United States. The private 3,500-foot airstrip at Crooked Island Lodge is complimentary for hotel guests. Nonguests pay landing and parking fees. This airstrip is most convenient for private and charter flights if you're staying in the area of Pittstown and Landrail Point. Ask your hotel to make arrangements for picking you up at the airport in case there are no taxis.

Hotels will arrange airport transportation. Generally someone from even the smallest hotel will meet you at the airport, despite the fact that taxis are usually waiting on flights.

CONTACTS Acklins Island Spring Point Airport. ✉ *Midway along Acklins Island*

☎ *242/344–3169.* **Crooked Island Colonel Hill Airport.** ✉ *On northeast side of Crooked Island* ☎ *242/344–2357.*

BOAT
Mail boats that bring supplies to the islands each week make an adventurous mode of transportation. You'll ride with groceries, large and small appliances, automobiles, and sometimes even livestock. All boats depart from Potter's Cay in Nassau. Schedules change frequently. Three mail boats travel to Acklins Island, Crooked Island, and Long Cay, M/V *Sea Spirit II*, M/V *New G* and M/V *Vinase* with Captain Tom Hanna, for a fair of $118 one way.

Ferry service between Cove Landing, Crooked Island, and Lovely Bay, Acklins Island, usually operates twice daily on varying schedules between 9 and 4.

CONTACTS Mailboat Captain Tom Hanna. ☎ *242/341–3468.* **Ferry Service.** ☎ *242/344–2197 ferry, 242/344–2415 Island administrator's office.* **Mailboat Port/Dockmaster's Office in Nassau.** ✉ *Potter's Cay, Nassau* ☎ *242/393–1064 Dockmaster's office, 242/394–1237.*

CAR
There are many car-rental operators. To get a good vehicle, reserve a car through your hotel prior to your arrival; even if you have a reservation you should be prepared for the possibility of the car not being there when you arrive. Gas is also not always available on the islands, as it's delivered by mail boats, which are sometimes delayed. Fortunately, it's easy to get a ride to most places with locals, who are friendly and often willing to help.

◉ Sights

Bird Rock Lighthouse
LIGHTHOUSE | The sparkling white Bird Rock Lighthouse (built in 1876) once guarded the Crooked Island Passage. The rotating flash from its 115-foot tower still welcomes pilots and sailors

Crooked and Acklins islands both have a lighthouse. Bird Rock Lighthouse (pictured) is the newer of the two, built in 1872.

to the Crooked Island Lodge, currently the islands' best lodging facility. This lighthouse is located 1 mile offshore and can only be reached by boat. ✉ *Bird Rock* ✛ *On separate island off northwest point of Crooked Island.*

🛏 Hotels

Casuarina Pine Villas

$ | **RENTAL** | Six modern cottages sit on a ½-mile stretch of white-sand beach between Landrail Point and Pittstown Point Landings. **Pros:** beachfront location; spacious economical accommodations; great place to hang out, fish, and relax. **Cons:** you need to arrange transportation to do anything; take plenty of insect repellent. $ *Rooms from: $155* ✉ *Landrail Point* ☎ *242/457–7005, 242/344–2036* ▭ *No credit cards* ⇨ *7 cottages* ⅰⓄⅰ *No meals.*

Chester's Highway Inn Bonefish Lodge

$$ | **B&B/INN** | For bonefishing enthusiasts, opportunity is never far away at Chester's Highway Inn, as each room faces

a pristine bonefishing flat that takes no more than 60 seconds to wade into. **Pros:** bonefishing flats directly opposite rooms; easy access to amazing outdoor activities; near Crooked Island ferry. **Cons:** unreliable Wi-Fi; limited dining options; distance from airport. $ *Rooms from: $245* ✉ *Chester's Hwy.* ☎ *242/357–4179, 242/225–1500* ⊕ *chestersbonefishlodge. com* ⇨ *4 rooms.*

Crooked Island Lodge

$ | **HOTEL** | A true anglers' paradise, this is one of the best fishing destinations in the Bahamas and Caribbean for bone- and deep-sea fishing. **Pros:** mind-bending ocean and beachfront location; bar and restaurant serves three meals a day; private airstrip for easy access. **Cons:** insect repellent necessary in this area; might be too remote for some; not all rooms offer sea views. $ *Rooms from: $195* ✉ *Pittstown Point Landing* ☎ *242/478–8989, 888/344–2507 toll-free in U.S. and Canada* ⊕ *www.crookedislandlodge.com* ⇨ *8 rooms* ⅰⓄⅰ *No meals.*

Ivel's Bed & Breakfast

$ | B&B/INN | FAMILY | When staying at Ivel's you are treated to gourmet meals, both Bahamian and American, and island hospitality that makes you feel like family. **Pros:** car rental available; water sports on-site; tranquil residential community. **Cons:** non-alcoholic facility; far from the best beaches. $ *Rooms from: $150* ✉ *Mason's Bay* ☎ *242/344–3199* ⊕ *www. ivelsbedandbreakfast.com* ⬈ *10 rooms and a cottage.*

🎿 Activities

FISHING

Crooked Island has a number of highly regarded bonefishing guides with quality boats and fly-fishing tackle. Most can be booked through Tranquillity on the Bay or the Crooked Island Lodge, but the guides also take direct bookings. Be aware that telephone service to and from Crooked and Acklins islands is not always operational.

You can stalk the elusive and swift bonefish in the shallows, or go deep-sea fishing for wahoo, sailfish, and amberjack.

Elton "Bonefish Shakey" McKinney (☎ *242/344–2038*), **Randy McKinney** (☎ *242/344–2326*), **Jeff Moss** (☎ *242/344–2029*), and **Clinton** and **Kenneth "The Earlybird" Scavalla** (☎ *242/344–2011* or *242/422–3596*) are all knowledgeable professional guides. **Captain Robbie Gibson** (☎ *242/457–7017*) has a 30-foot Century boat and is the most experienced reef and offshore fishing captain on Crooked Island, where astounding fishing in virgin waters is the rule. Many wahoo weighing more than 100 pounds are landed each season with his assistance. Robbie's personal-best wahoo is a whopping 180 pounds. He's also a skilled guide for anglers pursuing tuna, marlin, sharks, barracuda, jacks, snapper, and grouper.

SCUBA DIVING

Captain Robbie Gibson

DIVING/SNORKELING | In addition to fishing expeditions, Captain Robbie Gibson offers scuba diving of wreck sites and wall dives, snorkeling, and day tours to see flamingos or explore land caves. You can rent gear from him and a two-tank dive with equipment runs about $100 per person. ☎ *242/457–7017, 242/422–4737.*

Inagua

Inagua does indeed feel like the southernmost island in the Bahamas' 700-mile-long chain. Just 50 miles from Cuba, it's not easy to get to—there are only three flights a week from Nassau, and you must overnight there to catch the 9 am flight. At night the lonely beacon of the **Inagua Lighthouse** sweeps the sky over the southern part of the island and the only community, **Matthew Town,** as it has since 1870. The coastline is rocky and rugged, with little coves of golden sand. The terrain is mostly flat and covered with palmetto palms, wind-stunted buttonwoods, and mangroves ringing ponds and a huge inland saltwater lake. Parts of it look very much like the Florida Everglades, only without the alligators and poisonous snakes.

Matthew Town feels like the Wild West, with sun-faded wooden buildings and vintage and modern trucks usually parked in front. It's obviously not a tourist mecca, but those who do visit witness the great spectacles of the Western Hemisphere: the 60,000-some West Indian pink-scarlet flamingos that nest here alongside rare Bahama parrots and roseate spoonbills. If you're not a bird lover, there's extraordinary diving and fishing off the virgin reefs. Although there are few tourists, this remote island is prosperous. An unusual climate of little rainfall and continual trade winds creates rich salt ponds. The Morton Salt Company harvests a million tons of salt annually at its Matthew

Deep-sea fishing in the Southern Out Islands

Town factory, where most of the 1,000 Inaguans work.

GETTING HERE AND AROUND

AIR

Inagua has one airport: Matthew Town Airport (IGA). Bahamasair has flights on Monday, Wednesday, and Friday from Nassau. Hotels will arrange airport transportation. Generally someone from even the smallest hotel will meet you at the airport, but taxis sometimes meet incoming flights.

CONTACTS Inagua Matthew Town Airport.
✉ *Matthew Town* ☎ *242/339–1680 only answered Mon., Wed., and Fri. when a flight is expected, 242/339–1415 airport* ⊕ *www.bahamasair.com.*

BOAT

The M/V *Lady Mathilda* sails once a week or three times a month, first to Abraham's Bay, and then to Matthew Town, Inagua. Not only is the boat characteristically cluttered with all sorts of cargo, the service is sporadic—so, always call the captain on the scheduled sailing day,

Thursday, or the Potter's Cay Dockmaster's Office in Nassau to check sailing times. She departs from Potter's Cay in Nassau and the journey in good seas takes 36 hours and costs $100 one way. If bad weather is approaching, she may not even leave harbor, skipping a week and leaving you stranded. The whole process is an authentic Bahamian adventure. Take your camera!

CAR

You can rent a car for about $80 a day, but there are few rental cars on the island, so call in advance. If you are driving outside Matthew Town, you will need an SUV or truck to navigate dirt roads. If you plan to stay in Matthew Town, you can easily walk everywhere.

CONTACTS Ingraham Rent-A-Car.
☎ *242/225–3933, 242/339–1515.*

Triple R Car Rental
Cars and SUVs available at affordable rates starting at $60 per day. ✉ *Matthew Town* ☎ *242/453–8018, 242/443–6671.*

◉ Sights

Erickson Museum and Library

LIBRARY | The Erickson Museum and Library is a welcome part of the community, particularly the surprisingly well-stocked, well-equipped library. The Morton Company built the complex in the former home of the Erickson family, who came to Inagua in 1934 to run the salt giant. The museum displays the island's history to which the company is inextricably tied. The posted hours are not always that regular. The Bahamas National Trust office, and the office of the Inagua National Park, is also here, but hours are unpredictable. ✉ *Gregory St. on northern edge of town across from police station, Matthew Town* ☎ *242/339–1863* ✑ *Free* ⊗ *Closed Sun.*

Inagua Lighthouse

TOUR—SIGHT | From Southwest Point, a mile or so south of Matthew Town, you can see Cuba's coast—slightly more than 50 miles west—on a clear day from atop Inagua Lighthouse, built in 1870 in response to the number of shipwrecks on offshore reefs. It's a grueling climb—the last 10 feet are on a ladder—but the view of the rugged coastline and Matthew Town is worth the effort. Look to the west to see the hazy mountains of Cuba. Be sure to sign the guest book just inside the door to the lighthouse. ✉ *Gregory St., 1 mile south of Matthew Town, Great Inagua Island.*

★ Inagua National Park

NATIONAL/STATE PARK | Nothing quite prepares you for your first glimpse of the West Indian flamingos that nest in Inagua National Park: brilliant crimson-pink, up to 5 feet tall, with black-tipped wings. A dozen flamingos suddenly fly across a pond, intermixed with fantastic pink roseate spoonbills.

It's a moving sight, and because of the island's remote location, few people get to see it. By 1952, Inagua's flamingos had dwindled to about 5,000. The gorgeous birds were hunted for their meat, especially the tongue, and for their feathers. The government established the 183,740-acre wildlife sanctuary and national park in 1963, and today more than 60,000 flamingos nest on the island, the world's largest breeding colony of West Indian flamingos. The birds thrive in the many salt ponds (owned by the Morton Salt Company) that supply their favorite meal—brine shrimp. Bird-watchers also flock here to spy gull-billed terns, egrets, herons, burrowing owls, pintail ducks, sandpipers, snowy plovers—more than 130 species in all. The Inaguan lyre-tail is one of the world's most recently announced species. Wild boar and feral donkeys left here after a brief French occupation in 1749 are harder to see.

To make reservations, you must contact the Bahamas National Trust's office (☎ *242/393–1317*) or Warden Henry Nixon (☎ *242/395/0856*). All visits to the park are by special arrangement. ✉ *Matthew Town* ✚ *10 miles west of Matthew Town* ⊕ *www.bnt.bs* ✑ *From: $25 per person. Rates include: park user fee and BNT warden's time. Not included: vehicle rental and fuel and park warden gratuity (optional).*

Morton Salt Company

FACTORY | Marveling at the salt process lures few visitors to Inagua, but the Morton Salt Company is omnipresent on the island: it has more than 47 square miles of crystallizing ponds and reservoirs. More than a million tons of salt are produced every year for such industrial uses as salting icy streets. (More is produced when the northeastern United States has a bad winter.) Even if you decide not to tour the facility, you can see the mountains of salt, locally called the Salt Alps, glistening in the sun from the plane. In an unusual case of industry assisting its environment, the crystallizers provide a feeding ground for the flamingos. As the water evaporates, the concentration of brine shrimp in the ponds increases, and the flamingos feed on these animals. Free tours are available by reservation at the salt plant in Matthew Town. ✉ *Matthew Town* ☎ *242/339–1300, 242/457–6000* 🌐 *www.mortonsalt.com.*

Beaches

Collin's Beach

BEACH—SIGHT | In addition to visiting this remove beach to chill in solitude, Collin's Beach is an ideal location to snorkel Inagua's offshore reefs. Casuarina trees provide shade in some areas, but that is about all you will find on this beach besides the sandy coastline and mesmerizing turquoise waters. It is about ten miles north of Matthew Town, so be sure to bring sunscreen, bug spray, umbrellas or portable shade, lots of fluids in a cooler, and some beach toys and snorkeling gear. Every year, a few luxury cruises make winter stops in Inagua and bring their guests to Collin's Beach. **Amenities:** none. **Best for:** solitude; snorkeling.

Restaurants

Cepigel

$ | **BAHAMIAN** | **FAMILY** | Vegan menus are hard to come by in The Bahamas on the whole, so it is a rare treat to find vegetarian options and a focus on fresh ingredients in Inagua, the most southern island in the archipelago. Cepigel has that covered. **Known for:** Bahamian staples; intimate space; homemade desserts. [$] *Average main:* ✉ *Astwood St., Matthew Town* ☎ *242/339–1227* 🌐 *cepigel.wixsite.com/cepigel.*

Lighthouse Restaurant Bar and Grill

$$ | **BAHAMIAN** | Although Lighthouse Restaurant is casual and intimate like Inagua's overall character, it is considered the best high-end restaurant on the island. Known for its stunning sunsets, the octagon shaped restaurant overlooks the ocean and the historic lighthouse. **Known for:** oceanfront location; great sunset views; traditional Bahamian food. [$] *Average main: $18* ✉ *Lighthouse Rd.* ☎ *242/453–2277, 242/453–1200.*

★ **S sinn L Restaurant & Bar Lounge**

$ | **BAHAMIAN** | The best spot to dine and even party is at S sinn L in Matthew Town, which becomes Inagua's dance hot spot on the weekend. In a comfortable, smart, air-conditioned dining room, you can enjoy delicious fresh Bahamian breakfasts, lunches, and dinners with some American fare as well. **Known for:** live calypso and Bahamina Goombay; go-to spot for dancing; Bahama Mama cocktails. [$] *Average main: $15* ✉ *East St., Matthew Town* ☎ *242/339–3923, 242/339–1515* 💳 *No credit cards.*

Hotels

The Great Inagua Outback Lodge

$$ | **B&B/INN** | The Great Inagua Outback Lodge is the dream of Inaguan Henry Hugh who wanted to relax in his own quiet island paradise. **Pros:** comfortable with modern amenities; right on water and close to beach and flats; full meals in stay/fish/dine packages. **Cons:** long and extremely bumpy road; remote; no pool. [$] *Rooms from: $284* ✉ *Matthew Town* ✥ *15 miles from Matthew Town, along northern road and the beach road* ☎ *716/479–2327 in U.S. and Canada* 🌐 *www.ccoflyfishing.com/greatinagua.html* 🛏 *2 rooms* 🍴 *All meals.*

Sunset Apartments

$ | **RENTAL** | These two spacious apartments seated on a rocky shoreline on Matthew Town's southern side are your only option for a room with a water view, and a great place to watch sunsets. **Pros:** great place for bonefishing; Ezzard is a wonderful host and a top fly-fishing guide; fully equipped kitchens. **Cons:** no Internet; little to do but fish and birdwatch; you need to pay in cash or wire transfer. [$] *Rooms from: $150* ✉ *Matthew Town* ☎ *242/339–1362* 💳 *No credit cards* 🛏 *2 apartments* 🍴 *No meals.*

♈ Nightlife

Da After Work Bar
BARS/PUBS | This local bar on Gregory Street is the most popular hangout in town. ⊠ *Gregory St., Matthew Town* ☾ *Usually closed Sun.*

The Fish Fry
GATHERING PLACES | A collection of fish shacks next to the water is open on weekends, with DJs occasionally playing music in the covered pavilion next door. ⊠ *Matthew Town.*

🏃 Activities

BIRD-WATCHING
Great Inagua Tours
FISHING | Mr. Colin Ingraham has been a tour guide for more than 22 years, and while he specializes in birding and island sightseeing, he can also take you fishing for tuna or wahoo, or snorkeling on the reefs. ⊠ *Matthew Town* ☎ *242/339–1336, 242/453–0429 cell.*

FISHING
Ezzard Cartwright
FISHING | Inagua's only bonefishing and deep-sea fishing guide, Ezzard Cartwright has been featured on ESPN Outdoors shows. He is the only local with access to Lake Windsor, home to tarpon, snook, and bonefish that can only be reached by boat. Reserve early for bonefishing from January to July. ⊠ *Matthew Town* ☎ *242/339–1362, 242/453–1903 cell.*

Index

Photo Credits

Front Cover: Daniel Piraino/EyeEm [Description: Black Point, Bahamas]. **Back cover, from left to right:** Maurice Brand/Dreamstime,Bicho_raro/iStockphoto, Henrik Landfors/iStockphoto. Spine: Kovnir Andrii/Shutterstock. **Interior, from left to right:** The Bahamas Ministry of Tourism (1). Ray Wadia/The Bahamas Ministry of Tourism (2). The Bahamas Ministry of Tourism (5). **Chapter 1: Experience the Bahamas:** Reinhard Dirscherl/agefotostock (6-7). Ray Wadia/The Bahamas Ministry of Tourism (8). Bahamas Ministry of Tourism (9). Bahamas Ministry of Tourism (9). Bahamas Ministry of Tourism (10). Ron Nickel/agefotostock (10). Beltsazar/Dreamstime (10). BlueOrange Studio/Shutterstock (10). Worachat Sodsri/Shutterstock (11). Bahamas Ministry of Tourism (11). Bahamas Ministry of Tourism (12). Stephen Frink Collection/Alamy(12). Bahamas Ministry of Tourism (12). Worachat Sodsri / Shutterstock (12). Jocrebbin/Dreamstime (13). Danita Delimont/Alamy(14). Bahamas Ministry of Tourism (14). Bahamas Ministry of Tourism (14). Danielbothaphoto/Dreamstime(15). Danielbothaphoto/Dreamstime (15). Stanislav Simonov (18). DwayneTucker.com (19). dam@seaphotoart.com (20). Jimi world (20). johnandersonphoto/iStockphoto (20). Courtesy of The Bahamas Ministry of Tourism and Aviation (21). Nassau Paradise Island Promotion Board (21). The Bahamas Ministry of Tourism and Aviation (22). Maria Victoria Herrera/Shutterstock (22). Vytalis Arnoldus/Shutterstock (22). Shane Gross/Shutterstock (22). Nassau Paradise Island Promotion Board (23). Dirscherl Reinhard/agefotostock (27). The Bahamas Ministry of Tourism (28). The Bahamas Ministry of Tourism (29). The Bahamas Ministry of Tourism (29). frantisekhojdysz/Shutterstock (30). The Bahamas Ministry of Tourism (32). The Bahamas Ministry of Tourism (33). The Bahamas Ministry of Tourism (34). The Bahamas Ministry of Tourism (35). Ray Wadia/The Bahamas Ministry of Tourism (35). The Bahamas Ministry of Tourism (35). **Chapter 3: New Providence and Paradise Islands:** Macduff Everton (55). The Bahamas Ministry of Tourism (69). Graycliff Hotel (75). Laurin Johnson/iStockphoto (82). Remedios Valls Lopez/agefotostock (84-85). Lars Topelmann/The Bahamas Ministry of Tourism (91). Ramunas/Dreamstime (94). Ramona Settle (101). **Chapter 4: Grand Bahama Island:** Denis Jr. Tangney/istockphoto (103). DEGAS Jean-Pierre/agefotostock(106). Thomas Lorenz/Shutterstock (107). The Bahamas Ministry of Tourism (107). FLPA/Michael Gore/age fotostock (115). The Bahamas Ministry of Tourism (120). Our Lucaya Beach and Golf Resort (123). Davis James/age fotostock (126). The Bahamas Ministry of Tourism (128). Dirscherl Reinhard/age fotostock (130). Walter Bibikow/agefotostock (137). Jef Nickerson/Flickr (138). biskuit/Flickr (138). The Bahamas Ministry of Tourism (139). Peter Adams/agefotostock (139). Shane Pinder/Alamy (140). Erkki & Hanna/Shutterstock (141). Shane Pinder/Alamy (141). **Chapter 5: Andros, Bimini, and the Berry Islands:** Greg Johnston/agefotostock (149). Juliet Coombe/agefotostock (153). Tiamo Resort (167). BARBAGALLO Franco/agefotostock (171). Mark Conlin/Alamy (174). Larry Larsen/Alamy (178). Amy Strycula/Alamy (184). **Chapter 6: Eleuthera and Harbour Island:** The Bahamas Ministry of Tourism (187). The Bahamas Ministry of Tourism (198-199). Greg Johnston / age fotostock (202). Bahamas Ministry of Tourism (212). Alvaro Leiva / age fotostock (215). Ian Cumming / age fotostock (218-219). **Chapter 7: The Exumas:** ARCO/F Schneider / age fotostock (223). The Bahamas Ministry of Tourism (226). Ray Wadia/The Bahamas Ministry of Tourism (227). The Bahamas Ministry of Tourism (227). Cheryl Blackerby (231). Cheryl Blackerby (236). Ramona Settle (239). Staniel Cay Yacht Club (243). Bahamas Ministry of Tourism (245). Staniel Cay Yacht Club (246). **Chapter 8: The Southern Out Islands:** Greg Johnston/age fotostock (249). Cheryl Blackerby (252). Patrick Swint/flickr (253). stephan kerkhofs/Shutterstock (253). Jeff Greenberg/Alamy (254). Cheryl Blackerby (255). mweichse/Shutterstock (255). Michael DeFreitas /age fotostock (267). Greg Johnston / age fotostock (269). The Bahamas Ministry of Tourism (271). Greg Johnston / age fotostock (274). Greg Johnston/Cape Santa Maria Beach Resort (284). BARBAGALLO Franco / age fotostock (287). Bahamas Ministry of Tourism (292). Greg Johnston/Cape Santa Maria Beach Resort (294).**About Our Writers:** All photos are courtesy of the writers.

Every effort has been made to trace the copyright holders, and we apologize in advance for any accidental errors. We would be happy to apply the corrections in the following edition of this publication.